Human Sexuality

Making Responsible Decisions

SAUNDERS COLLEGE PUBLISHING

Philadelphia New York Chicago
San Francisco Montreal Toronto
London Sydney Tokyo Mexico City
Rio de Janeiro Madrid

HUMAN SEXUALITY

Making Responsible Decisions

Linda Brower Meeks
Philip Heit
Ohio State University

Illustrated by
James C. Brower

Address orders to:
383 Madison Avenue
New York, NY 10017

Address editorial correspondence to:
West Washington Square
Philadelphia, PA 19105

This book was set in Palatino by Ruttle, Shaw and Wetherill.
The editors were John Butler, Lee Walters, Sally Kusch, and Jessie Raymond.
The art & design director was Richard L. Moore.
The text design was done by Nancy E. J. Grossman.
The cover design was done by Richard L. Moore.
The artwork was drawn by Jim Brower.
The production manager was Tom O'Connor.
This book was printed by Von Hoffman.

Cover credit: The sculpture, "ETERNAL SPRINGTIME" by Rodin, 1884.
  Photograph by William T. Moore, Jr.

HUMAN SEXUALITY

ISBN 0-03-058366-7

234   032   98765432

CBS COLLEGE PUBLISHING
Saunders College Publishing
Holt, Rinehart and Winston
The Dryden Press

Preface

A person's sexuality is everything that makes that individual a sexual being physically, psychologically, mentally, socially, and emotionally. Although many factors influence sexual well-being, research reveals that accurate information has the most profound positive effect. Knowledge forms the basis for understanding this sensitive and controversial aspect of life, and this understanding enables us to (1) make healthy, appropriate decisions about our sexuality and take full responsibility for them, (2) understand and accept the sexuality of others, and (3) form intimate, satisfying relationships. *Human Sexuality: Making Responsible Decisions* is a text written for college students with these purposes in mind.

In this book we stress the importance of being responsible for one's sexuality. This is reflected by our inclusion of the decision-making process along with the basic content that forms the core of each chapter. We have incorporated this theme because we believe that making appropriate responsible decisions promotes good health, happiness, and satisfaction, not only in sexual areas but in one's overall sense of well-being.

The four steps in this process are as follows: (1) a look at your lifestyle, (2) gathering information, (3) evaluating the information, and (4) making responsible decisions. This format encourages the students to think about how the issues under discussion affect their sexuality in light of their individual lifestyle, to collect accurate, complete information based on current findings, to assess all available options along with the consequences of each, and to make the appropriate choice that best suits their needs and then accept full responsibility for the consequences of the decision.

Each chapter consistently begins with this format, which is used to preview the content and offer a rationale for learning the material, pose questions to be considered as the chapter is studied, and point out the areas in which needs for sexual understanding exist by suggesting goals or objectives for learning the chapter content.

At the ends of chapters are exercises, called I-Openers. They could also be called eye-openers. They are intended to open students' eyes to sexual issues that pertain to that particular chapter. Each I-Opener presents a situation related to the chapter content and then "walks" the student through the decision-making process through open-ended questions that are thought-provoking and stimulating. We have found these particularly effective in encouraging open classroom discussion. This is a unique feature of the text, and one which we have found effective in our own teaching experiences.

This leads us to an important area of emphasis in this text: communication. We begin in Chapter 1 by discussing methods of effectively sending, receiving, and clarifying messages. We encourage students to develop communication skills in order to be able to discuss their feelings as well as understand the feelings of others.

Throughout the text, we have included counseling notes from our files. These are comments from a variety of persons, including our students and those we have counseled privately. These comments express individual subjective feelings concerning common issues and situations that may be familiar to many students. They are included to aid communication and to enhance the understanding of others, as well as to clarify personal questions students may have.

We have tried to focus upon intimate, healthy, satisfying relationships. This is the first text to include chapters on Liking, Loving and Intimacy; Marriage and the Family; The Single Lifestyle; and The Parenthood Option. In these chapters there are practical considerations for examination in regard to each individual's lifestyle. The latest findings from research are presented, while students are asked to consider the question, "What can I do to improve my relationships?"

Additional learning aids that appear in our text are the Summary Statements and Suggested Readings at the ends of chapters; also, there is a complete Bibliography as well as a Glossary at the end of the text.

This text is written in a personal style that is easy to read. Obviously, sexuality is an area in which students are highly motivated, but there is much to be learned. Thus, it is not a matter of generating interest but of making accurate information more accessible. Our extensive teaching and writing experience has enabled us to clearly describe the detailed information that needs to be included.

As will be evident from a brief glance within this text, we have provided excellent artwork consisting of original, accurate anatomical drawings. There are numerous photographs interspersed throughout. As an additional teaching/learning aid, a set of slides taken from the drawings in the text will be made available to those adopting this text.

Finally, there is an Instructor's Manual to accompany this text. This contains ideas for introducing each chapter, including an overview of the chapter, chapter outline and objectives, key terms, and related audio-visual resources. Also included are teaching strategies, additional I-Openers, and carefully designed test questions. There are overhead transparency masters of the line drawings from the text.

We hope that those using this book will find it to be as rewarding an experience as it was for us to write it.

Linda Brower Meeks

Philip Heit

Acknowledgments

Many people helped bring this book to completion. First and foremost, we thank our families for their love, patience, and support.

The reviewers of this book performed their job with great care, providing us with many useful ideas. Among these reviewers were Jean Byrne, Kent State University, Katherine W. Ellison, Montclair State College, Irene Frieze, University of Pittsburgh, Glen G. Gilbert, Portland State University, Nicholas K. Iammarino, Rice University, J. Glenn Lohr, Western Kentucky University, Gideon E. Nelson, University of South Florida, Valerie Pinhas, Queens College, A. J. Pope, Central Michigan University, James H. Price, University of Toledo, Murray Vincent, University of South Carolina, Robert A. Walker, Pennsylvania State University, William L. Yarber, Purdue University, and Michael Young, University of Arkansas.

We are especially grateful to the following reviewers who went well beyond the scope of their responsibilities and spent many hours helping to polish the manuscript: Philip A. Belcastro, Southern Illinois University, Nan G. Hubbard, University of North Carolina at Greensboro, and Marvin R. Levy, Temple University.

The "team" at Saunders College Publishing was fantastic. John Butler, our sponsoring editor, guided this project from beginning to completion. His support and enthusiasm were contagious. Lee Walters, the developmental editor, provided special guidance in helping to organize the manuscript. Lee proved to be a developmental editor who is competent and professional as well as a most pleasant person with whom to work. We appreciate the support our publisher, Don Jackson, provided us throughout the project. He helped make working with Saunders an enjoyable experience. Leesa Massey deserves thanks for helping us take care of the little details. Sally Kusch deserves plaudits for her excellent work as project editor.

James C. Brower deserves special recognition. He spent many hours drawing the excellent illustrations in this book.

We are also grateful to Ann Gabriel for her "on the spot" typing and handling of the manuscript.

Finally, we owe a great deal to our students — both past and present. Their ideas and experiences were used throughout this book.

Linda Brower Meeks

Philip Heit

Contents Overview

Table of Contents

Chapter Seven BIRTH CONTROL, STERILIZATION, AND ABORTION

Chapter Eight HOMOSEXUALITY AND BISEXUALITY

About the Authors

LINDA BROWER MEEKS

Professor Meeks has been a faculty member of the Health Education Department at The Ohio State University since 1969. Before coming to OSU she was at the University of Wisconsin and the University of Toledo. Her graduate work was in the area of human sexuality, family life education, and counseling, health education, and sociology. Professor Meeks is the co-author of *Education for Sexuality*, an extremely successful text on teaching sexuality which has been published in six languages. She is also the co-author of *Toward a Healthy Sexuality, Group Strategies in Understanding Human Sexuality: Getting in Touch*, and *Toward a Healthy Lifestyle Through Health in the Elementary School*. She is an avid tennis player and has competed on the Ohio Wightman Cup team. She has an eight-year-old daughter, Kristen Ann. Professor Meeks is committed to a healthy, dynamic lifestyle.

PHILIP HEIT, Ed.D.

Philip Heit has been a member of the Health Education Department faculty at The Ohio State University since 1976. Prior to coming to OSU, Dr. Heit taught in the New York City public school system and the state college system in New Jersey. Dr. Heit has written numerous articles and conducted extensive research in the area of human sexuality. Dr. Heit and Professor Meeks are the co-authors of the following books: *Health: Focus on You; Teaching Health Science in Middle and Secondary Schools; Human Sexuality and Family Living; Venereal Diseases; Death, Dying, and Aging*. Phil Heit is committed to a dynamic, healthy lifestyle. He is a marathon runner and has competed in the prestigious Boston and New York City marathons more than twenty times. He is married to Sheryl Heit and they are the parents of Yve and Gay.

ONE

Sex Education: Making Responsible Decisions

In your vision of the world is the image of yourself.

—Morgan

Shut your eyes for a moment and think of the most rewarding lifestyle that you might have. Keep your eyes closed long enough to get a clear vision of yourself. What would you be doing? With whom would you be? How would you feel about yourself and others?

The vision that you have of yourself and of your possibilities is very important. It is one of the main reasons that you are reading this book. You have a vision of what you are or what you want to be. You connect this vision with your personal feelings about happiness.

Most of us want to have a healthy, happy lifestyle. Our chances for success in this endeavor are greatly influenced by our vision of what health and happiness are. Do you have a clear vision of happiness that is attainable?

WHAT IS HAPPINESS?

Immanuel Kant wrote, "The three grand essentials to happiness in this life are something to do, someone to love, and something to hope for." The authors like this vision because it clarifies the indescribable word *happiness*. Happiness, according to Kant, has three dimensions. These three dimensions can be further described.

If each of us needs something to do to be happy, then it is important to find satisfying work. To do this, you need to develop skills that will enable you to find a profession that makes you happy. You might teach, work in a bank, raise children, or engage in a number of other activities. You probably have recognized the importance of finding something to do. Most likely that is why you are attending school.

If you need someone to love to be happy, then you need to find ways to become closer to others. Certain skills can be developed that will enable you to gain the tools with which you can form meaningful relationships. You may be reading this book in the hope that you will gain these skills. You may already recognize the importance of self-understanding and self-awareness about your sexuality as it relates to establishing close relationships with others.

If you need something to hope for to be happy, you will want to examine your reasons for living. When you are able to answer the question, "What is the purpose of life?" you will be able to direct your life in a meaningful way, one that will make you happy.

HUMAN SEXUALITY EDUCATION PROMOTES A HAPPY, HEALTHY LIFESTYLE

After you have examined the essential ingredients of happiness, you might ask, "How can an appreciation and understanding of my sexuality promote happiness?" The authors believe that your sexuality — everything that makes you a sexual being physically, psychologically, mentally, socially, and emotionally — is important in your discovery of something to do, someone to love, and something to hope for. Let us examine these three essential ingredients of happiness and their relationships to your sexuality.

Something to Do

As you look for something to do to make you happy, you will be accompanied by your sexual self. No matter what you do, your maleness or femaleness will radiate from you. The vision that you have of your sexual self and the vision that others have of your sexuality will influence your life's work.

For example, what are your feelings about male and female roles? Some people feel that men should have certain jobs and that women should have certain other jobs. They may even feel that women and men who have the same job should be paid different amounts of money. A limited understanding of the sex roles of men and women certainly does not promote happiness. It blocks the human potential of both men and women.

Sexual harassment is another issue that has been a topic of concern for men and women who work together. Misunderstanding in the form of harassment will also block happiness and the achievement of human potential. The authors suggest that work and working relationships are more likely to promote happiness when you accept fully your sexuality and understand the sexual preferences of others.

Someone to Love

The next essential ingredient of happiness, someone to love, is more directly related to the need to study human sexuality. If loving someone is one of three essentials of happiness, then the study of loving relationships is quite important. Erich Fromm, author of *The Art of Loving* (1963), says that you *learn* the ability, or art, of loving. This is one justification for education about human sexuality. To fulfill this essential of happiness, you need to learn

- to accept your body
- to love yourself
- to care about others
- to be intimate
- to communicate your innermost needs to someone else
- the ingredients of a good relationship
- how to raise children
- the needs and desires of other men and women
- to deal with loneliness
- to discover what a commitment to a loving lifestyle means

Something to Hope for

The final essential ingredient of happiness identified by Immanuel Kant is something to hope for. A person who has a philosophy of life that identifies a reason for living has the greatest chance for happiness. When you have a philosophy of life, you can develop a life principle.

> A life principle is a generalized, accepted intention of purpose that is applied to specific choices and circumstances. This life principle runs through the fabric of our choices like the dominant theme in a piece of music: it keeps recurring and it is heard in different settings. Having a life principle is a matter of psychological economy. It diminishes the wear and tear of having to make all decisions from the ground up.

(Powell, 1976)

When you have a life principle, you have a framework to use when making decisions about your sexuality that promote happiness.

THE GOAL OF HUMAN SEXUALITY EDUCATION IS LEARNING A PROCESS FOR MAKING RESPONSIBLE DECISIONS

Consider the following questions: Should I have sexual intercourse? Should I abstain from sex? What characteristics might I look for in a person if together we want to form a long-term, mutually satisfying relationship? What form of birth control is the most effective for me? Am I ready and willing to be a parent?

You might answer these questions without carefully examining them. In fact, you may not be aware of plausible alternatives, pertinent information about these alternatives, or the consequences of your chosen sexual behaviors. A hasty decision may be self-destructive, and it may harm someone else.

Making responsible decisions that promote your health and happiness and that of others is a difficult task. The first and most important thing to learn is a *process* that you can use. The authors have written this book using a process as a framework for each chapter. The process includes

a look at your lifestyle
gathering information
evaluating information
making responsible decisions

A Look at Your Lifestyle

The study of human sexuality involves a careful examination of the issues that will confront you, the data relevant to the issues, others who are close to you, and society. These issues will have an impact on lifestyle that may promote health and happiness in you and others or that may be destructive. A look at your lifestyle involves

identifying the key issues and problems
stating these issues and problems as clearly as possible
identifying the alternatives available for dealing with each issue or problem

In the beginning of each chapter, the authors clearly state the issues and questions that need your attention. You are able to examine a topic with an awareness of the impact an issue may have.

Gathering Information

The next step in the process of making responsible decisions involves

• gathering information

The study of human sexuality includes basic factual information that gives you the background that you need to understand maleness, femaleness, sexual arousal, sexual response, contraception, abortion, homosexuality, sexually transmissible diseases, and so forth.

Information is a key ingredient. Attitudes, values, and decisions should not be based on myth, fallacy, or prejudice but on an accurate assessment of the information available. Each chapter in this text contains background information about an important sexual topic.

Evaluating Information

To make an accurate assessment, information is evaluated by

- examining each alternative carefully
- listing the physical, psychological, and spiritual consequences of each
- testing each alternative with your value system

The authors suggest that you consider the following life principle when you examine your values: "I am responsible and caring in my sexual lifestyle."

One way of testing your decisions is to use the values clarification process. Values, according to Raths (1966), are composed of several sub-processes:

PRIZING one's beliefs and behaviors

1. Prizing and cherishing
2. Publicly affirming when appropriate

CHOOSING

3. Choosing from alternatives
4. Choosing after consideration of consequences
5. Choosing freely

ACTING on one's beliefs

6. Acting
7. Acting with a pattern, consistency, and repetition

When you apply the values clarification process to your decisions, you are able to ascertain whether or not your decisions are in accordance with your life principle.

Making Responsible Decisions

The final step in making responsible decisions involves

- selecting the alternative that best suits your needs and standing accountable for the consequences

The process that you use for *making responsible decisions* will have a profound influence upon your lifestyle. Many people spend too much time in confusion, self-doubt, and depression. They become "stuck" and are not able to get their lives moving along in a happy, healthy manner.

You can avoid being "stuck" by using this approach in your daily living. You can identify the issues that affect your lifestyle, look at possible alternatives, gather information, evaluate the information, make a decision, and move on. Your life will be fuller and richer, and you will feel that you are in control.

Taking responsibility for your decisions is one of the most important things that you can do. It gives you higher self-esteem. It enables you to say, "No matter what happens, I have some ways of coping. I have alternatives. I can choose." This approach to living more fully can be a positive approach to your sexual lifestyle. Examples of this process are included in Tables 1.1 and 1.2.

Throughout this book the authors interject counseling notes from their files. These counseling notes include comments made by the authors' students and clients about the impact of their sexuality on their lifestyles and the process of making responsible decisions. You can learn and gain a great deal of insight from these comments.

TABLE 1.1 AN EXAMPLE OF THE PROCESS FOR MAKING RESPONSIBLE DECISIONS

A Look at Your Lifestyle

John and Mary are participating in sexual intercourse and want to avoid pregnancy. John and Mary have decided to use the decision-making process to explore alternatives to preventing a pregnancy.
- John and Mary identify the key issue or problem: to select a method of birth control that is effective, safe, and mutually satisfying.
- John and Mary identify as many alternatives as possible. They make a list of alternatives: abstinence, pill, IUD, sterilization, condom, foam, diaphragm, rhythm.

Gathering Information

- John and Mary consult reliable sources. They find out the effectiveness, cost, contraindications, mechanism of action, side effects, and noncontraceptive benefits of each.

Evaluating the Information

- John and Mary examine each alternative. What are the advantages, disadvantages, health consequences? They begin at the top of their list with the pill. What are the physical effects of the pill? What is the theoretical effectiveness? What are the advantages? Disadvantages? John and Mary look at the next alternative and ask the same questions. They proceed down the list until each alternative has been carefully examined. They then apply the values clarification process to each of the alternatives. They ask whether each is "responsible and caring."

Making Responsible Decisions

- John and Mary select the alternative that best suits their needs and agree to stand accountable for the consequences. In this case, John and Mary select the pill. John and Mary are saying, "After carefully examining each alternative, we are willing to select the pill with full knowledge of the possible side effects and their consequences."

TABLE 1.2   AN EXAMPLE OF THE PROCESS FOR MAKING RESPONSIBLE
DECISIONS

A Look at Your Lifestyle

You are sitting on the end of your bed talking to your best friend. Your best friend (of the same sex) tells you that (s)he is homosexual. You are taken by surprise. You talk briefly, and then your friend leaves. You are puzzled, confused, and not certain how to react. You need to sort some things out.

- You identify the key issue: My best friend is homosexual, and I don't know what this means to our relationship.
- You identify as many alternatives for dealing with the situation as you can think of: (a) tell my friend that I don't approve, (b) avoid my friend, (c) tell my friend that I will see him/her but never with a homosexual friend, (d) not see my friend again and not tell him/her why, and (e) tell my friend that we have different sexual preferences but that I value the friendship and want to talk openly about its effect on our relationships.

Gathering Information

- I will gather information from reliable sources so that I can learn about homosexuality. For example, one of my fears is that my friend will make a pass at me. The sources I consulted say that if I tell my friend my preferences, (s)he will *not* make a pass at me. My fear is therefore unrealistic and based on a myth.

Evaluating the Information

- I evaluate each alternative. For example, if I avoid my friend, I will be cutting off a relationship in which someone helps me out and has my best interests in mind. That would be giving something up. Yet if I keep my friend, there will be many things I will want to talk about, and at times I might feel uncomfortable. I list all the pros and cons of each alternative, and when necessary I use the information that I have gathered. I also use the values clarification approach. Am I proud of my decision? Am I willing to tell others? Then I apply my life principle: What is the responsible and caring way to handle this situation?

Making Responsible Decisions

- I decide to tell my friend that we have different sexual preferences but that I accept him/her and value the friendship. I have worked through my feelings and have pledged that when confusion gets in the way of the friendship, I will talk openly about it with my friend.

LEARNING TO COMMUNICATE IS VITAL TO HUMAN SEXUALITY EDUCATION THAT PROMOTES A HEALTHY, HAPPY LIFESTYLE

Taking responsibility for your sexual decisions is necessary for good mental health and for positive living. You also need to take responsibility for communicating your sexual needs, feelings, attitudes, and knowledge to other persons. Many people find it easy to talk about the weather, politics, books, and gossip; but they are "speechless" when approaching topics that deal with feelings, especially intimate feelings.

I had it all planned. We'd been dating for six months. I wanted to tell him that I loved him and that I didn't want to date anyone else. We were sitting at dinner. The words just wouldn't come out. I just can't talk about how I feel. It really hurts.

Loneliness and isolation from others may be attributed to an unwillingness to share what you are thinking and feeling. Lack of communication blocks self-growth and the growth of relationships. Herbert Otto, Director of the Human Potentialities Institute, has said, "Change and growth take place when a person has risked himself/herself and dares to become involved with experimenting with his/her own life" (Buscaglia, 1972).

Self-disclosure and Communication

This self-experimentation involves self-disclosure and effective communication. Self-disclosure is the act of revealing what you are thinking or feeling so that others will have an opportunity to respond genuinely to you.

I really value the relationship. For the first time in my life, I can tell someone everything. She sits and listens. She accepts me. She responds and tells me how she feels. I used to feel so bottled up inside. By getting my feelings and thoughts out, my whole life is better. And I am learning so much about myself.

Communication is the process by which you send and receive messages. Although you can send and receive messages in a number of ways, this discussion will focus on talking and listening. There are two rules to follow that enhance effective talking and listening skills. First, be open and honest when you talk. Openness facilitates sending a clear message. Second, avoid making judgments or evaluations about the message or the person to whom you are listening. As a listener, acknowledge and accept what someone has said before explaining your feelings. The following discussion of sending and receiving messages will help to clarify these rules and enhance your communications skills.

Sending Messages

Let's examine the types of messages that you send when you are dealing with your sexuality. Most likely you are sending two types of messages. The first type of message is called *information gathering* and the second type is called a *responsibility message*.

Let us further clarify what is meant by each type of message. When you evaluate your sexual behavior and your sexual lifestyle, you will need information about how certain behaviors influence your sexuality. You will be examining factual information. This type of sending focuses on messages that are conveyed objectively. These objective messages are sent without added feelings because their content is factual. The data are sent and received for the purpose of gathering information so that you can make wise decisions.

A very important second type of message then evolves. You will be evaluating this information at a personal level, reflecting your attitudes, beliefs, and values. How you feel becomes very important. Unfortunately, many persons cannot communicate on this level. The inability to communicate personal attitudes, beliefs, values, and feelings leads to misunderstandings and to the breakdown of relationships. Healthy sexuality necessitates taking responsibility for open communication.

I-Messages

Another term for responsibility messages is *I-Messages.* I-messages are statements about the self, revelations of inner feelings and needs, information not processed by others. An I-message has three parts (Gordon, 1970):

1. The first component involves the identification of a specific behavior
2. The second component pins down the tangible or concrete effect of the specific behavior described in the message's first part
3. The third part states the feelings generated by the effect

Simply stated, I-messages contain a behavior, an effect, and a feeling. An I-message facilitates open communication because you take responsibility for feelings and actions rather than shifting responsibility to someone or something else. I-messages give you a framework or structure for expressing your sexuality openly. An I-message can be contrasted with a *you-message.* A you-message, or a blaming and shaming message, closes off this needed openness.

The following examples clarify the difference between a responsibility-taking- or I-message and a blaming- or you-message.

> Mary is talking to her steady boyfriend, John.
>
> I-message—When I do not get a phone call from you each day, I wonder how you feel about me and I feel insecure.
>
> You-message—When you do not call me each day, you are thoughtless and selfish and I know that you do not care about me.

In the first example, Mary sends an I-message, and John understands the feelings she is experiencing. Mary has dealt with

1. the *behavior* of John that troubles her (When I do not get a phone call from you each day. . .)
2. the *effect* of that behavior (I wonder how you feel about me. . .)
3. the *feelings* that result (I feel insecure. . .)

In the second example, Mary sends a you-message. John may feel blamed and on the defensive. John may have had a reason for not calling daily. But instead of dealing with Mary's feelings about his calling, John will probably respond to her attack and be angry about being called "thoughtless" and "selfish." The real issue is lost, and a lack of communication results.

Let's examine another set of messages.

Mary is talking to her steady boyfriend, John.

I-message—When we have sex without using any form of contraception, I worry about an unwanted pregnancy and I feel guilty.

You-message—When we have sex without using any form of contraception, it proves to me that you are irresponsible and trying to trap me.

The I-, or responsibility-, message opens communication, and Mary and John can discuss the use of a contraceptive and their feelings about their lack of planning. The second message downgrades John, and it is more likely to elicit a conversation about who is at fault, rather than build the relationship.

There is probably no more important area in which to send clear messages than the area of human sexuality. The lack of communication that results from unclear messages, and the breakdown that can result, may be devastating.

After messages are sent, it is important for you to know whether they have been received clearly. You need only to listen to gossip to realize the possible changes in or interpretations of your messages to others. Effective receiving, or listening, skills complete the communication process.

Receiving Messages

When you receive a message, you will want to be certain that you heard the message clearly and that you have enough information to respond. Two important skills that enhance your ability to receive messages are (1) feeding back, or active listening, and (2) clarifying responses.

When you listen or receive a message, state clearly what you have heard. The process of "feeding back," or "active listening," achieves this purpose. Here is an example of active listening, the process where you feed back what you have heard to the person talking.

Mary is talking to her steady boyfriend, John.

Mary—When we have sex without using any form of contraception, I worry about an unwanted pregnancy and I feel guilty.

John (active listening)—Did I hear you say that you are worried about getting pregnant and that you feel that we should plan to use some form of contraception?

If John shows Mary that he has indeed heard what she has said, Mary can then clarify her feelings in a nonthreatening atmosphere. Mary does not feel that she has been ignored. Mary might, on the other hand, learn that her message was not clear. She might, for instance, be trying to tell John that she no longer wants to be sexually active. Active listening clarifies the intended message. When further clarification is needed, a clarifying response may be used to obtain more information or to help another person understand what he or she is saying.

Mary is talking to her steady boyfriend, John.

Mary (I-message)—When we have sex without using any form of contraception, I worry about an unwanted pregnancy and I feel guilty.

John (active listening)—Did I hear you say that you are worried about getting pregnant and that you feel that we should use some form of contraception?

Mary (knows that John has received her message clearly)—Yes, I am concerned.

John (clarifying response)—How long have you felt this way?

A clarifying response is a useful skill. Sometimes we are trying to make responsible decisions for ourselves or are trying to reach a mutually acceptable decision. Table 1.3 includes a list of clarifying responses that may assist you in your communication with others.

TABLE 1.3 CLARIFYING RESPONSES

1. Where do you suppose that you first got that idea?
2. How long have you felt that way?
3. Are you getting help from anyone? Do you need more help? Can I help?
4. Are you the only one in your crowd who feels this way?
5. Is there any rebellion in your choice?
6. What else did you consider before you picked this?
7. How long did you look around before you decided?
8. Was it a hard decision? What went into the final decision?
9. Are there some reasons behind your choice?
10. What choices did you reject before you settled on your present idea or action?
11. What's really good about this choice that makes it stand out from the other possibilities?
12. What would be the consequences of each alternative available?
13. Have you thought about this very much? How did your thinking go?
14. Is this what I understand you to say. . . (interpret the statement)?
15. What assumptions are involved in your choice?
16. Is what you say consistent with what you said earlier?
17. Where will it lead?
18. For whom are you doing this?
19. What will you have to do? What are your first steps?
20. For whom are you doing this?
21. Have you weighed your choices fully?
22. Are you glad you feel this way?
23. Why is it important to you? What purpose does it serve?
24. Is it something you really prize?
25. In what way would life be different without it?
26. Would you be willing to sign a petition supporting this idea?

TABLE 1.3   CLARIFYING RESPONSES continued

27. Are you saying that you believe. . . (repeat the idea)?
28. Do people know that you believe that way?
29. Are you willing to stand up and be counted for that?
30. I hear what you are for. . . now, is there anything you can do about it?
31. Are you willing to put some of your time, energy, and resources behind that idea?
32. Have you made any plans to do more than you have already done?
33. Who has influenced you on this?
34. Where will this lead you? How far are you willing to go?
35. How has it already affected your life? How will it affect you in the future?
36. How long do you think you will continue?
37. How did you decide which had priority?
38. Did you run into any difficulty?
39. Will you do it again?
40. Are there some other things you can do that are like it?

Reprinted with permission from Louis E. Raths, Merrill Harmin, and Sidney B. Simon. *Values and Teaching*. Columbus, Ohio: Charles Merrill Publishing Company, 1966, pp. 51–82.

I-OPENERS: PRACTICING THE PROCESS

The authors believe that your sexuality has the greatest probability of being healthy and happy when you learn to communicate effectively with others and when you make responsible decisions. Effective education in human sexuality affords you an opportunity to practice these essential skills. There is a special feature called an "I-Opener" at the end of each chapter in this book. These special features could also have been called "Eye-Openers." They are intended to open your eyes to sexual issues that are pertinent to your lifestyle. Each I-Opener deals with *making responsible decisions* as well as with communication.

When you make responsible and caring decisions and communicate effectively, your sexuality will be dynamic, healthy, and invigorating and will promote happiness.

SUMMARY STATEMENTS

- According to Immanuel Kant, "The three grand essentials" of happiness in this life are something to do, someone to love, and something to hope for."
- A process of making decisions about your sexuality that promote your health and happiness and that of others includes (1) a look at your lifestyle, (2) gathering information, (3) evaluating information, and (4) making responsible decisions.
- The values clarification process may help you ascertain whether or not your decisions are in accordance with your life principle.

- Communication is the process by which you send and receive messages.
- I-messages are statements about the self that contain a behavior, an effect, and a feeling.
- Active listening is a process of feeding back what you have heard to the person sending the message.
- A clarifying response can be used to obtain more information or to help one person understand what another is saying.

SUGGESTED READINGS

Buscaglia, Leo. *Love.* New Jersey: Charles B. Slack, 1972.

Fromm, Erich. *The Art of Loving.* New York: Bantam Books, 1963.

Gordon, Thomas. *Parent Effectiveness Training.* New York: New American Library, 1970.

Gortman, John, Cliff Notorius, and Howard Markman. *A Couples Guide to Communication.* Champaign, Illinois: Illinois Research Press, 1976.

Powell, John. *Unconditional Love.* Niles, Iowa: Argus Communications, 1969.

Powell, John. *Why Am I Afraid To Tell You Who I Am?* Niles, Iowa: Argus Communications, 1969.

Powell, John. *Fully Human, Fully Alive.* Niles, Iowa: Argus Communications, 1976.

COMMUNICATION

A LOOK AT YOUR LIFESTYLE

You have met someone at the bookstore and decided to take a walk and stop for a drink. The afternoon was well spent. You really enjoyed the other person's company. You agree to meet in front of the bookstore the following day. However, there is a thunderstorm that day. You go to the bookstore but (s)he does not show.

Write an I-message describing your reactions:
When (s)he was not in front of the bookstore, I _____.

1. Identify the key issue or problem_____

2. Identify three possible solutions or alternatives.

_____

_____

_____

GATHERING INFORMATION

Is there any information that you would like to have about any of the alter-

natives?_____

EVALUATING THE INFORMATION/ALTERNATIVES

Give at least one pro and one con for each alternative.

_____

MAKING RESPONSIBLE DECISIONS

Which alternative best suits your needs?
What are the possible consequences?

_____

_____

TWO

Male Anatomy and Physiology

A LOOK AT YOUR LIFESTYLE

I had a lot of questions about my body, especially when I started having wet dreams. I wondered why my bed was wet and if there was something wrong with me. In the morning I'd pull the covers up and tuck them in tight. I didn't want my mother to see the wet sheets. Somewhere I learned that guys didn't ask questions about their body. Guys were supposed to know.

A lack of knowledge about the male reproductive organs and their functions is a disservice to both men and women. Neglect of the sexual education of men stems from some very unhealthy assumptions in our society. The first assumption is that men know everything there is to know about sex. Traditionally, certain characteristics have been attributed to men that place them in this "all-knowing" role. Men have been described as "leaders," "heads of the household," "superior," "logical," and "dominant." The list of characteristics that affirm this "all-knowing" role is endless. It is assumed that a man should know everything and be able to do everything. A man who admits to himself, to other men, or to women that he is unsure of himself or that he needs more information about his sexuality feels uncomfortable.

Another faulty assumption often perpetuated in our society is that women need not know anything about male sexuality, the male organs, or their function. Why would a woman need to know about a man's organs or how they worked? Further, if she wanted to know, she could learn from a man with whom she became involved.

I remember mom sitting on the end of my bed telling me the facts of life. She told me all about Kotex and tampons and cramps. The kinds of things that girls learn in their mother-daughter talk. I wanted to ask her things I wanted to know. How big did guys get when they had an erection and how often did they come? But I wasn't supposed to be interested in that. I just sat there and listened.

Fortunately, our attitude about knowledge and understanding of ourselves and others is changing. No longer are men expected to know everything. Today a man can feel comfortable asking questions about his sexuality. He can feel comfortable exploring and learning about his body. He has the opportunity to discuss his sexuality and his organs and their functions with other men, and with women as well. He can learn to accept and appreciate the differences between men and between men and women. He has the opportunity to develop a responsible, caring attitude toward sexuality.

A responsible and caring woman also learns about male sexuality. She thus better appreciates the male body, male questions and concerns, and the differences between men and women. A woman's knowledge of a man's body is helpful to her in (1) appreciating what it means to be male, (2) pleasing herself sexually, (3) pleasing him sexually, (4) planning for contraception, and (5) discovering disease.

GATHERING INFORMATION

The sexuality of the male is very complex. He is a sexual being from head to toe. His brain functions in arousal as much as his penis. His neck and earlobes are as much sexual parts as his testes and scrotum. To understand him, it is important to learn about his body, his organs and their functions, his thoughts, his psychological makeup, and his feelings. The list of things to examine would be endless.

Although the entire male body is sexual, this discussion of male anatomy and physiology is limited to the organs involved in reproduction. Other aspects of male sexuality are included in the chapters that follow. The structure and function of the following organs are discussed: scrotum, testes, seminiferous tubules, epididymis, vas deferens, seminal vesicles, ejaculatory duct, prostate gland, bulbourethral (Cowper's) glands, urethra, and penis. In the section on male physiology, there is a discussion of erection, orgasm, and ejaculation.

EVALUATING INFORMATION

An examination of the information about male sexuality will assist you in being responsible and caring. As you learn about each of the organs and their functions, you can evaluate how this information will enhance your lifestyle. Consider the following questions:

1. What complications may result from a man's having had mumps during adolescence?
2. What are the advantages and disadvantages of circumcision?
3. What factors affect sperm production?
4. How might male hernia be avoided?
5. What would I do if I had a male child and his testes had not descended before birth?
6. What are the benefits of male self-examination?
7. How does penis size affect sexual satisfaction?
8. What would happen to the sexual life of a male with a spinal cord injury?
9. Why do some men develop secondary sex characteristics sooner than others?

Information is provided for you to evaluate. Your personal preferences will influence your decisions. Your personal preferences may differ from the preferences of others. Your decisions may also differ. What is important is that you take time to evaluate what you have learned. Careful evaluation will provide reasons for your decisions.

> I didn't know much about circumcision. Then shortly after the birth of our son the doctor asked my wife and me to make a decision. I guess we said yes because I am circumcised. But I am not certain what the advantages and disadvantages might be.

The evaluation of information will also enable you to form healthier attitudes about yourself and others.

> I've always been embarrassed about the size of my penis. When I learned that guys who are big and guys who are small are all about 6 inches when they're erect, I was really relieved. I'd have felt a lot better if I'd learned that sooner.

MAKING RESPONSIBLE DECISIONS

You might ask, "How can I be responsible for decisions about male anatomy and physiology? After all, the organs are already there!" The care of the male organs involved in reproduction deserves the same attention as the care of the rest of the body. Frequent self-examination and regular examination by a doctor need to be a part of one's lifestyle. A woman can encourage self-examination and even participate in the examination.

Both men and women can assume responsibility for the development of healthy attitudes toward the male body. Learning the names of the organs, their location, and their function should be helpful in discussing sex more freely (Figure 2.1). Rather than avoid discussions about circumcision, erection, penis size, ejaculation, or sperm production, men and women can talk openly. Without communication, it is difficult to make responsible decisions.

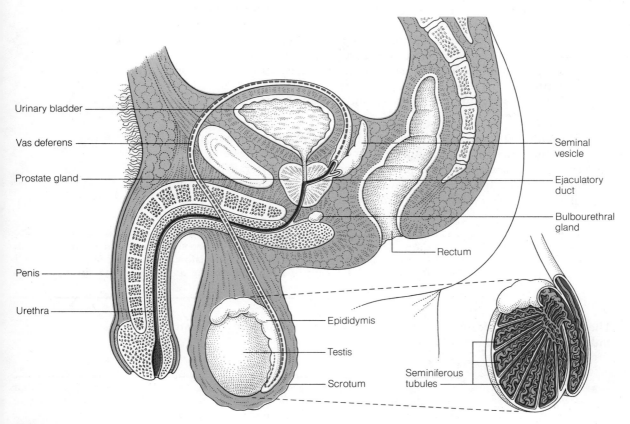

FIGURE 2.1 Organs of the male reproductive system.

The scrotum is a saclike pouch in the groin area that contains the testes. It is divided into two compartments. Each of these compartments contains one of the testes. Each testis is held in the scrotum by a spermatic cord. The spermatic cord contains blood vessels, nerves, and muscles. It also contains the vas deferens, which we will discuss later in this chapter.

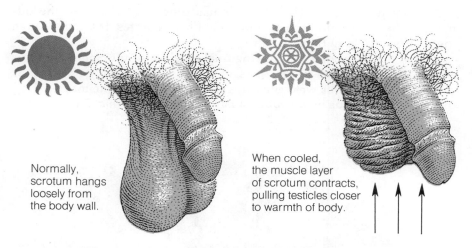

Normally, scrotum hangs loosely from the body wall.

When cooled, the muscle layer of scrotum contracts, pulling testicles closer to warmth of body.

FIGURE 2.2 Effect of temperature on scrotum and position of testicles.

FUNCTIONS OF THE SCROTUM

The *scrotum* has two basic functions: (1) to hold the testes and (2) to regulate temperature. Sperm cannot be produced at internal body temperatures. They are produced at a temperature that averages 3°C lower than normal body temperature. The scrotum acts as a temperature regulator in two ways (Figure 2.2). First, the scrotum perspires freely. The evaporation of perspiration has a cooling effect. Second, there are muscles attached to the testes that can contract, pulling the testes closer to the body, thus warming them, or relax, lowering the testes away from the body, thus cooling them. These are called the *cremasteric muscles*.

A man will notice that his testes are close to his body when he has just taken a cold shower, when he has been outside skiing on a cold day, or when he has just climbed out of a swimming pool. The testes are lower on a very warm day or after a warm bath or shower.

Sometimes men do things that interfere with the natural physiological process. For example, when a man is exercising, he is usually warm. The natural physiological reaction would be for the cremasteric muscles to relax, lowering the testes away from the body and cooling them. However, during exercise, many men wear athletic supporters, or jock straps, which keep the testes close to the body. The higher temperature temporarily inhibits sperm production (but does not cause sterility). Tight underwear and bathing in very hot water also have the same effect.

The Testes

There are two *testes*. They develop inside the body just below the kidneys. In the eighth month of intrauterine life, the testes descend through the inguinal canal to the scrotum.

After the testes descend, the inguinal canal closes off. Sometimes this area is left weak. Later in life, stresses such as lifting heavy objects may cause problems in this weakened area. Some of the intestine may push on this area and eventually protrude, causing an *inguinal hernia* (Figure 2.3).

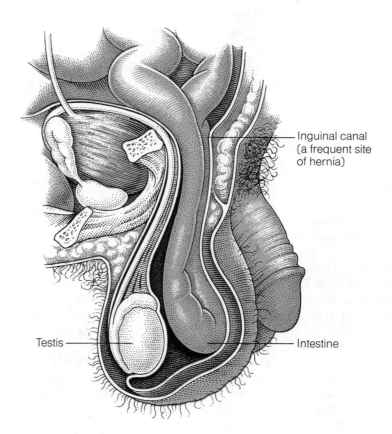

Inguinal canal (a frequent site of hernia)

Testis

Intestine

FIGURE 2.3 A frequent site of hernia.

CRYPTORCHIDISM

Cryptorchidism is a condition that can arise when the testes do not descend through the inguinal canal to the scrotum before birth. This condition may occur as a result of low hormonal stimulation, or it may result from a blockage in the canal. The most frequent cause of cryptorchidism is premature birth. In many cases, cryptorchidism is temporary and the testes descend shortly after birth. When the testes do not descend, they are relocated with hormone treatments or surgery to prevent sterility.

FUNCTIONS OF THE TESTES

The testes have two basic functions: (1) secreting the male hormone testosterone and (2) producing sperm. Around the age of 10, the pituitary gland secretes *follicle-stimulating hormone (FSH)* and *interstitial-cell-stimulating hormone (ICSH)*. These hormones initiate puberty. Interstitial-cell--stimulating hormone stimulates a special group of cells in the testes, the interstitial cells (cells of Leydig), to produce testosterone.

THE SECRETION OF TESTOSTERONE When testosterone is released into the bloodstream, many changes occur (Figure 2.4). These

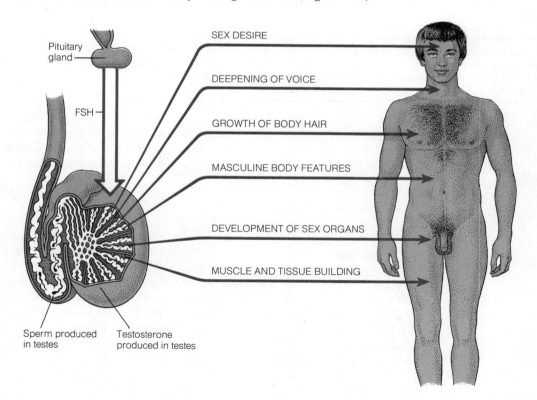

Pituitary gland

FSH

Sperm produced in testes

Testosterone produced in testes

SEX DESIRE

DEEPENING OF VOICE

GROWTH OF BODY HAIR

MASCULINE BODY FEATURES

DEVELOPMENT OF SEX ORGANS

MUSCLE AND TISSUE BUILDING

FIGURE 2.4 Male secondary sex characteristics.

changes are referred to as the male secondary sex characteristics. The male organs such as the penis and the testes will grow. The voice will become deeper. Hair will grow on the body, especially in the groin and on the chest. The torso will become more V-shaped as the male develops muscle mass and longer and heavier bones. These characteristics develop at an individual rate, and sometimes this development may be uncomfortable for the growing male.

I remember when all the other guys would shower and I'd try and sneak to the wash basin instead. They all had larger penises and many pubic hairs. I could only count a couple of hairs.

Because the male hormone initially increases weight, muscle mass, and aggressiveness, some coaches have given it to their teams, in the hope that it would improve athletic performance. However, there is no evidence that testosterone will affect athletic performance. The Join Committee on the Medical Aspects of Sports of the American Medical Association advises against its use, because it may cause shrinking of the testicles, loss of sex drive, dizziness, muscle aches, and liver damage.

Until I took this class I always thought that it would be neat to get some shots to make me more of a man. It sure made sense; the more male hormone — the more manly I could be. I didn't know it could be dangerous, let alone that I could be less of a man.

SPERMATOGENESIS Puberty is also the beginning of the production of sperm (spermatozoa) — *Spermatogenesis.* Sperm production will be discussed in more detail when we discuss the seminiferous tubules.

SELF-EXAMINATION

After puberty, a man should regularly examine his testes (Figure 2.5). First, he should look at his testes in the mirror. The two testes are approximately equal in size (about 2 by 1 by 1¼ inches). One testis, usually the left one, normally hangs slightly lower than the other. A man should feel his testes once a month, just as a woman should examine her breasts once a month. He should feel the entire testes. If the testes are sensitive to touch, he may have an infection or a sexually transmitted disease. A growth or mass on the testes may be a sign of cancer or a cyst. One percent of all cancers that occur in men involve the testes. Testicular cancer may occur in the twenties or thirties, and may be detected by self-examination. Self-examination should begin at puberty because it familiarizes the growing male with his body and helps him to establish a permanent habit.

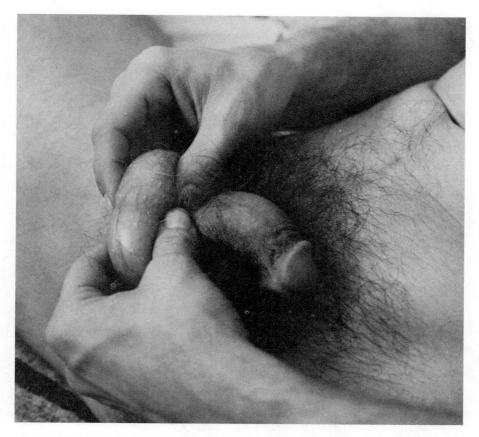

FIGURE 2.5   A growth or mass on the testes may be a sign of cancer. (Photo by Teri Leigh Stratford, 1981)

The Seminiferous Tubules

A whitish, fibrous sheath surrounds each testis and divides the testis into several sections. Each section is filled with a coiled network of tubes called the *seminiferous tubules.*

With the onset of puberty (Figure 2.6), FSH begins to stimulate these seminiferous tubules to produce sperm. Sperm production is called spermatogenesis. Spermatogenesis usually begins at age 12, but mature sperm are not found in the growing male until he is nearly 14 years of age.

THE CHARACTERISTICS OF SPERM

The characteristics of mature sperm are:

1. They are very tiny, only about 0.0024 inch.
2. They have a head, a neck, a midpiece, and a tail.

3. The hereditary material is located in the head of the sperm.
4. The tail of the mature sperm propels it, makes it able to move.
5. The mature sperm has 23 chromosomes.
6. The mature sperm carries either an X or a Y chromosome.

FACTORS AFFECTING SPERM PRODUCTION

Several factors affect the production of sperm. As mentioned before, higher temperatures inhibit the production of sperm. Stress tends to reduce sperm production, as do high altitudes. Radiation may completely block sperm production.

ORCHIDITIS A male should have the mumps vaccine prior to puberty to avoid a condition called *orchiditis*. When a male gets mumps after puberty, the mumps virus causes the seminiferous tubules to swell. As they continue to swell, they are crushed by the white fibrous sheath

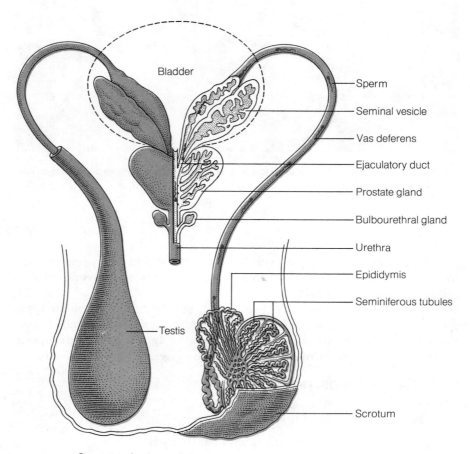

FIGURE 2.6 Sperm production and transport.

that divides the testes. The seminiferous tubules lose their function, and the male may become sterile.

The Epididymis

After sperm are produced by the seminiferous tubules, they move to the *epididymis*. The epididymis is a comma-shaped structure found on the back and upper surface of the testes. Sperm mature in the epididymis for about 2 to 6 weeks. Some sperm will remain for storage, but most move on to the vas deferens.

The Vas Deferens

The *vas deferens* are two long, thin cords that go from the epididymis in the scrotum, up through the inguinal canal, into the abdomen. Eventually each vas deferens turns downward. They are joined by the ducts of the seminal vesicles to form the ejaculatory duct.

The vas deferens functions as a passageway for sperm and as a place for sperm storage. Male sterilization, a vasectomy, is the cutting of the vas deferens so that the sperm have no passageway. A vasectomy is described in greater detail in Chapter 7.

The Seminal Vesicles

The *seminal vesicle* is a small gland at the end of each vas deferens. These two glands produce an alkaline fluid that is very rich in fructose, a simple sugar that provides nutrition for the sperm. The amount of this fluid in the seminal vesicles at the time of ejaculation is thought to be related to the intensity of the experience: the more seminal fluid, the more satisfying the experience. Thus, if a male has multiple ejaculations, usually the first climax will be the most intense. In subsequent climaxes there is less seminal fluid.

The Ejaculatory Duct

The *ejaculatory duct* is a short, straight tube that passes into the prostate gland to open into the urethra.

The Prostate Gland

The *prostate gland* lies just beneath the bladder and surrounds the urethra. It produces a fluid that makes up most of the quantity of semen. This fluid is very alkaline, and it aids the sperm in its route to fertilize the egg. The vagina is very acidic, and thus affects the longevity and movement of the sperm. The alkaline prostatic fluid neutralizes the acidic vagina as well as the acidity in the male urethra.

CANCER OF THE PROSTATE

The prostate gland may become a frequent site of cancer in the male. In the early stages of cancer of the prostate, hard lumps or masses can be felt during a rectal examination (Figure 2.7). Although many men are squeamish about having a rectal examination, it should be done yearly after 30 years of age.

Because the prostate surrounds the urethra, the following signs may indicate an enlarged prostate and perhaps cancer.

1. loss in the force of the urinary stream
2. dribbling
3. increased frequency of urination
4. blood in the urine
5. passing urine at night

The Bulbourethral Glands (Cowper's Glands)

The *bulbourethral*, or *Cowper's, glands* are two small pea-sized glands that are located one on each side of the urethra. Small ducts from these glands open into the urethra. When a man becomes sexually excited, the bulbourethral glands secrete a slippery fluid. A drop of this fluid can be noticed at the tip of the penis.

This fluid is sometimes called *precoital* (before intercourse) fluid. It is alkaline and may aid in lowering the acidity in the urethra, making it easier for the sperm to live. Although this fluid precedes ejaculation, sperm have sometimes been found in it and can cause pregnancy.

The Urethra

The *urethra* is a tubelike passageway that runs from the urinary bladder to the outside tip of the penis. The urethra goes through the prostate

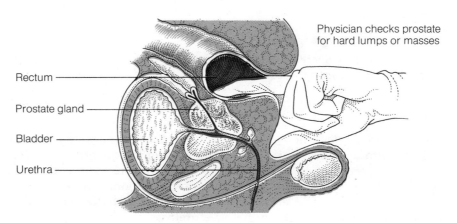

FIGURE 2.7 Checking for hard lumps or masses during rectal examination of the prostate.

gland, where it is joined by the ejaculatory duct. The urethra is about 9 inches long . It serves as a passageway for semen and urine. Before ejaculation, the opening of the bladder closes off so that the urine and semen are not in the urethra at the same time.

The Penis

The *penis* is the male organ of sexual pleasure, reproduction, and urination. The part of the penis that is attached to the pelvic area is called the root. The main part of the penis is called the *body* or *shaft*. The tip or head of the penis is called the *glans*. The *corona* is the rim or crown where the glans rises slightly over the shaft. A circular fold of skin, called the *foreskin* or *prepuce,* covers the glans in uncircumcised men. The *frenulum* is the underside where the glans is attached to the foreskin.

CIRCUMCISION

Circumcision is the removal of the foreskin from the penis (Figure 2.8) for a variety of ritual, religious, physical, or hygienic reasons. Whether or not circumcision is necessary is controversial. Aside from religious or ritual reasons, the main arguments for and against circumcision, focus on its hygienic value and its effect on the sensitivity of the glans.

When a man is circumcised, the sensitive glans is left exposed. Some people believe that this makes the penis more sensitive and that the man will respond to touch more quickly. However, in uncircumcised men, the foreskin retracts during sex play, and the glans is exposed. Therefore, sensitivity is not lessened. Other people believe the contrary: that circumcised men are *less* sensitive, because the glans is toughened by constant exposure. Masters and Johnson (1966) found no significant difference in the sensitivity of the glans of circumcised men and that of uncircumcised men.

Probably the most popular reason for circumcision is the belief that it is more hygienic. There are a number of small glands located in the foreskin that discharge their secretions on the glans. The accumulation of these secretions on the glans is called *smegma*.

Although the cause-and-effect mechanism is not completely understood, some researchers have found a relationship between men not circumcised and cancer of the penis and of the cervix in women. Cancer of the penis, although uncommon, is more common in uncircumcised males (Hand, 1970). Some physicians recommend circumcision as a hygienic means of avoiding the accumulation of smegma. However, an uncircumcised man can also avoid smegma accumulation by pulling back the foreskin and carefully cleansing the glans.

Circumcision is the treatment of choice for males who have *phimosis,* a condition in which the foreskin is long, tight, and not retractable.

PENIS SIZE

Our culture is preoccupied with penis size and the belief that a large penis is more satisfying to the female. It seems that our movies and best-

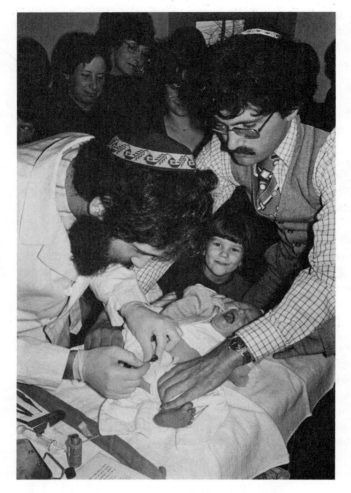

FIGURE 2.8 Circumcision is the removal of the foreskin from the penis. (Photo by Bill Aron, 1978, Jeroboam, Inc.)

selling books tend to provide vivid descriptions of the sex act. These descriptions usually include men with enormous penises. The man in the movie may have some other noticeable physical characteristic, such as large feet or long fingers, and the faulty conclusion is drawn that "large feet mean a large penis."

I can remember sitting around with the girls in the dorm discussing our dates. We'd all laugh when we'd talk about how big his shoes were or how tall he was. . . as if it made a difference.

These descriptions create an unnecessary emphasis on penis size and make both men and women believe that a man needs a large penis to be a good lover. This worry can be alleviated with accurate information about penis size and female sexual satisfaction. The female vagina stretches to accommodate the size of the penis. In addition, the labia and the clitoris are the most excitable parts of the female, and they are not affected by penis size. Further, a penis that appears smaller when flaccid (not erect or hard) tends to increase more in size during erection than an already large penis (Masters and Johnson, 1966) (Figure 2.9). Thus, penis size is relatively unimportant in sexual performance.

The penis cannot be enlarged with surgery, through exercise, or by hormonal injections. In fact, injections of silicone and other substances have been found to destroy a man's ability to have an erection.

MALE PHYSIOLOGY

The male organs involved in reproduction (1) produce sperm, (2) transport the sperm to the female, and (3) provide sexual satisfaction. In this section we will discuss erection, orgasm, and ejaculation. Male sexual response will be covered in Chapter 4.

Erection

The penis is composed of three cylinders, each containing erectile tissues. The top two cylinders are called the *corpora cavernosa,* and the single one beneath is called the *corpus spongiosum.* Each of these three cylinders contains many spaces, or cavities, and resembles a sponge. Thus, these three cylinders are also referred to as the three spongy layers. These spongy layers are richly supplied with blood vessels and nerves. The spaces in them are separated by cross-bars of smooth muscle.

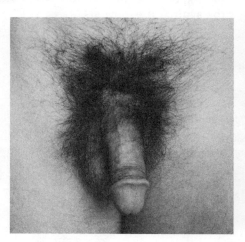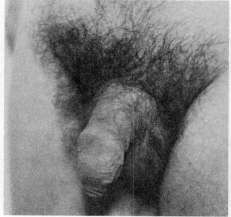

FIGURE 2.9 A penis that is smaller when flaccid tends to increase more in size during erection. Left, a circumcised penis. (Photo by Teri Leigh Stratford) Right, an uncircumcised penis. (Photo by K. Bendo)

Erection is produced by an involuntary spinal reflex. There are receptors in the penis, scrotum, and thighs that, when touched, produce a neural signal that is sent to the sacral, or lowest, portion of the spinal cord. This signal causes the smooth muscles to become relaxed. It also causes the parasympathetic nervous system to send a message to the arteries leading into the penis, telling them to dilate or expand. Blood rushes into the arteries in the spongy layers under relatively high pressure, having the same effect as soaking a sponge with water. At the same time, the flow of venous blood away from the penis is partially reduced. The mechanism of erection is summarized in Figure 2.10.

The penis is made up of loose folds of skin. When the penis is engorged with blood, it swells, elongates, and becomes erect. The nonerect penis, which is usually 2½ to 4 inches long, will increase in size to about 6 inches long.

SPINAL CORD INJURY

The spinal reflex involvement in erection has implications for male physiology. If a man's spinal cord is severed above the reflex center in the sacral area, he can still have an erection by tactile stimulation of his penis, thighs, and scrotum. There is another location higher in the spinal cord that also produces an erection and is responsive to fantasy and psychological factors.

An erection is an involuntary process. Although an erection is usually associated with sexual excitement, the two are not necessarily connected. The capacity for an erection begins at birth. The small baby boy may have an erection when his mother or father bathes him, when he explores his body, or when he rubs his genitals against something. As boys grow and develop, they may experience an erection when riding a bike or when tight clothing rubs against the genitals.

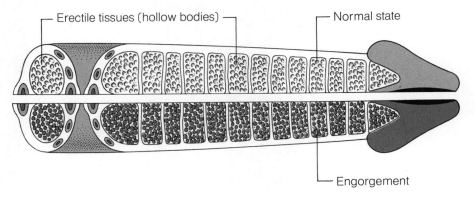

Erectile tissues (hollow bodies) — Normal state — Engorgement

FIGURE 2.10 Parasympathetic impulses during sexual excitement cause arteries leading into penis to dilate; blood engorges erectile tissues and penis swells and becomes erect. Venous blood flow away from penis is reduced during erection.

> I remember babysitting for a little boy. Every time I'd change his diapers and sponge him, he'd get an erection. I worried that I was a sex pervert and since we were both males that he'd be homosexual.

MORNING ERECTION

It is also common for a man or boy to wake up with an erection. A *morning erection* may be due to a full bladder. In addition, a morning erection often accompanies the rapid eye movement (REM) or dreaming stage of sleep (Karacon, 1970). If a man wakes up during the REM stage he may have an erection.

Orgasm

The culmination of sexual stimulation in the man is called *orgasm* and involves a pleasurable feeling of physiological and psychological release. Orgasm is usually accompanied by ejaculation (Hole, 1978).

Ejaculation

Ejaculation is the sudden expulsion of seminal fluid from the erect penis. The reflex action producing ejaculation operates in the following manner. When the penis is stimulated orally, manually, or coitally, messages are transmitted to the lumbar and sacral portions of the spinal cord. These messages may also be a result of psychological stimulation. As a result of spinal reflexes, the sympathetic nervous system sends a message to the smooth muscles in the internal organs involved in ejaculation.

Rhythmic contractions occur in the smooth muscles in the walls of the testes, epididymis, vas deferens, and ejaculatory ducts. At the same time, there are rhythmic contractions in the seminal vesicles and prostate gland, as well as in the skeletal muscles at the base of the erectile tissue. The pressure within the erectile tissue aids in forcing the semen through the urethra.

SEQUENCE OF EVENTS

The order of events during ejaculation serves to facilitate the safe passage of sperm:

1. The fluid from the bulbourethral glands is secreted. This fluid lubricates the tip of the penis and lowers the acidity of the urethra.
2. The fluid from the prostate gland is released. This fluid is alkaline and neutralizes the acidity of the seminal fluid and later will neutralize the acidity of the vagina, enhancing the sperm viability. Most of the seminal fluid comes from the prostate gland.

3. The sperm cells, which are formed in the testes (seminiferous tubules, epididymis), travel along the vas deferens.
4. Fluid is ejected from the seminal vesicles. The seminal fluid is alkaline, and it contains fructose, a nutrient, which nourishes the sperm.

The mechanism that results in ejaculation is summarized in Figure 2.11. The seminal fluid leaves in spurts that correspond with the rhythmic

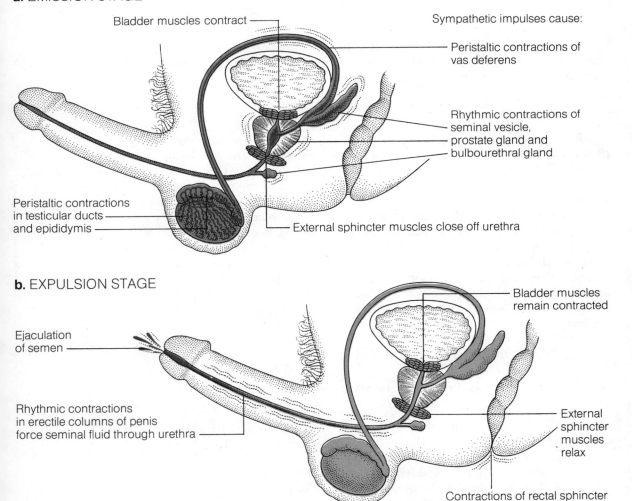

a. EMISSION STAGE

Bladder muscles contract

Sympathetic impulses cause:

Peristaltic contractions of vas deferens

Rhythmic contractions of seminal vesicle, prostate gland and bulbourethral gland

Peristaltic contractions in testicular ducts and epididymis

External sphincter muscles close off urethra

b. EXPULSION STAGE

Ejaculation of semen

Bladder muscles remain contracted

Rhythmic contractions in erectile columns of penis force seminal fluid through urethra

External sphincter muscles relax

Contractions of rectal sphincter

FIGURE 2.11 Ejaculation is the sudden expulsion of seminal fluid from the erect penis.

contractions. The first contractions occur at 0.8-second intervals. Normally, 3 ml of semen are secreted during ejaculation. Each milliliter contains about 120 million sperm. The normal male ejaculate may vary from 35 to 200 million sperm per milliliter. The average male ejaculate of 3 ml (less than a teaspoon) contains approximately 300 million sperm.

After ejaculation, sympathetic impulses cause constriction of the arteries leading to the erectile tissue in the penis. The blood flow is reduced. The smooth muscles within the vascular spaces contract, enabling the veins to carry the excess blood from the spaces in the spongy layers. The penis returns to the flaccid or nonerect state.

NOCTURNAL EMISSIONS, OR WET DREAMS

Spontaneous ejaculations may occur during sleep. Such ejaculations are called *nocturnal emissions,* or "wet dreams." Wet dreams are caused by the changes in hormonal concentrations that accompany puberty and adolescent development. Young men who have not learned that wet dreams are normal may be frightened, uncomfortable, and embarrassed by their occurrence.

SUMMARY STATEMENTS

- *The scrotum is a saclike pouch in the groin area that (1) holds the testes and (2) regulates temperature for sperm production.*
- *The testes develop inside the abdomen, near the kidney, and pass through the inguinal canal to the scrotum during the eighth month of intrauterine life. Cryptorchidism, undescended testes, causes male sterility because sperm cannot be produced at body temperature.*
- *Puberty begins around the age of 10. The testes begin their important functions: (1) to secrete the male hormone testosterone, which causes secondary sex characteristics to appear, and (2) to produce sperm.*
- *Beginning at puberty, a man should regularly palpate his testes. A lump or mass may be an early warning of testicular cancer.*
- *Spermatogenesis, sperm production, takes place in the seminiferous tubules. Although spermatogenesis usually begins at age 12, mature sperm are seldom found in the male until age 14.*
- *The epididymis is a comma-shaped structure found on the back and upper surface of the testes where the sperm mature.*
- *The vas deferens are two long, thin cords which function as a passageway for sperm and as a place for sperm storage.*

- *The seminal vesicles are two small glands at the ends of the vas deferens that secrete an alkaline fluid that is rich in fructose, a sugar nutrient that provides energy for the sperm.*
- *The ejaculatory duct is a short, straight tube that passes into the prostate gland to open into the urethra.*
- *The prostate gland produces an alkaline fluid, which makes up most of the quantity of semen. Because it is a frequent site of cancer in men over 50, a man should have an annual rectal examination to check for lumps or growths.*
- *The bulbourethral, or Cowper's, glands are two small pea-sized glands located on either side of the urethra that secrete a slippery fluid that can be noticed on the tip of the penis when a man is sexually aroused.*
- *Inside the penis is the urethra, a 9-inch tube that runs from the bladder to the outside tip of the penis. The penis is the male organ used for sexual pleasure, reproduction, and urination.*
- *Circumcision is the surgical removal of the foreskin from the penis.*
- *Penis size is relatively unimportant in satisfying a woman, because a penis which is smaller when flaccid will increase more in size than a larger one, and the vagina stretches to accommodate the size of the penis.*

- *An erection occurs when the spongy layers inside the penis are engorged with blood and the penis swells and elongates.*
- *The culmination of the male sexual experience is called an orgasm, which is usually accompanied by ejacula-tion, the expulsion of the seminal fluid from the urethra of the erect penis.*
- *Seminal fluid is composed of prostate secretion, which is whitish and alkaline; secretions of the seminal vesicles, which act as a nutrient; and sperm.*

SUGGESTED READINGS

Blank, Joani. *The Playbook: For Men/About Sex.* Burlingame, California: Down There Press, 1975.

Kinsey, Alfred C., Wardell Pomeroy, and Clyde Martin. *Sexual Behavior in the Human Male.* Philadelphia: W. B. Saunders, 1948.

Lewis, Alfred Allan. *The Male: His Body, His Sex.* Garden City, New York: Anchor Press, Doubleday, 1978.

Masters, William, and Virginia Johnson. *Human Sexual Response.* Boston: Little, Brown, 1966.

Zilbergeld, Bernie. *Male Sexuality: A Guide to Sexual Fulfillment.* Boston: Little, Brown, 1978.

MALE ANATOMY AND PHYSIOLOGY

A LOOK AT YOUR LIFESTYLE
You and your partner are seeing a movie. During a lovemaking scene, you are surprised at the size of the actor's penis. You think his penis is unusually large.

Write an I-message describing your reaction to this situation:
When I see a large penis, I ————————————————————— .

1. Identify the key issue or problem.
Given:
I am wondering what my partner's feelings are.

———————————————————————————————————

2. Identify three different ways to initiate a discussion about penis size with your partner.

———————————————————————————————————

———————————————————————————————————

———————————————————————————————————

GATHERING INFORMATION
Identify three facts related to penis size.

———————————————————————————————————

———————————————————————————————————

———————————————————————————————————

EVALUATING THE INFORMATION
Complete the following I-message:

After carefully evaluating the information about penis size, I _____

_____

MAKING RESPONSIBLE DECISIONS
If I heard someone making fun about the size of someone else's penis, I would _____

_____

THREE

Female Anatomy and Physiology

A LOOK AT YOUR LIFESTYLE

Several years ago eleven women formed a group to write *Our Bodies, Ourselves,* a book by and for women. In their book they discuss why knowledge about the female body is essential for a healthy, energetic lifestyle:

> For us, body education is core education. Our bodies are the physical basis from which we move out into the world; ignorance, uncertainty—even, at worst, shame—about our physical selves create in us an alienation from ourselves that keeps us from being the whole people that we could be. Picture a woman trying to do work and to enter into equal and satisfying relationships with other people—when she feels physically weak because she has never tried to be strong; when she drains her energy trying to change her face, her figure, her hair, her smells, to match some ideal norm set by magazines, movies and TV; when she feels confused and ashamed of the menstrual blood that every month appears from some dark place in her body; when her internal body processes are a mystery to her and surface only to cause her trouble (an unplanned pregnancy or cervical cancer); when she does not understand or enjoy sex and concentrates her sexual drives into aimless romantic fantasies, perverting

37

and misusing a potential energy because she has been brought up to deny it. Learning to understand, accept, and be responsible for our physical selves, we are freed of some of these preoccupations and can start to use our untapped energies. Our image of ourselves is on a firmer base, we can be better friends and better lovers, better people, more self-confident, more autonomous, stronger and more whole.

(The Boston Women's Health Book Collective, March 1973)

Self-knowledge is a necessary part of a whole person. Certainly knowledge of the female anatomy and physiology is a necessity for a woman who desires self-acceptance and self-love. It is one of the ingredients that is needed for a responsible and caring lifestyle. There is validity in the statement made by the Boston Women's Health Book Collective that "body education is core education."

Men also need to learn about the female body as a part of their core education. It would be difficult indeed for a man to have responsible and caring sexuality without any knowledge or appreciation of the female body and how it functions. A man's knowledge of a woman's body is helpful to him in (1) appreciating what it means to be female, (2) pleasing himself sexually, (3) pleasing her sexually, (4) planning for contraception, and (5) preventing and discovering disease.

I was really scared until after the first time I had sex. I wasn't sure about her body. I didn't know what to say. I met a girl who was five years older than me. She taught me it all. I guess because she was older I felt I could talk straight out with her.

Gathering Information

Although the entire female body is sexual, this chapter is limited to a discussion of the anatomy and physiology of the reproductive system. Other aspects of female sexuality are included in the chapters that follow. The structure and function of the following organs and structures will be discussed: the mons veneris, the labia majora, the labia minora, the clitoris, the vestibule, the urethral opening, the introitus, the hymen, the perineum, Bartholin's glands, the breasts, the vagina, the uterus, the oviducts, and the ovaries. The diseases and disorders that affect these organs and structures will be carefully examined. In addition, there is a discussion of the phases of the menstrual cycle, conditions affecting menstruation, and menopause. A special section is included on the annual physical examination.

Evaluating the Information

An examination of the information about female sexuality may assist you in being responsible and caring. As you learn about the female organs and structures and their functions, you can evaluate how this information will affect your lifestyle. Consider the following questions:

1. Why do some women have larger breasts than others?
2. Is a woman still a virgin if her hymen breaks while she is riding a bicycle?
3. How often and when should a woman examine her breasts?
4. What should a woman do if she discovers a lump in her breast?
5. When does ovulation occur?
6. Is menstrual blood clean?
7. What can a woman do about severe menstrual cramps?
8. Is it all right to have sex during menstruation?
9. Do all women have problems during menopause?
10. What can a woman expect during the annual checkup?

Information is provided for you to evaluate. Your personal preferences will influence your decisions. Careful evaluation will provide reasons for your decisions. Information can dispel myths.

Making Responsible Decisions

Body knowledge is indeed "core knowledge." A woman needs to understand her body and its functions so that she can give herself the attention that she needs. She needs to participate in regular self-examination and to have a regular examination by her physician. She needs to recognize the symptoms of diseases and disorders that affect the reproductive system. She needs to have knowledge and a healthy attitude about her menstrual cycle, menopause, and pelvic examination. More important, she needs to take appropriate action when necessary—to make responsible decisions.

I had very irregular periods for about eight months. Each month I'd talk about seeing the doctor after my menstrual flow. Somehow I just didn't call. Today I picked up the phone and called. I feel good inside. It's like a gift. I'm going to do something for myself. I guess that's what you meant when you said that the goal of our sex class was to make responsible decisions.

Every responsible and caring man also learns the functions of a woman's body. Part of a woman's self-acceptance is the acceptance that she receives from significant others. A man can be very supportive if he is well informed about the menstrual cycle, menopause, and the diseases and disorders of the reproductive system.

My father discovered a lump in my mother's breast. She kept saying it was nothing. We were very concerned. He encouraged her to see a doctor. She didn't want to. I think she was scared. He ended up taking off from work and going with her to the doctor's office. When we found out that she had cancer and needed surgery, we spent a lot of time talking about what it meant. I never knew how women felt. We are all a lot closer now.

THE EXTERNAL FEMALE ANATOMY

The term *vulva* refers to the female external genitalia. The external genitalia consist of the mons veneris, the labia majora, the labia minora, the clitoris, the vestibule, the urethral opening, the introitus, the hymen, the perineum, and Bartholin's glands (Figure 3.1).

The Mons Veneris

The mons veneris consists of pads of fatty tissue over the front of the pubic bone. This fatty tissue between the bone and skin serves as a protective cushion for the female reproductive organs. The term *mons veneris* comes from Venus, the goddess of love and beauty. *Mons veneris* is Latin for "mountain of love."

During puberty, hair covers the mons veneris in a triangular fashion. When the female is sexually aroused, the vagina secretes moist lubricants. The pubic hair covering the mons may trap the scent of these secretions and further arouse both male and female.

The Labia Majora

The *labia majora* are the outer lips, or heavy folds of skin, surrounding the opening of the vagina. The labia are richly supplied with nerve endings and blood vessels and are sensitive to touch. During sexual arousal, the labia become engorged with blood.

The Labia Minora

The *labia minora* are two smaller lips or folds of skin located between the labia majora. The labia minora extend from the clitoral hood downward, past the openings to the urethra and the vagina. They vary in size, shape, and color. These smaller lips contain sweat and oil glands. They are richly supplied with nerve endings and blood vessels.

The Clitoris

The *clitoris* is a small cylindrical body (about 2 cm long and about 0.5 cm in diameter) projecting between the labia minora. The clitoris is com-

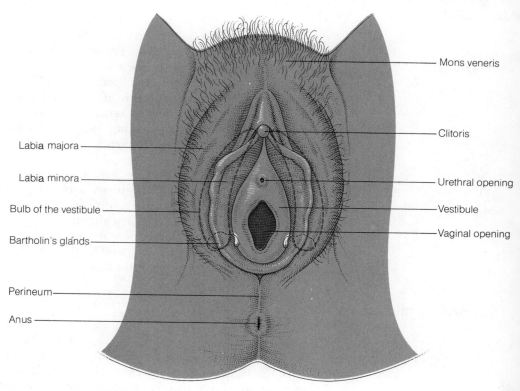

FIGURE 3.1 Female external reproductive organs.

posed of an external shaft and glans covered by the clitoral hood. The hood covering the shaft and glans is similar to the foreskin covering the glans of the penis. The hood covers the very sensitive glans, which is richly supplied with blood vessels and nerve endings.

The shaft of the clitoris contains two small spongy bodies, the cavernosa bodies. These spongy bodies become engorged with blood during arousal and are responsible for what some call clitoral erection.

The Vestibule

The *vestibule* is a space between the labia minora into which opens the urethra, the vagina, and the ducts of the Bartholin's glands.

The Urethral Opening

The *urethra* is a short tube that serves as a passageway for urine from the bladder to the outside of the body. The urethra opens into the floor of the vestibule, midway between the glans of the clitoris and the vaginal opening.

CYSTITIS

The urethral opening is in close proximity to the vaginal and anal openings. Therefore, bacteria from defecation and infectious agents from sexual contact are easily transmitted from the anus and vagina to the urethra. They may travel up the urethra and infect the bladder. The bladder may become inflamed, a condition termed *cystitis*. It is also possible to cause cystitis by irritating or damaging the urethra. Because this type sometimes occurs during first intercourse, it has been termed "honeymoon cystitis."

The symptoms of cystitis include pain during intercourse, frequent urination, blood and/or pus in the urine, a burning sensation during urination, and pelvic pain. To avoid cystitis, a woman can (1) be careful to wipe with toilet paper from front to back after urinating or having a bowel movement, (2) drink several glasses of water each day, (3) make sure that she and her partner wash their hands and genitals before and after intercourse, and (4) urinate before and after intercourse.

The Introitus and the Hymen

The vaginal opening is called the *introitus*. The *hymen* is a thin membrane that stretches across the introitus. There is a circular perforation in the center of the hymen. It is through this perforation that the menstrual flow leaves the body and that tampons are inserted during menstruation. Sometimes (rarely) there is no central perforation and the menstrual flow is blocked. This is called an *imperforate hymen*, and the hymen must be opened by incision.

The hymen varies in thickness and extent, and sometimes it is absent. There are many unnecessary concerns about the presence or absence of the hymen.

When I was a kid, probably seven or eight, I remember taking a spill on my bike. The seat jammed up between my legs. I had some blood on my panties. It was just a few drops but it scared me. My mom had a funny reaction. I wasn't sure what to think. Later, when all the kids said that girls had a "maidenhead" or "cherry" to prove their virginity I was scared. What did this mean? I wondered how breaking my hymen would affect my life. I wondered if anyone would believe me.

For centuries, people have erroneously believed that the presence of the hymen proved a woman's virginity. Such proof would be demonstrated at first coitus by the bleeding that would occur from the rupture or tearing of the hymen. In some tribal communities, it is customary to place a white pillow under the buttocks of the female on her wedding night to collect blood stains as proof of virginity.

The purpose of the hymen is to protect the vagina until puberty. Prior to the secretions of estrogens at puberty, the vaginal walls are not as tough, and the internal genitalia are more susceptible to infection.

Because the hymen varies in thickness and extent and may be absent at birth, there may or may not be bleeding when it is torn or ruptured. Generally there is slight bleeding, but not always. In some cases the hymen is resistant to coital rupture. To prevent pain and difficult insertion of the penis, a physician can make an incision in the hymen. Some physicians recommend a natural stretching of an intact hymen prior to coitus, done by the insertion of a finger through the perforation and a downward push toward the anus.

The Perineum

The *perineum* is the area between the vaginal opening and the anal opening. It is a smooth area of skin that is richly supplied with nerve endings. Thus, the perineum is very sensitive.

Bartholin's Glands

Bartholin's glands are a pair of bean-shaped glands, the ducts from which empty the secretions near the middle of the labia minora. The secretions from these glands provide the genital scent that contributes to sexual arousal.

It used to be believed that the secretions from the Bartholin's glands were needed for lubrication so that the penis could be easily inserted into the vagina. Research has dispelled this belief. There is not enough secretory material to sufficiently lubricate the vaginal introitus (Masters and Johnson, 1966).

The Breasts

The *breasts* are not considered to be a part of the female external genitalia. They are included in our discussion because of their function in sexual arousal.

The breasts respond to hormonal stimulation at puberty and begin to grow and develop. In a mature woman, the breasts consist of two types of tissue—fat tissue and glandular tissue. The glandular tissue is mammary, or milk-producing, tissue. All women have nearly the same amount of mammary gland tissue and are able to produce nearly the same amount of milk during lactation, so that the overall size of a woman's breasts has little bearing on her ability to nurse her baby.

MAMMARY GLAND TISSUE

Mammary gland tissue responds to hormones and when hormonally stimulated may be sensitive or may swell. Women experience sensitivity and swelling (1) during the phase of the menstrual cycle prior to bleeding, (2) during pregnancy, (3) during breast-feeding, and (4) while taking birth control pills.

MASTODYNIA

Mastodynia is the term used for the swelling and painful tenderness of the breasts accompanying the menstrual cycle. Each month there is a build-up of fluid and fibrous tissue in preparation for pregnancy. When conception does not occur, the body must reabsorb these substances. There are many lymphatic vessels running through the breasts. These vessels empty into the lymph nodes, where these substances are drained. Sometimes drainage is difficult, and there is congestion. When fluid becomes trapped in a lymph duct, it forms a sac called a *cyst*. When these substances form a lump, it is called a *fibroadenoma*. Both cysts and fibroadenomas occur less frequently with advanced age. However, they are often of concern to women who confuse them with malignant growths. About 80% of lumps and swellings in the breast area checked by physicians are either cysts or fibroadenomas.

FAT TISSUE AND BREAST SIZE

Surrounding the mammary or glandular tissue is fat tissue. The fat tissue protects and cushions the mammary glands. The amount of fat tissue varies in women and is responsible for variations in breast size (Figure 3.2). There may also be more fatty tissue in one breast than in the other. Women with very small breasts and women with large breasts may both be self-conscious.

I've always been concerned with my breasts. Why couldn't they just be a little bigger? I'm always self-conscious when I wear a bathing suit around a guy for the first time.

I'd give anything to get rid of a couple of inches. Everywhere I go I get stares. I'd like to go unnoticed.

NERVE ENDINGS, AREOLAS, AND NIPPLES

The breasts are richly supplied with nerve endings. There are the same number of nerve endings in small breasts as there are in large breasts. Thus, small breasts are more sensitive per square inch than are larger breasts.

In the center of each breast is a darkened area called the *areola*. The areola contains oil-producing (sebaceous) glands. The secretions from the sebaceous glands lubricate the nipples, keeping them from cracking during breast-feeding.

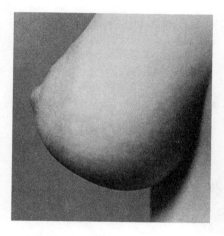

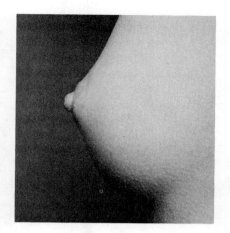

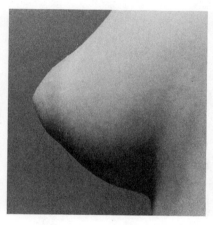

FIGURE 3.2 All women have nearly the same amount of mammary gland tissue and produce nearly the same amount of milk during lactation.

In the center of the areola is the nipple. The *nipple* is the tip of the woman's breast. Both nipples are richly supplied with nerve endings and are very sensitive to touch. The nipples may protrude, may be slightly turned inward, or may be level with the areola. The nipples may become erect when cold or during sexual arousal.

SELF-EXAMINATION OF THE BREASTS

A woman should begin self-examination as soon as she begins to menstruate regularly (Figure 3.3). Although problems are rare in the early teens, self-examination of the breasts establishes familiarity with the breasts, self-acceptance, and a lifelong habit.

The best time to do a breast examination is a few days after menstruation, when any swelling has subsided. The breast examination should be done at the same time each month. The breast exam consists of a visual exam and a palpating, or feeling, exam.

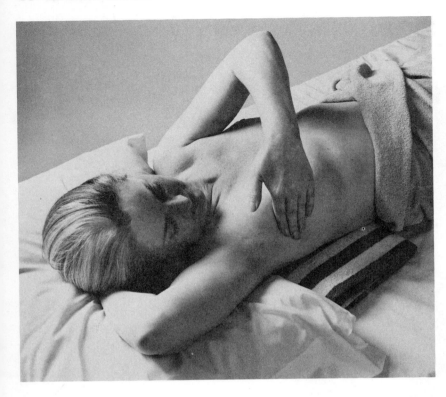

FIGURE 3.3 A woman should examine her breasts each month a few days after her menstrual flow has stopped. (Photo by Bernard Lawrence, American Cancer Society)

To do the visual check, stand in front of a mirror. Compare both breasts. Look for puckering or dimpling, any sores, pore enlargements, or skin color change, and any obvious flattening or thickening. Squeeze the nipple to check for a bloody or clear discharge. Lean forward, place your hands on your hips, flex your chest muscles, and raise your hands over your head. These actions will accentuate any abnormalities or differences between the breasts.

Palpate your breasts while you are lying down. Lie down flat on your back. Put a cushion or folded towel or pillow under the shoulder on the side of the breast you are examining in order to distribute the breast tissue more evenly. Raise your arm (on the side to be examined) over your head. Place the other hand gently but firmly over the breast. Using the flat of your fingers feel each breast in a clockwise fashion. Make small circles over the entire breast. The most common location of tumors is the outer fourth of the breast, between the nipple and the armpit. Pay close attention to this area. Continue your examination by palpating the armpit area.

A round, hard lump is most likely a noncancerous cyst or fibroadenoma but should always be checked by a physician. A cancerous, malignant lump is irregular and spreads. Its shape is responsible for the sign of Cancer, the crab.

When a lump is discovered, a physician should be seen at once. Although 80% to 90% of lumps are benign, only a physician can make a final determination of the cause of the lump and the extent of the problem.

BREAST CANCER

About one in 15 women will develop breast cancer, and the number is rising. Breast cancer kills 33,000 women annually. It is the most common type of cancer in women, and it is the leading cause of death in women 37 to 55. Treatment may include chemotherapy, radiation, and/or mastectomy, the surgical removal of the breast (Figure 3.4). Currently, many physicians are performing "lumpectomies." A "lumpectomy" is the removal of the cancerous growth and some of the nearby tissue. All women should examine their breasts regularly and see their physicians. Table 3.1 identifies women who are especially at risk.

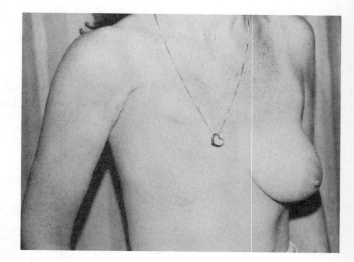

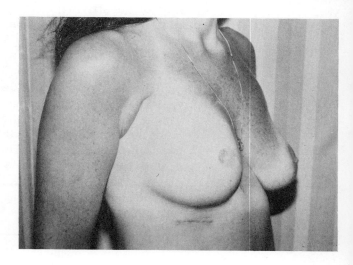

FIGURE 3.4 Above, a woman's breasts after right radical mastectomy. Below, after reconstruction. (Photos courtesy of Dr. Maja Reutschi, Geisinger Medical Center)

TABLE 3.1   BREAST CANCER RISK PROFILE

Approximately one woman in 15 will develop breast cancer, and this rate is still rising. In women under the age of 30, the risk is 10 per 100,000. This risk rises to 200 per 100,000 by age 70. The Breast Cancer Risk Profile can be used by a woman and her physician to determine potential risk factors:

If you are the daughter of a breast cancer victim, you have twice the risk.
If you are a sister of a victim, you have two and a half times the risk.
If you are infertile, you have one and a half times the risk (of a fertile woman).
If your first full-term pregnancy came after age 25, you have twice the risk (of women who became pregnant sooner); after 31, three times the risk of the women pregnant before 21.
If you began to menstruate very early and have been menstruating for a long time, you have twice the risk.
If you have fibrocystic disease, there is also twice the risk (doctors disagree strongly on this point, since the apparent link may be only statistical).

Adapted from Dr. H. P. Leis, Jr., New York Medical College, in a report to the International College of Surgeons, San Diego, 1974.

THE INTERNAL FEMALE ANATOMY

The internal female anatomy consists of the vagina, the uterus, the oviducts, and the ovaries (Figure 3.5). Each of these will be discussed along with the diseases and disorders that affect them.

The Vagina

The *vagina* is a muscular passageway lying between the bladder and the rectum. This 4- to 5-inch (10- to 12.5 cm) collapsed muscular tube leads from the vulva upward to the uterus. It is composed of three layers: (1) a mucous layer richly supplied with blood vessels, (2) a muscular layer, and (3) an elastic, fibrous layer.

The vagina serves as (1) the female organ of intercourse, (2) a passageway for the arriving sperm, (3) a canal through which the baby is born, and (4) a passageway for the menstrual flow.

VAGINAL SIZE

The vagina can best be described as a "potential space." Normally the vaginal walls lie closer together. However, when anything enters the vagina, the vaginal walls stretch apart. The walls extend to four to five times their size during childbirth. During sexual intercourse they stretch to accommodate the penis. Thus, there is no such thing as a penis too large or too small for the vagina.

I always worried that I would hurt her. She isn't even five feet tall. I think she weighs under 100 pounds. I'm all male! Over 6 feet 2 inches. She is so small next to me. Am I going to be able to get it in her?

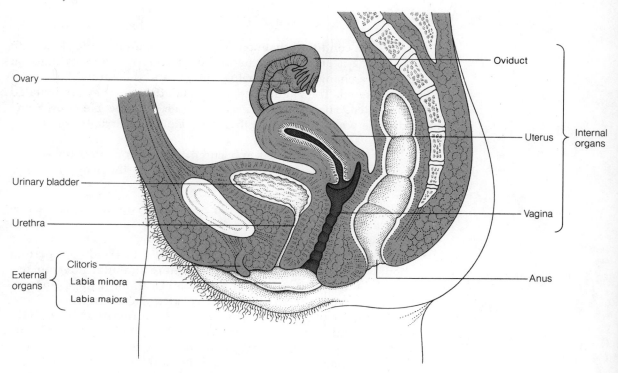

FIGURE 3.5 Organs of the female reproductive system.

VAGINAL MOISTURE

The vagina is usually moist and acidic. The pH in the vagina is approximately 4.0 to 5.0. The moisture increases during sexual excitement, when the walls of the vagina secrete a mucoid material by a "sweating phenomenon." This process will be discussed more thoroughly in Chapter 4. The moisture in the vagina also varies with the different stages of the menstrual cycle. There is a continuous secretion of dead cells mixed with lubricating fluid coming from the cervix and the vagina. This continuous secretion has a self-cleansing quality that, combined with a pH of 4.0 to 5.0, makes douching the vagina unnecessary except for prescribed medical reasons.

My mother told me that "nice" girls clean themselves out every day. She convinced me that if I didn't use a perfumed douche rinse, I'd have a funny smell. I douched daily. In a few weeks I had a very funny odor and I itched like crazy. Seemed like this wasn't what should happen to "nice" girls.

VAGINITIS

Vaginitis is a condition that occurs when the natural acidic (4.0 to 5.0) pH of the vagina is altered. This natural pH promotes a healthy mucosa. When there is a change, the normal secretions and the natural balance of bacteria are altered. The vagina and vulva are affected. They are irritated and begin to itch. The secretions may take on a disagreeable odor. Some women douche when they detect this odor. Douching irritates the lining and increases vaginitis further.

Vaginitis should be treated and cured. Sources of infection will be discussed in more detail in Chapter 11. Some of the ways to avoid vaginitis are:

- Wear cotton panties or nylon panties with a cotton crotch to allow ventilation.
- Eat a well-balanced diet low in sugar.
- Bathe regularly, washing the vulva carefully. You and your partner should wash the hands and genitals before and after intercourse.
- Avoid the use of Vaseline for sexual lubrication. It traps bacteria. Use a K-Y jelly instead. Always have adequate lubrication.
- Avoid the use of feminine hygiene sprays, perfumed douches, bubble bath, and similar products. A couple of tablespoons of white vinegar mixed with a quart of warm water is more effective as a douche, because it helps to restore the normal pH.
- Use a vinegar douche when taking antibiotics for an extended period of time.
- Have your partner use condoms whenever you or your partner experience a discharge or itching. Have your partner use condoms when either of you has sex outside the relationship.
- Focus on good toilet habits. Wipe carefully from front to back. Use white toilet tissue that is not perfumed.
- If chronic vaginitis exists and you are using the birth control pill, you may want to consider another form of contraception.

VAGINAL CANCER

Vaginal cancer used to be rare in our country, and then in the late 1960s and early 1970s it began to increase. In 1970, it was discovered that vaginal cancer was more likely to occur in women whose mothers had taken diethylstilbestrol (DES) during pregnancy to prevent miscarriage. A relationship between DES and vaginal cancer has now been confirmed. Thus, women who were born after 1940 should check with their physicians to see whether their mothers took DES and whether they are in the high-risk group.

Although a Papanicolaou (Pap) smear is recommended for high-risk women every six months and annually for all other women, it does not always confirm a malignancy in the vagina. A better test is painting the vaginal and cervical area with an iodine stain to highlight abnormal cells.

Treatment for vaginal cancer involves chemotherapy, radiation, and/ or surgery. Interestingly, some physicians also recommend preventive procedures for DES-exposed women, such as using contraceptive jellies on the cervical and upper vaginal area. Physicians also recommend avoiding any exposure to estrogens, such as the use of birth control pills.

The Uterus

The *uterus,* or womb, is a hollow, muscular, pear-shaped organ in the pelvic cavity between the bladder and the rectum. In the nonpregnant state, the uterus is about 3 inches long and 2 inches wide at the top, narrowing down to the cervix where it is normally about ½ to 1 inch in diameter.

The uterus is divided into three anatomical parts. The *corpus,* or body, is the upper muscular division of the uterus. Below the corpus is the constricted area of the uterus, the *isthmus.* During pregnancy the isthmus lengthens and thins out. It helps the corpus to enlarge the womb for the growing embryo.

The *cervix* is the lowest part of the uterus. The narrowed cervix keeps the growing embryo inside the womb during pregnancy. There are no nerve endings in the cervix. The cervix contains mucus-secreting glands. There is a continuous secretion of dead cells and mucus from the cervix. These secretions can be examined to detect abnormal cells (cancer) in the uterus by means of a Pap smear. The Pap smear will be discussed in the section on gynecological examinations.

CERVICAL CANCER

Although the cause of *cervical cancer* is unknown, there appears to be a relationship between cervical cancer and sexual intercourse. Women who appear to be at higher risk are those who began to have intercourse at an early age, those who engage in intercourse frequently, and those who have many sexual partners. Also at high risk are women whose mothers took diethylstilbestrol (DES) to prevent miscarriage and women who have had genital herpes.

High-risk women should have a Pap smear every six months. Other women should have a Pap smear annually. If the Pap smear is positive, a second smear is done, followed by a biopsy. Cancer of the cervix is treated with radiation, chemotherapy, and hysterectomy.

TWO UTERINE LAYERS

Besides the three anatomical divisions of the uterus, there are two uterine layers: the myometrium and the endometrium. The *myometrium* is the muscular layer of the uterus. There are many interweaving fibers within the myometrium, with arteries and veins lying between them. During pregnancy the uterus has a spongy appearance known as *stratum vasculare*. At the culmination of pregnancy, these arteries are kept from hemorrhaging by the constriction of the muscle fibers.

The *endometrium* is the inner lining of the uterus. It consists of soft, spongy tissue that is richly supplied with secretory glands and blood vessels. It is 3 to 4 mm in thickness. The endometrium grows each month to prepare a home for the fertilized egg.

ENDOMETRIOSIS

Sometimes the endometrial tissue grows somewhere other than in the lining of the uterus. This condition is called *endometriosis*. It may grow in one of the genital, urinary, or intestinal organs and is a frequent cause of infertility. Physicians recommend that women with endometriosis have their children as early as possible, because this extra lining is stimulated to grow by hormonal secretions each month. Treatment consists of the removal of the tissue.

ENDOMETRITIS

Endometritis is the inflammation of the uterine lining. The symptoms include pelvic pain, a foul-smelling discharge, and a tenderness during examination. Sometimes there are no symptoms. A frequent cause of endometritis is an intrauterine device (IUD) that has become lodged in the uterine lining. This condition requires treatment. Ampicillin and tetracycline are taken orally. Treatment also includes bed rest and no sexual intercourse for at least two weeks. In most cases, the IUD must be removed.

POLYPS

Polyps are long, tubelike protrusions that grow from mucous membranes inside the uterus or along the cervix. They are rarely malignant. The symptoms that indicate possible polyps are irregular menstrual periods, a heavy menstrual flow, and bleeding between periods. The treatment for polyps is dilation and curettage (D & C).

FIBROIDS

About 20% to 25% of women of childbearing age have benign, slow-growing growths in the uterus called *fibroids*. Rarely do these fibroids become malignant or cancerous. They are most likely to occur when tissue builds up in the endometrial lining each month and is not completely sloughed off. Fibroids may pose problems during a pregnancy, and they may make delivery difficult. Fibroids may also push against the bladder and rectum, or they may cause urinary tract infections. Sometimes they are the cause of menstrual irregularities and a heavy menstrual flow. They may make a woman feel bloated in her abdominal area. When menopause occurs, fibroids shrink because of the diminished secretion of estrogen.

UTERINE CANCER

Uterine cancer is rare but is more frequent in certain women. Women at higher risk are those who have (1) a history of uterine cancer in their family, (2) diabetes, (3) delayed menopause, (4) irregular bleeding, and (5) obesity. Irregular bleeding is the most common symptom and usually occurs after menopause. The physician generally performs a D & C to confirm the diagnosis.

DILATION AND CURETTAGE (D & C) *Dilation and curettage* is a surgical procedure in which the cervical opening is dilated by means of probes of increasingly larger sizes until a metal loop curette can be inserted to scrape away the uterine lining (Figure 3.6). The procedure can be performed with a local anesthesia on an outpatient basis. In this case recovery will take 8 to 24 hours. If general anesthesia is needed, the procedure is performed in a hospital, and the recovery time is longer.

There is bleeding for several days following a D & C. Sanitary napkins are used to collect the blood rather than tampons, to avoid any unnecessary infection. Danger signals following a D & C are excessive bleeding and/or cramping and a high fever.

The D & C is performed for several reasons:

1. as a cleansing procedure before any gynecological surgery
2. for a diagnosis of cancer of the uterus or oviducts
3. for a diagnosis when there is abnormal bleeding or blood clotting
4. for a diagnosis when infertility is suspected
5. as a follow-up procedure when an incomplete abortion is suspected
6. for an abortion

HYSTERECTOMY

The surgical removal of the uterus is referred to as a *hysterectomy*. This surgery may be performed by an abdominal incision or through the vagina. A *partial hysterectomy* is the removal of most of the uterus. Part of the cervix remains, and the ovaries and oviducts are left in place and continue to function. Ovulation occurs each month, and the ovary secretes estrogen into the bloodstream. There is, however, no menstrual period. A regular Pap smear is required every six months. A *complete hysterectomy* is removal of the uterus including the cervix. Sometimes it is necessary to remove the ovaries and the oviducts. This will curtail the secretion of hormones, and estrogen replacement therapy (ERT) will be needed. There is a 4- to 6-week recovery period after a hysterectomy. Major complications may include shock, hemorrhage, and psychological depression due to

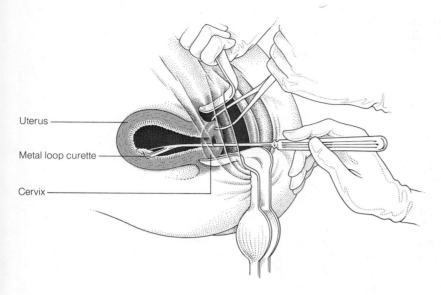

Uterus ——————

Metal loop curette ——————

Cervix ——————

FIGURE 3.6 The cervix is dilated with various probes, and the uterine lining is scraped away with a metal loop curette.

organ loss or the permanent end of childbearing. Most women have no side effects from a hysterectomy. In fact, many women say they've never felt better. They enjoy the freedom from menstrual periods and from concern about contraceptives.

The Oviducts

The *oviducts*, also called the uterine tubes and fallopian tubes, are 3- to 5-inch trumpet-shaped tubes. They lie in close proximity to the ovaries and extend to the corners of the uterus. At the end of each tube are fingerlike projections called *fimbria.*

The purpose of the oviducts is transporting the ovum to the uterus. Although scientists are not certain about the action of the tube, it most likely occurs in this manner:

> When ovulation occurs, the musculature of the fallopian tubes and the ligaments by which it is suspended tend to draw the flaring end of the tube and the ovary together. Contractions of the muscular walls of the fallopian tube create a suction that directs the ovum into the tube. The process is further aided by the constant beating of hair-like projections found on the inner surface of the fallopian tubes. These projections are called cilia, and their beating action creates a constant current into the uterus. Ordinarily, ova from the right ovary enter the right fallopian tube and those from the left enter the left tube. However, there are numerous cases on record to support the observation that cross-over occurs (e.g., the left tube may move over to pick up an ovum from the right ovary).

(Burt, 1975)

The ovum may also float to one of the tubes. Once inside the tube, the ovum is transported by the peristaltic contractions of the tube itself. The ovum moves at a rate of 1 inch every 24 hours. The ovum is viable (healthy and alive) for approximately 24 to 48 hours; thus, fertilization usually occurs in the upper 2 inches of the oviduct.

ECTOPIC PREGNANCY

An *ectopic pregnancy* occurs when implantation takes place outside the uterine lining. The most common site for an ectopic pregnancy is in the oviduct (uterine tube). Implantation of a fertilized egg in the oviduct is called a *tubal pregnancy*. About one out of every 200 pregnancies is tubal Hellman, 1971).

Tubal pregnancies are more common in women with IUDs. The symptoms are abdominal pain, a late or missed menstrual period, irregular bleeding or spotting, and a pelvic lump or mass. A tubal pregnancy can be dangerous if not detected. The oviduct cannot expand and will eventually rupture. This may result in severe infection, severe bleeding, and possibly shock and death.

The Ovaries

The two *ovaries* lie at the brim of the pelvis. Their shape resembles that of an almond. Each ovary is about 1 inch wide, 1½ inches long, and one-quarter of an inch thick. The ovary has two functions: (1) to produce ova and (2) to secrete hormones.

PRIMARY FOLLICLES

At birth the ovary contains many podlike structures that contain immature or unripened ova. These podlike structures are called *primary follicles*. It is estimated that there are between 200,000 and 400,000 of these primary follicles in each ovary at birth. These follicles continually degenerate. There are about 10,000 left at puberty, and by age 50 most have disappeared. During the reproductive years about 375 of the primary follicles are sufficiently developed to expel ova.

PUBERTY

Around eight years of age, the pituitary gland at the base of the brain secretes follicle-stimulating hormone (FSH). Follicle-stimulating hormone travels to the ovary via the bloodstream to initiate puberty. In a woman, *puberty* is the period when the ovaries begin to secrete estrogens and the secondary sex characteristics develop. Somewhere between the ages of 10 and 14 the influence of estrogens on the female body becomes noticeable. The accompanying changes are referred to as secondary sex characteristics (Figure 3.7). These changes make the female body ready for

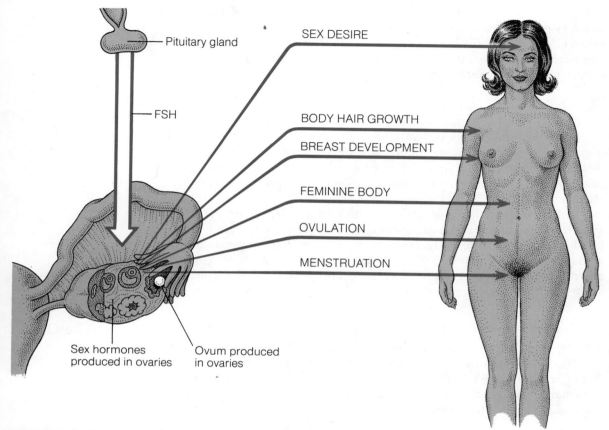

FIGURE 3.7 During puberty, estrogen secretion makes the female body ready for reproduction.

reproduction. The oviducts, uterus, and vagina all increase in size and physiological maturity.

The secondary sex characteristics include (Burt, 1975):

1. deposition of fat in the breasts, accompanied by development of an elaborate duct system
2. broadening of the pelvis, which changes from a narrow, funnel-like outlet to a broad oval outlet
3. development of soft and smooth skin
4. deposition of fat in buttocks and thighs
5. development of pubic hair with a flat upper border (a triangular border is characteristic of the male)
6. early uniting of the growing end of long bones with the bone shaft (in the absence of estrogens, females usually grow several inches taller than average).

Accompanying these anatomical changes during puberty, there are important physiological changes. These physiological changes begin with ovulation and menstruation. Ovulation and menstruation will be discussed later in this chapter.

OVARIAN CYSTS

Sometimes one of the primary follicles grows and does not rupture to release an egg. The result is a *cyst*. The cyst will usually fill with fluid, although some just become hard. When cysts develop, there may be unexplained abdominal swelling, pain during the menstrual period, and irregular cycles. Sometimes there are no symptoms.

In many cases, the cyst will disappear after one or two cycles. If not, the physician will do a biopsy (take a tissue specimen) of the cyst to determine whether or not surgery is needed.

OVARIAN CANCER

Ovarian cancer accounts for about 1% of all cancers in our country. Certain women have a higher risk of this type of cancer than other women. These women (1) are at least 40 to 50 years of age, (2) have a history of infertility, (3) have a history of ectopic pregnancy, or (4) have endometriosis. Treatment for ovarian cancer is the removal of the ovaries, an *oophorectomy*.

THE MENSTRUAL CYCLE

The *menstrual cycle* prepares a woman's body for the possibility of pregnancy each month. The cycle is dependent on the levels of several hormones in the bloodstream. These hormone levels fluctuate in rhythmic cycles of approximately a month. Each monthly cycle is divided into three phases: the proliferative phase, the secretory, or progestational, phase, and the menstrual phase (Figure 3.8).

The Proliferative Phase

The word *proliferate* means "to grow by the rapid production of new cells." During the proliferative phase of the menstrual cycle, new cells are growing.

FSH SECRETION

Each month shortly after menstruation begins, the pituitary gland secretes follicle-stimulating hormone (FSH). Follicle-stimulating hormone travels to the ovaries via the bloodstream and stimulates about 15 to 20 of the primary follicles in the ovaries to grow. The follicles enlarge because of an accumulation of fluids similar to the swelling of a blister. These growing follicles secrete estrogens, which cause the uterine lining, the endometrium, to grow. The endometrial lining attains a thickness of 2 to 3 mm.

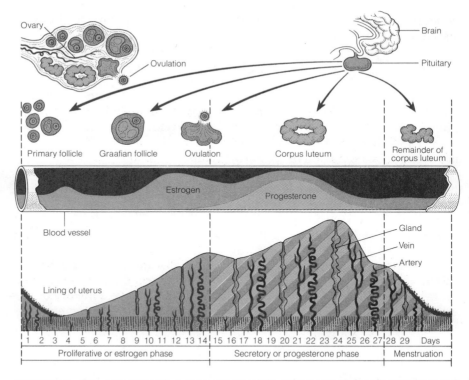

FIGURE 3.8 The menstrual cycle prepares a woman's body for the possibility of a pregnancy each month.

OVULATION

As the middle of the cycle nears, one of the immature primary follicles balloons outward into full maturity. This follicle is called the *Graafian follicle*. A small dot or nipplelike protrusion called the *stigma* develops on the surface of the Graafian follicle. As the stigma develops, the pituitary gland secretes luteinizing hormone (LH). Luteinizing hormone causes the stigma to disintegrate, and this disintegration causes the Graafian follicle to rupture and release an egg. This process is called *ovulation*. Ovulation, the release of an egg, generally occurs on the 14th day prior to the first day of the next menstrual cycle. The other primary follicles that have started to grow, degenerate. It is interesting to note that variation in the length of a woman's menstrual cycle occurs in the proliferative phase.

The Secretory, or Progestational, Phase

The newly released egg is very fragile, and a woman's body must make some changes to prepare for its possible fertilization. The follicular cells from the ruptured Graafian follicle are transformed into a temporary endocrine gland by the action of LH. This yellow glandular body, formed in the ovary from the follicular remains, is called the *corpus luteum* (yellow body).

CORPUS LUTEUM SECRETION

To prepare the female reproductive system for the reception of the ovum, the corpus luteum secretes the important hormones: (1) estrogens and (2) progesterone. The secretion of progesterone is what gives this part of the menstrual cycle its name.

PROGESTERONE SECRETION

Progesterone from the corpus luteum initiates the secretion of glands in the walls of the oviducts. These secretions nourish the ovum, or egg, as it passes through the oviduct. Progesterone also inhibits the contraction of the muscular layer of the uterus, the myometrium, as a precautionary measure, to prevent the egg from being expelled. The ducts in the mother's breasts begin to develop to nourish the newborn in response to progesterone secretion.

ESTROGEN SECRETION

The corpus luteum also secretes additional amounts of estrogens. Estrogens and progesterone work together to cause the endometrium to continue to increase in thickness. They cause an increase in the blood supply in the lining of the uterus, and they cause glands in the lining to secrete endometrial fluid. Estrogens and progesterone also inhibit the release of FSH and LH, so that no new primary follicles begin to mature.

The Menstrual Phase

If fertilization does not occur, the *menstrual phase* is initiated. The menstrual phase, like the proliferative and secretory phases, is under hormonal influence. It is related to the function of the corpus luteum.

The corpus luteum remains active for about 10 to 12 days. During this time, it secretes estrogen and progesterone, which work together to prepare the lining of the uterus and to block FSH and LH so no new primary follicles begin to grow. However, when fertilization does not occur, the corpus luteum degenerates after 10 to 12 days.

THE CORPUS LUTEUM SHUTS DOWN

Two days before the end of the cycle, the secretion of estrogens and progesterone decreases sharply as the corpus luteum degenerates. The lining of the uterus, the endometrium, is no longer stimulated. The endometrial cells shrink to about 65% of their previous state. The day before the menstrual flow begins, the blood vessels to the lining of the uterus are closed off. Without a fresh supply of blood, the lining of the uterus dies.

MENSTRUATION

This dead layer of cells separates from the rest of the uterus. The dead tissue and the small quantity of blood in the uterine cavity cause uterine contractions. These contractions expel the contents of the uterus as the *menstrual flow*. During menstruation approximately 35 ml of blood, 35 ml of fluid, and the lining of the uterus are expelled (Burt, 1975). The bleeding lasts from 2 to 8 days, the average being 4 to 6 days. The menstrual flow marks the end of the three-phase female cycle.

Unless some abnormal condition exists, the menstrual period will not drastically alter a woman's life. She will not bleed heavily nor feel tired and run-down. She will need some form of protection to absorb the menstrual flow. Two commercial products can be used for this purpose: sanitary pads (napkins) and tampons.

TOXIC-SHOCK SYNDROME (TSS)   Toxic-shock syndrome (TSS) is a serious flu-like illness that begins with a high fever, vomiting, and diarrhea and is followed by a sunburn-like rash and peeling of the skin ten days later. These symptoms may progress to a dangerous drop in blood pressure. Circulatory shock and respiratory distress may occur within 24 to 48 hours.

Toxic-shock syndrome is caused by *Staphylococcus aureus*, a bacterium. The *S. aureus* bacterium may be present as a result of a localized infection of the skin, bone, or lung. This fact accounts for TSS in men and boys and a few cases in women and girls. However, approximately 95% of all reported cases of TSS in women and girls occur in those who are menstruating. The *S. aureus* bacterium is localized in the vagina. The bacteria probably make and secrete a toxin, which enters the bloodstream, causing TSS.

In June 1980, the Center for Disease Control examined the risk factors for this disease. Findings paralleled those in a study done by the Wisconsin State Health Department. A significant relationship was shown between TSS and tampon use. Tampons may play a contributing role by 1) carrying the organism from the fingers or the introitus into the vagina in the process of insertion, 2) providing a favorable environment for growth of the organism or elaboration of toxin regardless of the manner in which the organism is introduced, 3) traumatizing the vaginal mucosa and thus facilitating local infection with *S. aureus*, or 4) absorbing of toxin from the vagina (Center for Disease Control, Atlanta, Georgia, September 19, 1980).

Although the exact role that tampons play is not clearly understood, women can almost entirely reduce their risk of TSS by not using tampons. If tampon use is desirable, tampons could be used for only a portion of the menstrual period, for example, during the daytime only. It is unclear whether or not superabsorbent tampons are more likely to cause TSS than tampons with regular absorbency. In addition, it is unclear whether the frequency of changing tampons is a risk factor. It may be that women who select the superabsorbent tampons change them less frequently.

It is important to remember that toxic-shock syndrome can be serious as early as 24 to 48 hours after the onset of symptoms. When symptoms of TSS occur, tampon use should be discontinued immediately and a physician should be consulted. The physician will perform a vaginal examination and will remove any retained tampons. Cervical and vaginal cultures will be made for *S. aureus*. The TSS victim is usually placed in intensive care and given fluids. Because 30% of the women who have had TSS have had a recurrence, tampons should not be used until the *S. aureus* bacterium has been eradicated from the vagina.

Menstrual Conditions

Several terms are used to describe the various aspects of the menstrual cycle: menarche, amenorrhea, dysmenorrhea, menorrhagia, and menopause.

MENARCHE

Menarche is the term used to describe the first menstrual cycle. The age of menarche has been decreasing in the United States. It is not uncommon for menstruation to begin as early as the age of 9. There is no reason for thinking, however, that a girl who does not menstruate early is not healthy. Many girls begin their periods as teenagers.

I was so uncomfortable waiting for my period to come. All of the other girls talked about it. I had Kotex and a carrying case in my purse. I thought the day would never come.

AMENORRHEA

Amenorrhea is the absence of menstruation. There are two classifications of amenorrhea. *Primary amenorrhea* is the term used when there has not been a menstrual period by age 18. Primary amenorrhea may be caused by malformed or underdeveloped female organs, glandular disorders, general poor health, and emotional factors. *Secondary amenorrhea* is the term for the condition when menstruation ceases after at least one menstrual period. Secondary amenorrhea is normal during pregnancy and while breast-feeding. It may occur sporadically during the first and last months of a woman's childbearing years. Amenorrhea is a symptom of infertility. It may be caused by stress, disease, cysts, tumors, hormone imbalances, extreme weight loss, and congenital defects. Medical assistance is needed when amenorrhea persists.

DYSMENORRHEA

Dysmenorrhea refers to painful menstruation. Many women experience mild discomfort during their menstrual periods. Dysmenorrhea is more than this mild discomfort. The causes are poorly understood. They include inflammation, constipation, psychological stress, and hormone imbalance.

CONGESTIVE AND SPASMODIC DYSMENORRHEA

In her book *The Menstrual Cycle,* Dr. Katherine Dalton (Dalton, 1969) distinguishes between congestive and spasmodic dysmenorrhea, both caused by hormonal imbalance. *Spasmodic dysmenorrhea* is more common between the ages of 15 and 25 and is related to too much progesterone in relation to estrogen. The symptoms include sharp pain in the lower abdomen, cramping, and nausea. To alleviate this condition, Dr. Dalton recommends hormone therapy. Spasmodic dysmenorrhea is less likely to occur after a woman has experienced pregnancy and childbirth.

Congestive dysmenorrhea refers to what we popularly call "premenstrual tension." The symptoms are produced by too much estrogen in relation to progesterone. This situation results in increased congestion. There may be a feeling of heaviness, and fluid may be retained in the breasts, ankles, and abdomen. "The blues" occur about a week before the menstrual period and are accompanied by irritability, tension, depression, headache, fatigue, and the urge for simple carbohydrates. This type of dysmenorrhea may worsen with age. Again, Dr. Dalton recommends hormone therapy.

PROSTAGLANDINS

In addition to the possible problems resulting from estrogen and progesterone levels, there is a hormonelike substance that may be a cause of dysmenorrhea. This substance is called *prostaglandin.* Prostaglandins are manufactured in the uterine lining, the endometrium. There is a sharp increase in the amount of prostaglandins produced before the menstrual period. The prostaglandins increase contractions in the uterine lining, and these contractions may be painful and cause dysmenorrhea (Connell, 1972).

RELIEF FROM CRAMPS

If the cause of dysmenorrhea is pinpointed and believed to be a hormonal imbalance, then hormone therapy may be helpful. But hormonal imbalance is not always the cause, and many women prefer not to take hormones. The following suggestions may be helpful:

- Reduce your intake of beverages containing caffeine (colas, coffee).

- Reduce your intake of sugar and of carbohydrates.
- Reduce your salt intake.
- Increase your intake of potassium by drinking orange juice and eating bananas.
- Engage in mild exercise such as walking.
- Sit in a warm bath tub, whirlpool, or sauna, or use a hot-water bottle.
- Ask your doctor about the use of a mild painkiller.
- Try masturbating to increase blood flow.

These suggestions may help alleviate the discomfort. However, very painful menstruation needs the attention of a physician. It may be a symptom of a disease or disorder.

MENORRHAGIA

Menorrhagia refers to an abnormally heavy menstrual flow. Menorrhagia may be a symptom of disease, endocrine disorder, or abnormalities of the sexual organs. Excessive bleeding should be reported to a physician.

Sexual Activity During Menstruation

There is no physiological reason to avoid sexual intercourse during the menstrual period. In fact, orgasm during menstruation may help to reduce a feeling of fullness, and in some women it may alleviate backache.

When I have a feeling of being bloated during my period, I masturbate. This tends to release my tension and I feel a lot better.

SEXUAL AROUSAL

The menstrual flow appears to have varying effects on sexual arousal. Some women feel especially aroused when the estrogen level in the body is high. The peak estrogen level occurs at midcycle and just prior to menstruation (Weideger, 1976). Other women have a greater interest in intercourse during their periods because of the reduced likelihood of pregnancy. Yet other women feel the need to turn inward and enjoy being alone and less intimate at this time.

ATTITUDES

Men also have varied reactions to sexual intercourse during menstruation. Some men find menstruation sexually arousing while others would rather avoid sexual intimacy. These feelings may be connected with the myths regarding uncleanliness. There is nothing unclean about menstrual blood (and only a few ounces of blood flow during the entire period).

Couples who wish to have sexual intercourse without any evidence of the menstrual flow can use a diaphragm to collect the blood.

MENOPAUSE

Cause

Menopause is the time in a woman's life when menstruation ceases permanently. It occurs somehere between the ages of 48 and 52 as a natural process accompanying aging. During this time, the ovaries stop producing a monthly egg. The circulating levels of both estrogens and progesterone are thus decreased. Previously, these hormones were needed to prepare the female body for a pregnancy. But without an egg and without estrogens and progesterone, the lining of the uterus no longer builds up. Eventually menstruation ceases entirely.

It is not true that women who begin their periods early will go through menopause earlier, nor is it true that women who take birth control pills build up an excess of eggs and menstruate years beyond other women.

I used to think that each woman had so many eggs in her that had to be used. I thought that if I took birth control pills for 10 years, I'd be menstruating til I was 60. In this class I learned that the eggs disintegrate with age.

Menopause may result from an oophorectomy, removal of the ovaries. However, if only one ovary is removed, the other ovary will increase its secretion of estrogens, and there will be no effects.

Symptoms

There are two rather common symptoms that may accompany menopause: "hot flashes" and a decrease in the moisture and elasticity of the vagina.

HOT FLASHES

Hot flashes are an indication that the body is trying to adjust to changing hormone levels. When estrogens and progesterone decrease, the secretion of FSH and LH increases. FSH and LH appear to upset hormonal balance and thus trigger a vasomotor response. The arteries dilate, and blood rushes quickly to them. The increased blood supply makes the woman feel hot and sweaty. Usually this sensation lasts from several seconds to a minute and may occur as often as five times a day. Sometimes hot flashes are followed by a chilly feeling, and the same vasomotor response may cause dizziness, swollen ankles, and rapid heartbeat.

VAGINAL DRYNESS AND ELASTICITY

Another symptom accompanying menopause is vaginal dryness, also a response to diminishing estrogen levels. There is a loss of elasticity in the vaginal walls, the mucous membranes in the vagina thin out, and the width and length of the vaginal barrel decrease.

With increased dryness intercourse may be more difficult, and with the thinner vaginal wall, some women may experience pain. The dryness can be combatted with a lubricant, preferably a K-Y jelly. An estrogen cream can be used to provide lubrication, as well as some hormone therapy. Frequent sexual activity is also helpful.

With lowered estrogen levels, the vagina is no longer as acidic and has increased susceptibility to infection. Whenever intercourse is painful or vaginal infection persists, medical attention should be sought.

OTHER SYMPTOMS

Other symptoms that may also accompany menopause include insomnia, headaches, fatigue, and depression.

About 10% of women experience serious depression. In most cases, the depression is a result of feelings and environmental factors rather than a direct result of physiological changes.

Treatment

Although some physicians treat depression during menopause with hormone therapy or with tranquilizers or other mood-modifiers, many focus on counseling as therapy. During therapy, a woman is helped to establish new life goals and to examine her role in the middle years. Ideally, of course, if every woman made this examination of her role a part of her lifestyle, menopause would not be a crisis. Research indicates that the better the mental health of a woman before menopause, the fewer unpleasant symptoms she will have when it occurs (Coleman, 1972).

THE REGULAR EXAMINATION

Every adult woman should have a regular examination, especially if she is over 35 or taking birth control pills. A semiannual (twice a year) exam is recommended for women who are at high risk for one reason or another.

The regular examination is not to be viewed as a check to see what is wrong, but rather as an opportunity to gather information, record important findings, restore confidence, and continue optimal care. A healthy reproductive system depends upon the general health of a woman. The following examinations provide the information needed for a health profile:

- health history
- thyroid palpation
- breast examination
- blood tests and a blood pressure check
- lung tests
- urinalysis
- pelvic examination including a Pap smear and a test for gonorrhea.

Health History

Before the examination it is a good idea for a woman to update her health history. In order to keep files current and helpful, a woman should keep a personal calendar from the time she begins to menstruate. She should simply record the days when she is menstruating. She should write down any additional information about her periods. Did she have cramps? Was it a heavy flow?

I went to see my doctor because I've been having menstrual cramps. She asked me when my last period started, how long it lasted, and how many tampons I used the first day. I don't really know much about my own body!

If she is sexually active, she should make a check on the days she has had intercourse and make a note about what type of contraception, if any, was used. She should record any noticeable changes — a vaginal discharge, a lump in the breast or groin. If she is taking birth control pills, she should indicate when she began her pill pack and mark down any day that she forgot a pill.

I kept going back to the health center because of a nuisance infection. I became a "regular." Finally, the doctor asked me to make a check somewhere whenever I had sex. He also asked me to write down the first day I noticed symptoms. I found out that Bob kept giving me trichomoniasis. He was having sex with someone else.

Thyroid Palpation

The *thyroid gland* is an endocrine gland located just below the larynx (voice box) and in front and to the side of the trachea (windpipe). This gland secretes hormones that influence growth and stimulate activity in the nervous system. During the young adult years, the thyroid gland may enlarge, or lumps or tumors may develop on it. These conditions affect thyroid function, which in turn affects growth and the functions of the reproductive system. During the annual examination, the physician palpates, or feels, the thyroid to determine whether there are any lumps or tumors, and also determines whether or not the thyroid gland is enlarged.

Breast Examination

It is important for a woman to examine her breasts each month after her period. The physician and patient can discuss what a woman feels and what questions she has about her breasts. The physician can tell the patient if she is doing the examination correctly.

> I've been doing self-examinations since I took a basic health class. But to be perfectly honest, I wouldn't know if I found a lump in my breast or not. I find bumps here and there. Nothing seems abnormal, but how would I know?

Blood Tests and a Blood Pressure Check

Blood tests and a blood pressure check can help each of us, male and female, get a picture of our general health status. These are particularly important to a woman. The use of several contraceptives is accompanied by risks to the circulatory system.

BLOOD TESTS

A woman should have a complete blood count. A blood sample should be sent to a laboratory to determine the hemoglobin level. During the reproductive years many women fail to get enough iron, and anemia may result. Some women may need iron or other supplements.

Every woman of childbearing age should know her Rh factor. The Rh factor will be discussed more thoroughly in Chapter 6.

Some investigators link the level of triglycerides and cholesterol (fats) in the bloodstream with heart disease. As part of a complete blood count, the triglyceride and cholesterol levels can be checked. When the triglyceride or cholesterol level is high, a woman can discuss dietary changes with her physician.

In addition to these blood tests, some women have their blood tested for syphilis during their regular examination.

THE BLOOD PRESSURE CHECK

Changes in blood pressure can indicate an improved state of health or stresses upon the body that can lead to a variety of problems. Levels of hormones circulating in the bloodstream can affect the circulatory system. That is why physicians do not like to prescribe birth control pills or estrogen replacement therapy for women who have high blood pressure or a history of high blood pressure.

Blood pressure will vary within a normal range. It is important to know your normal blood pressure so that you will be able to detect changes.

Lung Tests

The physician will listen carefully to your heart and lungs. If you are a smoker, you may want to discuss a smoking-cessation program with your physician. Smoking during the childbearing years is accompanied by increased health hazards, including lung cancer. Smoking during pregnancy affects the developing embryo (see Chapter 6), and smoking while taking birth control pills increases the risk of blood clots.

Urinalysis

A *urinalysis* is a chemical or microscopic examination of the urine. Usually a woman collects a urine sample in a cup at the laboratory or at the physician's office. There are directions for collecting the sample. The urine is analyzed for several reasons, but the information the obstetrician–gynecologist needs is twofold. First, whenever cystitis is suspected, the urine is checked. Second, the urine is checked for excess sugar as a test for diabetes.

The Pelvic Examination

The *pelvic examination* includes (1) an inspection of the external genitalia, (2) a speculum examination, (3) a bimanual vaginal examination, and (4) a rectovaginal examination. A pelvic examination can be done by a physician or a nurse practitioner.

INSPECTION OF THE EXTERNAL GENITALIA

The first part of a thorough pelvic examination is a careful inspection of the external genitalia. A check is made for any irritations, lumps, swelling, or discoloration. Of particular concern is a vaginal discharge or any adhesions of the clitoris. Then the physician or practitioner inserts a finger into the vagina to see whether (1) urine will flow involuntarily, (2) there is pus in Bartholin's glands, and (3) the muscles in the pelvic floor are strong.

THE SPECULUM EXAMINATION

A metal or plastic speculum is inserted inside the vagina to hold apart the vaginal walls. The metal speculum may feel cold. During speculum insertion, it is important to relax.

Someone told me that it would really hurt. I always tense up right before she puts that metal thing in. I found that it helps to take a deep breath through my mouth.

With the speculum in place it is easy for the physician or nurse practitioner to do a visual internal examination to look for (1) evidence of lesions, (2) an unusual discharge, (3) any inflammation of the vaginal walls, (4) infection, (5) growths, and (6) abnormal mucous membrane. Then two routine tests are done.

The first test is a *Papanicolaou smear*, commonly called a Pap smear (Figure 3.9). For a Pap smear, tissue is gently scraped from the cervix with a spatula. This tissue is sent to the laboratory and tested for cancer and other abnormal conditions. A Pap smear is not recommended during menstruation, because menstrual blood makes accurate examination of the tissue difficult. It is best not to douche before having a Pap smear.

The second test involves collecting the vaginal discharge with a long cotton swab. This specimen is collected for a microscopic examination and for a culture to test for gonorrhea.

SELF-EXAMINATION

Many women want to take greater responsibility for their health and would like to do their own speculum examinations.

A physician or nurse practitioner can show a woman her cervix and how to use a speculum. Many women have joined self-care groups to learn about their body and its care. Table 3.2 is a discussion of self-examination techniques. You should remember, though, that self-examination should not replace thorough, regular, medical examinations.

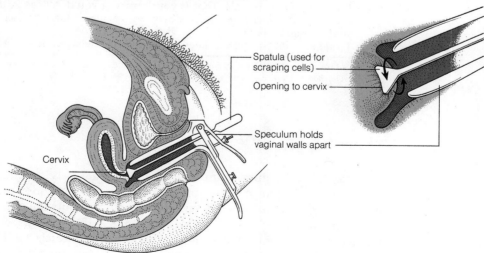

FIGURE 3.9   During the speculum examination, a spatula is used to scrape cells for a Pap smear.

TABLE 3.2 SELF-EXAMINATION TECHNIQUES

You need for self-examination:

> Directional light (a strong flashlight)
> Speculum (plastic ones are inexpensive and easier to obtain)
> K-Y jelly (or similar lubricant)
> Long-handled mirror
> Firm bed or table, or floor

It's a good idea to have your own plastic speculum to prevent the transfer of infection. Be sure to wash it in warm water and an antibiotic soap after each use. You should go through the motions of opening and locking the speculum before you actually examine yourself.

1. When you are familiar with manipulation of the speculum, position yourself comfortably on the bed or table, sitting or lying down with knees bent and feet placed far apart. You may want to prop yourself up on a pillow.
2. Lubricate the speculum with a small amount of K-Y jelly. Holding the speculum closed, gently insert it sideways into your vagina, at the same angle at which you would insert a tampon.
3. When it is in all the way, slowly turn it so that the handle points up.
4. Then grasp the handle and firmly push the shorter, outside section of the handle toward you. This will open the blades of the speculum inside you.
5. Now, steadily holding the part of the handle next to your pubic hair, push down the outside section until you can hear a click. The speculum is then locked open.
6. If you have never done this before, or are in an awkward position, your vagina may tend to reject the speculum. Also, you might have to move the speculum around or reinsert it before the cervix pops into view. Sometimes a friend can be very helpful here, particularly if your cervix is off to one side (a common occurrence).
7. It is often easier to have the light pointed at the mirror and the mirror held so that you can see into the tunnel that your speculum has opened up. This pink area, which looks much like the walls of your throat, is your vagina. At the end of the tunnel is a pinkish, bulbous area that you'd think was surely the head of a wet penis. That is your cervix. If you don't see it, then gently draw out the speculum, push down with your stomach muscles, and try again. The cervix will pop into view.
8. To remove the speculum, keep it open and slowly pull it straight out.

Adapted from *Second Wave*, Vol. 2, No. 3 (Summer, 1973). As found in Boston Women's Health Book Collective, *Our Bodies, Ourselves*. New York: Simon and Schuster, 1979, 122–123.

BIMANUAL PELVIC EXAMINATION

After the speculum examination, a bimanual pelvic examination is done. The physician or nurse practitioner inserts the index and middle finger of one hand into the vagina (Figure 3.10) and puts the other hand on the abdomen. The hands are pressed together so that the size, shape, consistency, and position of the uterus, ovaries, and oviducts can be felt and any unusual growths or inflammation detected. Any source of pelvic pain and its location can be determined.

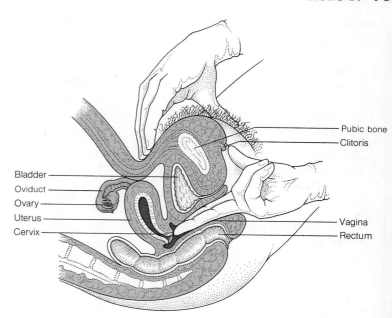

Pubic bone
Clitoris

Bladder
Oviduct
Ovary
Uterus
Cervix

Vagina
Rectum

FIGURE 3.10 Feeling for the size and shape of organs and any unusual growths or inflammations.

RECTOVAGINAL EXAMINATION

The examiner places one finger in the vagina and another finger in the rectum to do a rectovaginal examination. By pressing together, the examiner can check for rectal lesions. The tone of the rectal sphincter muscle (important in bowel movements) can also be checked, as well as the alignment of the organs in the pelvis.

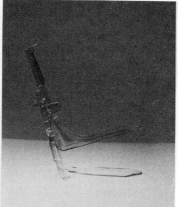

FIGURE 3.11 Many women want to participate in their health care. Left, a woman examining herself with a plastic speculum and mirror. Right, the instrument being used. (Photos courtesy of Feminist Health Works, New York)

SUMMARY STATEMENTS

- *The term* vulva *refers to the external female genitalia and includes the mons veneris, the labia majora, the labia minora, the clitoris, the vestibule, the urethral opening, the introitus and the hymen, the perineum, and Bartholin's glands.*
- *Breasts consist of fatty tissue and mammary gland tissue. Women have variations in breast size due to the fatty tissue but have nearly the same amount of mammary gland tissue to produce milk.*
- *Mastodynia is the term for painful, tender breasts that result from inadequate drainage of fluid and fibrous tissue. This condition may result in the formation of cysts or fibroadenomas, which account for roughly 80% of lumps discovered by women in their breasts.*
- *About 1 out of 15 women develop breast cancer; thus, self-examination of the breasts should be done monthly a few days after menstruation, when any swelling has subsided.*
- *The internal anatomy consists of the vagina, the uterus, the oviducts, and the ovaries.*
- *The vaginal walls stretch to accommodate the penis and extend to four to five times their size during childbirth.*
- *Vaginitis is a condition that occurs when the natural acidic pH of the vagina is altered. A woman can*
avoid it by wearing cotton panties, eating a diet low in sugar, bathing regularly, avoiding the use of Vaseline, having her partner use condoms when there is a discharge or itching, having good toilet habits, using a vinegar douche when taking antibiotics, and discontinuing the use of birth control pills.*
- *Women whose mothers took DES during pregnancy need a Pap smear every six months, because their risk of vaginal cancer is higher.*
- *Women whose mothers took DES and who began having interco .rse at an early age, engage in intercourse frequently, nave many sexual partners, or have had herpes are more likely to have cervical cancer and should have a Pap smear every six months.*
- *The menstrual cycle prepares a woman's body for the possibility of a pregnancy each month. Each month is divided into three phases: proliferative; secretory, or progestational; and menstrual.*
- *Toxic-shock syndrome (TSS) is a flulike illness (caused by* Staphylococcus aureus*) that is followed by a sunburnlike rash ten days later and may be accompanied by circulatory shock as soon as 24 hours after onset.*
- *Menopause is the time in a woman's life when menstruation ceases permanently.*

SUGGESTED READINGS

Blank, Joani. *My Playbook: For Women/About Sex.* Burlingame, California: Down There Press, 1975.
Boston Women's Health Book Collective. *Menstruation.* For a copy send stamped, self-addressed, business-size envelope to: BWHBC, Dept. BB, P.O. Box 192, Somerville, MA 02144. Eight-page brochure including information on attitudes, examining your cycle, menstrual sponges, and home remedies for menstrual problems.
Boston Women's Health Book Collective. *Our Bodies, Ourselves.* New York: Simon and Schuster, 1979.

Dalton, Katherine. *The Menstrual Cycle.* New York, Pantheon, 1969.
Friday, Nancy. *My Mother, Myself.* New York: Delacorte Press, 1977.
The Diagram Group. *Woman's Body: An Owner's Manual.* New York: Paddington Press, 1977.
Weideger, P. *Menstruation and Menopause.* New York: Alfred A. Knopf, 1976.

A LOOK AT YOUR LIFESTYLE

A close girlfriend of yours tells you that she has discovered a lump in her breast. She tells you that it is a nuisance and she can't wait for it to disappear. The lump persists, and your girlfriend continues to do nothing about it.

FEMALE ANATOMY AND PHYSIOLOGY

Write an I-message describing your reaction to this situation.

When you told me that you discovered a lump in your breast, I _____ .

1. Identify the key issue or problem.
Given:
I would like my girlfriend to visit her physician and to have the lump checked.

_____

2. Identify (describe) how you would demonstrate your concern for your girlfriend. What would you say when you began a discussion about her lump? _____

_____

GATHERING INFORMATION
What are three facts that you know about lumps found in the breast?

_____

EVALUATING THE INFORMATION
Complete the following I-message:
After carefully examining the information about lumps in the breast, I would

_____

MAKING RESPONSIBLE DECISIONS
If I discovered a lump in my breast (or someone very close to me), I would

_____

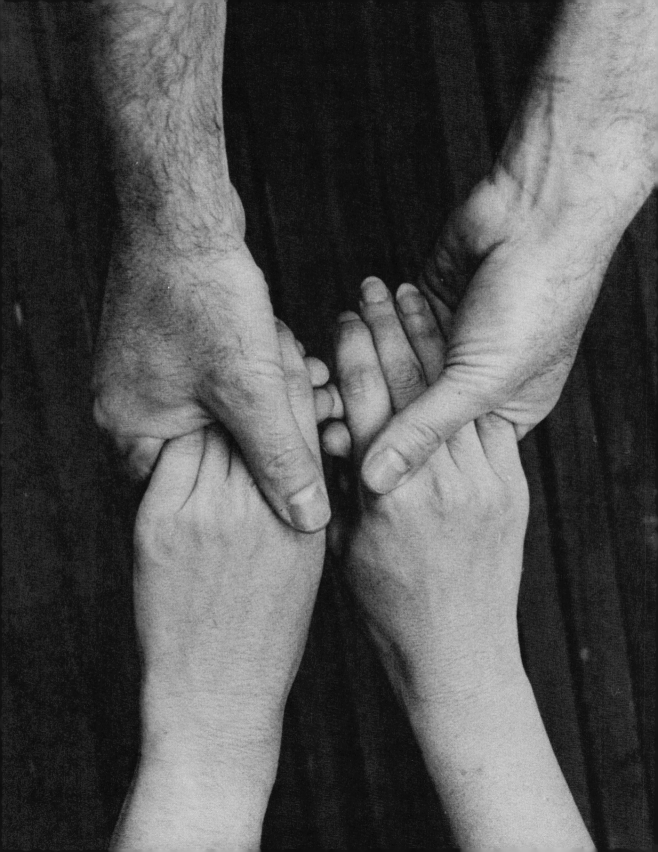

FOUR

The Physiology of Sexual Response

A LOOK AT YOUR LIFESTYLE

One of the important concerns expressed throughout this book is that a sexual relationship between two people can have deep psychological overtones. Writers throughout the years have described these emotional factors with great detail so that many of us have been made aware of the psychological play of love and affection, ego satisfaction, the need for novelty and variety, the pleasures of mutual respect and esteem, and the joy of giving and receiving. The theme of this chapter sheds light on the importance also of the *physiological* factors that play a role in the understanding of our sexuality. That is, an awareness of bodily responses can contribute much toward the total sexual satisfaction of individuals and their partners.

During the sexual response cycle, a number of common physiological changes occur. Masters and Johnson categorized these changes into four basic stages: excitement, plateau, orgasm, and resolution. While these stages make up the sexual response cycle, one should be careful not to use them as individual progress checklists during sexual encounters. Focusing upon what is "supposed to happen" often detracts from the enjoyment of the sex act. The sexually active person should be able to

1. look at the sex act as an enjoyable experience without the *fear* of "knowing I have to satisfy my partner"
2. accept as "normal" the changes that occur in the body, from excitement to resolution
3. gain some general knowledge about the sexual response cycle to better understand its complexities
4. understand that different people may have different variations within the sexual response cycle

GATHERING INFORMATION

Physiological factors discussed in this chapter are the sexual response phases, clitoral and vaginal orgasm, and multiple orgasms.

Before the research of Masters and Johnson, the phases of sexual response were not so succinctly categorized. However, their observations showed that people go through four phases during sexual response—excitement, plateau, orgasm, and resolution. Throughout each phase, changes occur within the body that make each phase unique.

For years, researchers felt that the female experienced two types of orgasms—clitoral and vaginal. The research by Masters and Johnson, however, refuted the idea that these two different types of orgasms exist, and today it is generally accepted that there is no distinction between the clitoral and vaginal orgasm. Masters and Johnson have also collected vast data that indicate that the female is capable of having multiple orgasms.

EVALUATING THE INFORMATION

In this chapter you will gain a better understanding of questions such as:

1. Why does the penis become flaccid after ejaculation?
2. Can a woman have consecutive orgasms within a short time period?
3. What happens to one's body from the moment of excitement until the time of orgasm?
4. Can the male have multiple orgasms?
5. What causes the penis to become erect?
6. What does the latest research say about the human sexual response?

In evaluating the information in this chapter, you must remember that the points made regarding sexual response do not constitute a checklist. While the information might be clear and concise, sexual response in reality may not be. The information is to be used as a means of understanding your body.

MAKING RESPONSIBLE DECISIONS

After understanding the information in this chapter, it is important that you take responsibility for making the information work for you. For example, if a man understands that a woman is capable of more than one orgasm during the sexual response cycle, he does not have to cease all lovemaking after the woman's first orgasm. Of course, he also does not have to set preconceived goals of having the woman achieve a predetermined number of orgasms in a certain period of time. Communication between the two people is the best way for them to fulfill needs.

The greater our knowledge about what happens to us during our sexual behavior, the greater the chance that we will understand our own and our partner's needs. Accordingly, we hope you can react responsibly to the following kinds of situations:

1. understanding your partner's uncomfortableness at having spoken irrationally during orgasm
2. accepting your partner's satiation point during sexual encounters
3. understanding why you may be limited in the number of times you can become sexually aroused

Ever since Masters and Johnson published their famous work in 1966, *Human Sexual Response,* their research and terminology have become those most adopted among sex educators, researchers, therapists, and counselors.

THE STAGES OF SEXUAL RESPONSE

According to Masters and Johnson, sexual responses in the human body in both men and women begin with a sexually arousing stimulus, proceed through orgasm, and finally end with a return of the body to a sexually unstimulated state. Known as the *response cycle,* this process is divided into four phases: the *excitement* phase, the *plateau* phase, the *orgasmic* phase (also known as *orgasm*), and the *resolution* phase (also known as *recovery*). Since the stages of sexual response, for the most part, differ between men and women, our discussion of each phase will isolate the characteristics indigenous to each group.

The Excitement Phase

MEN

The excitement phase in men begins with sexual arousal, which leads to erection. The erection may be caused by direct stimulation of the penis, by a sexually stimulating sight, sound, smell, or train of thought, or by kissing or touching the erogenous zones. The erection can take place within seconds of the stimuli.

Erection occurs because more blood flows into the penis than flows out of it. The increased engorgement of blood in an area is also known as *vasocongestion*. *Myotonia*, a secondary response, also occurs. Myotonia is an increase in muscle tension that is a result of sexual stimulation.

I remember when I was a student in elementary school. My friends and I thought that we got erections from a bone that grew in the penis. One day, while one of the boys in the class had an erection, a girl happened to walk by and accidentally bumped hard against the penis. My friend complained that it hurt and soon the rumor around the school was that Joey has a broken penis.

It should be noted that vasocongestion and myotonia can occur in men and women and are not necessarily related only to sexual response.

During erection, the penis can double in length. That is, a small penis in the flaccid state may double in size, whereas a large penis in the flaccid state may just harden and not necessarily double its length.

I remember as a teenager, it was very easy for me to get an erection. If I saw a sex-related movie, read *Playboy* magazine, or fantasized about my girlfriend I would become erect. Now that I am 30 years old, it takes physical contact from my wife to get an erection. Just reading a book does not do what it used to. Yet I enjoy sex just as much now as when I was a teen.

Changes are also noted in the testes and scrotum. The skin of the scrotum thickens and tenses during excitement, and the scrotal sac is flattened toward the body. Usually one of the testes rises closely to the body before the other (Figure 4.1).

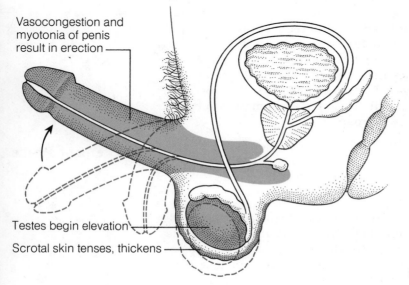

Vasocongestion and myotonia of penis result in erection

Testes begin elevation

Scrotal skin tenses, thickens

FIGURE 4.1 Changes in the testes, scrotum, and penis during sexual excitement.

WOMEN

The first sign of sexual response in women is a moistening of the vagina with a lubricating fluid that occurs within 10 to 30 seconds of the onset of sexual arousal. As in the male, the lubrication can occur from direct stimulation of the genital area or the breasts or from sights, sounds, smell, or thoughts that arouse one's erotic train of thinking. The vaginal lubrication is due to a "sweating reaction" that occurs on the walls of the vagina. Of course, there are no sweat glands in the vagina and the lubricant is not sweat. The pressure of blood in the vaginal walls forces droplets of lubricant to be pushed through the walls as sexual tension increases. The lubrication prepares the vagina for the entrance of the erect penis.

The appearance of vaginal lubrication at this point deserves some emphasis. An unlubricated vagina can make penile insertion uncomfortable or even painful, while a lubricated vagina can make penetration much easier. However, many more changes occur in the woman between the onset of excitement and orgasm. One such change occurs in the clitoris.

Before my girlfriend and I have sexual intercourse, we often engage in mutual oral–genital sex. When this happens, I do not know if she is lubricated from her own body or from my saliva. However, we communicate very well and she tells me when she feels ready for sexual intercourse.

The clitoral glans swells and may double in size. The amount of swelling is not related to sexual responsiveness or the ability to achieve orgasm. As in the penis, the swelling of the glans in the clitoris is a result of an engorgement of the blood vessels there. The clitoral shaft also increases in diameter.

The type of sexual stimulation a woman receives determines the nature of her response. Naturally, engorgement of the clitoral glans and shaft will occur more quickly when the mons is directly stimulated than it will when only the breasts are directly stimulated.

During the excitement phase, a series of changes also occurs in the female breasts (Figure 4.2). First the nipples become erect due to contraction of muscle fibers. Both nipples do not necessarily become erect at the same time. Second, they increase in length and diameter as a result of blood vessel engorgement (vasocongestion). In addition, the veins that are usually visible on the surface of the breasts become more distinct.

Third, the female breasts increase in size during the latter part of the excitement phase. This sign of increased sexual tension is a prerequisite for transition to the next phase of sexual response. Late in the excitement phase, the areolas on the breast swell as a result of vasocongestion. In many men, the nipples also become erect, although this occurs with less consistency than in women.

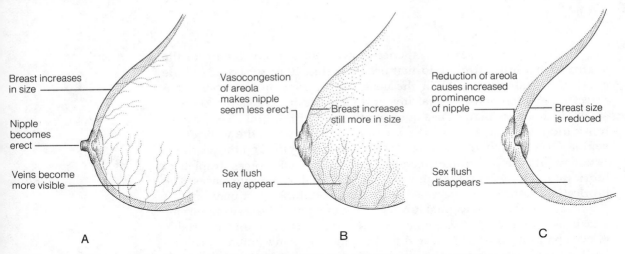

Breast increases
in size

Nipple
becomes
erect

Veins become
more visible

Vasocongestion
of areola
makes nipple
seem less erect

Breast increases
still more in size

Sex flush
may appear

Reduction of areola
causes increased
prominence
of nipple

Breast size
is reduced

Sex flush
disappears

A   B   C

FIGURE 4.2 Breast changes during female sexual response. (A) Excitement: Breast size increases, the nipples become erect, areolas swell, and the veins become more distinct. (B) Plateau and orgasm: Breasts and areolas increase in size and nipples become less erect. (C) Resolution: The breasts return to their unaroused state.

> The idea that the nipples are an erotic part of the body is something I always associated with women. One time I was making out with a girl and she sucked my breasts the same way I did hers. I found that to be a super "turn on," and since that time, I expect my partners to return the same favors as I perform on them.

Upon arousal, the labia majora spread apart more and are displaced somewhat upward toward the clitoris. For women who have not had a baby, the labia majora thin out and flatten themselves against the surrounding tissues, whereas in women who have given birth they become stretched and engorged with blood instead of flattening. In some cases, the labia majora can increase in size two to three times. The labia minora (inner lips) also swell during this phase (Figure 4.3).

During excitement, the inner two-thirds of the vagina expand and then relax. Gradually the walls expand again, and thus the vagina becomes more accommodating to the erect penis. When the upper two-thirds of the vaginal walls expand, the uterus and cervix are pulled up, forming a "tenting effect" in the vaginal walls that surround the cervix. The result of this is a "ballooning" of the inner two-thirds of the vagina. The total length of the vagina may be increased as much as one full inch.

There are also other occurrences in the body which indicate sexual arousal in men and women. Some groups of voluntary and involuntary muscles may become tense. In addition, the heart rate and blood pressure are increased, and a "sex flush" may appear on the skin, appearing at first on the abdomen and spreading up to the breasts. It usually looks like a measles rash. According to Masters and Johnson, the sex flush appears on about 75% of women and about 25% of men.

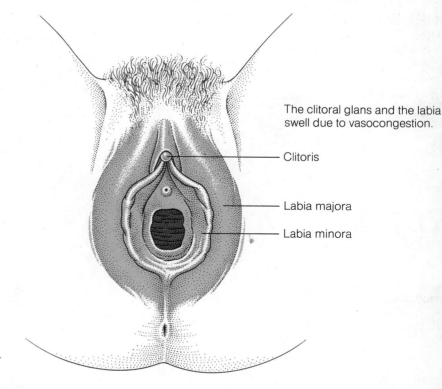

The clitoral glans and the labia swell due to vasocongestion.

—— Clitoris

—— Labia majora

—— Labia minora

FIGURE 4.3 Female sexual response during excitement.

The Plateau Phase

MEN

Since full erection of the penis takes place during the excitement phase, few additional changes will occur in this phase with regard to erection. However, there may be a slight increase in the diameter of the coronal ridge of the glans. On occasion, the glans may turn a deeper reddish purple color (Figure 4.4).

The testes may increase about 50% over their unstimulated size and may be pulled up further into the scrotum because of a shortening of the spermatic cords. When the testes have reached their highest elevation, orgasm is imminent. If the nipples were not erect earlier, they may be so now.

During this phase, a few drops of moisture may emerge from the urethra. This fluid most likely comes from the Cowper's glands. Although not semen, this fluid may contain large numbers of sperm cells. Thus, it is possible for a woman to become pregnant even when her partner does not ejaculate or withdraws his penis before ejaculation. A man may not always emit this pre-ejaculate.

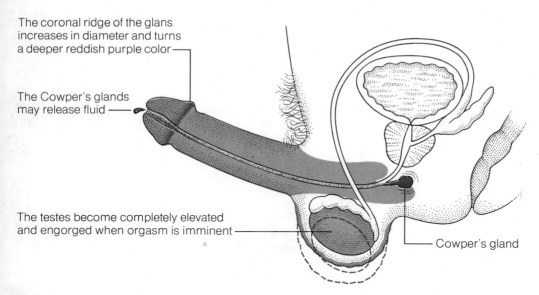

The coronal ridge of the glans increases in diameter and turns a deeper reddish purple color —

The Cowper's glands may release fluid —

The testes become completely elevated and engorged when orgasm is imminent —

Cowper's gland

FIGURE 4.4 Male sexual response during the plateau phase.

WOMEN

The most dramatic change that occurs to the woman during the plateau phase (Figure 4.5) is the appearance of what Masters and Johnson call "the orgasmic platform." This is a vasocongestion of the tissues that surround the outer third of the vagina. As a result, the diameter of the outer third of the vagina can be reduced by as much as 50%. This reduction enables the vagina to "grip" the penis, thereby increasing the arousal level of the man. However, the occurrence of this vasocongestion does not necessarily indicate that the woman is ready to experience orgasm. With the onset of the orgasmic platform comes a further elevation of the uterus, which also becomes enlarged during this phase. These changes may not be experienced subjectively. The second most dramatic change is the elevation of the clitoris. During this process, the clitoris is retracted into the clitoral hood and shortened by as much as 50%. However, it does continue to respond to stimulation by either direct stimulation of the mons or indirectly via the thrusting of the penis into the vagina.

Vasocongestion of the labia majora may continue to increase, especially in women who have given birth. The labia minora will usually change color late during this phase. This color change often indicates that orgasm will occur, provided that erotic stimulation is encountered.

As readiness for orgasm takes place, the two major processes of vasocongestion and myotonia will continue.

For both men and women, the plateau phase brings on a further increase in blood pressure, heart rate, and breathing rate. The sex flush may now appear to be more widespread than it was. Voluntary and invol-

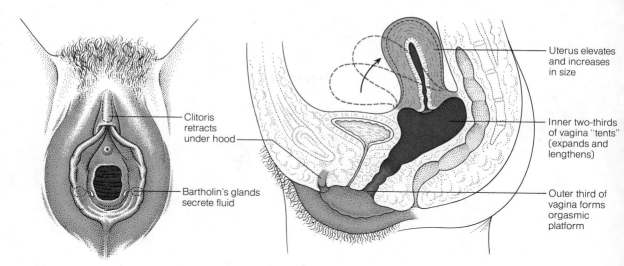

FIGURE 4.5 Female sexual response during the plateau phase.

untary muscles may become more tense, and some of the muscles in the face, ribs, and abdomen may contract.

Orgasm

MEN

The male orgasm is a series of rhythmic contractions that occur at intervals of about four-fifths of a second (Figure 4.6). After the first few contractions, subsequent contractions tend to become longer, with diminishing intensity.

> The kind of sensation I get from an orgasm varies. Usually, the first time with any woman is more intense because the experience with someone new as well as the desire is likely to be more intense. The intensity of my orgasm will also vary with different women. The more excited a woman gets, the greater will be my excitement.

Prior to orgasm, the fluid containing the millions of sperm cells collects in the seminal vesicles, which, upon rhythmic contractions, expel the contents into the urethra. At the same time, the prostate expels its fluids into the urethra. These occurrences constitute the first stage of ejaculation.

During the second stage of ejaculation, the contractions of the urethral bulb and the penis itself project the semen outward. The pressure exerted

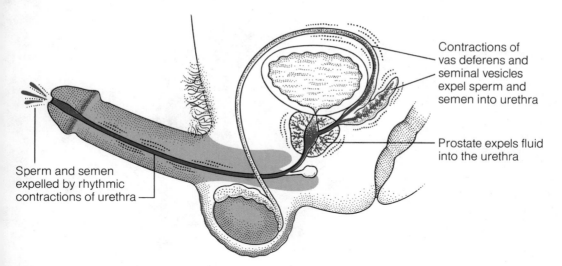

Contractions of
vas deferens and
seminal vesicles
expel sperm and
semen into urethra

Prostate expels fluid
into the urethra

Sperm and semen
expelled by rhythmic
contractions of urethra

FIGURE 4.6 Male sexual response during orgasm.

is sometimes strong enough to project the semen 2 feet. If the man has had an ejaculation shortly before, i.e., perhaps an hour before, the contractions will not be quite as strong. Also, in older men, contractions are less vigorous; therefore, the pressure of expulsion is somewhat reduced.

I remember when I was 17 and I would masturbate. When I would ejaculate, my semen would spurt as far as a foot or two. Now that I am in my late twenties, I still masturbate (only occasionally), but I notice that my ejaculate travels no further than a few inches from my penis.

WOMEN

The most observable feature of the female orgasm is a series of rhythmic contractions of the orgasmic platform (Figure 4.7). The outer third of the vagina and its vasocongested tissues undergo muscular contractions. While the initial contractions occur at intervals of approximately four-fifths of a second, subsequent contractions are longer and less intensified. The intensity of the woman's orgasm can vary from three to five contractions for a mild one, eight to twelve for an intense one.

The onset of an orgasm occurs with an initial spasm of the orgasmic platform preceding the rhythmic train of contractions by a few seconds. Along with these contractions, the uterus rhythmically contracts. Contractions begin at the upper end of the uterus and, in wavelike motions, move through the uterus downward to the cervix. The greater the severity of the contractions, the greater the intensity of the orgasm. Other muscles, such as the anal sphincter, may also undergo contractions.

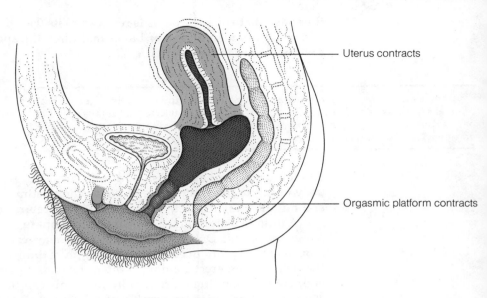

Uterus contracts

Orgasmic platform contracts

FIGURE 4.7 Female sexual response during orgasm.

> During a good orgasm, I let go of reality. When it's really good, I don't know who I am, whom I am with, or how I got there. I just go on a trip. My body begins to feel hot and I experience a radiating flash throughout my body. My vagina has a series of throbs that can number anywhere from three to twenty. It's just the greatest feeling I have ever experienced.

Occasionally the woman may feel an urge to urinate during or immediately following orgasm.

During orgasm, the blood pressure, heart rate, and breathing rate in men and women reach a peak. The sex flush will also be most observable. Orgasm will also cause a tightening of the muscles in the neck, buttocks, abdomen, and arms and legs. Most men and women are not usually aware of the extreme muscular tension that occurs during orgasms. Sometimes their bodies will be sore the next day due to muscle aches.

It is difficult to describe the sensation of orgasm in men and women. Among some of the generalities used to detail the feelings of orgasm are "a warm glow," "a tingling sensation," and "a total release."

Resolution

MEN

In men, the most obvious sign that the resolution phase has set in is the rapid loss of the erect state of the penis. In this two-stage process, the penis begins to shrink quite rapidly. In the second stage, the remainder of the somewhat enlarged penis is reduced to its flaccid state. This reduction is a result of an emptying of blood that filled the spongy tissue (corpora cavernosa) of the penis (Figure 4.8).

It takes no more than a minute after I ejaculate during sexual intercourse that I can feel my penis becoming flaccid. It then becomes so flaccid that it falls out of my partner's vagina. At one time this made be feel embarrassed, but knowing what I do now, I realize this is normal.

If the male had a sex flush, it disappears. The testes and scrotum gradually return to the position held during the unstimulated state. After several minutes, the nipples, if they were erect, return to the normal state.

A unique feature in the male resolution phase is what is known as the *refractory period*. During this period, the man cannot become sexually aroused to the point of erection. The length of time it would take to arouse the penis to the erect state most often depends upon the man's age. The younger the man, the more rapidly the penis can be brought to the erect state. Some men may be capable of becoming erect again in a matter of minutes, while other men may need as much as a day's rest before erection can be achieved again. The refractory period may last for several days in very old men.

WOMEN

In women, the first significant occurrence during the resolution phase is the reduction in the size of the breasts. The reduction in the size of the

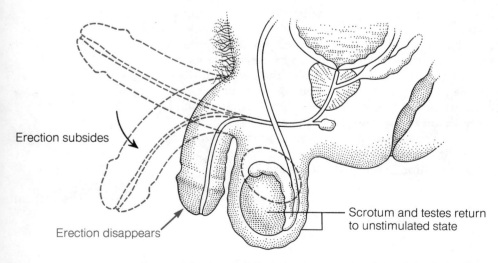

Erection subsides

Erection disappears

Scrotum and testes return to unstimulated state

The penis is reduced in size due to the emptying of blood that filled the corpora cavernosa.

FIGURE 4.8 Male sexual response during resolution.

breasts causes the nipples to stand out further than usual. The increased prominence of the nipples may be an indication that the woman has experienced orgasm. This change in the breasts, along with the rapid disappearance of the sex flush, may indicate that the woman experienced orgasm. Of course, one would have to look at the change of nipple and breast size very soon after the female orgasm.

Of the women Masters and Johnson observed, about a third showed a film of perspiration over the entire body. Sometimes the perspiration appeared only on the soles of the feet or on the palms of the hands.

Another major change that occurs during the resolution phase is a reduction of the size of the clitoris within five to ten seconds after orgasm. However, five, ten or more minutes may elapse before the clitoris returns to its unaroused state (Figure 4.9). Also soon after orgasm, the outer third of the vagina begins to increase in diameter. The ballooning of the vagina diminishes, and the uterus begins to shrink. At this point, the cervix drops slowly to its unaroused position. The opening of the cervix, the *os*, enlarges. This perhaps makes it easier for sperm to travel to the uterus.

Unlike the man, the woman does not enter a refractory period. The woman is capable of achieving multiple orgasms, to be discussed later in this chapter.

> After I have an orgasm, I love to just hold my husband tight. I also like him to hold me tight. Usually we have some good conversations. Both of us are not uptight and we can communicate real well. At other times we just lie alongside each other and let the quietness put us to sleep.

The processes that take place for the woman's body to return to normal may vary, depending on whether or not orgasm occurred. As much as

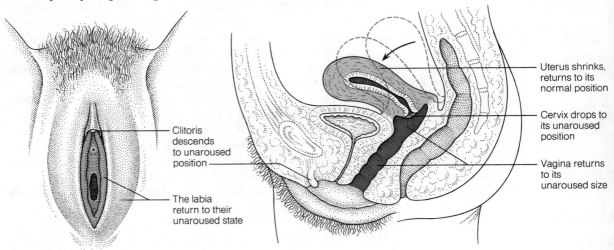

Clitoris descends to unaroused position

The labia return to their unaroused state

Uterus shrinks, returns to its normal position

Cervix drops to its unaroused position

Vagina returns to its unaroused size

FIGURE 4.9 Female sexual response during resolution.

a half hour may elapse before the woman's body can return to its un-aroused state.

In both men and women, blood pressure, pulse rate, and breathing rate soon return to normal.

In analyzing the processes that take place during the response cycles, it should be noted that each phase is not sharply defined, especially the phase between excitement and plateau. It should also be noted that the four phases that have been described occur in most but not *all* men and women. Individuals may vary from the model presented, and the variances do not, in any manner, constitute abnormality.

MALE AND FEMALE SEXUAL RESPONSIVENESS

Male

The process by which an erection occurs is dependent upon a myriad of factors. The psychic reflexes such as thoughts and emotions, the nervous reflexes such as those emanating from the tip of the penis, as well as the nerve cell activity that takes place throughout the central nervous system, all play a role in the erection process. In the male, each of these processes can work independently or interdependently toward achieving an erection. That is, the brain as a controlling variable over nerve cell activity can be an integral force in causing a man to experience an erection. Conversely, thoughts and emotions have the ability to interfere with the automatic nervous and vascular sexual responses (De Lora and Warren, 1977).

PSYCHIC AND REFLEX ACTIONS

An erection can be due to either a *psychic* or a *reflex* action. A man can have a psychic erection if he sees a sexually arousing movie, fantasizes, or reads a sexually stimulating novel (Figure 4.10). In other words, a psychic erection occurs because of thought and not tactile stimulation to the body. This occurrence is caused by an impulse that has originated in the brain and has traveled to the penis via the spinal cord.

Conversely, a reflex erection is caused by effective tactile stimulation to the penis or genital area (Figure 4.11). In this case, the nerve impulse will travel from the site of the touch, through the lowest part of the spinal cord (sacral area), and back to the muscular walls of the blood vessel which in turn triggers the erectile process. A man who has a spinal cord injury and is confined to a wheelchair will probably not be capable of experiencing a psychic erection. However, he may be able to experience a reflex erection.

Some reflex erections are stimulated by nonsexual activities. One such type of reflex erection is that of the man who wakes up each morning with his penis in the erect state when erotic thoughts had not entered his mind. Probably this was due to a full bladder or possibly an unconscious friction between the penis and the bed. Morning erection is also associated with rapid eye movement (REM) sleep during which neural stimuli occur.

ORGASM

Most specialists in human sexuality recognize that orgasm is a total body response (de Moya and de Moya, 1973). According to Kinsey (1948), *orgasm* is an explosive discharge of neuromuscular tensions at the peak of sexual response. Men for the most part achieve orgasm more easily through masturbation and coitus than through any other means.

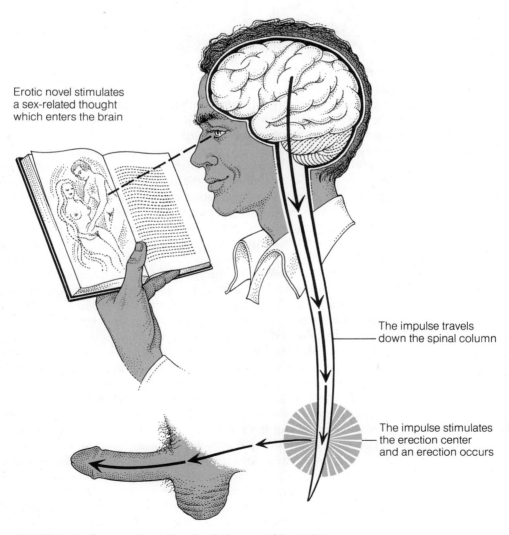

Erotic novel stimulates
a sex-related thought
which enters the brain

The impulse travels
down the spinal column

The impulse stimulates
the erection center
and an erection occurs

FIGURE 4.10 Passage of nerve impulse during a psychic erection.

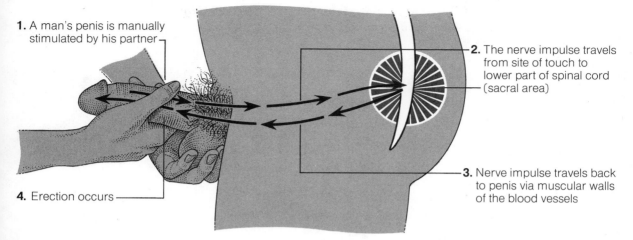

1. A man's penis is manually stimulated by his partner

2. The nerve impulse travels from site of touch to lower part of spinal cord (sacral area)

3. Nerve impulse travels back to penis via muscular walls of the blood vessels

4. Erection occurs

FIGURE 4.11 Passage of nerve impulse during a reflex erection.

Some researchers differentiate between ejaculation and orgasm in the male (De Lora and Warren, 1977). Ejaculation does not necessarily indicate orgasm. A man may be nonorgasmic, in that ejaculation brought with it very little emotional or physical release. This condition is also called *ejaculatory anhedonia.* Some men, on the other hand, may experience orgasm without ejaculation, a condition known as *retrograde ejaculation* (Figure 4.12). Retrograde ejaculation often occurs because of prostate surgery. It can also be due to an illness or to the use of certain depressant drugs. In retrograde ejaculation, or "dry orgasm," the ejaculate, instead of passing through the penis, enters the bladder by a reverse mode of operation of the sphincters that are involved in urination and ejaculation. In the normal man, the internal sphincter closes off the entrance to the bladder during ejaculation and the external one opens, allowing semen to flow out of the penis through the urethra. In retrograde ejaculation, the action of the two sphincters is reversed. The external sphincter closes and therefore prevents the ejaculate from passing through the penis. The internal sphincter opens, therefore permitting the ejaculate to go into the bladder. This condition is harmless, and the man is still capable of achieving and enjoying orgasm, although he cannot fertilize an ovum.

MALE AND FEMALE ORGASMIC EXPERIENCE In the past, it has been assumed that there are basic differences between a man's experience of orgasm and a woman's experience of orgasm. The difference that is most obvious is the fact that men ejaculate and women do not. To help differentiate between male and female orgasm, Proctor et al. (1974) conducted a study in which college students were asked to write a brief statement indicating what an orgasm felt like. The students' descriptions were then submitted to a panel of medical students, obstetrician–gynecologists, and clinical psychologists, who were then asked to identify the sex to which the description belonged. The results of the study showed that none of the

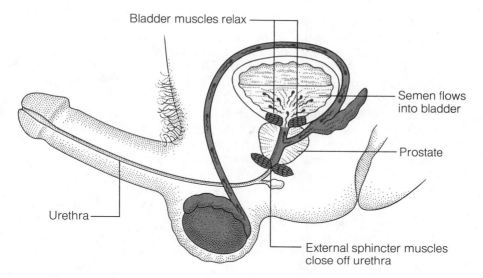

Bladder muscles relax

Semen flows into bladder

Prostate

Urethra

External sphincter muscles close off urethra

FIGURE 4.12 The passage of semen during retrograde ejaculation.

professional groups were able to distinguish the sex of a person from that person's written description of his or her orgasm. More importantly, serious questions were raised about the assumption that orgasm as experienced by men is something different from orgasm experienced by women. Unless there is empirical evidence to the contrary, it is not unreasonable to assume that the experience of orgasm for men and women is basically the same. The research of Kinsey (1948) and Masters and Johnson (1966) also emphasized the similarities and not the differences between male and female orgasm.

Female

STAGES OF THE FEMALE ORGASM

In their research, Masters and Johnson (1966) have identified three distinct stages of a woman's subjective progression through orgasm. The stages are as follows:

STAGE I During this stage orgasm has its onset, with a sensation of suspension or stoppage. Although it lasts for an instant, this sensation is accompanied or followed immediately by an isolated thrust of intense sensual awareness. Although this awareness is clitorally oriented, it radiates up into the pelvis. A number of women describe the first stage of orgasm as a strong sense of bearing down or expelling. Often a feeling of receptive opening is expressed.

STAGE II At the second stage of progression through orgasm, a sensation of "suffusion of warmth," specifically felt in the pelvic area first and then spreading throughout the body, was described by almost every woman in the Masters and Johnson study who experienced orgasm.

STAGE III   In the final stage of subjective progression, a feeling of involuntary contraction focusing specifically in the vagina or lower pelvis was mentioned consistently. Often this sensation was described as "pelvic throbbing."

The work of Singer and Singer (1972) sheds light on a different view of female orgasmic response. The Singers described three types of female orgasm experience. The first type, called *vulval orgasm,* is similar to the "involuntary rhythmic contractions of the orgasmic platform" noted by Masters and Johnson. The second type, known as *uterine orgasm,* is characterized by a cumulative gasping type of breathing that culminates in an "involuntary breath-holding response, which occurs only after considerable diaphragmatic tension has been achieved." Upon orgasm, the breath is violently exhaled, after which there is a feeling of relaxation and sexual satiation. This type of response appears to be dependent upon deep stimulation involving penis–cervix contact. This contact is thought to displace the uterus and cause stimulation of the peritoneum (the membrane lining the abdominal cavity).

The third type, the *blended orgasm,* is a combination of the first two types. It is characterized by both the breath-holding response and contractions of the orgasmic platform. According to Singer and Singer, the different types of orgasms will cause different types of satisfaction, and individual interpretation of that satisfaction determines which is the most preferable.

ACHIEVING ORGASM: THE FEMALE VARIANCE

Helen Singer Kaplan, a well-known sex therapist, developed a continuum to indicate the difficulty women have in achieving orgasm. In looking at the continuum starting at the "easy to reach orgasm" end, the following were the progressive stages:

1. A small number of women are able to achieve orgasm through erotic fantasy.
2. Some women are able to achieve orgasm by rhythmically pressing together their thighs. This rhythmical movement can stimulate the clitoris.
3. At the next part of the continuum are women who become orgasmic in response to kissing and petting. However, in this stage, petting is limited to the breasts and not to the genital area.
4. Next are women who, after they have had a sufficient exposure from foreplay, can attain orgasm soon after the penis is inserted into the vagina. Perhaps only a few coital thrusts are needed before orgasm occurs.
5. In the middle of the continuum are women who can achieve orgasm in the missionary position (man on top). Usually, orgasm does not occur until an extended period of sexual intercourse.

6. In this part of the continuum are women who can achieve orgasm by taking the "female on top" position. In this position, increased clitoral stimulation can occur.

7. One step farther on the continuum is the woman who needs her partner to supply manual stimulation during sexual intercourse. Often this will take place in the female superior position, and the man will manually stimulate the clitoris. Manual stimulation can also be given to the breasts.

8. Many women fit into the category in which direct stimulation to the clitoris, either manually or orally, can produce orgasms.

9. Toward the latter part of the Singer continuum are women who require the following to achieve orgasm: lengthy and intense clitoral stimulation, fantasy along with the clitoral stimulation, self-masturbation, and prolonged application of a vibrator.

10. At the furthest extreme are those women who cannot experience orgasm, regardless of the behavior employed.

While many studies of the female orgasm have been conducted, the Kinsey data remain the most quoted. According to Kinsey (1948), the woman experiences her first orgasm at an average age of 20. This is six years later than the man, who has his first orgasm at around age 14. Unlike the man, whose first ejaculation was usually brought on by solitary masturbation, the first orgasm for the woman was brought on by social sex. That is, 59% of women experienced their first orgasm with a partner—30% in marital intercourse, 18% in petting, 8% in premarital coitus, and 3% in homosexual contact. Thirty-seven percent of women experienced their first orgasm by masturbation, while only 4% did so by dreams.

It may very well be that the Kinsey data, in some cases, are not applicable to today's women. Shere Hite's study (*The Hite Report*, 1976) has been criticized for poor research design and poor sampling methods, but her book has received widespread attention. According to this study, 83% of the women surveyed masturbated, 95% of these women able to achieve orgasm. However, only 30% of the women surveyed were able to achieve orgasm through sexual intercourse. These figures are similar to the Kinsey data in that Kinsey also found that 95% of women who masturbated achieved orgasm.

The data of Hite and Kinsey bring out some interesting points. According to Hite, half the married and unmarried women surveyed indicated they would like to or did masturbate after intercourse to achieve orgasm. Kinsey found that 70% of women achieved orgasm during their first year of marriage and that eventually 95% of married women did go on to develop the ability to have orgasms.

THE CLITORAL VERSUS THE VAGINAL ORGASM

The work by Masters and Johnson opened up new insights into the controversy that once existed regarding clitoral versus vaginal orgasms.

For purposes of clarification, *clitoral* and *vaginal* are used to indicate the type of stimulation. The terms do not mean that the vagina or the clitoris experiences orgasm.

One time I went to bed with this guy and he asked me if I had clitoral or vaginal orgasms. I didn't know what the hell he was talking about. The next time I had an orgasm, I tried to focus on whether or not it was clitoral or vaginal. Frankly, I didn't know one from the other. All I know is that it is enjoyable having an orgasm, period.

The basis for the theory that women can experience two kinds of orgasms, one clitoral and the other vaginal, was presented by Freud in his work *Three Essays on the Theory of Sexuality*. Freud reasoned that everyone goes through certain psychosexual stages, one of which involves masturbation. He explained that some girls discover that they can achieve orgasm by stimulating the clitoris. As the child becomes older, she changes toward heterosexual genital maturity or, more specifically, desires sexual intercourse. The female is supposed to transfer her sexual responses from the clitoris to the vagina. Some women fail to make this transfer. Therefore, they may continue to experience orgasm upon stimulation of the clitoris while being "vaginally frigid." As a result, masturbation, which results from stimulation to the clitoris, becomes thought of as immature, while sexual intercourse becomes the mature behavior. Using this rationale, since masturbation is infantile, pleasures achieved by touching the clitoris are infantile. A sexually mature woman, according to Freud, will move from having orgasms produced by touching the clitoris to having orgasms produced by the penis in the vagina.

After Freud wrote his doctrine of vaginal orgasm as distinct from clitoral orgasm, the sexual literature adopted these theories in its analyses of sexual functioning. Many psychoanalytic writers accepted the idea that the clitoral orgasm was an expression of immaturity, neuroticism, masculinity, or frigidity, or some combination, while vaginal orgasm denoted femininity, maturity, and normality.

The most remarkable biological feat of the mature woman is being able to deflect and displace the masculine libido of the clitoris to the purely feminine channels of the vagina.

(Bonaparte, 1953)

Clitoral activity is masculine and immature while vaginal responsiveness is feminine and mature. . . . the sexual act for a woman may be profoundly cathartic. . . [but] only under the condition that it is experienced in a feminine, dynamic way and it is not transformed into an act of erotic play or sexual equality.

(Deutsch, 1945)

Freud's theory, which acted as a spark for other theorists, caused much trouble for many women. Because of the ideas presented in the above excerpts, many women underwent a great deal of stress and anxiety trying to figure out why they could not achieve vaginal orgasm, yet at the same time enjoy the pleasures produced by clitoral stimulation. The results of the Masters and Johnson studies were able to show that there is no difference between a vaginal orgasm and a clitoral orgasm. They found that an orgasm always consists of contractions of the orgasmic platform as well as contractions of the muscles around the vagina, regardless of whether stimulation was centered on the vagina or the clitoris. Further, if we reflect upon our discussion of the Kaplan continuum, we find that women can experience orgasm without any clitoral or vaginal stimulation — i.e., through fantasy or intense kissing or fondling of the breasts.

Another reason to discount Freud's theory is based upon the process that occurs during the act of sexual intercourse. In their research, Masters and Johnson were able to show that features of the female anatomy come into play in orgasm. During sexual intercourse, the thrusting of the penis causes motion of the labia minora at the entrance of the vagina. These lips come together above the vaginal opening to form the "hood," or what is also known as the prepuce, of the clitoris. The rhythmic motion of the inner lips produced by the coital thrusting slides the hood rhythmically back and forth against the sensitive glans of the the clitoris. The clitoris then becomes stimulated through light touch. Therefore, we can see that the clitoris participates fully in sexual intercourse even though it is not stimulated directly. It seems that clitoral stimulation can be the factor that initiates orgasm.

While there is no scientific basis to distinguish between clitoral and vaginal orgasm, in some circles, the differentiation persists.

> The present-day reader acquainted with scientific method might, after reading the above [psychoanalytic account of clitoral versus vaginal orgasm], ask to see the experimental data or, lacking that, request the opportunity to review in some detail case material from which Freud drew his conclusions. Neither of these conditions can be met, and one is forced to regard the theory as unsupported opinion of a very gifted man, but unsupported nevertheless. Another complication in this matter is that none of the proponents of the clitoral-vaginal transfer theory, Freud included, have stated signs or symptoms by which one may distinguish between these presumably different types of orgasms . . . *the final demolition of the old transfer notion came with the research of Masters and Johnson* [italics added]

> (Hastings, 1963)

MULTIPLE ORGASMS

Another aspect of female sexual response studied by Masters and Johnson was the *multiple orgasm,* or the capacity in some women to experience orgasm more than one time during a single sexual response cycle.

In the past, it was believed that, like the male, the female was capable of one orgasm during a sexual response cycle. However, some researchers prior to Masters and Johnson had collected data that indicated that women were capable of achieving more than one orgasm. One study found that 13% of married women reported having multiple orgasms (Terman, 1951). Kinsey found that 14% of the women in his study with 25 or more coital experiences, irrespective of marital status, experienced multiple orgasms.

I had always thought that one orgasm was all I could have during one sexual encounter. Then one day, I was with this guy who turned out to be a delayed ejaculator. It turned out to be the best thing that ever happened to me. After I had my orgasm, I continued making love to him and found that the longer he stayed in me without ejaculating, the more turned on I got. That was my first experience with multiple orgasms. Believe me, it won't be my last.

Yet after considerable data had shown that multiple orgasms in women existed, other researchers raised concerns about the validity of such findings. These concerns were usually raised by men who no doubt were influenced by male standards.

> One of the most fantastic tales the female volunteers told Kinsey (who believed it) was that of multiple orgasm. Allegedly 14 percent of these women claimed to have experienced it. . . . Multiple orgasm is an exceptional experience. The 14 percent of Kinsey's volunteers, all vaginally frigid, belonged obviously to the nymphomaniac type of frigidity where excitement mounts repeatedly without reaching a climax. . . . Not being familiar with this medical fact . . . Kinsey was taken in by the near-misses which these women represented as multiple orgasm.
>
> (Bergler and Kroger, 1954)

THE PHYSIOLOGY OF MULTIPLE ORGASM After a woman's first orgasm, a series of changes take place. Her clitoris descends to its resting position and the orgasmic platform relaxes and loses its engorgement, as do the labia minora and the labia majora. However, all of these events can be reversed. With continued erotic stimulation, the clitoris can again elevate, the veins refill with blood, engorgement takes place, muscles contract, and another orgasm is thus initiated.

For some women, continuous stimulation without a time lapse is preferred, while for other women, a retreat backward to the plateau or excitement phase is preferred before stimulation is started again.

Some guys I have sex with play a numbers game. A few years ago, the famous line, after having sex, would be "Did you come?" The guys today now ask, "How many orgasms did you have?" Why can't guys understand that some women are satisfied with one orgasm?

Masters and Johnson reported that a woman may "experience 5 to 20 recurrent orgasmic experiences with the sexual tension never allowed to drop below a plateau phase maintenance level until physical exhaustion terminates the session." In their clinic for infertile couples, Masters and Johnson worked with five men who were fully sexually potent but who were not able to have orgasm during sexual intercourse. As a result, these men were able to maintain the act of sexual intercourse for a period of upwards of 60 minutes at any given opportunity. In three of these five cases, the wives were able to benefit in that they were able to be multiorgasmic. As in the case of other women who can self-stimulate themselves to multiple orgasms, coitus was terminated by the female partner's admission of sexual satiation, only after the woman was able to have multiple orgasms.

In summary, multiple orgasm is not a characteristic of self-stimulation. Rather, it is a characteristic of any effective stimulation that is prolonged enough to induce multiple responses. According to Masters and Johnson, the average woman with optimal arousal will usually be satisfied with 3 to 5 manually induced orgasms. With a mechanical stimulator such as an electric vibrator, the woman may have 20 to 50 consecutive orgasms. These figures do not mean that man must be capable of bringing the female to orgasm several times during each sexual encounter. First, the statement "The average female with optimal arousal will usually be satisfied with three to five manually induced orgasms" probably does not apply to most women. Masters and Johnson would probably be safer saying that "some women are capable of multiple orgasm." Second, while *some* women may be capable of multiple orgasms, they may feel that one orgasm is pleasurable enough and that continuance of sexual intercourse is not desirable. Much more research needs to be undertaken so that we can identify just how many women are capable of achieving multiple orgasms and what conditions must be present. It should not be assumed that the more orgasms a woman has, the more satisfied she will feel.

SUMMARY STATEMENTS

- *There are four phases of the sexual response cycle: excitement, plateau, orgasm, and resolution.*
- *Each phase is marked by changes in the body.*
- *A man can have a psychic or a reflex erection.*
- *Some men can achieve orgasm but not ejaculate, and vice versa.*
- *It is usually easier for a man than for a woman to achieve orgasm.*
- *According to Masters and Johnson, there is no difference between clitoral and vaginal orgasm.*
- *Women are capable of achieving multiple orgasms.*

SUGGESTED READINGS

Kinsey, Alfred C., Wardell B. Pomeroy, and Clyde E. Martin. *Sexual Behavior in the Human Male*. Philadelphia: W. B. Saunders, 1948.

Kinsey, Alfred C., Wardell B. Pomeroy, Clyde E. Martin, and Paul A. Gebhard. *Sexual Behavior in the Human Female*. Philadelphia: W. B. Saunders, 1953.

Masters, William, and Virginia Johnson. *Human Sexual Response*. Boston: Little, Brown, 1966.

**THE PHYSIOLOGY
OF SEXUAL
RESPONSE**

A LOOK AT YOUR LIFESTYLE

While having a conversation about sex with a group of your friends, the following question is asked by a male and female in the group: *"What actually takes place in my body that makes me sexually aroused?"*

Write an I-message describing your reaction to this question:

When you asked me "What makes you feel sexually aroused?," I _____

1. Identify the key issue or problem:

_____

Given:
I need to decide how to react to my friend's questions about sexual arousal.

_____

2. Identify the possible solutions or alternatives:
Given:
A. *Ignore my female friend.*
B. *Ignore my male friend.*
C. *Ignore both my male and female friends.*
D. *Discuss sexual response with both friends.*

GATHERING INFORMATION

You have decided to select alternative D, "Discuss sexual response with both friends." Make up a chart like the one shown. Outline sexual response in the spaces.

PHASES	MALE	FEMALE
Excitement		
Plateau		
Orgasmic		
Resolution		

EVALUATING THE INFORMATION

What is the most important thing that your female friend should know about sexual response?

_____

What is the most important thing that your male friend should know about sexual response?

_____

MAKING RESPONSIBLE DECISIONS

Identify one aspect of human sexual response that is related to making responsible decisions.

_____

FIVE

Sexual Arousal

Throughout our lives, we are bombarded with a wide range of sexual stimuli. These stimuli may take the form of seeing an attractive man or woman passing us on the street, smelling a perfume or cologne that your partner happens to be wearing, holding hands with someone toward whom you feel intimate, hearing a voice on the radio, or having a fleeting thought about a particular person or event. Each of us may have different experiences that trigger a state of being sexually "turned on." In the previous chapters on anatomy and the physiology of sexual response, some of the details of what happens inside the body during sexual arousal were covered. However, our discussions and thoughts about sexual arousal need not be limited to our physiology.

Men and women need to look at their behavior and the behavior of others if they are to come to grips with the sexual side of their personal ties. The fully caring individual needs to ask and be able to respond to many issues and questions related to sexual arousal. For example:

1. Why do I often feel "horny"?
2. Is there a "right" way to be a good lover?
3. Do women get "turned on" as frequently as men?
4. Why don't I think much about sex?
5. Why do I often find sex with my partner boring?

I always thought that I was strange because I always felt sexually turned on. My girlfriend always told me that I had "strange hormones" because she felt I was horny all the time. Yet when I would speak with my friends, they would feel the same way I did. I then developed the attitude that guys, more so than women, had a desire for sex. Then a few months ago, I met this woman who functions on the same wavelength as I. Our sexual desires for each other are equally intense. No longer do I have the fear that "it's only me" when it comes to being sexually aroused.

Just what may *motivate* you to become sexually aroused and what *will* be sexually arousing are two concerns that will be dealt with in this chapter. What this chapter is *not* is a manual that will make you the ultimate lover.

The purpose of this chapter is to inform you about arousal in sexual behavior. You must also understand that sexual arousal and practices are highly individual. Understanding what makes you and others "tick" will enable you to be a more effective communicator as well as a more fully understanding sexual being.

GATHERING INFORMATION

Understanding sexual arousal entails a great deal more than knowing a sexual technique or a position in sexual intercourse. To limit our knowledge of sexual arousal to that of mechanistic technique is to deny ourselves the opportunity to reap the benefits of a total sexual experience. Therefore, the following will be discussed in this chapter:

1. the biological and psychological factors that play a significant role in sexual arousal and motivation
2. the role fantasy plays in our sexual behavior
3. the role various stimuli such as foods and chemicals and body senses play in our sexuality
4. techniques involved in one-person sexual arousal as well as in partner-to-partner sexual arousal

EVALUATING THE INFORMATION

The information provided in this chapter will enable you to understand the reasons you and/or your partner behave the way you do. As you examine the many factors that play a role in sexual behavior, you will evaluate the ways this information can enhance your lifestyle as well as that of your partner.

The purpose of this chapter is to present an overview of the processes involved in sexual motivation and arousal. While you may feel accepting in applying some of the information to your lifestyle, you may also feel uncomfortable recognizing that some of the mentioned facets may be a part of your sexual self.

One guy I dated wanted to prove to me he was a sexual acrobat. He was into trying every position in sexual intercourse — and in about an hour. I felt as if I were trying out for the U.S. Gymnastics Olympic Team. Frankly, I enjoy sex in the missionary position the best. I just cannot get as turned on if the guy is on the bottom, on the side, or any place else.

Not only is it important that you evaluate the information in this chapter as it applies to you, but that you share your thoughts and feelings with your partner. Denying your feelings and concerns by not telling your partner is to limit your potential to enjoy a healthy sexuality.

MAKING RESPONSIBLE DECISIONS

Many people are afraid to share their needs with their partners. Each individual must feel comfortable sharing his or her rights. The decision to say "no" or "yes" to another person's request is not only a right but a responsibility. If we accept the fact that we are sexual beings, then we must also accept the fact that we are the only ones responsible for the decisions we make. When you think but do not share your sexual concerns with your partner because your partner may think you're "weird," you may be denying your own as well as your partner's need for intimacy. Telling your partner, for example, "I like it when you touch me that way," not only can help you meet your needs but can serve to compliment your partner. And it is just as important to admit to your partner, "I don't like it when you touch me that way."

BIOLOGICAL AND BEHAVIORAL FOUNDATIONS OF SEXUAL AROUSAL

Looking at the many factors that may influence sexual arousal and motivation, biological, psychological, and sociological influences appear to be the most prominent. Just which of these factors is the most influential as well as what roles they all play has been the subject of many studies, theories, and controversies. The difficulty in establishing the impact of these various factors on sexual behavior is that each factor may work independently or they may work together in motivating sexual behavior. For example, is one's involvement sexually with another a result of an increase in hormone production, pressure from one's partner to perform, or a need to prove one's masculinity or femininity? The possibility is that one or all of these factors may be significant. In the sections to follow, factors that are thought to influence sexual motivation will be examined.

Biological Factors

In Chapter 2 we discussed male puberty. During puberty, a boy experiences an increased "sex drive" (libido) that is precipitated by increased "sex" hormones. These hormones cause changes in the genitals and reproductive system and result in the development of a "sexually mature" person. It appears that hormones have a distinct impact upon sexual behavior.

I remember when I entered the eighth grade. It seemed as if I always walked around with an erection. I did not know what sex was all about, nor did I understand the techniques of sexual intercourse. Yet I seemed to be horny all the time. All of the guys used to kid each other and say that our hormones were acting up.

Although theories have been raised that purport to show that increasing amounts of hormones cause humans to behave in a more sexual way, few are supported (Gagnon, 1977). The influences of hormones on sexual behavior are extremely complex. Androgens, male sex hormones, have been linked to sexual activity. It is assumed that if men during puberty have higher rates of sexual activity than women, they also have higher levels of androgens. Thus there is the assumption that increased androgens cause increased sexual activity. Yet Kinsey (1953) found that in the male, the upsurge of sexual responsiveness is more marked than the steady rise in the androgen levels. While Kinsey also found that no correlation existed between female androgen levels and sexual responsiveness and activity, his conclusions are being questioned today.

One theory regarding the effect of hormones upon sexual behavior indicates that bias on the part of researchers has an impact upon the extent to which hormones are said to be influential. The following example illustrates this point:

> Scientific experiments on this subject have been inconclusive, contradictory, and ambiguous. The majority of these experiments have been with hormones. In guinea pigs, one laboratory group showed that prenatally-administered testosterone resulted in adult pseudohermaphrodite females (that is, animals with female chromosome complements and internal but ambiguous external genitalia) (Phoenix et al., 1959). These animals were said to display less of the female receptive sexual posture than normal females in response to estrogen. Testosterone administered postnatally to these animals gave no conspicuous behavioral change, nor did testosterone administered to males. These animals did display male-type mounting behavior, but so did normal females. Female hormone, estrogen, when injected into castrated males, according to one group, resulted in increased male mounting activity; according to another group, similar experiments resulted in *decreased* mounting activity and increased receptive postures; whereas, according to a third group, similar experiments resulted in decreases of any kind of sexual behavior (Feder and Whalen, 1965; Ball, 1937; Keen, 1934; Whalen, 1964)! When three different laboratories get three different results on nearly identical experiments, observer bias, even in guinea pigs, is very likely .
>
> (Rosenberg, 1973)

Another researched aspect of sex hormone and its relationship to sexual arousal and motivation is that of *castration,* removal of the testes. In the past, castration was practiced in many cultures for a variety of reasons. Although not common today, castration is sometimes necessary for medical reasons, such as cancer of the prostate. This operation is called an *orchidectomy.* And until recently, castration was used in the United States to prevent severely retarded, criminal, or irresponsible individuals from becoming parents. Sex offenders were sometimes castrated as well. However, sterilization serves the same purpose without interfering with sexual pleasure.

According to Kinsey (1953), men who are castrated as adults are, in many cases, still capable of being aroused by tactile or psychologic stimuli. These men can exhibit all aspects of sexual response, including erection and orgasm. Other studies show that castration can lead to reduced sexual interest and activity (Bremer, 1959), highly variable interest in sexual activity (Hamilton, 1943), and continued desire and function in sexual activity (Beach, 1951).

In examining the evidence about castration and sexual arousal, the limitations of our interpretation need to be understood. For example, if a person is castrated and thus shows a decrease in sexual activity, how much of this decrease can be attributable to the reduction in hormone production, vis-à-vis psychological variables? Is it possible that the decrease in sexual activity can be due to embarrassment? The answer is not fully known yet.

We do know that hormone replacement therapy is appropriate for men who are *hypogonadal*—that is, lack androgens as a result of a disease of the endocrine system. These treatments are often effective, in that libido is increased. Hormones have also been prescribed to treat impotence, and used this way, hormones have been shown to increase libido (Reckless and Geiger, 1975). It should also be noted that hormone treatment increases the risk of atherosclerosis, coronary thrombosis, and cancer of the prostate.

The evidence with regard to women suggests that estrogens do not play a significant role in the abililty to become sexually motivated or aroused. Women who have reduced estrogen levels, either due to removal of the ovaries or as a result of menopause, show no significant reduction in libido (Masters and Johnson, 1966; Kinsey, 1953). While estrogen replacement therapy has been used by women with irregular menstrual cycles or difficulty lubricating vaginally, there is no marked increase in libido when estrogen replacement therapy is undertaken (Money, 1961). However, increased supplies of androgens in females do raise the level of sexual response.

On the basis of the discussion to this point, it appears that for both men and women, androgens are important in the sex drive. From current evidence it appears that the *amount* of androgens in the body may not be related directly the the "amount" of one's sexual activity. Androgens are needed as a starting point from which one can increase libido. Increased amounts may increase sexual satisfaction (Persky et al., 1978).

Behavioral Factors

I have never given any thought to what it means to be "turned on." Sure, I know my heart begins to beat faster, my vagina begins to feel wet, and I have just an overall urge to "get it on," but I have a difficult time coming up with the answer to "Why?"

Sexual arousal is a difficult and complex process to understand. We have discussed one aspect of this process—physical arousal. But many other factors, psychological and cultural, have an impact upon our behavior. There is more to an event than just an incident (stimulus) and a reaction to that incident (sexual arousal). Many factors may cause a particular event to be considered a sexual stimulus—religious beliefs, cultural background, health status, and education, to name a few.

The degree to which a person defines something as sexual is dependent upon what that person considers sexual. One man who may look at a woman with unshaven legs may think she is sexually arousing while another man may look at the same woman and find her to be totally unappealing. Just what causes different processes to take place between the stimulus (hairy legs) and the response (arousal) is the basis for further investigation.

Let's look at a case study exemplifying the stimulus–response syndrome. As a male, you notice an attractive female sitting next to you. You also notice she is wearing a dress which is raised above her knees. Your response to this female may appear to be automatic. You think of her legs exposed without any clothing over them. You then think of yourself lying in bed next to her, and then you think of sexual intercourse. In essence, the mere fact of seeing her legs has triggered a sexual fantasy to be played in your head. However, something had to happen that made you think the way you did. Somewhere along the line, you had to learn, practice, and perhaps experience. That is, what made you believe that legs were sexually arousing? What made you think that the setting would be lying together in bed? How do you know what sexual intercourse is?

The stimulus–arousal process is not nearly as simple as one might think. What makes us classify a particular event as sexually arousing is a myriad of influences that are based upon cultural experience.

When I was in elementary school, my friends and I would always go downstairs to the school library and look through all of the issues of *National Geographic*. We would always find the pictures of the bare-breasted women who lived in Africa and get turned on.

In our society, we have a tendency to accept models of sexually arousing events and then learn that these events are supposed to appeal to everyone. For the heterosexual man, undressing a woman is arousing—changes take place physically and psychologically. Yet ask the man to explain why he is going through changes, and probably he will be at a loss for words. A great deal of learning must take place if one is to integrate sexual activities in a sequence that is culturally appropriate.

Let us look at identical activities and their role in sexual response. For example, suppose a woman's gynecologist is giving her a yearly physical and checks her breasts for lumps. It is more than likely that she would not find the physician's manipulation of her breasts sexually arousing. But suppose her lover did the same thing. It is more than likely that she would find *his* touch sexually arousing. Sexual arousal is a process that incorporates the learning activities that have been experienced throughout life.

It should be noted that taking an in-depth look at the process of sexual stimulus and response does not interfere with one's ability to become aroused. Often people think that when they break down a whole to its components, the result is a loss of "excitedness." To make an analogy, if we analyzed why one person could ride a bicycle while another continued to fall, we would not lose our interest in bicycling. If anything, we might better be able to understand the principles of cycling, which in turn might help us to cope with adverse conditions ourselves. It should also be noted that careful analysis of a situation is not a prerequisite for active participation.

APHRODISIACS AND SEXUAL BEHAVIOR

Named after the Greek goddess of love and beauty, Aphrodite, *aphrodisiacs* are substances which supposedly increase sexual desire. In our discussion, aphrodisiacs will be limited to substances that can be consumed, such as foods and drugs, and to perfumes.

Foods

Foods head the list of substances that are often thought to contain sexually stimulating properties. Some of the foods that have been thought to increase one's sexual desire are dried salamander, fat of camel's hump, salted crocodile, wings of bees, the blood of executed criminals, turtle's eggs, and artichokes. There are two basic reasons that foods have been considered to have sexually stimulating properties. First, when a food is rare or new, people speculate that a sexual stimulant may exist within that food. Such was the case when the potato was first introduced in England. Second, if a food resembled a sex organ, it was often believed that sexual strength was contained within. Therefore, the banana, because it resembled a penis, and the oyster, because it resembled a vagina, were thought to be aphrodisiacs (MacDougald, 1961).

Folklore plays a significant role in beliefs that certain foods can increase the sex drive. For example, suppose someone told you that strawberry ice cream with lettuce would increase your sex drive. You might then "spread the gospel" and tell your friends that, indeed, lettuce with ice cream was an aphrodisiac. You might eat this combination and your sex drive might thereafter increase. But was the increase due to the food? In this situation, as in others that have arisen with aphrodisiac substances, the increased sex drive was due to the *belief* that the food would increase libido and not to the food *per se*.

Alcohol

Alcohol, perhaps more than any other drug, is considered a sexual stimulant. In Arab, Chinese, and Hindu "recipes" for aphrodisiacs, all the basic ingredients of the common liquors are listed (Dusek and Girdano, 1980). One need not look too hard at our society to find numerous associations between advertisements for alcoholic beverages and sex. Often we will see a beautiful woman with a low-cut dress, holding a glass of wine. The message presented is "Wine will make you mellow and romantic." For many, alcohol is an inducement for sex. Since alcohol is known to break down inhibitions, a person who may be uncomfortable engaging in sex may drink so as to remove the uncomfortable feeling. As a result, alcohol can be an excuse for doing something that might not ordinarily be done. However, that the alcohol *per se* will increase sexual performance is a myth. Shakespeare so succinctly wrote, "It [alcohol] provokes the desire, but it takes away the performance" (Macbeth, Act II, Scene 3).

Alcohol is a depressant drug. As such, it slows down the body processes and thus reduces a person's ability to perform.

Any time I would have a few drinks with my girlfriend, we would both get horny. Usually, I would be able to stay in her longer without ejaculating than I would had I not had a drink. If I had too much to drink, I just would not be able to get it up. My girlfriend rarely had an orgasm when she drank.

Yet one major study indicates that greater sexual enjoyment is experienced by many people after they have had something to drink (Athanasiou et al., 1970). This increased enjoyment may be because alcohol serves as a distraction from the everyday stresses that might inhibit sexual performance. Using alcohol to enhance libido is an issue of mind over matter.

Marijuana

Marijuana has been widely publicized as a substance that increases the sexual drive in a way similar to that of alcohol. Specifically, marijuana is known to suppress inhibitions.

> Sometimes my boyfriend and I smoke a joint before we have sex. When I get "high," I focus all of my energies on us. Sex seems as if it's endless. Not only does our lovemaking seem long, it is. My orgasms seem like they last for minutes. I always find sex better when we are both "high."

While at one time it was thought that marijuana was no more harmful than alcohol, today there is mounting evidence that marijuana may produce significant reproductive and hormonal damage. According to the National Institute on Drug Abuse (1980), several studies have shown that marijuana smoking can lower the level of testosterone in the blood, although it usually remains within the normal range. Abnormal sperm movement and shapes, as well as reduced numbers of sperm, have been found in relation to marijuana use.

The studies of the hazards of smoking marijuana are not conclusive. What we do know at this point is preliminary, and it may not be until the year 2000, if then, that we are able to arrive at more valid conclusions.

Stimulants ("Uppers")

Some people use stimulants as sexual enhancers. Amphetamines and cocaine are two common drugs that stimulate the central nervous system, so that one's mood may be elevated. This mood change, in turn, is thought to reduce inhibitions that interfere with sexual pleasure. Being "up" on stimulants can give one a false feeling of superiority and lead one to act in an uncharacteristic way. For example, a sexually inhibited person may become sexually aggressive. In any case, stimulants do not increase sex drive. In fact, continued use of these drugs can lead to dependence and eventually diminish sexual capacity (Kaplan, 1974).

Depressants

For the most part, barbiturates and tranquilizers ("downers") have not been used as sexual enhancers. These drugs, like alcohol, depress the central nervous system and, if anything, depress sexual desire. The reason alcohol may be used as a sexual inducer, and not depressants, is that depressants are much more dangerous—they are easier to become addicted to and they can have immediate damaging effects, especially when combined with alcohol. However, alcohol is also known to be dangerous when used irresponsibly.

Other Drugs

Several other drugs have been used as aphrodisiacs. One such drug is *amyl nitrite*, also known as "snappers" or "poppers." According to some people, amyl nitrite intensifies orgasm. What it does do is relax the smooth muscles in the body, resulting in vasodilation. Vasodilation may cause one to feel dizzy, have a headache, or faint. This dizziness may cause time distortion—hence the sense of "prolonged orgasm." Since amyl nitrite relaxes the anal sphincter, it may facilitate anal intercourse.

L-dopa, a drug which is used to treat Parkinson's disease, a disease of the nervous system, created a stir several years ago when it was reported that men using this drug were in a constant state of sexual arousal. On occasion, it did produce *priapism,* which is a continual and pathological erection of the penis. In this condition, the corpora cavernosa becomes erect, but the glans of the penis does not. This condition is painful, and it is not accompanied by sexual desire (Walker, 1963).

Cantharides, more commonly known as "Spanish fly," is another drug that frequently has been called an aphrodisiac. This substance is made from the dried and heated bodies of beetles, which are ground into a fine powder. When taken internally, it passes through the urinary system and irritates the lining of the bladder as well as the urethra. This irritation can cause the genitals to become stimulated, which in turn can produce an erection. Whether taken by a male or a female, cantharides can be dangerous. Depending on the dosage taken, extensive tissue damage, and even death, can occur.

ANAPHRODISIACS AND SEXUAL DESIRE

Substances that supposedly inhibit sexual desire are known as *anaphrodisiacs.*

Perhaps the method most often mentioned as an inhibitor of sex drive is the use of *potassium nitrate,* also known as saltpeter. Many of us have heard that saltpeter was used in boarding schools to repress the sexual urge in boys. This idea could not be further from the truth. Potassium nitrate is a diuretic. A diuretic is a substance that causes one to eliminate water from the body. Hence it was supposed that if a person had a great desire to urinate frequently, he would not have a desire to be sexually active. Using this logic, it can be seen that potassium nitrate would be rather ineffective as an anaphrodisiac.

It has been experimentally shown that some drugs that are used in the treatment of hypertension can reduce erectile potency, the ability to ejaculate, and the intensity of orgasm (Money and Yankowitz, 1967). One such drug is called Ismelin.

Some physicians who prescribe tranquilizers such as Valium for their patients have also found that sexual desire will decrease. However, opposite effects can occur similar to the effects produced by alcohol. That is, inhibitions can be broken down, and, as a result, sexual desire can increase.

EROGENOUS ZONES

Erogenous zones are those parts of the body that are sexually sensitive to touch. Most often thought of as erogenous zones are the genital area, the breasts, the lips, the neck, the thighs, the buttocks, the ears, and the mouth. According to Kinsey (1953):

> ... the nape of the neck, the throat, the soles of the feet, the palms of the hands, the armpits, the tips of the fingers, the toes, the navel area, the midline of the lower end of the back, the whole abdominal area, the whole pubic area, the groin, and still other parts have been recognized as areas which may be erotically sensitive under tactile stimulation.

Kinsey also found that even nonliving structures such as teeth and hair are erogenous zones because these structures stimulate the sensitive nerves that are at their bases.

The manner in which our bodies and minds respond to stimulation is dependent upon the sense used. We will therefore discuss the roles of touch, sight, smell, taste, and sound in sexual arousal.

Touch

According to many writers, our entire body can serve as a source of sensual and sexual pleasure (Perls, 1969; Comfort, 1972). We can be touched by another's hands, body, lips, tongue, and mouth. We can also be touched by objects. The textures of the things that touch us are important. Are they rough or smooth? We can be touched gently or handled roughly. We can be touched by hands that are warm or ice-cold. The preferences we have may depend upon mood. Some people may wish to be touched one day in a very gentle and easy manner and then the next day in a hard, aggressive manner.

My partner and I could sometimes spend hours just touching. Sometimes I would start at the top of my partner's head and, only using my fingertips, spend one hour to get down to the toes. We would each take turns. At no time would we touch the genital area. Often we would only touch and not consummate the session in sexual intercourse. Our love for each other would be passed back and forth through the signals permeated by our fingers. We always have felt very much in love.

The belief of having erogenous zones makes touching a very important aspect of arousal. The context in which a person is touched is the determining factor in whether or not sexual arousal will occur. For example, during an examination, a doctor places his or her hands below a man's scrotum and asks him to cough. The man will probably not associate this act with sex and thus will not have an erection. However, if a person with whom he is intimate places a hand on the scrotum in exactly the same way (lovers seldom ask you to cough), there is a good chance that erection will occur, provided of course that he finds this person arousing.

Every part of the body can be an erogenous zone. We have probably been influenced by films, books, and our peers to think of only selected parts of the body as erogenous zones. Yet the parts of our bodies through which we can be sexually aroused are almost numberless.

> There are females in our histories who have been brought to orgasm by having their eyebrows stroked, or by having the hairs on some other part of their bodies gently blown, or by having pressure applied on the teeth alone.
>
> (Kinsey, 1953)

The anatomic structures of the body that are sensitive to touch are nearly identical in the male and female. Any form of tactile stimulation that can be applied to one sex can be applied to the other.

Smell

Among animals, smell is one of the initiators of sexual arousal. *Pheromones* are odors from the bodies of animals during fertile periods and serve as an important means of communication. The dog in heat secretes an odor that attracts as well as sexually arouses other dogs. However, there is no conclusive evidence to indicate that pheromones play a significant role in the control of human sexual behavior (Rogel, 1978).

Human beings, on the other hand, can become conditioned to become sexually aroused by certain smells. Many men feel "turned on" by women who wear perfume, and many women feel turned on by men who wear cologne.

In our society, some people feel that genital secretions are unappealing. Others feel that genital secretions are sexually arousing.

My partner has an odor from her body that I find is unique to her and sexually appealing to me. If you blindfolded me and lined up a hundred women, I would be able to pick out my lover just by her smell.

Taste

The sense of taste is closely associated with the sense of smell. How a person "tastes" may serve to increase or decrease one's sexual arousal. For example, if your lover has just brushed his or her teeth upon awakening in the morning, you may be more receptive to kissing, which in turn may lead to increased states of sexual arousal.

Sometimes the taste of genital secretions and perspiration can play a role in arousal. Another effect of taste is illustrated by the following case study:

My wife uses a foam when we have sex. Sometimes, she wants me to have oral sex with her after we have intercourse. Up until recently, I would refuse to "get down" on her because I couldn't stand the taste of her foam. Then she heard of flavored foam, which she then began to use. Now I have no problem.

Vision

One of the most important senses involved in sexual arousal is the sense of sight. The early research of Kinsey (1948) showed that the male is more aroused by visual stimuli than is the female. However, during the Kinsey years, visual materials were prepared mostly for men and women were taught that sexually arousing material was "bad." Today, the differences in the intensity of reactions of men and women have been reduced. While often not to the same degree as men, women *are* aroused by looking at pictures of nude men, as well as by pictures of women and couples.

Lately, I have been finding that I look at guys' crotches. A man who wears a tight pair of designer jeans really catches my eyes. I feel somewhat uncomfortable looking at crotches, so I very consciously make sure I don't look too hard.

Sound

Sound can also be sexually arousing. For many people, talking during lovemaking accentuates arousal.

I love it when my partner tells me what he is going to do to me. The greater the detail, the more enjoyable our lovemaking.

Many people enjoy describing to each other the things that make them feel good. Comments such as "You're a good lover," and "You fondle my breasts just the right way," can increase the state of arousal in both partners.

In many situations, there may be a conscious effort to suppress sound. There can be several reasons for this:

- The individuals may find each other boring and thus feel they have nothing in common other than sex.
- The individuals may feel inhibited in expressing their likes and dislikes out of embarrassment.
- Especially among females, the idea may exist that "nice" women should not emit sounds, just play a part.
- Some people find sound distracting.

If people suppress sounds, they may never know whether or not their partners are pleased by what they are doing. But while many people prefer sounds, there are others who find it distracting. Talking, television, a baby's crying, or people outside the bedroom talking or singing may distract you and keep you from becoming sexually aroused. Some people may feel that "I know what my partner likes and dislikes," and for *that* reason silence may be the preferred state.

I remember my first intense lovemaking session. Everything this guy was doing to me was physically annoying. He grabbed my breasts too roughly and massaged my vagina when I really preferred the massage to my clitoris. I felt as if I was not supposed to say anything.

SEXUAL EXPRESSION

The ways people express their sexuality vary dramatically. Chapter 12 describes the roles that love and intimacy play in our behavior. In this chapter we have examined the impact of psychological and biological stimuli on sexual motivation. In what follows we will look at some of the more frequent behavior patterns of sexuality.

Celibacy

Any human being who has the capacity for sexual behavior is considered a sexual person. Among the many ways in which one can express sexuality, there are the extremes, such as nymphomania and satyriasis at one end of the continuum, and the total lack of sexual activity at the other. *Celibacy,* which is a decision to refrain from sexual activity, is an alternative lifestyle practiced by many individuals, both men and women. (For clarity, when we refer to celibate persons, we refer only to adults.)

Complete celibacy is defined as refraining from any voluntary sexual activity or contact, including self-stimulation. It does not include involuntary sexual responses such as wet dreams.

The *interpersonal* or *partial celibate* permits himself or herself to masturbate but not to engage in any form of sexual activity with others.

The *experiential celibate* is a person who practices celibacy as a sexual option. In this case, the person practices celibacy before or after he or she has experienced other varieties of sexual behavior. For example, a married couple may be celibate for months, yet have engaged over a thousand times in sexual intercourse.

The *religious celibate* is a person who practices celibacy because of a specific ideology or belief. Most people seem to connect the word *celibate* with a religious devotion or order. Nuns, monks, those who choose priesthood in the Roman Catholic church, and some clergy of other religious traditions are expected to practice celibacy because of their role of having to give their attention to all of humanity.

Some people may also practice celibacy for health reasons. A heart attack victim may decide to abstain from sex because of the fear that sex could "overstrain" the heart and lead to another attack. While the thinking of the medical profession today has shifted (with precautions) from belief in abstention to belief in active participation in sex, many people continue to remain hesitant.

Many couples practice celibacy about two weeks out of each month. That is, the "rhythm system" of birth control is practiced, and for about two weeks, abstinence is the norm.

CHOOSING TO BE CELIBATE

Persons may choose to be celibate for some of the reasons that have already been mentioned. However, there may be other reasons that people may opt not to engage in sexual activity.

- Enhancement of creativity: Some persons feel that sexual activity interferes with creativity. As a result, celibacy facilitates creativity in these persons (Brown, 1980).
- Conveying a deeper love: Some people feel that celibacy can produce a loving relationship that is more intense and meaningful without sexual activity. Such couples may feel that sex is just another variable in a relationship and can detract from the focus that each can give the other.

When the topic of celibacy was featured on a television talk show,* some of the comments made by celibate people regarding their lifestyle were:

> My racquetball game has improved since I have not been sexually involved with anyone.
> Sex is only a biological experience which I consider to be only a small part of our relationship.
> I can have intimacy without sex.
> I have no sex hang-ups because I just don't think about it.
> My wife and I are more affectionate to each other than we have ever been. This began when we became celibate. Occasionally we will have sex, but usually we go about three or four months without intercourse. When we do have intercourse, it is unplanned. When it happens, it happens.

PROBLEMS RELATED TO CELIBACY

Many who choose to become celibate are pleased with their lifestyle. However, like other lifestyles that may deviate from those commonly valued by most of society, celibacy may have its problems.

One example is the single man who prefers not to have sex. In our society, if two adults have been dating for a period of time, it is often expected that sexual overtures will be made. The man is often placed in the role of initiator. Yet if the man does not wish to engage in sexual behavior, he may be looked at by his partner as "weird" or perhaps homosexual.

Another problem of celibacy is that of reengaging in sexual activities after abstaining for a lengthy period of time. In today's society, where sex is much more acceptable than it was in years past, getting back "in the swing" may be a difficult and uncomfortable undertaking for many persons. Yet proponents of celibacy claim that this is no problem. In this case, the motto "If you don't use it, you don't lose it," is probably apropos.

---

*The Phil Donahue Show, NBC-TV, July 22, 1980.

One of the key points to remember about celibacy is that a lack of sexual activity does not necessarily correlate with a lack of love. In many relationships in which people have been married for 30 or 40 years we often find a minimal amount of sexual activity or none at all. Yet the love each person has for the other may be most strong and the relationship most intimate. People may lose sexual interest in each other, while not losing their feeling for each other.

Masturbation

For the sake of clarity, *masturbation*, in this chapter, is defined as self-stimulation of the genitals, either manually or by an object, for the purpose of achieving sexual pleasure. *Mutual masturbation* is defined as stimulation of the genitals by another, either manually or by an object, for the purpose of achieving pleasure.

MASTURBATION: HISTORICAL PERSPECTIVES

I remember once when teaching a human sexuality class, we were involved in a discussion about communication between parents and children regarding sexuality. One older student in the class mentioned that she and her daughter had no barriers about discussing sexual matters. Suddenly, another student in the class asked this woman if she ever spoke with her daughter about masturbation. The woman replied, "Although my daughter and I speak about everything, we would never discuss *that!*"

When discussions about masturbation are brought up, a certain uneasiness often surfaces. Perhaps the major source of this uneasiness stems from historical accounts and beliefs.

It is known that even before man was created, masturbation existed throughout the animal world. Yet throughout history, we can see that, for example, Judeo-Christian views held that the purpose of sexual behavior was to procreate. Therefore masturbation as well as any act which did not include penile—vaginal intercourse was considered reproductively wasteful.

In the 18th century, the evils of masturbation were popularized by Tissot. In his medical view of masturbation, he stated that the fluids contained within the body had certain powers. An abundance or shortage of these powers created imbalances in a person's physical and mental status. Therefore, semen, being considered fluid in the body, could play a role in illness if too much was lost—whether lost through masturbation, sexual intercourse, or any other activity. Based upon this theory, Tissot argued that many illnesses that weakened the body were caused primarily by masturbation. Tissot's views were widely held by many people for many years. Although these views were not empirically tested, many people held the belief that avoidance of "unnecessary sex" was a key to good living.

In the 19th century, Benjamin Rush, a noted physician, convinced people that masturbation caused epilepsy and memory loss, among other maladies. Later in the 19th century, other physicians spread the belief that people who masturbated would develop weak muscles, sallow complexions, acne, and sunken eyes.

It was not until even later in the 19th century and early 20th century that physicians finally concluded that many of the diseases originally thought to come about through sexual excess were actually a result of physiological disorders.

CONTEMPORARY VIEWS OF MASTURBATION

Even today, there is a great deal of conflict regarding masturbation. The "Declaration on Masturbation," which was issued by the Vatican in 1975, stated:

> . . . masturbation constitutes a grave moral disorder. . .
> . . . it lacks the sexual relationship called for by the moral order, namely the relationship which realizes "the full sense of mutual self-giving and human procreation in the context of true love."

Yet, according to Kinsey (1948), only in rare circumstances is masturbation considered an abnormality.

> It is significant that those who had most often found moral objections to masturbation were the ones who most often insisted that physical and mental damage had resulted from their activity. Such rationalizations are of ancient standing, and they have been perpetuated into the present day by a surprising number of physicians, psychiatrists, psychologists, and educators. But such arguments are obviously attempts to justify the moral code, and are not supported by any examination of the physical fact.

> (Kinsey, 1948)

Masturbation is viewed as a problem when it disturbs or is used to disturb others. According to some researchers, people who have never masturbated are far more likely to be suffering from emotional or sexual problems than those who have masturbated.

I always had guilt feelings about masturbating. It wasn't until my friends very hesitantly admitted they did also that I began to be more accepting of my behavior.

It is well known that during adolescence masturbation is a frequent outlet for sexual satisfaction. By age 15, 82% of boys have masturbated, and by age 20, the percentage has increased to 92% (Kinsey, 1948). The figures for females are much lower: 20% have masturbated by age 15, and 33% by age 20. However, it has been found that there is an increase in the incidence of masturbation as a woman ages. By age 45, about 60% of women have masturbated.

Masturbation does not disappear when one marries. Hunt (1974) has shown that 72% of young husbands and 68% of young wives masturbate at least once per month. These figures indicate that 20- and 30-year-olds who masturbate are not unique.

I remember feeling very guilty about masturbating during marriage. Finally, I mentioned this to my husband, expecting him to explode. But he was the one who seemed the most relieved. It ended up that he had the same guilt feelings because he, too, masturbated. Our sexual relationship was and still is good. And we both continue to masturbate. Sometimes we will do it in front of each other. What a turn on!

WHY PEOPLE MASTURBATE

Many reasons have been given for why people masturbate. Among these are

1. Satisfaction. Achieving orgasm through any activity is enjoyable.
2. Simplicity. Self-arousal eliminates partners, which in turn eliminates commitments and other variables that may impinge upon one's desire for privacy.
3. Better performance. Some men may masturbate before having sexual intercourse. This may enable them to "last longer" once they do have sexual intercourse.

As kids, my friends and I would often go downtown to "get it on" with prostitutes. They were good at making us come quickly, and we always felt guilty afterwards because our ten dollars would seem to disappear all too soon. Then one day, right before our pick-up, we masturbated first. While each of us was better able to partake in sexual intercourse, we did not enjoy it as in the past.

---

4. Relaxation. Some people may masturbate as a means of reducing stress.

Sometimes I have a difficult time falling asleep at night. I tried all kinds of exercises—TM, yoga, and a host of relaxation exercises. None of them worked. Then one day I masturbated before I was to go to sleep. Afterwards, I found myself relaxed and was able to fall asleep. Now, it's a regular practice for me.

---

5. Discovery. Masturbation can be used by some people as a means of discovering what feels best to them. These discoveries can then be put into practice with a partner.

FEMALE MASTURBATION

The most common method used by women to masturbate is stimulation of the clitoral shaft, clitoral area, and mons with the hand or an object (Figure 5.1). Some women may stimulate the clitoris directly by holding the skin or lips stretched tight around the clitoral area with one hand and stimulating the clitoris with the other hand. Since the clitoris is very sensitive, direct stimulation for an extended length of time can become irritating (Masters and Johnson, 1966). Lubrication of some sort may be necessary to minimize this irritation.

> I masturbate different ways at different times, sometimes beginning in the clitoral area, sometimes on my breasts. I use circular motions in both cases, often using two hands, one on my breast, one on my clitoris; or one on my clitoris, one in vagina, or at its entrance. I achieve very large orgasms by running my finger between clitoris and vagina (in that channel) to stop orgasm before reaching it and then begin again until I cannot stop it any longer, all the while spreading my legs further and further apart. Except for raising my lower body up, up, up, my body per se does not move very much.
>
> (Hite, 1976)

FIGURE 5.1 A common method used by women to masturbate.

Direct stimulation may take place on the shaft of the clitoris. Some women may rub up and down one side, while others may use a circular motion around the clitoral shaft and glans. By pulling on the minor lips, a woman can become aroused, since this action can cause the loose skin covering the glans to slide back and forth. Sometimes clitoral stimulation may be accompanied by an in-and-out movement of the fingers in the vagina. At other times, vaginal penetration without stimulation of the clitoris can take place. However, vaginal penetration only is not frequently practiced.

For some women, masturbation may take the form of thrusting or grinding the genital area against an object such as the bed, pillows, or clothing. This can be done with the legs together or apart. This method spreads stimulation over a wide area. The woman can be lying on her back or stomach.

> Usually I masturbate on the corner of a chair or something similar with a pillow between my legs. I hump up and down with my legs together.
>
> (Hite, 1976)

Other ways that women masturbate include crossing the legs tightly and squeezing rhythmically; letting the running water from a faucet pass over the genital area; insering objects such as candles, carrots, or vibrators into the vagina; and manipulating parts of the body (i.e., breasts) other than those in the genital area.

For masturbation, I find that the bathtub can be a major source of excitement. I let warm water run from the faucet and I spread my legs up close so that the water skims my clitoris. When I begin to get more aroused, I turn the water up and let it run over my clitoris and vagina directly. I find I get a better orgasm this way than if I were to use a vibrator.

The methods described for female masturbation are contrary to what many men believe. Kinsey (1953) found that many men thought women masturbate mainly by direct insertion into the vagina. Most women, however, prefer stimulation to the clitoral area. This fact is meaningful to men, for if they feel that a woman will respond to direct stimulation to the vagina only, their lovemaking technique may be something less than that desired by their partners.

MALE MASTURBATION

Men show less variety in masturbating practices than women. Most men masturbate by gripping the penis around the shaft and moving the hand in an up-and-down motion (Figure 5.2). Variation takes place from man to man in that the pressure of the grip, the speed of hand movement, and the extent of contact with the glans may differ. Unlike the vagina, the penis does not become lubricated. As a result, some men may use saliva, a

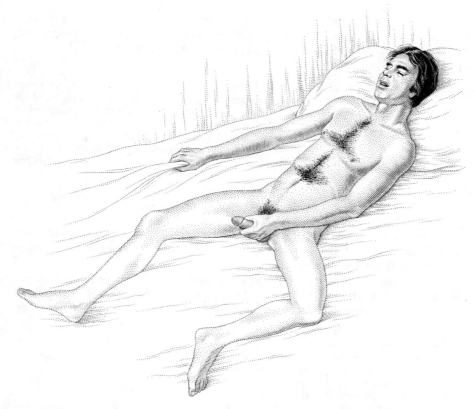

FIGURE 5.2 Male masturbation.

jelly or cream, or soap (during a shower or bath) on their penis at the time of masturbation. Such substances permit the hand to slide very easily over the penis. Many men find this to be highly sexually arousing.

When a man is approaching orgasm, he usually increases the speed by which he moves his hand up and down the penis. As orgasm occurs, this movement either slows down or stops (Masters and Johnson, 1966).

Some men, as a part of masturbation, may use a finger to rub the frenulum or the crown of the glans. Others may use vibrators.

A few men insert objects or their fingers into the anus while masturbating. Others may manipulate their breasts, while some can reach orgasm by lying on a pillow, stomach down, and thrusting in up and down rhythmical movements.

Fantasy

Fantasy alone can be a form of self-stimulation. For the majority of men and women, sexual fantasy is frequently accompanied by masturbation. However, it should be made clear that masturbation does not necessarily have to accompany fantasy. For example, if you are walking on campus and you meet a person who arouses sexual thoughts, you almost certainly would not masturbate right there and then. You might, however, go home and later on that day fantasize and masturbate.

> When I masturbate, I have a recurring "daydream" of a salesman approaching a lovely white cottage on a beach and finding the door partly open. He calls and, getting no answer, wanders through all of the rooms looking for some sign of occupancy. Finally, he comes to a closed door and hears water running within. Opening the door, he finds a woman showering and he proceeds to undress, climb into the shower, and make love to the woman. By this time, I usually have my climax.
>
> (Friday, 1973)

There are many people who do not fantasize and yet can masturbate to orgasm. The only thing these people think about is the act in which they are engaged at that moment.

The types of fantasies expressed by men differ from those of women (DeLora and Warren, 1977). Male fantasies are likely to include aggressiveness, impersonal encounters, and multiple partners.

I often fantasize that three women are keeping me captive. Each has fights over the other regarding who will have me for the night. Sometimes, one will sneak up on me without the other two knowing, and we will have sex. At other times, I fantasize that I am in a women's prison. Being the only male, all of the women want my body. I hand-select two for each lovemaking session and take them to a private room, where each does everything to me.

The common themes in female sexual fantasies are having intercourse with a stranger, multiple partners during a lovemaking session, doing things that may never be done in reality, being forced to have sex or forcing someone else to have sex, and engaging in sex with another woman (Hunt, 1974).

In general, women tend to be more romantic than men are in their fantasies. Culture has an influence, and we can see its correlation with the subjects of fantasy. Men have more aggressive fantasies than women because in our society men are "supposed to" play the role of the sexual initiator. Women, on the other hand, are "supposed to" be more timid and passive.

Fantasy should not be interpreted as hope for reality. While it may be so in some cases, it may not be so in others. For example, some men may think that if a woman has a fantasy of being raped, she actually desires to be raped. What these men do not realize is that in a rape fantasy, the woman *selects* and *controls* the rapist, the scene, and everything that happens. What occurs in reality is another story.

PURPOSES OF FANTASIES

Fantasies can serve a number of purposes:

1. They allow for rehearsals and planning. In the process of fantasy, people can mentally practice what they intend to do. They can arrive at alternative strategies to their sexual activities should their expectations not be fulfilled.
2. Sexual fantasies can be enjoyable. Sexual fantasies allow you to think about practicing sex with any person you wish. You can control what someone says, does, and thinks. You are the director, and everyone performs exactly the way you feel they should.
3. Sexual fantasies allow you to escape from activities you find unenjoyable. They serve as an outlet for those who have trouble dealing with things that may not, at the moment, seem enjoyable.

NONCOITAL TECHNIQUES OF AROUSAL

The process of sexual arousal encompasses more than just sexual intercourse. The information here provides a close look at some of the more common ways that sexual techniques play a role in sexual arousal. Techniques known as *foreplay* can be used in the preliminary stages of sexual intercourse. Foreplay usually involves partners stimulating each other by kissing, touching, and caressing.

Kissing

Just about every adult in our society has kissed someone at one time or another. Kissing, as described in this section, refers to mouth-to-mouth or mouth-to-body stimulation for the purpose of sexual arousal.

The simplest method of kissing is lips-to-lips with closed mouths. These kisses can be long or short in duration. In deep kissing, or what is known as a "French kiss" or "soul kiss," one or both partners can accept each other's tongue through open mouths. The tongues can be rubbed against each other or against the insides of the mouth, or they can be sucked by each partner.

The mouth is not the only part of the body that can be kissed. Depending upon a person's preferences, any part of the body can be kissed in a way in which sexual arousal will be enhanced.

Manual Stimulation of the Male Genitalia

Many of the techniques described for male masturbation can be applied to the discussion in this section. According to Comfort (1972), a couple who can skillfully masturbate each other can do anything else they wish.

> A woman who has the divine gift of lechery and loves her partner will masturbate him well and a woman who knows how to masturbate a man—subtly, unhurriedly, and mercilessly—will almost always make a superlative partner. She needs intuitive empathy and real enjoyment of a penis, holding it in just the right place, with just the right amount of pressure and movement, and timing her action in bursts to coincide with his feeling—stopping or slowing to keep him in suspense, speeding up to control his climax.
>
> (Comfort, 1973)

Men can be massaged on the penis or scrotum for sexual arousal. In addition, a man's partner can roll the penis between the palms of the hands, varying the pressure with the man's desires. Men also enjoy having the hand grasped around the shaft and moved up and down. Many men also enjoy being masturbated with one hand while his partner uses the other hand to fondle his breasts, perineum, testicles, or anus.

Manual Stimulation of the Female Genitalia

As stated previously, manual stimulation of the female genitalia can be more involved than stimulation of the male genitalia.

> For preparation as well as orgasm, the flat of the hand on the vulva with the middle finger between the lips and its tips moving in and out of the vagina, while the ball of the palm presses hard just above the pubis, is probably the best method.
>
> (Comfort, 1973)

It is a good idea to remember that the clitoris is very sensitive and thus can be easily susceptible to pain. Great care must be taken in manipulating this part, especially if it is dry. If the woman is aroused and her clitoris is dry, her partner can touch the inside of the vagina and pass its lubrication onto the clitoris. If the vagina has no lubrication, saliva can be used.

Those who are skilled enough can use the heel of the hand to rub the mons and clitoris, while at the same time, a finger can be moved in and out of the vagina. However, make sure that the fingernails have been cut, since jagged edges can be an irritant.

Some women may prefer that their partners use an open hand during manual stimulation, so that the mons and clitoris will be stimulated by the thumb, while at the same time, the middle finger can massage the anus, either internally or externally. If this practice is followed, the finger that was in contact with the anus should not be placed in the vagina afterwards, since bacteria from the rectal area can cause a vaginal infection.

Again, preferences in manual stimulation of the genital area will vary from person to person. Some couples may prefer mutual masturbation or simultaneous masturbation (Figure 5.3). Some may not like this practice, since it may be distracting. On the other hand, mutual masturbation may serve to arouse each partner to similar levels, heightening excitation.

For those who may not be sure *how* to stimulate their partners manually, Comfort (1973) suggests that each partner masturbate in front of the other. The assumption here is that a picture is worth a thousand words.

Oral–Genital Stimulation

Contact between the mouth and genitals, for many people, plays a significant role in sexual arousal.

However, there are many people, regardless of whether or not they partake in oral–genital contact, who have reservations about this behavior. There may be several reasons for their reservations, some of which were mentioned in our discussion of masturbation.

1. Because of religious beliefs, some individuals feel that any sex that does not result in the possibility of reproduction is immoral.
2. Some people feel that oral–genital contact is "dirty." This may be because the urinary openings are closely connected to the genitals. (But according to some experts, the vagina has fewer bacteria than the mouth.)
3. Some people feel that oral–genital contacts are acts practiced only by homosexuals. (Oral–genital contact is no more homosexual than it is heterosexual.)

FIGURE 5.3   Simultaneous manual stimulation of partners' genitalia.

CUNNILINGUS

Cunnilingus, which is derived from the Latin *cunnus*, "vulva," and *lingere*, "to lick," is defined as oral stimulation of the female's genitals. The focus of stimulation during cunnilingus is mainly the clitoris and also (though somewhat less) the labia minora, as well as the vaginal opening. The use of the tongue, through circular and back-and-forth movements can be highly arousing to a woman. The tongue can often stimulate the clitoris more than a finger can, since saliva can be used as a lubricant. Women often find the feeling of warmth and tenderness during cunnilingus enjoyable. Some women prefer that the partner's tongue dart quickly along the vaginal area, while others prefer to have the labia minora sucked or licked. Some men find that they can massage the clitoris with the tip of the nose and at the same time use the tongue to lick around the vagina. There are some women who prefer that their partners stimulate their vaginas, either with a finger, a vibrator, or another object, while at the same time licking the clitoris.

For some women, cunnilingus is the most enjoyable form of sex, since the partner may spend more time performing than he would during sexual intercourse, where he may "finish" in a minute. Also, the fear of pregnancy is eliminated. Often women will not achieve orgasm during sexual intercourse because they are distracted by fear of becoming pregnant.

While health problems due to cunnilingus are minimal, there are some concerns that need mentioning. First, sexually transmissible diseases can be spread from the vagina to the oral cavity. In Chapter 11 we discuss this problem. Second, a partner who blows air into the vagina of a woman who is pregnant risks the possibility of causing air to enter the uterine vein, with very serious consequences (Sadok and Sadok, 1976).

FELLATIO

Fellatio, which is derived from the Latin word *fellare*, which means "to suck," is defined as oral stimulation of the male's genitals.

Among the techniques used in fellatio are sucking on the glans and licking the glans and the frenulum. Usually these actions are enough to cause an erection. Once the penis is fully erect, the man's partner can slide the lips from the head of the penis, down the shaft to the base, and up again in rhythmic motions. Careful attention needs to be given so that the teeth do not scrape the penis, the most common mistake made by the novice. Along with the up-and-down motion, the tongue can be flicked back and forth along the glans or the frenulum.

Some men prefer to have their partners masturbate them while at the same time sucking the glans. If the penis is too small, the man's partner can encircle the shaft with a few fingers while performing fellatio.

Sometimes the entire shaft of the erect penis can be taken into the mouth. However, the person attempting this must learn to relax the throat muscles so that the penis can be taken deep into the throat. Without relaxation of the throat muscles, the gag reflex may be stimulated, since anything that comes in contact with the throat can trigger this reaction.

> One of the most arousing things you can do to a man is the Butterfly Flick. On the underside of the penis, about one to two inches behind the head, is a ridge called the corona. Just underneath the corona is a delicate vertical membrane. This the most sensitive area of the man's body. To drive him straight to ecstasy, take your tongue and flick it lightly back and forth across the membrane—like you were strumming a banjo. Now run your tongue down to the base of the penis and back up again a few times and then return to the Butterfly Flick, only this time flicking all the way up and down the underside of the penis. Continue until the man begs for mercy.
>
> ("J," 1969)

For most men, fellatio is a highly arousing experience. Many feel that it simulates sexual intercourse (the wet and warm mouth synonymous with the vagina) and yet produces more excitement (the movement of a tongue).

The major questions many people raise are, "What if he comes in my mouth?" "Should I let him?" One has several choices: Remove the mouth from the penis when ejaculation is imminent; allow the man to ejaculate in your mouth, but do not swallow the semen; allow the man to ejaculate in your mouth and swallow the semen. To alleviate any concern, ejaculate is basically protein and is not harmful to health. The best way to deal with this concern is to discuss beforehand what both partners' preferences are and come to a decision on how you intend to deal with these feelings.

MUTUAL ORAL–GENITAL STIMULATION

Fellatio and cunnilingus can be performed simultaneously by two partners (Figure 5.4). While this act can be performed in several positions, the one most frequently used is partner-on-top-of-partner. In this position, both abdomens will face each other but the partners' heads will be facing in opposite directions. The nickname for this position is "69" or "soixante-neuf," because the position of the bodies resembles the numbers six and nine. Sometimes couples prefer to partake in "69" lying on their sides.

Simultaneous oral–genital stimulation has the advantage of enabling each partner to enjoy the other at the same time. However, some couples find that simultaneous oral sex brings with it too many distractions. One partner may be too concerned about pleasing the other and, as a result, will not be able to relax. In addition, one or both partners may become aroused to the point where they get "carried away." Thus, the penis or vagina may be manipulated in a manner that is uncomfortable to one or both partners. In addition, if "69" is performed with the male on top of the female, the female may lose her oral control of the penis and possibly gag.

One more thing needs mentioning. If both partners differ in size (short and tall), mutual oral–genital stimulation can be an uncomfortable or impossible act in which to engage.

FIGURE 5.4   Mutual oral–genital stimulation.

Anal Stimulation

Stimulation of the anus is a pleasurable activity for a number of people. Since the anus has a fairly large supply of nerve endings, its role in sexual play can be significant (Masters and Johnson, 1970). Basically, there are three methods of stimulation of the anus: genital, manual, and oral.

GENITAL STIMULATION OF THE ANUS

Sodomy is another term for anal intercourse, although this term encompasses a wide range of sexual variations. As with oral–genital contact, the incidence of anal intercourse appears to have increased significantly over the past few years. Kinsey (1948) found that the incidence of anal intercourse was so rare that its inclusion in his studies was not warranted. In the 1960s, Gebhard et al. (1965) found that only 3% of married men and women have ever engaged in this activity. However, in the 1970s, Hunt (1974) found that 15% of heterosexuals aged 35 to 44 and 25% of heterosexuals under 35 had engaged in anal intercourse within the year previous to his study. Apparently, the number of people participating in anal intercourse has markedly increased.

The procedures for engaging in anal intercourse are somewhat more complex than those for sexual intercourse. First, the anus does not produce a lubricant that can facilitate penetration by a penis. Second, the anus is surrounded by tight muscles, which may serve as a barrier against penetration. Therefore, couples who decide to participate in this act must be able to communicate well with each other. The recipient needs to relax, and the inserter needs to be very gentle. The anus can be lubricated with a jelly such as K-Y, as can the penis, to help facilitate penetration. The position a couple decides to use for anal intercourse can be as varied as the couple decides. While the most common position is one person on top of another, abdomen down, the positions used in sexual intercourse can be adapted.

While anal intercourse is relatively safe, it does have two major drawbacks. First, the penis should not be inserted in the vagina after anal intercourse unless it has been washed thoroughly. If it is not washed, bacteria from the anus can cause vaginitis (see Chapter 3). Second, bacteria can enter the urethra of the male and cause an infection. To prevent infection, a condom can be used. If a man does not choose this alternative, he can urinate so as to increase the chance that any bacteria that have entered will be eliminated.

MANUAL STIMULATION OF THE ANUS

Manual stimulation can take the form of rubbing the anus with the hand or an object or inserting into the anus an object or a finger. Manual stimulation of the anus can take place during other sex acts, such as sexual intercourse, oral–genital stimulation, and masturbation, or it can be a prelude to other sex acts, including anal intercourse. As with anal intercourse, contact should not be made with the vaginal area if a finger or an object has been in close contact with the anus.

ORAL STIMULATION OF THE ANUS

Oral stimulation of the anus, also known as *anilingus,* is stimulation of the anus by the mouth or the tongue or both. For some couples, the warmth and moisture of oral contact with the anus is a highly satisfying and arousing experience.

COITAL TECHNIQUES OF AROUSAL

The word *coitus,* which is derived from the Latin word *coitio,* means "a coming together." Throughout this book, and particularly in the part that follows, coitus means sexual intercourse, or insertion of the man's penis into the woman's vagina. *Copulation* has the same meaning.

Coitus can be performed in any number of positions. We will describe the four most basic positions and mention some of their variations. Table 5.1 lists the advantages and disadvantages of each position.

Face-to-Face, Man-Above

The face-to-face, man-above position, more commonly known as the "missionary" position, is probably the most used today by American couples during sexual intercourse (Figure 5.5). In some states, old laws state that it is illegal to have sexual intercourse in positions other than this one.

In the man-above, face-to-face position, penile penetration in the vagina is usually easy to achieve, assuming the woman's vagina is some-

TABLE 5.1 ADVANTAGES AND DISADVANTAGES OF SEXUAL INTERCOURSE POSITIONS

Position	Disadvantages	Advantages
FACE-TO-FACE, MAN-ABOVE	May be uncomfortable with an obese male.	Entry into vagina is simple.
	May be uncomfortable for elderly couples.	It is sexually stimulating for man.
	Penile contact with vagina is minimal.	Penetration may be maintained after ejaculation.
	Manual stimulation of clitoris is difficult.	Each partner can see the other's face.
	Woman's movements may be restricted.	
	Inadvisable and difficult during latter part of pregnancy.	
	May facilitate quick orgasms for premature ejaculators.	
FACE-TO-FACE, WOMAN-ABOVE	May be uncomfortable with an obese female.	Man can manually stimulate clitoris and breasts.
	May be uncomfortable for elderly couples.	Woman can control the movements comfortable to her.
	Restricted movement of male may cause penis to slip from vagina.	Man can control his ejaculation.
	Man can make the woman feel uncomfortable if he penetrates too deeply.	Woman can control extent of penetration.
	Poor position for impregnation.	
FACE-TO-FACE, SIDE-BY-SIDE	Arm or leg can get pinned under the body.	More comfortable for the obese and elderly.
	Deep pelvic thrusts are difficult.	Both people equally regulate pelvic thrusts.
	Sometimes difficult to gain penile penetration.	Freedom for sex play.
		Good for late stages of pregnancy.
		Maximum contact to clitoris by penis.
REAR ENTRY	Cannot see partner's face.	Comfortable during pregnancy.
	May repulse some since it resembles anal intercourse.	Man's hands are free to stimulate woman's body.
		Woman can stroke scrotum.
		Good for conception.

what lubricated and the man is gentle and tactful. The woman can lie on her back and spread her legs. While she is in this position, the man can support himself on his knees and hands and insert his penis into the vagina, with or without using his hands. The woman can use her hands to manipulate the penis for comfortable penetration. The woman is usually in the best position to guide the penis, since she probably knows her body

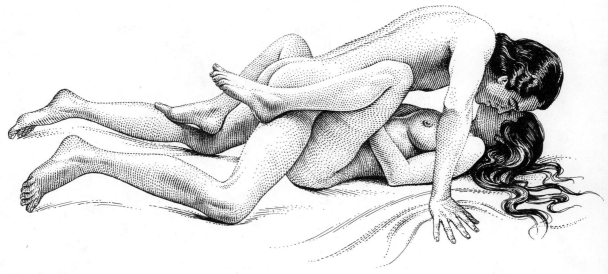

FIGURE 5.5 Face-to-face, man-above, intercourse position.

better than does her partner. Once the penis has been inserted, the woman can place her legs closer together, restricting the vaginal opening and providing more pressure against the penis.

In this position, the man has a great deal of control of the bodily rhythms and movements. He can move his hips up and down (pelvic thrusting), side to side, or around. This can be done in varying speeds and duration. The woman can also follow along with the same movements of her partner's.

Face-to-Face, Woman-Above

The woman-above position allows the woman to play a more "dominant" role in sexual intercourse (Figure 5.6). In this position, the woman can be either prone or sitting upright. Insertion of the penis can take place while the couple is in another position such as the man-on-top, and they can then roll over to the woman-on-top position. Another possibility is having the man lie on his back and the woman kneel over him, thereby guiding the penis into her. The guidance can be managed by the man or the woman.

In this position, the woman has a great deal of control of the body movements. She can move up and down, side to side, or around. She can also control the tempo of her movements better than if she were in the woman-below position.

There are many variations on the woman-above position. The woman can straighten her legs in front of her; she can position herself to face the

FIGURE 5.6   Face-to-face, woman-above, intercourse position.

man's legs; or, with the woman facing the man, the man can lift himself on his elbows or hands and orally stimulate the woman's breasts.

Face-to-Face, Side-by-Side

The side-to-side position is considered a "restful" position, since neither partner supports the other's weight (Figure 5.7). The movements in this position are controlled equally by the man and the woman. A couple can move into this position from another position or begin in it. Variations of this position rely on the position of the legs.

Rear Entry

In the rear entry position of sexual intercourse, penile penetration can take place with the man facing the woman's back (Figure 5.8). There are numerous ways of accomplishing this position. One common way is for the woman to kneel with her head down. The man then kneels with his legs between hers and he inserts his penis.

FIGURE 5.7 Face-to-face, side-by-side intercourse position.

The four major positions of sexual intercourse described do not represent, by any means, the full extent to which one can choose to enjoy copulation. Numerous varieties can be imagined and practiced. However, couples might be better off doing what their feelings indicate rather than trying to prove themselves "masters of mechanics." Sexual intercourse should be seen as a mutual act that can be highly satisfying physically and emotionally.

FIGURE 5.8 Rear entry intercourse position.

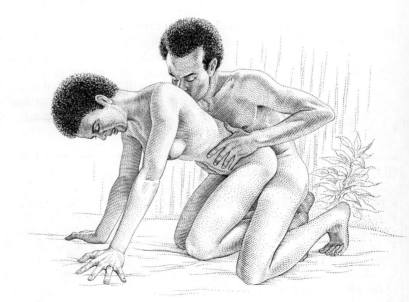

DEVICES USED IN SEXUAL AROUSAL

Dildos

A *dildo* is an artificial penis that is usually made of rubber. The dildo may be inserted into the vagina or anus by a partner or by oneself.

Vibrators

Vibrators, which come in a variety of shapes and colors, can be used in masturbation or in homosexual and heterosexual sex play. Some vibrators, which may be purchased in adult bookstores or through mail-order outlets, are penis-shaped. Other vibrators, which can be used for facial and body massage, can be purchased in ordinary retail outlets.

They can be placed inside the vagina, on the clitoris, or on the mons. The male can use a vibrator on the penis. Vibrators can also be used in anal stimulation. (When vibrators have not been available, electric toothbrushes have served as adequate substitutes for some people.) For some people, vibrators can be used in sex therapy (See Chapter 10).

Penile Aids

Many males are forever looking for the ultimate erection. As a result, they often seek out magazine ads that promise a longer penis. The fact is, there are no devices that can induce the erect penis to grow longer. However, some men do use penis extenders. These are rubber or plastic tips that are worn on the tip of the penis. They can be held in place by a condom or strap. In this manner, the penis can be "longer" by an inch or two than would ordinarily be possible.

The men who use extenders are those who may not be able to achieve an erection or who may feel their penis is too short.

Another penile aid that men may use is what is known as a "French tickler." These are rubber or plastic rings that fit over the glans or shaft of the penis and contain projections that supposedly provide increased stimulation for the female. Many women feel no added stimulation and sometimes find these devices irritating.

SUMMARY STATEMENTS

- *Hormones may affect one's sexual behavior.*
- *The psychological aspects of sexual arousal are complex.*
- *Aphrodisiacs and anaphrodisiacs do not affect sexual behavior.*
- *There are many erogenous zones, and all five senses are involved in sexual stimulation.*
- *Celibacy is a choice for some people.*
- *Masturbation is a common sexual behavior.*
- *There are many aspects and techniques of foreplay.*
- *Sexual intercourse can be performed in many positions.*
- *Some people use sexual aids to enhance arousal.*

SUGGESTED READINGS

Comfort, Alex. *The Joy of Sex: A Gourmet Guide to Love Making*. New York: Simon and Schuster, 1974.

Friday, Nancy. *My Secret Garden*. New York: Simon and Schuster, 1973.

Herman, Julia R. "The Physiology of Erotica: Women's Sexual Arousal," *Psychology Today*, April 1975.

Inkeles, Gordon, and Murray Todris. *The Art of Sensual Massage*. San Francisco: Straight Arrow Books, 1972.

O'Conner, L. R., and Albert Ellis. *The Photographic Manual of Sexual Intercourse*. New York: Pent-R Books, Inc., 1969.

Wilson, Glenn, and David Nias. *The Mystery of Love: How the Science of Sexual Attraction Can Work For You*. New York: Bantam, 1980.

Zilbergeld, B. *Male Sexuality*. Boston: Little, Brown, 1978.

A LOOK AT YOUR LIFESTYLE

Listed below in the left-hand column are 15 kinds of sexual behavior discussed in this chapter. In the right-hand column are two major areas—"With a Committed Partner" and "With My Husband or Wife." Place a check (✔) in the space that best expresses your degree of acceptance within each of the two major areas. For each behavior listed in the left column, you will have two corresponding checks.

SEXUAL AROUSAL

Behavior	With a Committed Partner			With My Husband or Wife		
	ACCEPTABLE	NEUTRAL	NOT ACCEPTABLE	ACCEPTABLE	NEUTRAL	NOT ACCEPTABLE
1. Both my partner and I practice celibacy						
2. Kissing my partner						
3. Caressing my partner's breasts						
4. Orally stimulating my partner's body						
5. Sharing a sexual fantasy with my partner						
6. Masturbating while in my relationship						
7. Masturbating my partner						
8. Being masturbated by my partner						
9. Using an object such as a vibrator during sex play						

Table continued on next page.

Behavior	With a Committed Partner			With My Husband or Wife		
	ACCEPTABLE	*NEUTRAL*	*NOT ACCEPTABLE*	*ACCEPTABLE*	*NEUTRAL*	*NOT ACCEPTABLE*
10. Performing fellatio/ cunnilingus on my partner						
11. Having fellatio/cun- nilingus performed by my partner						
12. Engaging in sexual in- tercourse in the face- to-face, man-above po- sition.						
13. Engaging in sexual in- tercourse in the face- to-face, woman-above position.						
14. Engaging in sexual in- tercourse in the face- to-face, side-by-side position						
15. Engaging in sexual in- tercourse in the rear entry position						

GATHERING INFORMATION
List five facts that support any five of your choices (one fact per choice).

_____

_____

_____

_____

_____

EVALUATING THE INFORMATION

Behavior # _____ was *most* acceptable to me for both major areas because

_____.

Behavior # _____ was *least* acceptable to me for both major areas because

_____.

MAKING RESPONSIBLE DECISIONS

On a scale of 1 (lowest) to 10 (highest), rate your comfort in dealing with these 15 behaviors in a relationship.

1. _____

2. _____

3. _____

4. _____

5. _____

6. _____

7. _____

8. _____

9. _____

10. _____

11. _____

12. _____

13. _____

14. _____

15. _____

SIX

Conception and Pregnancy

Choosing to become pregnant is a decision that *two* people must make. And this decision should be based upon well-thought-out reasons. Couples who choose to have children because they feel that doing so will make a poor marriage better or because mom and dad are eager to become grandparents stand less of a chance of raising children responsibly than couples who base their decision upon their own desire for a child.

> Tom and I had problems communicating in our relationship. We both felt a child would give us something in common that we both could share. But having a kid turned out to be a big mistake. Instead of our child bringing us closer together, he served as an escape from dealing with our lack of communication. Tom and I are now divorced.

Before deciding to have children, couples need to determine whether or not their lifestyles are compatible with the changes that will occur. Among the major considerations are:

COMMITMENT People in a relationship need to feel a sense of love and responsibility for each other if they are to raise a child responsibly.

139

ECONOMICS Raising a family requires being able to feed, clothe, and provide the child with basic material needs.

A SINCERE DESIRE FOR CHILDREN The decision to have children should be predicated upon a sincere desire. This decision should be a "we" decision (determined by the couple), as opposed to a "they" decision (determined by others).

The aforementioned three areas are but a few of the numerous factors that a couple must consider in their decision to begin a family. Yet making the decision is just one aspect of conception and pregnancy.

GATHERING INFORMATION

When conception is thought to have occurred, there are many decisions to be made and a great deal of information to consider. Among these are selecting an obstetrician, seeking good prenatal care, choosing a method of childbirth, determining the father's role in pregnancy and childbirth, knowing what occurs in the body during pregnancy, possible complications of pregnancy, and whether or not to breast-feed.

EVALUATING THE INFORMATION

In this chapter the following major areas are explored so that your future decisions can be made in a responsible manner:

- how pregnancy occurs
- how to select an obstetrician
- proper prenatal care
- the process of childbirth
- birthing alternatives
- postnatal concerns

The information provided will help you deal with the many questions that often arise about conception and pregnancy. Among these are:

- How will you feel about being told you are pregnant or that you are the partner to a pregnancy?
- Will you find pregnancy to be a detriment to physical appearance?
- Is the process of childbirth as awful as sometimes professed?
- Will you find your child the joy you think it will be?
- Will you have positive feelings about breast-feeding?

You have a right to receive accurate information. With accurate information, you are in a good position to understand your feelings, thoughts, and ideas more thoroughly. We hope the factual information in this chapter will help you make your decisions rationally.

MAKING RESPONSIBLE DECISIONS

After you have made a decision to have a child, it is important that this decision be one that is cherished. According to many women and men, childbirth can be the most joyous occasion that can be shared.

Even though I am a physician, I found witnessing the birth of my child to be the most wonderful moment I have experienced in my life. I cried as my child was entering the world.

The key to a happy and healthy pregnancy and childbirth is a mutual decision made by a couple, based upon accurate information, honest and open communication, commitment, and, most important, love. Continued possession of these attributes serves to reinforce your decision.

THE PROCESS OF CONCEPTION

The information presented throughout this chapter is based on the assumption that conception is a choice that has been made by the people affected. Once this choice has been made and the process begun, certain biological events will begin to occur.

Fertilization

As we have seen in Chapter 3, on about the 14th day before the expected beginning of the next period, the woman ovulates. The ripened egg is released from the ovary and enters the oviduct. Once in the oviduct, the egg takes approximately three days to reach the uterus. If the egg has not been fertilized, it disintegrates. Since normal sperm can retain their fertilizing power for up to 72 hours after being deposited into the vagina, it is possible for the woman to be on her way to pregnancy even though the egg has yet to be released by the ovary.

When the fertile sperm has met the ripe egg (ovum), the sperm penetrates the egg's surface and sheds its tail. Fertilization takes place in a fraction of a second.

Bob and I have been trying to have a baby for the past year. Yet month after month would pass, and I would get my period. Then one night it happened. We had intercourse and I just knew we had hit paydirt. There is no biological rationale for my feeling, yet I knew I was pregnant. Sure enough, I was right.

Often the question is raised, What happens to all of the sperm if only one fertilizes the egg? In a typical ejaculation, 150 to 300 million sperm are emitted. Most of these never approach the egg, and some may seep out of the vagina. Only one sperm will enter the egg (we do not know why only one fertilizes an egg), and many others may swim around it. However, after about 72 hours, almost all of the sperm will die and disintegrate.

INFERTILITY: ITS EFFECT ON CONCEPTION

The word *fertile* means "being capable of producing offspring." *Infertile* means "being incapable of producing offspring." A woman is fertile when she produces a ripened egg each month.

For 10% to 15% of couples, the woman's inability to become pregnant is a concern. If this condition exists for about a year, it is often wise to consult a physician. Either the male or the female, and in some cases, both, may be infertile.

Sterile, another word synonymous with *infertile*, is also often used to indicate the inability to produce sperm or eggs. A person who is sterile still has the same desire and ability to perform sexually, as opposed to one who is *impotent*, which means the inability to have an erection.

MALE INFERTILITY About 40% of fertility problems are a result of the male's inability to impregnate the female. The most frequent cause of infertility among males is a low sperm count. Another cause of infertility in men is the production of abnormal sperm cells. They may be abnormal in that they may not be *motile*, in other words, not have the ability to propel themselves to reach the ovum. Motile sperm have the ability to move about one inch an hour.

Other causes of sterility or infertility in the male are infectious diseases of the testes and sexually transmitted diseases affecting the reproductive system. As we have read in Chapter 2, undescended testes can be a problem at birth that, if not corrected before puberty, can cause infertility. In some cases, inadequate production of hormones can cause fertility problems. However, hormone therapy can often remedy the situation.

FEMALE INFERTILITY The most common reason for infertility in a woman is the failure to ovulate at the same time each month. This irregular ovulation can be due to any number of reasons, such as a change in diet, physical and emotional stress, illness, and hormonal imbalance.

If the woman's partner has been diagnosed as fertile, the next step a physician takes is to ascertain the cause of the woman's infertility. A physician may wish to determine, assuming that tests have shown that the woman does ovulate, whether the sperm is being denied passage to the egg. Infections, which may or may not be caused by sexually transmitted diseases, can cause the oviducts to be blocked. This blockage can prevent the egg from passing down into the uterus. Infections in the vagina and uterus may also prevent the sperm from reaching an egg. These infections can be due to pelvic inflammatory disease (see Chapter 11), which causes scar tissue to form in and around the oviducts as well as the ovaries.

Through medication or surgery, many of the problems related to female infertility can be remedied.

I remember visiting my gynecologist. He told me I couldn't bear children. We had been trying for six years with no success. Finally, we adopted a newborn child. Two months later, I became pregnant. I think that my emotions must have played a factor because I figured "the hell with it" after I was told I couldn't bear children. Maybe changing my frame of mind helped me become pregnant.

Many of you have heard stories of women who were told by their doctors that they could not have children and shortly thereafter became pregnant. This type of situation has led people to believe that whether or not one can become pregnant is to a large degree dependent on "frame of mind." The truth of this situation is highly controversial. Science has not shown that there is a significant relationship between the ability to become pregnant and one's emotional and mental state, but the possibility of some influence cannot be discounted.

INCREASING FERTILITY AND CONCEPTION

The majority of students reading this chapter are probably more concerned about the prevention of pregnancy than about increasing the chances of pregnancy. Yet many of you may sometime want to become pregnant and yet not be able to. There are several methods and techniques that can be used to increase the chances of conception.

TIMING SEXUAL INTERCOURSE The time of the month is an important factor to consider in conception. The rhythm method of birth control (see Chapter 7) can also be used to enhance the chances of conception. By using a *basal body temperature chart,* the woman can determine when she is ovulating. Once an ovulation pattern is established, the woman may wish to have intercourse about one to two days before she ovulates, since sperm can survive for up to 72 hours in the womb.

FREQUENCY OF INTERCOURSE To enhance the chances of pregnancy, the frequency with which a couple has intercourse should be reduced. The male needs to maintain a high sperm count. During each subsequent ejaculation by the male, the number of sperm cells is reduced. It takes at least 24 hours to replenish all 300 million sperm. If a woman is about to ovulate, the male should not ejaculate for about 2 days before this time. Put simply, save the sperm for when it counts.

POSITION OF INTERCOURSE The position in which a couple chooses to engage in sexual intercourse is an important factor in conception. The man-on-top, face-to-face position (see Chapter 5) is considered the position most beneficial for increasing the chances for pregnancy. Before ejaculation has occurred in this position, the woman may wish to draw her knees up to her chest. She should remain in this position for at least 20 minutes after the man has ejaculated. It may also be helpful if a pillow is placed under her buttocks to prevent the semen from running out of the vagina, since the process of gravity usually plays a role. During ejaculation, the man should also penetrate as deeply as possible and not thrust. He should keep his penis in the vagina for several minutes, and when he does remove his penis, he should do it as gently as possible.

UNUSUAL FERTILIZATIONS

Not all conception takes place in the traditional penis—vagina technique of sexual intercourse. Many other techniques are now used which can make conception and pregnancy possible.

ARTIFICIAL INSEMINATION *Artificial insemination* involves introducing semen into the vagina or uterus of a woman by artificial means so that conception can occur. Artificial insemination was practiced on animals as long ago as the 14th century. It is now being used by men and women as well. Estimates indicate that in the United States, 1% of all babies born are conceived by artificial insemination (Francoeur, 1974).

The semen for artificial insemination can be from a husband or a donor. In either case, it is used when a husband has a low sperm count or none. The husband's sperm or the sperm of a donor is placed in the woman's vagina. If the husband's sperm is used, several ejaculates can be collected and held under proper conditions. However, most cases of artificial insemination use donor sperm.

Sperm banks have risen in popularity over the past number of years. Since it is now possible to freeze sperm, many people have decided that artificial insemination is a viable option for the future.

One sperm bank opened in 1980 with the idea of freezing the sperm of well-known scientists. Although several have already donated their sperm, most have sought to remain anonymous and thus removed from controversy. One who has chosen not to remain anonymous is William Schockley, a Nobel laureate.

TEST-TUBE BABIES Scientists now have the ability to unite an egg and sperm outside the human body and in a laboratory—hence the name *test-tube baby*. This technique can be used in instances where the woman's oviducts are blocked. In test-tube fertilizations, the woman's egg is removed from her body and placed in a Petri dish with artificially capacitated sperm from the husband. The fertilized egg is then placed inside the uterus for growth and development. This technique was used successfully in England in 1978. Louise Brown, the first test-tube baby, is now a healthy child.

DETECTING PREGNANCY

The first sign that indicates pregnancy is the absence of the menstrual period when it is expected. However, the missed period does not necessarily indicate that conception has occurred. In fact, most women at one time or another may skip a period for a month or be late because of "nerves," diet, physical activity, or a host of other circumstances. However, if conception did occur, the woman may experience tenderness in the breasts, nausea, vomiting, fatigue, and a change in appetite. Some women may experience spotting, or a light irregular flow of blood.

When a woman has not had her period and has other accompanying symptoms of pregnancy six weeks after the first day of her last menstrual cycle, she may wish to have a pregnancy test.

One of the most common methods used to determine pregnancy is a urine test. The woman should collect her urine in a small jar as soon as she awakens in the morning and bring it to a clinic, a laboratory, or her physician. In this test, *human chorionic gonadotropin* (HCG), which is found in the urine of pregnant women, should be detectable if fertilization has occurred. This test should be done about ten days to two weeks after the woman's period was expected.

Blood tests can also be used to detect traces of HCG, which may be present in the blood about 10 days after conception has occurred.

Several companies now sell "do-it-yourself" pregnancy tests, which can be purchased without a prescription. While many of them claim to be accurate, there is always the problem that users may not follow the instructions carefully, thereby causing false readings. Even if procedures are properly followed, these tests often produce false-negatives. In one study, 20% of all pregnant women who used home tests obtained false-negative results (*Test Yourself,* 1978).

Regardless of the method used to diagnose pregnancy, a woman should be aware of the possibility that she may be pregnant if she is sexually active and has some of the obvious symptoms of pregnancy.

THE DEVELOPMENT OF THE EMBRYO AND THE FETUS

Once conception has occurred and the decision has been made to take the pregnancy to term, many events will be taking place that affect the baby and its mother. To understand these events, it is important to know how the baby is developing.

The Basic Development of the Fertilized Egg

Certain basic changes take place as soon as fertilization occurs. The fertilized egg divides into many cells and becomes a *morula* as it travels down the oviduct. It then becomes a *blastocyst* and afterward attaches itself to the wall of the uterus. The *trophoblast*, which maintains the embryo, becomes a *placenta*.

THE PLACENTA

The *placenta* is the organ that exchanges nutrients and waste products with the mother. The blood vessels of the placenta are connected to the circulatory system of the mother through blood vessels in the uterine wall. However, the circulatory system of the fetus and the mother are separate. While the mother's blood and the fetus's blood do not mix, except in rare instances, some substances can be exchanged through a thin membrane. Among these substances are oxygen and nutrients, which supply the fetus with the substitutes for breathing and eating. The waste products and carbon dioxide of the fetus pass from the fetal blood back to the mother.

While the membrane between the fetus's and mother's blood prevents the exchange of blood, other substances may be exchanged. Some examples are depressant drugs such as alcohol and heroin. This is why babies born to mothers who use these drugs must be detoxified at birth. For this reason, a woman must be concerned about taking drugs while she is pregnant. Some disease-causing organisms can also be passed from mother to fetus, such as the organisms responsible for German measles (rubella) and syphilis.

Another function of the placenta is to produce human chorionic gonadotropin. This hormone stimulates the production of progesterone. Elevated levels of this hormone are suspected of causing many of the physical changes associated with pregnancy.

THE UMBILICAL CORD

The *umbilical cord* is a semitransparent jelly-like rope that is attached to the placenta from the fetus's navel. It contains two arteries and one vein. Oxygen and essential nutrients reach the fetus through the umbilical vein, and waste products from the fetus travel to the mother from the two umbilical arteries.

AMNION

The *amnion* is a thin membrane that forms a sac, or "bag of waters." It surrounds the unborn child in the uterus and contains *amniotic fluid*, in which the child floats. The amniotic fluid serves to maintain a constant temperature for the child and acts as a cushion to help prevent injury to the child.

Table 6.1 outlines the major changes that occur from conception to birth throughout each third, or trimester, of pregnancy.

PRENATAL CARE AND CONSIDERATIONS

To facilitate the most healthy pregnancy possible, the pregnant woman should seek appropriate care that will enhance her well-being and the well-being of her unborn child. This care should begin before pregnancy occurs. A complete physical examination by a physician is a wise start.

TABLE 6.1 DEVELOPMENT OF THE CHILD—CONCEPTION THROUGH BIRTH

First Trimester	Second Trimester	Third Trimester
Week 1 — Ovum becomes embryo Week 2 — Embryo is 1.5 millimeters long Week 3 — Embryo is ½ inch long Week 4 — Nervous system forms — Eyes and ears are visible — Digestive system forms 2nd month — Heart appears as four-chambered structure — Upper and lower limb buds appear — Nose and upper lips form — Tail becomes less distinct — By end of second month, embryo has large head, brain, facial characteristics, fingers, and toes — At the end of Week 8, embryo is called fetus 3rd month — Fetus is 3½ inches long and weighs 1.6 ounces — Face becomes more apparent — First external signs of the sex of the fetus appear — Excretory system develops rapidly	4th month — Fetus kicks its legs and moves its arms — Fetus is 3½ inches long and weighs 7 ounces — Skin begins to develop 5th month — Rate of growth slows — Fetus weighs 1 pound — Fetus becomes perceptible to mother — Fetal heartbeat becomes audible to stethoscope — Fine hair (lanugo) develops 6th month — Fetal movements become more vigorous — Can respond to external sounds and pressure in having an increased heartbeat	7th month — Fetus is fully developed — Fetus weighs about 4 pounds 8th month — Development of almost all organic systems is complete — Weight is 5 pounds and length is 18 inches 9th month — Fetus is fully developed — Skin has smooth and polished look — Eyes are slate-colored — Gains 1 pound per week — Is born weighing about 7 pounds and is about 20 inches long

Selecting a Physician

One of the most important decisions in pregnancy is selecting a physician. In the majority of cases, a doctor who is an *obstetrician* will deliver the baby. An obstetrician is a physician who specializes in the care of women during pregnancy, labor and delivery, and the period immediately following. The obstetrician is usually also a *gynecologist,* a physician who specializes in the treatment of the problems of the female reproductive and sexual organs. In selecting a physician there are certain factors to consider.

RECOMMENDATIONS FROM OTHERS

One of the best ways to select an obstetrician is to consult people whom you feel you can trust and whom you believe are knowledgeable about medicine, especially as it relates to childbirth.

PHILOSOPHY OF THE OBSTETRICIAN

With the diversity of philosophies that exist today—the Lamaze method, home birth, the partner's desire to take pictures—it is important that a couple select an obstetrician whose philosophy is compatible with theirs.

HOSPITAL AFFILIATION

When you select an obstetrician, you also select a hospital. An obstetrician is given privileges at selected hospitals. Thus, if you find that a hospital near you has a new birthing center but the obstetrician you are considering is affiliated with a hospital too far away, you may place yourself in an undesirable situation. You can always call a hospital for a list of those doctors with whom it is affiliated.

PARTNERSHIP

Some obstetricians work with partners so that someone is always available. In this situation, you may visit and meet each of the obstetricians and become comfortable with each. If your obstetrician is then out of town, at least you will have someone whom you know deliver the baby.

The obstetrician you select should be one who will be patient and will listen to and respond to your questions. Adequate medical care is your right. You are employing the obstetrician to provide you with services you believe are essential for a healthy pregnancy and delivery.

Examinations by the Obstetrician

Once pregnancy has been confirmed, it is important that a woman begin to care for her baby. This means visiting an obstetrician.

During her first visit, the doctor or the nurse will ask for a medical history. The last date of the woman's menstrual cycle will need to be known so that the approximate delivery date of her baby can be ascertained. To figure out the expected date of delivery, the woman should count back three months from the first day of the last menstrual period and add seven days plus one year. Thus, if the first day of the last menstrual period was August 5, 1981, she would compute the date of delivery as follows:

August 5, 1981 (first day of last menstrual period)
− 3 months
May 5, 1981
+ 7 days and one year
May 12, 1982, (expected date of delivery)

The figures used for computing the expected date of delivery are based upon the average length of a human pregnancy, which is 266 days, or approximately nine months.

While the woman will be given her due date during her first visit, statistics show that chances are she will not deliver on that date. Only 4% of deliveries occur on the due date, while 60% occur within five days of the predicted date.

In addition to being given a date of delivery during her first visit, the woman will be weighed, so that the doctor can keep a record of how much weight she is gaining throughout her pregnancy. The doctor will also check her blood type as well as record pertinent information such as allergies and any unusual physical conditions. The doctor will give her a physical examination, checking her heart, lungs, breasts, and abdomen.

The doctor will also perform an internal examination. Two fingers will be inserted into the vagina, and at the same time the abdomen will be pressed lightly. In this way, changes in the uterus that occur during pregnancy can be determined. The doctor can also determine the location of the ovaries and uterus, whether they are normal or enlarged, or whether there is a tumor or other obstacle that might hinder the growth of the baby.

Around the fifth month, some doctors may examine the woman's abdomen, using a *sonograph*. This recording device, by means of ultrasound, produces a picture on a screen that provides the physician with a great deal of information. This method, which is safe and is practiced routinely by many obstetricians, can be used to ascertain the baby's weight and position in the uterus as well as possible complications.

During visits to the doctor, a pregnant woman will be provided with valuable information concerning diet and proper health habits to follow. Pregnancy usually calls for one visit a month. However, many physicians prefer a woman to visit every two weeks during the eighth month and weekly during the last month.

With proper guidance from the obstetrician and responsibility and follow-through on the part of the woman, pregnancy will most likely be a safe road from conception through delivery.

THE STAGES OF PREGNANCY: EFFECTS UPON THE MOTHER

As with the development of the fetus, the stages of pregnancy can also be viewed in trimesters. Throughout her pregnancy, the mother goes through many changes. We will describe the changes that occur within each of the trimesters.

The First Trimester

It is during this period that the suspicion and confirmation of pregnancy takes place. Most of the physical changes that occur in the woman are due to increased production of estrogens and progesterone.

PHYSICAL CHANGES

BREASTS The mammary glands are further developed as a result of the increased production of hormones. The breasts will swell, and a tingling sensation will often be felt. The nipples as well as the areolas may become darker.

URINATION AND BOWEL MOVEMENTS Hormones cause more water to be retained in the body. As the uterus grows, it may press against the bladder. As a result, the woman will urinate more frequently. Bowel movements may become irregular because of the pressure that may be exerted upon the rectum by the uterus, or the woman may become constipated. This condition may cause the woman to reduce her activity, which in turn can cause her to feel tired most of the time.

MORNING SICKNESS Although it may occur at any time of the day, "morning sickness," — nausea and vomiting — is a condition experienced by many women during the first six to eight weeks of pregnancy.

FATIGUE Early in pregnancy, a woman may feel very tired and wish to sleep more frequently. This can be due to the effects of morning sickness, depression (if she does not wish to be pregnant), or the production of high levels of progesterone.

PSYCHOLOGICAL CHANGES

The psychological state of a woman during the first trimester is dependent upon a number of factors. If a woman is pregnant because she wants to be, she may be effervescent and "up." This is often true of women who have tried for a long time to conceive. When they finally learn they are pregnant, they are joyous.

The happiest moment of my life was when I found out I was pregnant. We tried for two years and nothing happened. Now I have never been happier.

Some women may feel very depressed. This state of depression may be due to uncertainty in a relationship. A woman who finds out she is pregnant at a time a relationship is at its low ebb will probably be depressed.

Some women may suffer through a depression during this trimester because they may feel physically fatigued. One's mental and physical state often go hand in hand.

Some women show no changes at all. Their attitude and behavior show that they feel pregnancy is a condition that should not and will not hamper their way of life.

Some women's partners experience a *sympathetic pregnancy*, also known as *couvade*. This is a phenomenon in which the man experiences nausea, vomiting, and labor pains along with the woman.

SEXUAL ACTIVITY

Sexual relations during this period can continue as they were before conception. Yet for many couples, morning sickness and fatigue can act as deterrents. Except for women who are pregnant for the first time, decreased sexual interest during the first trimester is not common.

Some physiological changes that are a result of pregnancy may affect sexual relations. For example, if a woman is anxious about her pregnancy, she may not be able to be aroused. This lack of interest in turn may make sexual intercourse painful, because she may not become lubricated. Also, since the breasts become more sensitive during the first trimester, the woman may be averse to having her breasts touched.

Some women are concerned that sexual intercourse may cause a spontaneous abortion. There is no evidence to support this notion. The unborn child is well protected within the confines of the uterus.

The Second Trimester

During the second trimester positive proof of pregnancy exists, in that the fetal heartbeat can be heard. Many physical changes take place that indicate to the woman that her pregnancy is observable.

PHYSICAL CHANGES

The pregnant woman becomes very much aware that she is expecting a baby. Her waistline begins to expand, and she can experience *quickening,* or feeling the fetus kicking and moving in her uterus. It is during this trimester that maternity clothes become a part of the woman's wardrobe.

The physical symptoms associated with the first trimester—morning sickness—disappear or become minimal. However, the woman's hands, face, ankles, wrists, and feet may swell as a result of the retention of water in the body. This condition is known as *edema.*

During this trimester, the woman's breasts are ready to be used for nursing, even though there are several more months before birth. Sometimes *colostrum,* a yellowish fluid, is secreted from the breasts.

PSYCHOLOGICAL CHANGES

The second trimester is often the most peaceful trimester. Since many of the physical problems of the first trimester are gone, the woman may feel better mentally. She may feel joyous because she can wear her maternity clothes and "show off" her condition. Barring any complications, she can continue to do many of the things she has been doing all along.

SEXUAL ACTIVITY

Masters and Johnson (1966) have shown that increased sexual response is common for women during this trimester. In fact, some women may experience orgasm for the first time, while others may develop a multiorgasmic response. This experience may be due to the increased pelvic vascularity which is brought on by pregnancy.

During the second trimester, the woman can use the full range of coital positions, provided she and her partner do not find them awkward or uncomfortable.

The Third Trimester

During the last three months of pregnancy, the expectant mother cannot help but be aware of her condition almost constantly.

PHYSICAL CHANGES

During this trimester, the fetus is very active. It kicks, turns, and pushes against the mother's abdomen.

During this trimester, the woman may also have an increased desire to eat. This appetite may be caused by hormonal changes throughout pregnancy. The gain in weight should be carefully monitored. Most physicians believe that the ideal weight to gain during pregnancy is approximately 20 pounds. These 20 pounds are usually dispersed as follows: 7.5 pounds for the average weight of the infant; 1 pound for the placenta; 2 pounds for the amniotic fluid; 2 pounds for enlargement of the uterus; 1.5 pounds for enlargement of the breasts; and 6 pounds for retained fluid and fat accumulated by the mother.

Excessive weight gain during pregnancy may cause medical complications, in that excessive strain may be placed on the heart and blood pressure may be unduly elevated.

This trimester is perhaps the most uncomfortable trimester of a woman's pregnancy. She may feel short-winded because of pressure on the lungs, and indigestion and heartburn may be common because of pressure exerted on the stomach.

Because the weight gain is at its peak during the third trimester, the pregnant woman's equilibrium may be off-center. She may try to compensate for the weight of her abdomen by trying to keep her shoulders and back straight. Overcompensation causes the "waddling" walk during the eighth and ninth months of pregnancy, as well as back pains.

During the third trimester of pregnancy, a woman may experience irregular, painless contractions of the uterus, called *Braxton–Hicks contractions.* Many women often mistake these contractions for the onset of labor.

At the beginning of the ninth month, the uterus may begin to descend. This occurs in most pregnancies and indicates that the child has begun to sink into the pelvis. In lay terms this is called *lightening* or *dropping*. This phenomenon is known medically as *engagement of the fetus*. This event occurs earlier in first pregnancies because of the greater pressure that surrounds the fetus. This pressure is greater in first than in subsequent pregnancies because the abdominal wall and the uterus have not been stretched by a previous childbirth.

PSYCHOLOGICAL CHANGES

For many women, this trimester can be more difficult than the first. Whereas many women find that the first two trimesters pass relatively quickly, the third seems to last forever, especially the ninth month. As a result, the woman may feel anxious and impatient. She may begin to worry and wonder whether her baby is unhealthy or has a physical problem. These concerns are even more magnified during a woman's first pregnancy. If the due date has passed, she may worry all the more. As a result, she may find she becomes easily irritated at things that usually are of no concern. In times like this, it is important that the woman's partner be understanding and supportive.

SEXUAL ACTIVITY

For many couples, the third trimester brings with it abstention from sex. Some people believe that sexual intercourse during this time may cause premature labor pains. However, that is not true. While orgasm in the woman may trigger contractions, these contractions are not indications of the onset of labor.

Many physicians feel that sexual relations are in no way harmful during pregnancy. However, some advise their patients to refrain from sexual activity during the last four to six weeks of pregnancy. Each couple should check with their physician regarding this recommendation.

Regardless of the physician's advice, sexual activity decreases among many couples during the third trimester because many women may feel unattractive and awkward. However, sexual intercourse does not have to be halted for those who continue to have the desire. The third trimester is often a good time to practice new positions in intercourse, since the man-on-top, woman-below position becomes uncomfortable. The side-to-side position is the most suitable one during this trimester. Other positions can be experimented with, provided each partner finds them comfortable (Figure 6.1).

In addition to sexual intercourse, couples can continue to satisfy each other during the third trimester using a variety of techniques such as mutual masturbation and oral–genital contacts. However, as was stated in Chapter 5, cunnilingus practiced on a pregnant woman can present a danger if air is blown into the vagina.

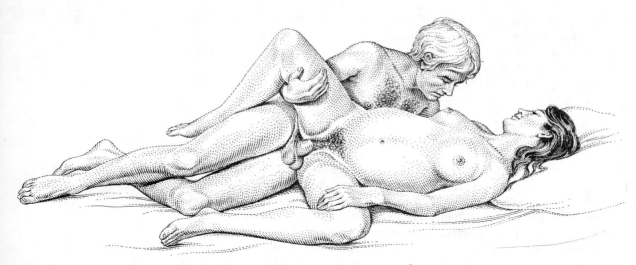

FIGURE 6.1   Rear entry position of sexual intercourse for pregnant woman.

DRUGS AND PREGNANCY

Legal as well as illegal drugs can have an effect upon the unborn child. According to *Consumer Reports* (1976), about 92% of women have used a prescription drug during pregnancy. While some of these drugs may indeed be helpful, they may also be harmful. For example, tranquilizers, if taken early in pregnancy, may cause birth defects. Heavy use of aspirin may interfere with blood clotting in both mother and infant.

The use of alcohol during pregnancy has been well documented. Alcohol, like other drugs, can pass through the placenta and harm the fetus. Excessive alcohol consumption can cause *fetal alcohol syndrome* — abnormal smallness in the size of the head, poor coordination, behavior problems, and often heart defects. According to the March of Dimes, there are one million alcoholic women of childbearing age in the United States. Some research also indicates that pregnant women who take one or two drinks daily stand an increased risk of spontaneous abortion (NIAAA, 1981).

Pregnant women might also be concerned about the effects of cigarette smoking on the unborn child. Research indicates that women who smoke have smaller babies. In addition, these babies are predisposed to heart attacks during adulthood (*Pregnant Women and Smoking*, 1980).

Although the data on caffeine use and pregnancy are not conclusive, the Center for Science in the Public Interest (1979) has requested the FDA to require coffee and tea manufacturers to include on their labels a warning about caffeine use by pregnant women. Animal studies indicate that heavy caffeine dosages cause birth defects.

THE ROLE OF THE FATHER DURING PREGNANCY

Whereas at one time pregnancy was thought to be a woman's sole domain and responsibility, today she shares the experiences of pregnancy with her partner.

My husband and I became closer than we had ever been when I became pregnant. We thought a great deal about the phenomenon of our pregnancy. During this time, we shared decisions and partook in activities on an equal basis.

The prospective father can gain insight into a woman's pregnancy through various means. One way is by visiting the obstetrician with his partner. During office visits, the prospective mother and father can take turns listening to the baby's heartbeat. At home, both can feel the abdomen and some of the accompanying movements from within. Later in this chapter, we will look at the role the father can play along with the mother during preparation for childbirth and the birth.

Many decisions must be made regarding the newborn. The crib, the nursery, the roles the prospective parents expect to play, employment, and health needs are within the realm of decisions that should be shared. The father-to-be is usually anxious about the health of the mother-to-be. He should be permitted to be reassuring, strong, and comforting from conception through delivery. All too often, the father is the "forgotten man" during pregnancy and childbirth.

NUTRITION AND PREGNANCY

One of the keys to delivering a healthy baby is a healthy diet. A healthy diet will provide the nourishment necessary for building new tissues in the fetus and replenishing cells in the woman's body that are being drained by the new life growing within.

Adequate nutrition means that the woman should eat a balanced diet with a daily caloric intake of 2500 to 2800 calories. The idea that a woman is "eating for two" and therefore must increase her intake of food during pregnancy is a myth. During pregnancy, emphasis should be placed on proteins, vitamins, and minerals. Deemphasis should be placed on fats, carbohydrates, sugar, and starches. Many obstetricians see no need for diet changes during pregnancy if the diet followed before pregnancy was sound.

BIRTH

The entire process of childbirth is called *parturition*. Before labor begins, one or more of three events will occur.

1. There will be a slightly bloody discharge known as the "bloody show," representing the plug of the mucus that was in the cervical opening during pregnancy.
2. In about 10% of women, the amniotic sac ("bag of waters") bursts, and the woman feels the amniotic fluid running down her legs. Labor usually begins within 24 hours. However, the "bag of waters" does not usually burst until the first stage of labor.
3. The woman will experience irregular contractions.

If the amniotic sac breaks or a bloody show is evident, the woman's doctor should be notified. A breaking of the amniotic sac can increase the risk of infection to the mother. The prospective parents should not hesitate to call the obstetrician, if it is warranted, even in the middle of the night.

Assuming labor has begun, the woman and the father-to-be may arrive at the hospital expecting to be admitted to a labor room automatically. However, this is not always the case. Usually, after the woman goes through the usual procedures of completing admissions papers, she is given an admission examination. Her blood pressure is taken, and her heart and lungs are examined. Her abdomen is palpated (felt by hand) to determine the baby's position. The fetal heart is then located, and its heart rate is counted. Finally, a vaginal examination is performed to determine how far labor has progressed. The progress of labor is determined by two criteria: the extent to which the cervix is dilated (opened) and the depth to which the baby has descended to the birth canal. The physician can determine the degree of dilation with the fingers. A single-finger breadth is the equivalent of 2 centimeters ($4/5$ of an inch). Two centimeters' dilation is a good indication that labor has begun. Ten centimeters represents a completely dilated cervix.

If the admission examination indicates that labor has begun, the genital area will be washed and, in many cases, the pubic hair will be shaved. An enema will also be administered to prevent fecal matter from interfering with the delivery.

Stages of Labor

Labor is divided into three stages. In each stage, distinct events take place.

STAGE 1: CONTRACTION AND DILATION

The first stage of labor is the longest. It can last anywhere from two hours to an entire day. Stage 1 labor can be divided into three phases.

STAGE 1, PHASE 1   In this phase of labor, contractions can be spaced 15 to 20 minutes apart and can last 30 seconds to 1 minute. The contractions in this phase are not very strong. During this phase, *effacement*, which is a thinning out of the cervix, takes place. At the same time, *dila-*

tion, or opening of the cervix, occurs. In this phase, the cervix can be dilated 2 to 5 centimeters (⁴/₅ inch to 2 inches).

STAGE 1, PHASE 2   In this stage, the contractions may be about 8 to 10 minutes apart. These contractions will last for about 20 to 30 seconds and will be more intense than the contractions in the previous phase. The cervix will dilate 5 to 8 centimeters (2 to 3 inches).

STAGE 1, PHASE 3   This is the final phase of Stage 1 and is known as *transition.* In this phase, the contractions are very strong and short. These contractions can last about 10 seconds, yet begin every minute or two. During this stage, the cervix will dilate from 8 to 10 centimeters (3 to 4 inches). The cervix can be completely dilated without being completely effaced. The reverse is also true.

STAGE 2: DELIVERY

This stage of labor begins with the cervix completely dilated and terminates with the delivery of the newborn. When this stage occurs, the woman is taken into the delivery room and prepared for birth. By this time, the baby has dropped further down into the birth canal, head first (assuming a normal delivery is taking place). This stage of labor can last from several minutes to a few hours.

During this stage of labor, the woman has an urge to push the baby out. When the doctor begins to see the head emerge *(crowning),* an *episiotomy* may be performed. An episiotomy is a cut made in the perineum to facilitate easier passage of the baby's head through the vagina and to prevent the vaginal tissues from being overstretched (see Chapter 3). This procedure is currently being questioned by many women, who feel that an episiotomy is often performed more for the convenience of the doctor than for the patient. Yet doctors contend that the episiotomy is needed to prevent the anal muscles from ripping and causing future complications in the process of defecation.

Once the baby has been eased out of the birth canal (Figure 6.2), the physician or nurse will extract any mucus that may be in the baby's air passages. At this time, the baby will usually begin to cry. Once the baby begins to breathe on its own, the doctor will cut the umbilical cord, which is still attached to the placenta inside the woman. The umbilical cord will be clamped and cut a few inches from the baby's navel, where it will dry up and fall off in about a week. After delivery, drops of silver nitrate will be put in the baby's eyes to protect them from damage caused by possible gonorrheal infection.

STAGE 3: AFTERBIRTH

In the final stage of labor, the placenta, also called the *afterbirth,* must be removed. The uterus will continue to contract, and with a few pushes, the placenta will be expelled. If the placenta is not expelled by the contractions, the doctor can remove it by hand. (It is important that the placenta

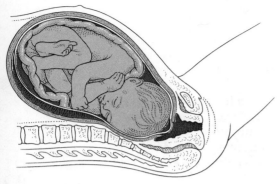

1. Beginning descent

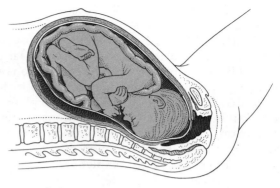

2. Further descent, rotation

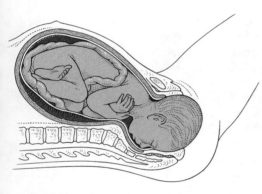

3. Extension . . . emergence begins

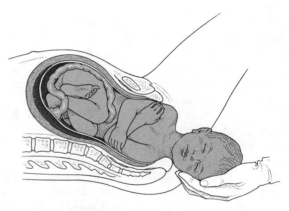

4. Anterior shoulder delivered

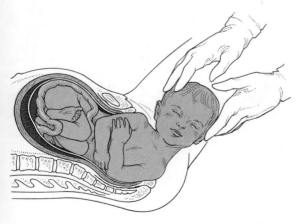

5. Delivery of posterior shoulder

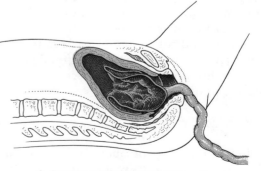

6. Placenta separates from uterine wall

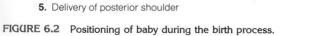

FIGURE 6.2 Positioning of baby during the birth process.

be intact and that no placental fragments remain in the uterus.) The placenta is then examined, and the mother is cared for. She is washed, and her episiotomy incision is sutured.

In many cases, almost immediately after birth, the baby is placed next to the mother's breast. While there may not be any milk as yet, there will be colostrum, which is nutritious for the baby. The closeness of the baby to its mother soon after birth promotes *bonding,* or the development of closeness between the baby and its parents, which provides the baby with a feeling of love.

Although the baby will be examined by the obstetrician immediately after birth, a pediatrician will usually give the baby a more thorough examination. In many hospitals, babies are given an *Apgar score,* which is a health status rating, immediately after birth. The Apgar score rates the baby's health on the basis of factors such as weight, color, alertness, and posture. The score ranges from 1 (unhealthy) to 10 (very healthy).

PROBLEMS IN CHILDBIRTH

For 99% of the babies born, the position in which they will be delivered is *longitudinal.* Ninety-six percent of these will have a *cephalic,* or head-first, presentation. In this position, the baby will be delivered head first and face rotated to the side as the rest of the body is presented.

Four percent of all longitudinal births are *breech,* or buttocks-first, presentations (Figure 6.3). If the doctor is aware of a breech position, he or she may try to manipulate the baby so that the head will be presented first.

In 1 in 200 births, the fetus may lie across the canal, in what is known as the *transverse* position, the shoulder, arm, or hand entering the birth canal first.

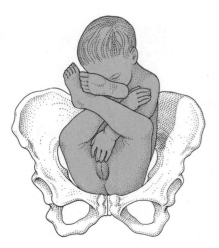 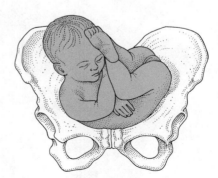

FIGURE 6.3   Baby in breech position **(left).** Baby in transverse position **(right).**

The physician may wish to deliver the baby in a breech or transverse position via a cesarean section.

Cesarean Section

A *cesarean section,* or *C section,* is the surgical removal of the baby through an incision made in the uterus and through the abdomen.

INDICATIONS FOR CESAREAN SECTION

The most common reason for cesarean section (Figure 6.4a) is a contracted pelvis. In this condition, the baby is not able to pass into the vagina. Cesarean sections may also be performed if the baby is in a breech or transverse position, if the cervix does not dilate, if the placenta prematurely separates from the uterus, if there is infection in the vaginal tract, if the mother is totally exhausted, if the fetus is under distress, or if the mother is severely incapacitated due to injury or trauma.

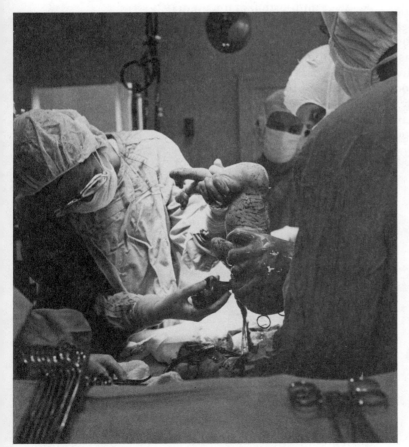

FIGURE 6.4a Cesarean section delivery. (Photo by Charlotte Brooks)

REPEAT CESAREAN SECTIONS

Having a cesarean section once does not necessarily mean that future deliveries will have to be via the same method. Vaginal deliveries can be performed if a woman has had a C section. However, if the C section was performed because of a small pelvis, subsequent deliveries will probably be handled in the same manner. Most women who have given birth by cesarean section the first time will do so subsequently (Guttmacher, 1962).

PERFORMING A CESAREAN SECTION

It takes about 45 minutes to perform a cesarean section. In most instances, the woman will be given a spinal anesthesia. Then either a longitudinal midline incision is made through the skin, fat, and fascia from just below the navel to the pubic bone, or a low, wide, transverse incision is made just above the pubis (Figure 6.4b). The latter is made in the area covered by pubic hair, so that the scar is not visible when the hair grows back. The abdominal muscle fibers are then separated, and the abdominal cavity is made visible. An incision is made in the lower midportion of the uterus.

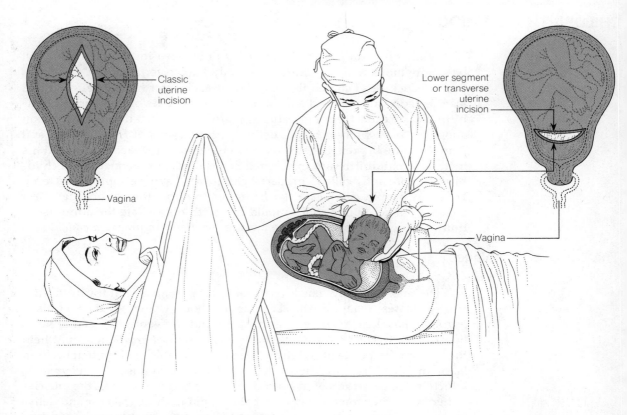

FIGURE 6.4b Procedure for cesarean section delivery.

The infant's head is removed first, and the rest of the body follows. The umbilical cord is clamped and cut, and the baby is handed to the nurse. The placenta is manually removed from the uterus, and the wound is stitched with absorbable sutures. The time from the beginning of the skin incision to the delivery of the baby is about five or six minutes. The repair of the uterine and abdominal wounds is what takes up most of the time.

Fetal Monitors

Fetal monitors are used when a physician believes complications may arise during labor. Wires hooked through the woman's vagina to the head of the fetus enable the fetal monitor to print data about the baby's heart rate. The data produced by the fetal monitor can provide the doctor with information that can aid in determining whether or not a cesarean section will be necessary.

Some women have complained about the use of these monitors because they may be used indiscriminately, or by an obstetrician lacking expertise in interpreting the signals. Moreover, the monitor is prone to readings that indicate problems where none exist.

CHILDBIRTH TECHNIQUES

While the term *prepared childbirth* will be used in this section, it will be synonymous with the more commonly known term, *natural childbirth*. Grantly Dick-Read coined the term "natural childbirth." He believed that fear, tension, and a lack of education were the causes of the pain of childbirth. Dick-Read's theory of natural childbirth was that through education about the birth process before delivery, these cycles of fear, tension, and pain could be broken. Several years later, Fernand Lamaze introduced his method of childbirth into the United States. The Lamaze method of childbirth is more aptly called "prepared childbirth," a more appropriate term. For many people, *natural childbirth* implies "without the use of drugs." Yet a woman is not "unnatural" should her birth necessitate the administration of drugs. Therefore, our preference for the term *prepared childbirth*.

The Lamaze Technique

The most widely used technique of prepared childbirth in the United States today is the Lamaze method. Using what he calls a *psychoprophylactic* method, meaning "mind prevention," Lamaze believed that two techniques, *relaxation* and *controlled breathing,* could help the woman dissociate herself from the uncomfortable feelings that occur in labor and delivery. This dissociation is not to be confused with *hypnosis,* which is a *passive* form of dissociation. By learning to relax all the muscles in her body, the woman may be capable of going through labor and delivery without the use of drugs. Lamaze believed that a woman, using controlled breathing exercises, could control the tension that accompanied the pain (Figure 6.5).

> My natural childbirth course proved to be helpful. I was at home alone, and I went into labor. My husband was at work, and before I knew it, the baby was coming out of my vagina. I delivered the baby myself. I was only able to do this because of the information I learned in my prepared childbirth course.

Many people believe that prepared childbirth classes are valuable only if the woman gives birth without using drugs. Such an idea could not be further from the truth. A major benefit of these classes is the knowledge gained about what happens to one's body and what can be expected during childbirth.

As for the concern about drugs and what is "natural" and "not natural," Dick-Read (1959) succinctly states:

> Natural childbirth is not:
> —necessary painless childbirth.
> —an endurance test (anesthesia is used if needed or wanted);
> —a failure if an anesthetic is used.
> —a denial of the achievements of modern obstetrics.
> —a step backward.
> —a denial of the importance of the doctor for physical care during pregnancy and labor, but a belief that psychological care is also important.
> —hypnosis.
> —connected with "birth control" or "planned parenthood."
> —a cult, nor does it have any religious, political, or racial affiliation or bias.

FIGURE 6.5 Lamaze training. (Photos, left by Erika Stone; right by Elizabeth Hamlin)

The LeBoyer Technique

In 1975, Frederick LeBoyer introduced his philosophy and method of childbirth to the United States. Unlike Dick-Read and Lamaze, LeBoyer's approach focuses on the birth experience of the infant.

LeBoyer believed that the process of birth is traumatic. He based this theory on the following:

- When a baby is born, it goes from a curled position (fetal position), in which it has been for nine months, to a straight-backed position, in which it lies on its back.
- The baby goes from nine months of darkness to glaring lights.
- The baby goes from quietness and the sounds of its mother's heartbeat to noise.
- The baby goes from an environment of warmth to an environment that may be more than 20 degrees cooler.

LeBoyer's position is that the newborn's transition from the inner world to the outer world should be made as nontraumatic as possible. To best mediate this transition, LeBoyer advocates that the following conditions should be met in the delivery room:

- When the baby is born, it should be placed in a tub of water at body temperature.
- The lights used in the delivery room should be dimmed.
- Soft music and low voices should be the kinds of sounds to which the newborn is exposed.
- The umbilical cord should be cut *after* it ceases to pulsate.
- The newborn should have skin-to-skin contact on the mother's abdomen.

While LeBoyer's philosophy sounds very rational, the fact remains that many hospitals in the United States are not predisposed to set up such an environment. There are some, however, that have adopted this method. What effect delivering a baby in such a way has is strictly speculative.

ANESTHETICS IN CHILDBIRTH

Obstetrical anesthesia is used commonly in childbirth today. Anesthetics, used to prevent pain in childbirth, can be divided into two major types: general and local.

General Anesthesia

A general anesthetic affects the whole body, creating anesthesia by temporary but complete unconsciousness. General anesthetics are absorbed quickly into the bloodstream via the lungs. Among the more widely used anesthetics is sodium pentothal. The major argument against general anesthesia is that it enters the baby's circulation through the placenta. The baby then is born sleepy, not alert. Respiration is also sluggish. In rare cases newborn babies have died from the effects of anesthetics, and some mothers have become ill.

Local Anesthesia

Local anesthesia, although it acts locally, may enter the mother's bloodstream. Local anesthesia can be used three main ways:

1. *By local infiltration.* When the baby is ready to be delivered, an injection of an anesthetic into the lower part of the vagina can numb the perineum.
2. *By injection into the spinal fluid surrounding the lower spinal cord.* The needle is introduced into the lower vertebral canal. This can anesthetize the lower nerve trunks. Often called a *saddle block,* the parts of the body that would ordinarily sit on a horse's saddle are numbed.
3. *By injection into the base of the "tail" or caudal space.* Known as *caudal* anesthesia, this method of injection eliminates labor as well as birth pain. Injections are begun after labor has been well established and the cervix is partially dilated.

There is no doubt that drugs can be and have been a tremendous asset in the process of childbirth. Indeed, many women need drugs during childbirth. The complaint of some women as well as those in the medical profession is that anesthetics are sometimes used unnecessarily, therefore increasing the chances of harm to the woman or her child. Some people also believe that administering anesthetics to a woman may take away her feeling of experiencing the excitement of birth.

BIRTHPLACE ALTERNATIVES

Not all women today are content to give birth in the traditional hospital setting. As a result, there has been an increase in recent years in the number of women who have decided to opt for an alternative.

Alternative Birth Centers

Alternative birth centers are beginning to appear throughout many parts of the country. Alternative birth centers may be connected with a hospital, although some are not. The birth center is supposed to simulate the home environment. In this environment, a couple, along with their obstetrician and pediatrician, will draw up a plan that directs the staff of the birthing center. This plan will take into consideration the use of intravenous infusions, anesthetics, and the needs and preferences of the mother.

The room may consist of a double hospital bed and chairs, a living room, a dinette, and a nurse's station.

The homelike atmosphere of the birthing center is conducive to relaxation with friends, family, or siblings. During labor, the mother may walk around and have the support of those close to her. Usually, no unexpected interns or other visitors are allowed to enter unless an emergency arises. In such cases, emergency medical equipment is readily available, and the mother can be moved to the maternity area.

Home Birth

Home birth is becoming more and more popular. With proper prenatal care, screening for complications, preparation, availability of a skilled assistant, and emergency transportation, home births can be a safe venture. With the availability of midwives as well as greater acceptance by some obstetricians, this method of delivery may become more popular in the years to come. But there may be difficulty getting doctors to deliver in a home, because many hospitals would revoke the doctor's hospital privileges. Several cases are now being tested in the courts.

Among the advantages of home birth are:

- It provides a familiar surrounding.
- It places the decision-making responsibility on the couple.
- It costs much less than a hospital delivery.
- It may enable a woman to be less anxious that she would be in a hospital.
- It avoids procedures the woman considers objectionable and unnecessary.

The major drawback of home birth is the lack of emergency medical treatment should it be needed. This is the reason given by groups who support legislation to prevent home births.

THE POSTPARTUM PERIOD

The first several weeks after birth is known as the *postpartum period.* During this time, the mother may undergo many changes. The process of birth is strenuous and tiring. The mother may find that the first few days after the birth of her child, she may want to rest in her hospital bed. However, at this time she is often inundated with telephone calls and visits from friends. At times this may be annoying and distracting, particularly if she is breast-feeding. At times, the new mother may have spur-of-the-moment episodes of crying or depression, known as *postpartum blues.* On the other hand, she may find the first few days after the birth of her child to be a "high." She may be glad that her 9-month state has finally ended.

Many factors may contribute to a woman's feeling "let down" after the birth of her child. She may feel physically tired from the stresses and strains of birth, and a person who is tired can be irritable.

The newborn may also cause the mother problems in relationships with the father and siblings. The father may feel jealous because the mother is devoting a great deal of time to the newborn. The older brother or sister may feel rejected. As a result, the mother may feel torn between the baby and her family. On the other hand, the newborn can make a happy family even closer.

When the baby first returns from the hospital, it does not sleep throughout the night. As a result, the mother and father may find themselves tired from awakening several times during the course of a night. If the baby is being bottle-fed, formula may have to be prepared. If the mother is nursing, she may find the baby will have a difficult time adjusting to her breasts. These situations can put additional stress and strain on the parents.

Since the woman also experiences a sharp decline in her hormone levels after birth, she may feel tired and distressed. Therefore, it appears that postpartum changes can be due to physical as well as social factors.

BONDING

The first few minutes after birth can be very important for the child. Bonding, as we previously stated, can begin immediately after birth. The attachment and attention that a baby receives from its mother can help each adjust to the other. If the baby receives soft touches, is spoken to, and is looked at as often as possible by the mother as well as the father during the first few days of life, it will cry less and smile and laugh more (Klaus and Kennel, 1976). Newborn babies can communicate. But they need to be given attention. The future happiness of a baby begins immediately after birth.

BREAST-FEEDING

The production of milk in the mother's breasts following childbirth is known as *lactation*. As soon as the placenta is removed during childbirth, the hormone *prolactin* will stimulate the breasts to produce milk. However, the milk will not be produced until two or three days after the baby is born. In place of milk, *colostrum*, which is the yellowish fluid produced by the breasts, will suffice to nourish the baby. Colostrum is especially designed for the newborn baby. It is easier to digest because it is low in carbohydrates, and it is richer than milk in immunity factors. Since it has a slightly laxative effect, it helps the baby clear out the *meconium* (the dark green or blackish matter discharged from the baby's bowels) and readies the digestive tract for the milk to be received in a few days.

The Case for Breast-feeding

In the United States today, we see an increase in the number of women who have decided to breast-feed their newborn. Breast-feeding can last from several months to years. The advantages are numerous:

- Human milk is best. Breast milk is more adaptable to the human body. Because it is easy to digest, the baby's energy is conserved for better growth.
- Breast-feeding delays menstruation. Mothers who nurse their babies can have their periods delayed for 9 months or longer. However, this does not mean they cannot become pregnant. Nursing is not a very effective method of contraception.
- Sexual interest. Masters and Johnson (1966) have shown that nursing mothers return more rapidly to sexual interest after childbirth than non-breast-feeding mothers.
- Allergies. Mother's milk will not cause allergic reactions such as eczema or colic in a baby.
- Shrinking of the uterus. Breast-feeding aids in shrinking the uterus.
- Simplicity. Mothers who breast-feed do not have to spend time sterilizing bottles and preparing formulas—and they can save money by not buying formula.
- As an expression of sexuality. Breast-feeding provides intimate and sometimes sensuous contact for the mother. She may find the baby's sucking on the breast to be sexually arousing. Sometimes this gives the mother guilt feelings, and she may decide not to breast-feed any longer. However, arousal is a normal occurrence.
- Properties of breast milk. Breast milk is always the right temperature, has the right mixture of nutrients, contains antibodies that protect the baby from disease, and is free from bacteria.
- Defective formula. In the past, there has been at least one instance when formula was not up to standard. As a result, many infants became mysteriously ill.

> The problem materialized last year when numerous babies around the country began suffering mysterious ailments. They stopped eating, lost weight at alarming rates and developed severe blood disorders. Doctors suspected a rare kidney problem.
>
> Then doctors found the real problem: The babies were being fed a Syntex formula that was seriously deficient in chloride, a vital nutrient.
>
> The flaw in the Syntex formula arose when the company decided in 1978 to eliminate salt from its two brands of soy-based formula, Neo-Mull Soy and Cho-Free, because of concern about salt's role in causing high blood pressure.
>
> But eliminating salt also eliminated much of the chloride, an element of salt.
>
> (The Wall Street Journal, August 8, 1980)

The Case Against Breast-feeding

Some women feel that breast-feeding is not for them. These women will usually be given an injection after the birth of their child so as to dry up the milk. Some of the objections to breast-feeding are:

- Effects of substances. Some substances that a mother may take can affect her baby, since they can be passed through the milk. Among these substances are alcohol, nicotine, and other drugs. Certain foods can also cause negative effects on the baby.
- Swollen breasts. Some women may develop swollen breasts if the baby does not drink enough milk. As a result, the excess milk stored in the breasts may cause tenderness. However, the excess milk can be removed with a suction cup.
- Annoying dripping. Some women complain that their breasts drip milk. However, a woman can insert pads inside her bra or wear a nursing bra to absorb any excess.
- Not knowing how much the baby consumes. It may be difficult for a woman to tell whether the baby is drinking enough. However, the baby's weight can be monitored and diapers can be checked. Six or eight wet diapers per day is a good indication that the baby is getting enough.
- Sore nipples. In spite of prenatal care of the nipples, they can still become sore. This can usually be remedied by exposing them to air as much as possible and, if necessary, rubbing them with lanolin or cocoa butter.
- Inverted nipples. Some women have *inverted nipples,* or nipples that are held in as opposed to protruding. During lactation, pain may be present. Sometimes a suction cup will draw the nipples out. Contrary to what some believe, women with inverted nipples can breast-feed.
- The father's concern. Some fathers complain that nursing denies them the right to feed their child. They argue that if the baby were bottle-fed, they would have the opportunity to share in the feeding process.
- The mother's concern. Breast-feeding may tie the mother down, thereby preventing her from participating in certain activities, like returning to work.

ATYPICAL CONDITIONS IN PREGNANCY

Multiple Births

Multiple births, or more than one child born at a time, may occur unexpectedly. Though heredity seems to play a role, multiple births are not definitely known to be an inherited trait. Fertility drugs are also thought to be a cause. Often, a doctor can detect multiple heartbeats during pregnancy, and a sonograph can usually show if more than one fetus is in the uterus. Multiple births can be in the form of twins, triplets, and quadruplets, but multiple births of more than four are extremely rare. The Dionne quintuplets, born in 1934, were the first quintuplets to survive. However, many children born in multiple births die because of low birth weight.

There are two types of twins—identical and fraternal (Figure 6.6). *Identical twins* develop from a single fertilized egg. They possess the same chromosomes, and they are always of the same sex. They share the same placenta, but they have separate amniotic sacs as well as separate umbilical cords.

Fraternal twins develop from two separate ova that are fertilized at the same time. Fraternal twins can be of the same or of different sexes. They have separate umbilical cords, amniotic sacs, and placentas. Fraternal twins look no more alike than any brothers or sisters, because they do not share the same chromosomes. The probability of twin births is one in 80 to 90 births.

Siamese twins are twins who are born joined. This occurs when a cell mass does not separate completely. As a result, the twins may be joined at any part of the body. Not long ago Siamese twins who were born fused at the head were successfully separated in Salt Lake City.

While *triplets* can result from the fertilization of three different ova, in most cases two eggs are involved. One separates and develops into identical twins. The probability of triplets is once in 7000 to 8000 births.

Quadruplets are most often the result of two ova that separate and form two sets of identical twins. The probability of quadruplets is one in 700,000 births.

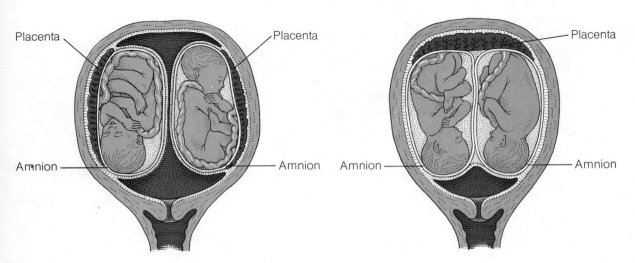

Placenta   Placenta   Placenta

Amnion   Amnion   Amnion   Amnion

FIGURE 6.6 Fraternal twins **(left)** and identical twins **(right)** in the uterus.

Miscarriages

A miscarriage, or *spontaneous abortion,* is an expulsion of the embryo or fetus before it has reached the point of development at which it can survive. This is not the same as an *induced abortion,* which is described in Chapter 7. Ten percent to 15% of all pregnancies result in spontaneous abortion, three in four occurring during the first trimester.

"Spotting," or vaginal bleeding, is the first sign that a woman may miscarry. If the signs of pregnancy disappear and the woman has cramps in the area of the pelvis, the fetus is often expelled. About half of miscarried fetuses are defective.

The reasons for miscarriages are varied. Females who conceive at an early age (under 18) are more likely to miscarry than women who are in their twenties. Women older than 35 years of age also have an unusually high incidence of miscarriage (Kiser et al., 1968). Some causes of miscarriage are illness, malnutrition, syphilis, and trauma. However, most miscarriages have no known cause.

Premature Births

When a newborn baby weighs less than 5½ pounds, it is considered a *premature* infant. By this definition, no reference is made to the duration of pregnancy because it is so difficult to determine with exactitude.

In about half of all premature births, the cause is unknown. Some of the known causes of premature delivery are *toxemia* (a disease during pregnancy characterized by high blood pressure, edema, and rapid weight gain, all frequently resulting from malnutrition), an abnormality of the uterus or cervix, and premature separation of the placenta from the uterine wall. Some of the more common conditions of the mother associated with premature births are heavy cigarette smoking, poor nutrition, and generally poor health.

Pseudocyesis

A woman who believes that she is pregnant and shows some of the signs and symptoms of pregnancy even though she is not pregnant is said to have a *false pregnancy,* or *pseudocyesis.* She may experience absence of menses, breast changes, nausea, and vomiting. Her abdomen may even swell (due to gaseous distention of the bowel). Despite medical assurance to the contrary, the patient may insist that she is pregnant. In fact, she may "go into labor" at the end of nine months. More frequently, she has a heavy period and claims to have miscarried.

Most of the women who experience pseudocyesis are emotionally unstable, childless women who have a longing for a baby (Hellman and Pritchard, 1971). These women can be treated by psychotherapy.

Ectopic Pregnancy

An *ectopic pregnancy* occurs when a fertilized ovum implants itself in any place other than in the lining of the uterus. About 96% of these implantations occur in the uterine tubes (oviducts); thus the term *tubal pregnancy*. Ectopic pregnancies can also occur in the abdominal cavity.

A tubal pregnancy is ordinarily diagnosed by the occurrence of lower abdominal pain several days or weeks after a period is missed. Vaginal bleeding may occur, which may be mistaken for a period. Since these conditions can be typical of many problems, a tubal pregnancy is difficult to diagnose.

Some embryos may spontaneously abort and be released into the abdominal cavity. In this case, if the embryo is young enough and the uterine tube has not been damaged, the embryo may disintegrate and surgery will not be required. However, if the embryo stretches the tube and ruptures it, the woman may hemorrhage and possibly die. In such instances, surgery is required.

Rh Factor

When a woman first becomes pregnant, her doctor will determine whether her blood has the Rh factor, so named because it was first discovered in the blood of rhesus monkeys. A person who has the Rh factor is said to be Rh-positive (Rh+), and a person who does not have it is said to be Rh-negative (Rh−).

If an Rh− woman is pregnant with an Rh+ fetus, a possible health problem may arise. If Rh+ blood mixes with Rh− blood, the Rh− blood will form antibodies against the Rh factor. While the blood of the fetus and the mother do not usually mix, there can be some interchange during birth. Thus, the mother's Rh− blood can build up antibodies. In a subsequent pregnancy, the woman's antibodies may enter the fetus's blood by crossing the placenta, attacking the fetus's red blood cells. The result may be a stillborn baby. There is little risk of this occurring in a *first* pregnancy. In a second pregnancy, however, through proper prenatal care and an injection of *RhoGam*, the production of these antibodies can be prevented.

Rubella

A pregnant woman should take precautions to prevent exposure to rubella (German measles), because she may expose her fetus to blindness, deafness, heart defects, and mental retardation. If a woman contracts rubella during the first month of pregnancy, there is a 50% chance her baby will be born with an abnormality. The later in pregnancy she contracts this disease, the lower the chance of a congenital malformation to the baby.

According to the March of Dimes, an organization concerned with the well-being of the newborn, 7% of all babies are born each year with some sort of birth defect. These defects can be physical or mental.

One procedure used to diagnose abnormalities in a fetus is *amniocentesis*, performed during the 14th to 16th week of pregnancy (Figure 6.7). The doctor inserts a needle through the woman's abdominal wall into the uterine cavity and withdraws a sample of amniotic fluid, which contains cells from the fetus. These cells are then analyzed, and many fetal abnormalities, such as sickle-cell trait and Down syndrome (mongolism), can be detected. Not all defects in the fetus can be diagnosed through this procedure, however.

Amniocentesis is not a routine procedure, since risks are involved. Only high-risk mothers should undergo this procedure. Women older than 35 years of age, women who have or whose partner has a parent with a chromosomal defect, women with a previous child with certain defects, and women in whose families there is a predisposition toward birth defects are considered at high risk. With some of the research today that indicates marijuana use may be suspected as a cause of birth defects, some women who use this drug are requesting amniocentesis. Although there is a relationship between cigarette smoking and its damaging effect on the fetus (i.e., a slowdown in fetal growth and lower-than-normal birth weight), amniocentesis cannot be reliable in this instance as a predictor of fetal problems due to tobacco.

If a woman is made aware that her fetus is defective, she may elect to have an abortion. Therefore, amniocentesis is performed between the 14th and 16th week of birth.

Although amniocentesis can indicate the sex of the fetus, it is not performed strictly for this purpose.

FIGURE 6.7 Amniocentesis: withdrawing a sample of amniotic fluid.

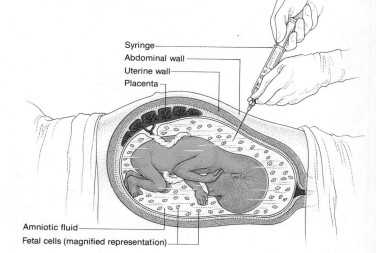

Syringe

Abdominal wall

Uterine wall

Placenta

Amniotic fluid

Fetal cells (magnified representation)

SUMMARY STATEMENTS

- *Fertilization takes place in the oviduct. The fertilized egg then grows in the uterus.*
- *Infertility problems may be caused by too few sperm or immotile sperm.*
- *A female may be infertile because of a failure to ovulate regularly or a blocked oviduct.*
- *Through artificial insemination couples who had difficulty conceiving can now increase their changes of parenthood.*
- *If a woman's period is two weeks late and she is sexually active, she may decide to be tested for pregnancy. However, a late period does not necessarily indicate pregnancy.*
- *Fetal development is divided into trimesters.*
- *Proper prenatal care is the key to having a healthy baby.*
- *During each trimester of pregnancy, the mother goes through physical and psychological changes.*
- *Pregnancy is a dual responsibility. The father needs to be a part of the experience.*
- *A healthy diet helps produce a healthy baby.*
- *Labor is divided into three stages. Stage 1 is the longest, consisting of contractions, effacement, and dilation. Stage 2 is the delivery of the newborn, and Stage 3, the expulsion of the placenta.*
- *Some babies may be in a breech or transverse position. In these cases, the baby may be turned around while in utero or delivered by a cesarean section.*
- *A cesarean section is the surgical removal of the baby through the abdomen.*
- *Among the most popular methods of childbirth is the Lamaze technique, a program in prepared childbirth.*
- *The LeBoyer technique is a method of delivery that emphasizes soft lights and sounds, submersion of the baby in warm water, and immediate skin-to-skin contact, all of which help the baby adjust to its new environment.*
- *Anesthetics are commonly used in childbirth.*
- *Today there is a tendency to use untraditional sites for childbirth.*
- *The first several weeks after birth are known as the postpartum period. During this period, the woman may undergo rapid changes in mood.*
- *Close parent-to-child contact, beginning immediately after birth, may make for a happier baby.*
- *There are advantages and disadvantages to breast-feeding.*
- *Multiple births can occur unexpectedly in 10% to 15% of all pregnancies.*
- *A premature baby is one who weighs less than 5½ pounds.*
- *Pseudocyesis is a false pregnancy. In this condition, a woman may exhibit the signs and symptoms of pregnancy.*
- *An ectopic pregnancy occurs when a fertilized ovum implants itself anywhere but in the uterus.*
- *Early in a woman's pregnancy, she will have a blood test to determine whether or not she has the Rh factor.*
- *A mother who contracts rubella in the first month of pregnancy stands a 50% chance of producing a defective child.*
- *In an amniocentesis, amniotic fluid is drawn from the amniotic sac and analyzed for genetic defects.*

SUGGESTED READINGS

Baldwin, Rakina. *Special Delivery, the Complete Guide to Informed Birth.* California: Celestial Arts, 1979.

Lamaze, Fernand. *Painless Childbirth: The Lamaze Method.* New York: Pocket Books, 1972.

La Leche League. *The Womanly Art of Breastfeeding.* Illinois: La Leche League International, 1980.

Nilsson, Lennart. *A Child Is Born.* New York: Delacorte Press, 1980.

The Boston Children's Medical Center. *Pregnancy, Birth, and the Newborn Baby.* New York: Dell Publishing Company, 1979.

CONCEPTION AND PREGNANCY

A LOOK AT YOUR LIFESTYLE

If you were to select the ideal conditions under which you could give birth, what would these conditions be? There are absolutely no restrictions on your thoughts, so feel free to fantasize. Think of such things as the site, people with whom you would wish to have contact, and any other conditions you choose to select. If you are a male, answer the question from your viewpoint.

GATHERING INFORMATION
List three advantages your selection would generate that may not occur in the birthing alternatives that exist today.

_____

_____

EVALUATING THE INFORMATION
If you were to give birth today, which option among the ones discussed in this chapter would you choose? List three reasons for your choice.

_____

_____

_____

The most important reason for my choice is _____.

I realistically believe that five years from now, the method of childbirth I select will have three major assets (Please list the assets.):

_____

_____

MAKING RESPONSIBLE DECISIONS
I believe the three most important facts to know in having a healthy pregnancy are (Please list):

_____

_____

_____

_____

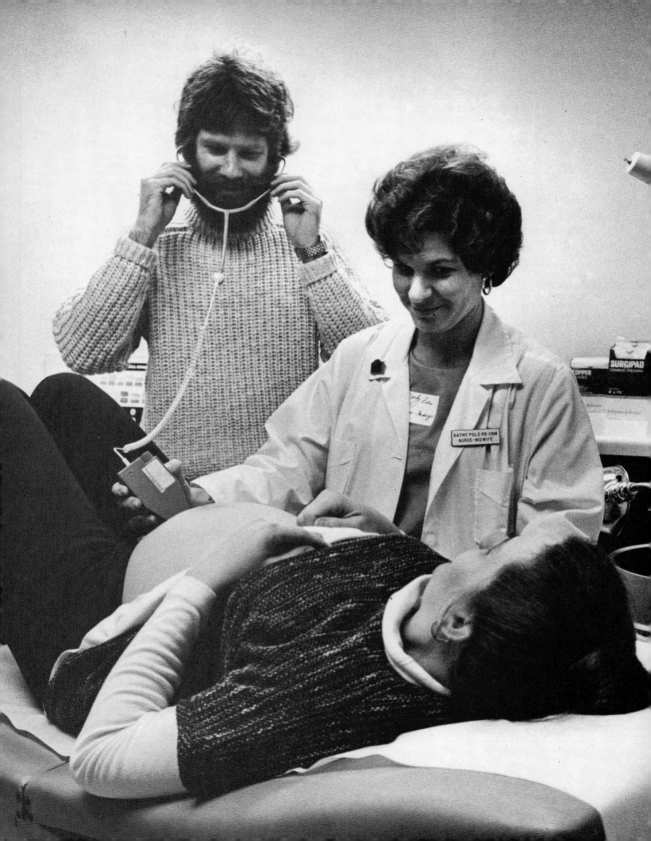

SEVEN

Birth Control, Sterilization, and Abortion

One of the most important questions that a sexually active person should ask is, "Would I be comfortable if my sexual behavior resulted in a pregnancy?" If we are to develop responsible, caring sexual attitudes, values, and behaviors, this question should be examined by both men and women individually and by men and women together.

For pregnancy to occur, several conditions must exist:

1. Semen must be deposited in a woman's vagina.
2. The semen must contain healthy sperm.
3. The sperm must find conditions in the vagina conducive to their life.
4. After being deposited, the sperm must be able to travel through the woman's uterus to the oviducts.
5. The sperm must meet a living egg in the oviduct that is ready for fertilization.
6. The fertilized egg must be able to travel to the uterus and implant itself.

177

If these conditions occur, a pregnancy will result. When normal sexual intercourse occurs, it is highly likely that without any means of contraception or birth control these conditions will be met and a pregnancy will result. Statistics have been carefully worked out to predict the probability of conception and pregnancy. These statistics are referred to as the *pregnancy rate*.

The pregnancy rate is established by the determination of how many women out of 100 would get pregnant if they participated in sexual intercourse for a year, using a particular means of birth control. The pregnancy rate with no means of contraception is 80%.

I'm shocked. Why me? I didn't think that you needed to use birth control the first time you had sex. And I only did it once!

The fact that unprotected sexual intercourse often leads to pregnancy is an issue deserving careful examination. Sexually active men and women need to examine the following questions:

- Do I want my sexual behavior to lead to a baby and parenthood?
- Does my sexual partner(s) want our sexual behavior to result in a baby and parenthood?
- Can I talk to my partner(s) about how I feel about having a baby and being a parent at this time in my life?
- If I do not want to have a baby or my partner(s) does not want to have a baby at this time, what birth control methods are available?
- How do I feel about each of these birth control methods? How does my partner(s) feel about each of these birth control methods?
- If I never want to have children or I have the number of children I want, how do I feel about sterilization? How does my partner(s) feel about sterilization? What sterilization alternatives are available?
- If I used a birth control method or sterilization and still became pregnant or got my partner pregnant, what would I do? What would my partner(s) want to do about an unwanted pregnancy?

Men and women who are responsible and caring in their sexuality are willing to examine these questions. They are willing, no matter how difficult the situation, to be open and honest about their answers.

GATHERING INFORMATION

When pregnancy is desired, there are many things to consider. These considerations are highlighted in the chapters dealing with pregnancy and parenthood.

When a pregnancy is *not* desirable, men and women need to examine the available alternatives. These alternatives fall into three categories that will be covered in this chapter:

- birth control methods
- sterilization
- abortion

Birth Control Methods

As mentioned previously, if a pregnancy is to occur, several conditions must exist. Altering these conditions makes it possible to decrease the likelihood of pregnancy. Birth control methods that involve contraception and interception may be used.

Contraception is the prevention of conception by a variety of chemical, physical, and surgical means or by abstention from intercourse during the fertile period. *Interception* is the prevention of implantation of the fertilized egg. The following birth control methods involve contraception and/or interception:

- Combination birth control pill
- Progestin-only pill (mini-pill)
- Progestin injections (the shot)
- Diethylstilbestrol (the morning-after pill)
- Intrauterine devices (IUDs)
- Condoms (rubber)
- Diaphragm
- Spermicidal preparations
- Basal body temperature method (BBT)
- Calendar method
- Mucus method
- Coitus interruptus (withdrawal)
- Douche

Sterilization

Sterilization is any procedure (usually surgical) by which an individual is made incapable of reproduction. The procedures include:

male sterilization
   vasectomy
female sterilization
   tubal ligation
     laparotomy
     colpotomy
   tubal cauterization
     laparoscopy
     culdoscopy

Abortion

An abortion is the premature expulsion of the product of conception (fertilized ovum, embryo, or nonviable fetus) from the uterus. An abortion can be therapeutic or elective. A *therapeutic abortion* is an abortion that is performed because the mother's life is in danger or because there is a possibility of fetal abnormality. An *elective abortion* is done at the request of the woman who is carrying the child but who has no compelling *medical* reasons for abortion. The different types of abortions are:

vacuum curettage (vacuum suction, vacuum aspiration, dilation and evacuation, D & E)
dilation and curettage (D & C)
induced labor or miscarriage
hysterotomy

EVALUATING THE INFORMATION

In this chapter, the following factual information is included to help you evaluate carefully each of the alternative methods or procedures identified:

1. How it works: the mechanism of action; the changes that may occur in the body
2. Instructions for effective use: directions for using the method correctly
3. Effectiveness: how this method or procedure is rated; the chances of its being successful or effective
4. Benefits: the positive results that this method will have, contraceptive or noncontraceptive
5. Side effects: the nuisance effects that may accompany this method or procedure; the risks that are assumed
6. Contraindications: a discussion of reasons for not using this method or procedure
7. Cost: an estimate of the cost for this method or procedure

In addition to the factual information that is provided in this chapter, you will want to explore your feelings, attitudes, and values about each method and procedure. Ask yourself:

- How do I feel about this method or procedure?
- Would I be comfortable with this method or procedure?
- Will this be effective for me? Will I be able to follow the instructions for effective use?
- Will this method or procedure be comfortable for me in my relationships?
- Will this be effective and comfortable for my partner(s)?
- Is this method or procedure congruent with my value system?

When evaluating each alternative, remember that it is best to base your decision on factual information, health status, and effectiveness *and* personal acceptance in accordance with your attitudes, values, and feelings.

MAKING RESPONSIBLE DECISIONS

After you have made a decision, it is important to follow through in your behavior and to be accountable. You will need to act on your decisions and to know and accept the probable consequences.

Unfortunately, many persons fail to act upon their decisions about birth control. There are a variety of reasons:

I am really angry with myself. Here it is our senior year. We both have accepted good jobs, and she turns up pregnant. We'd talked about it and even gone to the clinic for condoms and foam. But sometimes I'd forget them.

I know that I need to use something, but I'm just plain embarrassed. When I call for an appointment, I hang up when the nurse answers.

If I bring my diaphragm with me, what will he think? Maybe he'll think I sleep with everyone. I don't want him to think I'm "ready."

She should use something. It's not up to me. After all, *she* is the one who will get pregnant.

I've known our family doctor since I was a kid. How do I tell him I'm having sex? He'd probably tell me not to, and maybe he'd tell my parents.

I just hate all that mess from the foam. When it's sort of safe I don't use it. Sex seems so much better without all the fuss.

Whenever you make a decision and fail to act on it, you need to examine your reasons. In addition, you need to have enough information to make informed decisions. You are then able to accept knowingly the possible consequences. The following factual information on birth control methods, sterilization, and abortion will provide you with the knowledge you need to understand the consequences of each alternative, the cost, the risks, or the benefits.

BIRTH CONTROL METHODS

Birth control methods are designed to alter the conditions that are necessary for a conception and/or pregnancy to occur. Birth control methods involve *contraception*, prevention of conception by a variety of chemical, physical, and surgical means, and *interception*, the prevention of implantation of the fertilized egg. Some birth control methods may be purchased over the counter, while others require a prescription and routine medical care. Detailed information on a variety of birth control methods follows.

The Combination Birth Control Pill

HOW IT WORKS

The most widely used oral contraceptive in the United States is the combination birth control pill (Figure 7.1). *Combination pills* contain estrogen and progestin, a synthetic progesterone. Together they alter the natural menstrual cycle to prevent ovulation.

In the normal, unaltered menstrual cycle, estrogen levels are low during and after the menstrual flow. Low estrogen levels trigger the pituitary gland to secrete FSH, follicle-stimulating hormone. Under the influence of FSH, a single ovum and its surrounding cells develop into a mature follicle over a two-week period. Around the middle of the cycle, the mature follicle ruptures, releasing an egg from the ovary into the area of the oviduct (ovulation).

The pill alters this natural cycle. A woman takes her first pill on the fifth day after she has begun to menstruate. The pill contains estrogen and progestin. Normally, the estrogen level is low, and the pituitary will be stimulated to secrete FSH. However, when a woman takes the pill, she raises her level of estrogen. Little, if any, FSH is secreted, and the follicles, which have the potential for releasing an egg, do not mature. Progestin, a synthetic progesterone, inhibits LH, further preventing ovulation. Progestin also makes the cervical mucus very thick, so that the sperm have difficulty passing through, and alters the lining of the uterus, making it unsuitable for implantation. When a woman completes her pill pack, her hormone levels drop, and the lining of the uterus disintegrates and is shed as the menstrual flow.

FIGURE 7.1 There are many different types of pills and pill packs. The most common is the combination pill. (Photo by Joel Gordon, 1981)

INSTRUCTIONS FOR EFFECTIVE USE

Pill directions may appear complicated and confusing. Understanding the instructions for effective and safe use is a necessity.

Most physicians recommend that a woman begin taking the pill on a Sunday, making record keeping for the doctor, patient, and clinic much easier. So the woman beginning the pill will take her first pill on the first Sunday (1) after her last period has begun, (2) after an abortion, or (3) after her newborn baby is 1 month old. The pill should be taken at the same time each day. One pill is taken from the pill pack each day until the pills are gone. If she is using a 28-day pill pack, she should begin a new pack immediately. If she is using a 21-day pill pack, she should wait 1 week (till the next Sunday) and begin a new pack.

The first month that the pill is used, another method of birth control should also be used. The pill may not sufficiently alter FSH secretion the first month, and ovulation may occur.

It is important to remember to use the pill according to the prescribed directions. Sometimes, however, mistakes are made. If a pill is missed, a pill should be taken as soon as possible. The next pill should be taken at the regular time that day. Missing one pill does not usually affect the pregnancy rate; however, as an extra precaution, a backup method could be used for the remaining days in the cycle. If two pills are missed, they should be taken as soon as possible. Two more pills should be taken at the regular time that day. It is important to use a backup method for the remaining days in the cycle. Sometimes spotting may occur. If three or more pills are missed, there is a good chance that ovulation will occur. No more pills should be taken from this pill pack, and it should be discarded. A backup method of contraception should be used. A woman should begin a new pill pack on Sunday even if she is menstruating. Because of the abrupt changes in hormonal levels, a backup method should be continued during the next cycle.

Some women stop having periods while they are taking the pill. The question then becomes, "Am I pregnant?" If a woman forgets to take a pill and then misses her menstrual period, she should see a physician and have a pregnancy test. If she has not forgotten to take any of her pills but misses two consecutive periods, she should also see a physician and have a pregnancy test.

Some women take oral contraceptives to regulate their menstrual periods. They hope that, eventually, by regulating their cycles, it will be easier for them to become pregnant. When pregnancy is desired, a woman should stop taking the pill and use a backup method of birth control until she has had three consecutive and spontaneous menstrual periods.

A woman should have a complete physical each year. The examination should include a Pap smear, a pelvic exam, a weight check, a blood pressure check, a test for sexually transmitted diseases, and a breast examination.

EFFECTIVENESS

The pill is theoretically 99% to 100% effective when it is taken as directed. The actual effectiveness by users is 97% to 98%.

BENEFITS

In addition to its high effectiveness, the pill has noncontraceptive benefits that many women enjoy. Because it regulates the cycle to 28 days, the pill makes life more predictable. It reduces the flow of menstrual blood and reduces the number of days of the flow (helpful in alleviating anemia). In addition, there tends to be less cramping from menstruation, and some women experience less anxiety and tension prior to menstruation. The effectiveness rating may also reduce anxiety about an unwanted pregnancy and make sex freer and more frequent. There are also medical benefits from pill use. The pill seems to help with endometriosis, a condition in which the lining of the uterus, or the endometrium, grows outside the uterus. Endometriosis is one of the leading causes of infertility. Pill users also have a decrease in ovarian cysts and in fibrocystic breast disease.

SIDE EFFECTS

More than one third of all women who use oral contraceptives have side effects. The Food and Drug Administration requires that all pill users read a pamphlet available at the pharmacy. Written by companies manufacturing the pill and approved by the FDA, the pamphlets discuss the possible side effects of the pill.

Many of the side effects are fairly minor. They are inconvenient, and the pill user who experiences them may decide to quit taking the pill because they become a nuisance. These fairly minor effects (Hatcher, Stewart, et al., 1980) are as follows:

- Nausea. Try taking the pill with your evening meal if this is a problem; if you vomit within two hours of taking the pill, take an extra one, because your original pill may have had no effect.
- Weight gain, fluid retention, breast fullness or tenderness.
- Mild headaches. Return to the clinic or physician if severe.
- Spotting—bleeding between periods.
- Decreased menstrual flow—not always a nuisance.
- Missed periods—more common with low-dose pills.
- More problems—yeast infection, vaginal itching, or discharge.
- Depression, mood changes, fatigue. Return to the clinic or physician if severe.
- Decreased sex drive. This effect is rare; women on the pill more often experience an increased libido.
- Acne. Again, more women experience a decrease in acne problems.
- Chloasma, or "mask of pregnancy." The skin darkens on the upper lip, under the eyes, or on the forehead; sun may make it worse, and it may become permanent.

In addition to these nuisance effects, the pill has been related to circulatory disease and disorders. A study of 46,000 British women by the Royal College of General Practitioners (Population Reports, 1979, A-133) found that

- Oral contraceptive users experienced higher death rates from circulatory system disease — 25.8 per 100,000 woman years of observation — than women who had never used oral contraceptives — 5.5 per 100,000 woman years.
- Women who used oral contraceptives for five years or more faced a tenfold greater risk of death from circulatory disease than women who had never used the pill.
- These risks do not apply to women equally. Women over 35 and women who smoke one and a half to two packs of cigarettes a day face far greater hazards. The death rate for oral contraceptive users aged 35 to 44 was 42.6 per 100,000 woman years and for oral contraceptive users who smoked, 39.5 per 100,000 woman years, compared with less than 9 oral contraceptive users who did not smoke.

There is no clear evidence that oral contraceptives cause any form of cancer. There is a lower incidence of benign breast tumors in users of oral contraceptives when compared with non-users. Long-term use of oral contraceptives seems to be associated with a higher incidence of certain types of benign liver tumors (Population Reports, 1977, A-91).

Side effects from pill use may be warnings of serious trouble. The pill user should learn the five warning signs of serious trouble. These are summarized in Table 7.1. The first letter of each symptom spells out the word *ACHES*.

CONTRAINDICATIONS

Certain women seem to be especially susceptible to the possible dangerous effects of the pill. Thus, many physicians will not prescribe the pill for women with certain conditions or with certain conditions in their families. In other cases, the physician will ask a woman to consider seriously the alternatives to the pill before choosing it as a form of birth control.

Women who have circulatory problems or a history of circulatory problems in their families are not good candidates for pill use. If a woman has a tendency toward coronary heart disease, hypertension (high blood pressure), stroke, or blood clot formation, the pill is not recommended. Women who are heavy smokers should not use the pill.

The pill is also contraindicated in women who have diabetes or a strong family history of diabetes or who have damage to or impaired function of their liver, kidneys, or gallbladder. Women with fibrocystic breast disease or with cancer of the breast or reproductive system should not use the pill; neither should women who are pregnant or who have migraine headaches or undiagnosed vaginal bleeding. Pill risks seem to increase in women over 40.

TABLE 7.1 WHICH ACHES AND PAINS MAY BE WARNINGS

Five Signals	Possible Problem
Abdominal pain (severe)	Gallbladder disease, hepatic adenoma, blood clot, pancreatitis
Chest pain (severe) or shortness of breath	Blood clot in lungs or myocardial infarction (heart attack)
Headaches (severe)	Stroke or hypertension or migraine headache
Eye problems: blurred vision, flashing lights, or blindness	Stroke or hypertension or temporary vascular problem of many sites
Severe leg pain (calf or thigh)	Blood clots in legs

Source: Robert Hatcher et al. *Contraceptive Technology: 1980–1981*. New York: Irvington Publishers, 1980, p. 33.

We've talked about it, and I'd just be too scared. Her mom has diabetes, and both of her aunts have had breast cancer. I'd rather use condoms and make sure nothing happens to her.

In summary, the pill has an effect on almost every organ in the body. Potential side effects and health hazards need to be examined carefully.

COST

The estimated cost of one pill pack (a one-month supply) is around five to seven dollars. However, the cost of combined orals may vary, depending on the brand, where a woman obtains them, and her ability to pay.

The Progestin-Only Pill—The Mini-Pill

HOW IT WORKS

The *progestin-only* pill is often referred to as the "mini-pill," although other pills are also referred to as such. This pill contains small doses of progestin, a synthetic progesterone. This is the same progestin that is used in combined oral contraceptives. The progestin-only pill *may* be safer than combined orals because it contains no estrogen.

The progestin-only pill has several mechanisms of action. First, it slightly modifies the function of the hypothalamus, the pituitary gland, and the ovaries, thus altering the secretion of FSH and LH and affecting normal ovulation. Second, by altering hormone levels, the progestin-only pill affects the lining of the uterus. Implantation of the egg is difficult. Third, the egg moves more slowly in the tubes. This slow movement may result in a tubal pregnancy or in a defective egg's being implanted. Fourth, progestin causes a thick cervical mucus to develop, causing the sperm to have a difficult time entering the uterus.

INSTRUCTIONS FOR EFFECTIVE USE

One pill should be taken daily. As soon as the pill pack is completed a woman should begin a new one. She must take a pill every day to avoid an unwanted pregnancy. If she misses a pill, she should take it as soon as she remembers. She should take the next one at the regular time *and* use a backup method until her next period. When she misses two pills, she should take one as soon as she remembers and another one at the regular time. She should take two pills the following day *and* use a backup method until her next period.

During the first 3 to 6 months, a backup method should be used. A woman should never allow more than 45 days between menstrual periods without having a pregnancy test.

A woman should always chart the number of days between her menstrual periods. This charting is particularly important during the first 3 to 6 months while she is using a backup method. During this time she can establish her bleeding patterns. Some women bleed regularly every 28 to 30 days. They are probably ovulating and should use a backup method mid-cycle (days 10 to 18). Some women bleed every 25 to 45 days. They may not be ovulating every month. Since the time of ovulation cannot be predicted, a backup method should be used throughout the cycle (Hatcher et al., 1980).

EFFECTIVENESS

The progestin-only pill is theoretically 98% to 99% effective. Its use effectiveness is slightly lower, particularly during the first 3 to 6 months of use.

BENEFITS

While taking the progestin-only pill, a woman usually experiences a decreased menstrual flow and diminished menstrual cramping.

SIDE EFFECTS

The changes in the menstrual cycle may also result in very irregular menstrual periods or no menstrual periods at all (amenorrhea). Some women notice more body hair than usual. There may also be a change in the function of the liver and some water retention (edema).

CONTRAINDICATIONS

Certain women should avoid using the progestin-only pill. If there is any undiagnosed genital bleeding or a history of ectopic pregnancy, this pill should *not* be used. The other contraindications are the same as those for the combined oral contraceptive pill.

COST

The pill packs cost from five to seven dollars and last for one cycle.

Progestin Injections—The Shot

HOW IT WORKS

"The shot" is an injection of a long-acting progestin. The most commonly used injectable progestin is Depo-Provera, referred to as DMPA. A 150-mg injection of DMPA lasts for more than three months and is as effective as combined oral contraceptives. The shot has not been approved by the Food and Drug Administration for use in the United States.

It works much the same as the progestin-only pill, by inhibiting or partially inhibiting ovulation, making the uterine lining unsuitable for implantation, producing a thick cervical mucus that blocks the passage of sperm, and slowing down the speed of the egg through the oviducts.

INSTRUCTIONS FOR EFFECTIVE USE

The instructions for the progestin injection are simple. You should see your physician every 3 months for an injection. In addition, you should have a thorough gynecological examination prior to use and annually thereafter; use another means of birth control for the first 2 or 3 weeks after having the first shot; and carefully watch your weight during the first 3 months.

EFFECTIVENESS

The progestin injection is theoretically 100% effective. Its use effectiveness is slightly lower.

BENEFITS

The benefits are the same as those of the progestin-only pill: decreased blood loss during menstruation and decreased menstrual cramping. After one year of injections, most women stop menstruating. Some women like the idea of having no menstrual period.

SIDE EFFECTS

The side effects from these injections include headaches, decreased sex drive, dizziness, allergic reactions, and weight gain. Women who have a weight gain of more than 10 pounds or who have blurred vision, severe leg pains, or chest pains should call a physician for an appointment. Prolonged or heavy bleeding also needs to be checked.

CONTRAINDICATIONS

The contraindications for progestin injections are nearly the same as those for combined oral contraceptives. Of particular concern is undiagnosed genital bleeding.

COST

The cost of a progestin injection is about five to ten dollars.

Diethylstilbestrol—The "Morning-After" Pill

HOW IT WORKS

Diethylstilbestrol, or *DES,* is a synthetic estrogen that is taken orally after a woman has had unprotected intercourse in the middle of her cycle. Because DES is taken after intercourse to prevent pregnancy, it is called the "morning-after" pill. This contraceptive has been approved by the Food and Drug Administration for emergency use only.

I was walking to the dorm and all of a sudden there he was. I can't tell you how awful it was. At the hospital, they gave me one of those pills that you hear about.

INSTRUCTIONS FOR EFFECTIVE USE

When a woman has had unprotected intercourse in the middle of her cycle, she will need to go to her physician or clinic within three days to begin treatment. The sooner she begins the DES pills, the more effective they will be.

Before taking the pills she should have a gynecological exam and a breast exam.

She will take two DES pills (25 mg each) each day for five days. The pills may cause nausea, however; if vomiting occurs the dosage will not be high enough to work.

Ten DES pills should produce a level of estrogen that will stop a pregnancy. A regular menstrual period will occur. If the regular period is two weeks late, a pregnancy test is needed. DES is not always effective. The egg may already have been implanted, the pill dose may be too low, or the drug simply might not work.

EFFECTIVENESS

It is difficult to obtain clear statistics on the effectiveness of DES.

BENEFITS

The morning-after pill is for emergency use only. It should not be used as a regular method of contraception.

SIDE EFFECTS

The side effects of DES include nausea, breast tenderness, and early or late menses. When these side effects are severe, they may be serious. Remember the ACHES symptoms: abdominal pain, chest pain, headaches, eye or vision problems, and severe leg pain.

Another serious consideration in using DES is its potential relationship to cancer. Although at present there appears to be no relationship between DES use and cancer in the user, some of the daughters of users have developed cancer of the vagina in their teens or early twenties (Herbst, 1972). Males whose mothers took DES while pregnant have been found to have changes in the sperm, testes, and epididymis.

CONTRAINDICATIONS

The morning-after pill should not be taken by a woman who has a history of serious estrogen-related side effects. A pregnancy test should be taken in order for the user to avoid exposing the fetus to high levels of estrogen.

COST

The ten pills (25 mg each) of DES cost about five dollars.

Intrauterine Device (IUD)

HOW IT WORKS

The *intrauterine device* is more popularly known as the IUD. The IUD is a small plastic device (that comes in various shapes and sizes) with a nylon string attached. The IUD is inserted into the uterus. The Food and Drug Administration has approved the following IUDs: Lippes Loop, Saf-T-Coil, Copper 7, Copper T, and Progestasert (Figure 7.2).

It is not completely clear how the IUD works. Many researchers believe that it causes an inflammation that prevents the lining of the

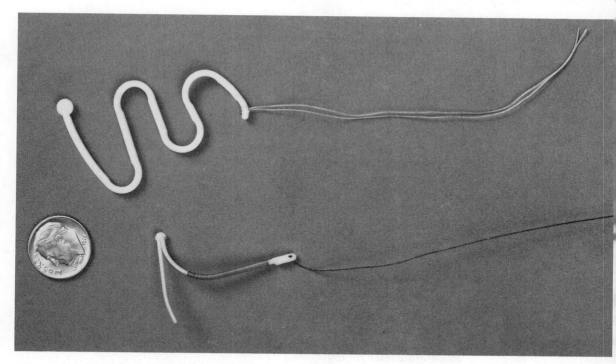

FIGURE 7.2 IUDs approved by the Food and Drug Administration. (Above) Lippes-Loop, (Below) Copper 7. (Photo courtesy of Planned Parenthood of NYC)

uterus, the endometrium, from developing, thereby hindering implantation. Or it is possible that the inflammation affects the fertilized egg. In the case of the Copper 7 or Copper T, the copper alters the functioning of the enzymes involved in implantation. The Progestasert increases the level of progesterone.

INSTRUCTIONS FOR EFFECTIVE USE

An IUD may be inserted any time during the menstrual cycle; however, many physicians feel that it is best to insert the IUD during the first few days of menstruation. There are two advantages of IUD insertion at this time. First, during menstruation the cervix dilates, making it easier for the physician to insert the IUD. Second, it is unlikely that a woman who is menstruating is pregnant. The disadvantage of IUD insertion during menstruation is the increased chance of infection.

IUD insertion may cause discomfort, pain, and cramping. Sometimes the physician will use a paracervical block of 1% lidocaine. In most cases, the insertion is done without a block.

When the IUD is inserted properly, the small nylon string can be located near the cervix. That is, a woman can check to see whether or not her IUD is in place.

After insertion, there are several guidelines for a woman to follow to have a safe, effective experience using an IUD.

The likelihood of expelling the IUD is greater during the first three months after insertion than it is thereafter. About 20% of IUD expulsions go unnoticed (Tietze, 1970), and approximately a third of pregnancies among IUD users occur after unnoticed expulsion (Mishell, 1974). Instructions for effective use include using another form of birth control with the IUD during this three-month period. The IUD may also be expelled during menstruation, when the cervix dilates. A woman should always check for the IUD after menstruation by putting her finger into the vagina and feeling for the IUD string. Whenever the string cannot be located, she should use a backup birth control method and return to her physician or clinic for a checkup. A backup method of birth control during midcycle when ovulation normally occurs will also increase the effectiveness of the IUD.

The Saf-T-Coil and Lippes Loop can be left in the uterus as a contraceptive method. The Copper 7 and Copper T must be replaced every 3 to 5 years. The copper diminishes gradually and will not be effective. The Progestasert should be replaced every year. An IUD should always be removed or replaced by a physician. It should be removed after menopause.

It is best not to remove an IUD in the middle of the cycle if a woman has had intercourse without a backup method (foam or condom) in the last 5 days. In this case, the fertilized egg could reach the uterus and implant itself after IUD removal.

Any pain or abnormal bleeding should be checked by a physician. These may be early signals of serious problems.

A heavy menstrual flow may accompany IUD use. A hematocrit (blood count) should be done with the yearly pelvic exam and Pap smear. Iron supplements may be advised.

A pregnancy test should be done when a period is missed. If there is a pregnancy, the IUD should be removed because of the danger of infection. There is about a 25% chance that removal will cause an abortion, whereas the chance is about 50% that spontaneous abortion will occur if the IUD is left in place (Hatcher et al., 1974).

EFFECTIVENESS

A woman's age, the number of pregnancies, the frequency of intercourse, and the type of IUD used will influence effectiveness. Theoretically, the IUD is 95% to 99% effective. In use effectiveness, the Food and Drug Administration says that there are fewer than six pregnancies per 100 woman years of use and fewer than 10 deaths per one million woman years of use (Population Reports, 1979, B-3). The Lippes Loop and Saf-T-Coil are about 97% effective. The Copper T and Copper 7 are also about 97% effective for the first three months. Their rate of effectiveness increases thereafter. The same can be said about the Progestasert.

BENEFITS

The IUD does not interrupt sexual activity and is very simple to use. There are no noncontraceptive benefits.

> I could never remember to take my pills. My diaphragm was always in its plastic container when I needed it. The IUD is just right for me. A lot of freedom and no hassle.

SIDE EFFECTS

Ten to twenty percent of women who have an IUD experience cramping, irregular bleeding, abdominal pain, and/or increased menstrual flow. These side effects are most prevalent right after the IUD is inserted. They are the major reasons women give for having the IUD removed.

Severe pain or an abnormal discharge may be a warning that the IUD has been expelled or that the uterus has been torn or perforated. A perforated uterus is very dangerous; thus, a woman who has these side effects should return to her physician or clinic.

An additional problem related to IUD use is the severity of any pelvic infection. Pelvic inflammatory disease, known as PID, is especially dangerous in women who have an IUD. A physician will remove the IUD while treating PID and will wait three months to insert another one. Because of the risk of PID, women who have several sex partners should probably not use an IUD.

The chances of a tubal pregnancy are increased with IUD use. Because of the risk of severe infection if one of the uterine tubes ruptures, a woman should see her physician whenever she misses her period. An ectopic pregnancy should always be suspected when a woman complains of severe pain.

To this date, the IUD has not been found to cause cancer.

CONTRAINDICATIONS

The IUD should not be used by women with the following conditions: pelvic inflammatory disease, sexually transmissible disease, pregnancy, history of ectopic pregnancy, a small uterus, fibroid growths in uterus, endometriosis, uterine deformities, an abnormal Pap smear, menstrual difficulties—heavy flow, cramps, intermenstrual bleeding, spotting—anemic problems, or problems requiring anticoagulant drugs.

COST

The IUD itself costs about five to eight dollars; however, the real cost is the charge for insertion, which varies between 25 and 50 dollars.

The Condom

HOW IT WORKS

A *condom* (also called a rubber, prophylactic, or safe) is a thin sheath that is placed over the penis to collect the man's semen so that it does not enter the vagina (Figure 7.3).

INSTRUCTIONS FOR EFFECTIVE USE

For the condom to be effective, the user must pay careful attention to instructions for use. The condom comes rolled up in a little packet. The man or his partner unrolls the condom on the penis. In doing so, there must be some room left at the tip of the condom to collect the semen. If not, the condom may tear during intercourse.

When a man becomes sexually aroused, his glands become active. The Cowper's (bulbourethral) glands begin to secrete fluid that will cleanse the urethra. There may be some sperm in the urethral canal. This small secretion may contain sperm. For the condom to be effective, it should be placed on the penis prior to penetration. Even this small secretion may impregnate the female.

The condom's effectiveness is increased considerably when it is used with foam. For the foam to be effective, it should be inserted into the vagina not more than 30 minutes before sexual intercourse.

The condom should not be removed until the penis is removed from the vagina. It is best to withdraw the penis soon after intercourse, before erection is lost, to avoid the loss of semen from the condom into the vagina. When withdrawing the penis, the man should hold the rim of the condom at the base of the penis so that it does not slip off. Additional contraceptive foam or jelly should be used if the condom slips off or is torn during intercourse.

A condom should be purchased at the drugstore to guarantee its quality. The quality of mail-order condoms cannot always be guaranteed. After

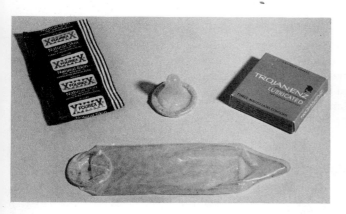

FIGURE 7.3 The condom should not be removed until the penis has been withdrawn from the vagina. (Photo by Russ Kinne)

purchase, a condom should not be kept more than two years. Old condoms may have undergone some deterioration and may tear during intercourse. Vaseline may also cause deterioration of the condom. K-Y jelly can be used for extra lubrication. Condoms should be stored in a cool place, since heat may also affect their quality (they should never be stored in a wallet). Most condoms can be worn only once safely.

EFFECTIVENESS

The condom is theoretically 97% effective when used with the preceding instructions. The effectiveness of the condom when not used carefully drops to 80% to 85%.

BENEFITS

The condom has other than contraceptive benefits. Because it provides a mechanical barrier, it keeps the male and female secretions separate and thus helps to prevent the spread of sexually transmissible diseases among the sexual partners. The reduction of various infections because of this mechanical barrier is also related to a lower incidence of cancer of the cervix in women whose partners use condoms.

> I know that a lot of guys don't like rubbers, but they make me feel safer. I like to have sex with different girls. I don't want to get anything.

The condom may also be helpful in treating males who ejaculate prematurely. There is less friction on the sensitive glans of the penis, and so the male wearing a condom may have more control and thus be able to delay his ejaculation.

Some women produce antibodies in response to a man's sperm, making conception difficult. The condom may help avoid this type of infertility problem. The condom is worn each time intercourse takes place for a half a year. When a pregnancy is desired, no condom is used during the fertile period.

One of the most beneficial uses of the condom is as a backup method. A couple can keep condoms on hand for the convenience of using them when other contraceptive methods are not available—when, for example, the woman forgets her pills for two or more days, a diaphragm has been torn, an IUD has been expelled.

SIDE EFFECTS

Rarely will there be side effects accompanying the use of the condom. There is relatively little incidence of an allergic reaction to the condom itself. The side effects are almost entirely psychological. Some men do not like to wear a condom because they feel it interferes with sensitivity. Some couples feel that stopping to put the condom on the penis interferes with the sex act, but other couples make it part of sex play.

CONTRAINDICATIONS

The condom is contraindicated if the psychological reaction of the male is severe enough to interfere with his erection.

COST

In summary, the condom is a safe, convenient, and inexpensive form of birth control. A condom can be purchased in many colors and patterns for about a dollar.

The Diaphragm

HOW IT WORKS

The *diaphragm* is a dome-shaped circular cup made of thin rubber with a flexible rubber-covered metal rim that is inserted into the vagina. When inserted properly, it fits snugly over the cervix and provides a mechanical barrier, preventing the semen from entering the uterus and the sperm from fertilizing the egg (Figure 7.4).

The diaphragm should always be used with a spermicidal cream or jelly. The spermicide is placed inside the dome of the diaphragm prior to insertion. A snugly fitting diaphragm will keep this spermicide in contact with the surface of the cervix. The spermicide provides a chemical protection that kills any sperm that come in contact with the cervix.

INSTRUCTIONS FOR EFFECTIVE USE

For the diaphragm to be as effective as possible, the woman must be certain that it is working both mechanically and chemically. Several instructions should be kept in mind.

The diaphragm should always be fitted by a physician or other trained professionals. Sample diaphragms are made available from many companies for this purpose. The doctor tries out many sizes until a diaphragm of the correct size is found.

The most effective diaphragm is the one with the largest rim that is still comfortable. When the rim is too large, a woman may experience discomfort. When the rim of the diaphragm is too small, it may not cover the cervix when the vagina enlarges during sexual arousal. After childbirth, an abortion, or a weight gain or loss of 10 pounds or more, the diaphragm should be rechecked for size.

A properly fitting diaphragm must also be inserted correctly. The diaphragm can be inserted while you are standing, sitting, or lying down.

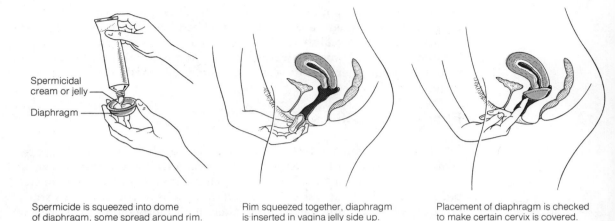

Spermicidal cream or jelly

Diaphragm

Spermicide is squeezed into dome of diaphragm, some spread around rim.

Rim squeezed together, diaphragm is inserted in vagina jelly side up.

Placement of diaphragm is checked to make certain cervix is covered.

FIGURE 7.4 A properly inserted diaphragm provides a mechanical barrier to sperm.

Hold the dome down and press on the rim to fold the diaphragm. Spread the lips of the vagina and insert the diaphragm into the vaginal canal. Push the diaphragm along the back wall of the vagina and secure the front behind the pubic bone. When inserted properly, the diaphragm cannot be felt. Run your finger along the rim of the diaphragm to see whether the cervix is covered. If you have any doubts, return to your physician to see whether you are correctly inserting the diaphragm.

The diaphragm must always be used with spermicidal cream or jelly. About one tablespoon of the spermicide is placed in the dome. Some of this is spread around the rim. This spermicide is effective for about six hours. Thus, the diaphragm with spermicide can be inserted two hours before intercourse. When intercourse takes place after this two-hour limit, a plastic applicator can be used to insert more spermicide. Two applicators of spermicide should be used. The diaphragm should not be moved or dislodged in any way. Also, if intercourse takes place more than once, two new applicators full of spermicide should be inserted. Some people believe that this much spermicide is messy, and they prefer to use a condom with the diaphragm for repeated intercourse.

The diaphragm should not be removed for 6 to 8 hours after intercourse. The sperm are still alive, and the contraceptive action of the spermicide is still needed. Also, there should be no douching during this 6- to 8-hour time period. When removing the diaphragm, hook your index finger behind the front rim and pull down and out.

The diaphragm needs to be cared for properly. It should be removed once every 24 hours, washed with warm soap and water, rinsed thoroughly, and dried with a soft towel. After it is dry, it can be dusted with cornstarch but not with perfumed powder or talc, because they damage the rubber and may irritate the cervix. While cleaning the diaphragm, check it for tears by visual examination and by running warm water in the dome. The diaphragm should be stored in its plastic container and kept away from heat.

The diaphragm must be used every time you have intercourse. Because the diaphragm user must "plan ahead," an unwanted pregnancy is most likely due to failure to plan for intercourse. The effectiveness rating for diaphragm use was established by women who used the diaphragm throughout the menstrual cycle and who used spermicidal creams or jellies.

EFFECTIVENESS

The diaphragm can be 97% to 98% effective when used with the preceding directions. In a 1976 study of 2175 women followed for two years at the Sanger Bureau in New York, an actual failure rate of two pregnancies per 100 users per year was documented. Most of the women in this study were under 30 and not married. It is likely their motivation not to become pregnant was a factor in their following the instructions for safe use closely. The effectiveness of the diaphragm is dependent on the user's being committed to its proper use. Theoretically, the diaphragm is 97% effective; in actual use, however, its effectiveness may drop to 75% to 80%.

BENEFITS

The diaphragm plus spermicidal jelly or cream has some other-than-contraceptive benefits. It is believed to afford *some* protection against sexually transmissible diseases. In addition, the diaphragm provides a mechanical barrier between the uterus and the vagina during menstruation. Some people find preventing the escape of blood from the uterus into the vagina during intercourse desirable.

SIDE EFFECTS

The side effects experienced with the use of the diaphragm and spermicidal jelly or cream usually have to do with the individual user's habits. A foul-smelling vaginal discharge may occur if the diaphragm is left inside the vagina for more than 24 hours or if the diaphragm is not washed with warm soapy water between the times that it is used. If the diaphragm rim is too large, cramping, pain or vaginal ulcerations may develop. When perfumed powder or talc is dusted on the diaphragm, the cervix may become irritated. Some spermicidal creams and jellies also may irritate the vagina and cervix. This side effect may be avoided by changing brands.

CONTRAINDICATIONS

As mentioned previously, many of the problems related to diaphragm and spermicidal jelly or cream usage can be alleviated or avoided by a change of brand or habit. However, in some cases the diaphragm and spermicidal jelly or cream may be contraindicated. Some women are allergic to the rubber from which the diaphragm is made. In this case, the woman might try the Ramses gum diaphragm before giving up on this method of birth control.

Other women or their partners are allergic to spermicide. If after switching brands there appears to be little or no relief from irritation or itching, the diaphragm should not be used.

The diaphragm should be avoided if a woman cannot achieve satisfactory fitting. An uncomfortable diaphragm may produce pain and detract from satisfactory sex. A large diaphragm may put pressure on the bladder and result in reoccurring urinary tract infections.

Most important, a diaphragm is contraindicated when a woman or her partner cannot insert it properly or when the couple will not use it regularly.

COST

The total cost of this method of contraception includes the visit for the fitting, the cost of the diaphragm, and the cost of the spermicidal cream or jelly. The visit to the doctor varies, averaging 20 to 40 dollars. Sometimes this cost includes the diaphragm. A diaphragm purchased at a pharmacy or clinic will usually cost about eight dollars. A 3- to 4-ounce tube of spermicide containing about 10 applications costs about four dollars. Thus, part of the cost—the spermicide—is dependent on the frequency of intercourse. The remaining cost is related to conscientious care of the diaphragm. A diaphragm should last about two years. A woman needs to see her physician annually and after the birth of a child to have her diaphragm and its fit checked.

Spermicidal Preparations

HOW THEY WORK

A *spermicidal preparation* is a foam, cream, jelly, or suppository containing a chemical that is deposited in the vagina near the cervix to immobilize or kill sperm. The cream or jelly should always be used with a diaphragm. A new suppository has recently gained attention and will be discussed separately.

FOAM

Spermicidal foam is purchased in a container and is used with an applicator. The foam is inserted into the vagina near the cervix. During intercourse, it is spread around, blocks the cervix, and becomes a mechanical barrier to sperm (Figure 7.5). The spermicidal agent in foam is a chemical that immobilizes or kills sperm.

INSTRUCTIONS FOR EFFECTIVE USE The mechanical and chemical contraceptive benefits of foam depend on the user's following directions carefully.

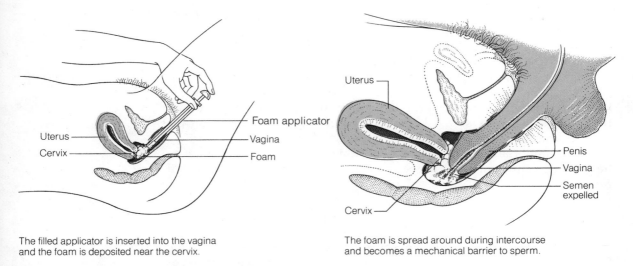

The filled applicator is inserted into the vagina and the foam is deposited near the cervix.

The foam is spread around during intercourse and becomes a mechanical barrier to sperm.

FIGURE 7.5 Spermicidal foam is inserted into the vagina near the cervix.

For foam to be effective as a mechanical barrier, it must be inserted at least 3 to 4 inches into the vagina. During sexual intercourse, the foam must be in contact with the cervix.

There must be sufficient foam, and it must be used correctly to function as a spermicide. Prior to using spermicidal foam, the bottle should be shaken vigorously to mix the chemicals so that they will act properly. The instructions should be read carefully. Some brands recommend inserting one applicator of foam, while others recommend two applicators. The foam will be effective only when used no more than 30 minutes prior to intercourse.

It is important to use another applicator (or two with some brands) of foam each time intercourse takes place.

The foam should be left undisturbed for eight hours after intercourse. Douching (rinsing the vagina with water) destroys its chemical effectiveness.

EFFECTIVENESS Studies report a range of effectiveness for spermicidal foam from 71% to 98%. An effectiveness rating of 78% appears most frequently.

BENEFITS Spermicidal foam decreases the transmission of gonorrhea and trichomoniasis. It may also lubricate the vagina, thus serving a dual purpose.

One of the main benefits of foam is its use as a backup method. Because it is readily available, a couple can use foam when first taking the pill or when stopping the pill; for repeated intercourse with the diaphragm; midcycle and during the first three months of IUD use; when using condoms.

> When Mom found out that we were having sex, she gave me that good old lecture I knew was coming. Then we talked about our relationship and my feelings about him. She wants me to be sure of what I'm doing. We talked about foam. She said it was good to use it when the other things weren't handy.

SIDE EFFECTS   There are seldom any side effects from using spermicidal foam. Occasionally one of the partners is allergic to the foam, and it will irritate the penis or the vagina. This problem can usually be solved by switching brands.

Some couples think that spermicidal foam is a nuisance. The foam may have an unpleasant taste for couples who have oral sex. In this case, use it after oral–genital contact. Some women feel that foam is messy, since douching is not allowed for 8 hours. A tampon might be used to absorb the moisture during this time.

CONTRAINDICATIONS   The use of spermicidal foam is contraindicated when either the male or female is allergic and experiences irritation to the cervix, vagina, or penis.

COST   Foam costs about three to four dollars for twenty applications. It can be purchased without a prescription.

SUPPOSITORIES

In 1977, a new spermicidal preparation, Encare or Encare Oval, was introduced in the United States. Encare is a spermicidal suppository. Encare is deposited high in the vagina at least ten minutes prior to intercourse. It effervesces, forming a thick mechanical barrier. It contains a strong spermicidal chemical. These mechanical and chemical effects last for an hour. A new suppository is needed after that time and when intercourse occurs more than once. After using Encare and having intercourse, a woman should not douche for 6 to 8 hours. The distributors of Encare claim that it is 99% effective (Salomon, 1977; Brehm, 1975), but many people question the company's authenticity in reporting such data. Two side effects noted are incomplete effervescence with less effective barrier and allergic irritation to the mucous lining.

Basal Body Temperature

HOW IT WORKS

The *basal body temperature (BBT)* method of birth control is based on the slight rise (0.5 to 1.0°F) in temperature that can be recorded 24 to 72 hours after ovulation has begun. This slight rise in temperature is caused by the secretion of the hormone progesterone.

INSTRUCTIONS FOR EFFECTIVE USE

A woman will need to follow instructions carefully to use the BBT method. She should discuss these instructions with a trained professional prior to its use.

The basal body temperature is the lowest temperature of a healthy woman during her waking hours. To obtain this temperature, a basal body thermometer is needed. It is marked in smaller intervals than those of the usual thermometer for accuracy in reading. It can be used orally or rectally, but when using this method the temperature should always be taken the same way. A woman takes her BBT in the morning after 6 to 8 hours of sleep and before rising, having sex or a snack, smoking a cigarette, or going to the bathroom. She waits 5 minutes to get an accurate reading. Then she records her BBT on a special BBT chart. She begins each new chart on Day 1, the day menstruation begins. By recording her BBT, she will notice a slight rise of .5 to 1.0°F or .3 to .5°C in the middle of the month (Population Reports, 1974, I-5). This is a sign that ovulation is occurring. When the BBT has been elevated for three consecutive mornings, it is safe to resume sexual intercourse until menstruation begins.

Some couples "risk" sexual intercourse at the beginning of the cycle (during menstruation) because they feel that conception is unlikely. The effectiveness of BBT diminishes when this happens. For effective use of BBT, a backup method of birth control should be used from Day 1 through three consecutive elevations of the BBT, or the couple should abstain from sexual intercourse.

A backup method should also be used when a woman has an elevation in her BBT because she is ill and has a fever, has not had much sleep, experiences stress in daily living, or uses an electric blanket. Also, a woman may experience an unexplained fluctuation in her BBT. During periods of fluctuation, the BBT is an unreliable means of predicting ovulation.

The basal body temperature method can be combined with the calendar method or with the mucus method for increased effectiveness. The BBT predicts the postovulatory (after ovulation) safe period, and the calendar method predicts the preovulatory (before ovulation) safe period.

EFFECTIVENESS

The effectiveness of the BBT method varies considerably, depending on a number of factors. It is probably somewhere between 65% and 85% effective, depending on the regularity of a woman's cycle and her ability to use the method according to the directions.

BENEFITS

The BBT method helps a woman with her fertility awareness. By keeping her BBT charts and sharing them with her physician, she has valuable information for the time when she desires a pregnancy. BBT can also be combined with other methods of birth control.

SIDE EFFECTS

When practiced solely as a means of birth control, the BBT method relies on abstinence which may be frustrating for about half the month.

CONTRAINDICATIONS

The BBT method relies on a woman's cycles being regular. It is contraindicated for women with irregular menstrual periods: young women, women who have just had a baby, women beginning menopause, women who have just had an abortion.

COST

A basal body temperature kit will cost approximately three to five dollars.

Calendar Method

HOW IT WORKS

The *calendar method* is based on predicting the time of ovulation by keeping a record, or calendar, of the number of days in each menstrual cycle for at least a year. The length of a menstrual cycle is the number of days between the beginning of one menstrual flow (Day 1) and the beginning of the next menstrual flow (Day 1). This record of the length of cycles is used to predict the time of ovulation and to estimate the days on which it is safe to have intercourse. These calculations are based on three assumptions: (1) ovulation occurs midcycle plus or minus two days, (2) sperm are able to fertilize the egg for 48 to 72 hours, and (3) the egg lives for about 24 hours. During the unsafe days, the fertile period, a woman abstains from intercourse or uses another method of birth control.

INSTRUCTIONS FOR EFFECTIVE USE

When a woman uses the calendar method, she must follow the directions for predicting the fertile period carefully. She must find the cycle with the longest number of days between menstrual flows and the cycle with the shortest number of days.

A woman should keep a record of her menstrual periods for one calendar year. She should record the number of days in each menstrual cycle, the number of days between the beginning of Day 1 of one menstrual cycle and the beginning of Day 1 of the next menstrual cycle. Let's suppose that a woman kept a record of the length of her cycles for one year and they turned out to be: 25, 24, 31, 24, 26, 27, 30, 28, 25, 26, 24, 26. With this example, the longest cycle was 31 days and her shortest cycle was 24 days.

The formula for using the calendar method to predict the fertile period is as follows:

Number of days in shortest cycle −18 = first fertile day

Number of days in the longest cycle −11 = last fertile day

Using our example, we would predict the fertile period to be

24 − 18 = 6 (first fertile day)

31 − 11 = 20 (last fertile day)

Her unsafe time for intercourse is from Day 6 after she begins menstruation until Day 20.

An easy way to calculate the first and last fertile days is to use Table 7.2. The important thing to remember when using the calendar method is that during the fertile period a woman should abstain from intercourse or use another method of birth control.

EFFECTIVENESS

The rate of effectiveness for the calendar method is difficult to predict. Theoretically it is 85% effective; however, it requires abstinence for several days during the cycle. Many couples do not follow the instructions and take risks or combine this method with others. Also, many women have irregular menses. The actual rate of effectiveness is closer to 65%.

BENEFITS

The calendar method may be helpful in predicting the fertile period when pregnancy is desirable. It may also be used with other methods.

SIDE EFFECTS

Unfortunately, strict adherence to the calendar method for a woman with a 28-day cycle means 8 days of abstinence midcycle. Women with longer cycles will need to abstain longer. Thus, the calendar method may be frustrating.

He says we'll use rhythm. Then when those couple of weeks roll around, he complains. I tell him that I probably won't get pregnant tonight. We keep on gambling. Sooner or later I'm going to be pregnant.

TABLE 7.2 HOW TO CALCULATE THE INTERVAL OF FERTILITY

If Your Shortest Cycle Has Been (No. Days)	Your First Fertile (Unsafe) Day Is	If Your Longest Cycle Has Been (No. Days)	Your Last Fertile (Unsafe) Day Is
21*	3rd day	21	10th day
22	4th	22	11th
23	5th	23	12th
24	6th	24	13th
25	7th	25	14th
26	8th	26	15th
27	9th	27	16th
28	10th	28	17th
29	11th	29	18th
30	12th	30	19th
31	13th	31	20th
32	14th	32	21st
33	15th	33	22nd
34	16th	34	23rd
35	17th	35	24th

*Day 1 = first day of menstrual bleeding.

Source: Robert A. Hatcher et al. *Contraceptive Technology: 1980-1981*. New York: Irvington Publishers, 1980, p. 103.

CONTRAINDICATIONS

The calendar method is not recommended for women with irregular menstrual cycles.

COST

There is no cost.

Mucus Method

HOW IT WORKS

In 1974, Drs. Evelyn and John Billings developed a method of birth control that was based on the changes in the mucus secretions that occur just before ovulation. The *mucus method* requires a woman to chart these changes in mucus.

A few days after menstruation begins, the vagina will appear to be dry. During this time, sexual intercourse is relatively safe. This period is followed by a mucous discharge that is white and cloudy. As midcycle nears, the amount of mucus increases. The mucus becomes clearer. There are one or two peak days when the mucus will look like raw egg white. On these peak days, the mucus is clear, slippery, and stringy and the vagina feels wet. Ovulation usually occurs within 24 hours of the last peak day.

Four days after ovulation, the mucus will appear cloudy and white. To avoid an unwanted pregnancy, a woman should abstain from sexual intercourse from the first day of the mucous discharge until 4 days after the last peak day.

INSTRUCTIONS FOR EFFECTIVE USE

A woman should not rely on the mucus method without first consulting a trained professional who can give her detailed instructions.

She should record observations on a special chart each day. Every time she uses the bathroom, she should put her finger into her vagina, feel for wetness, and collect mucus on her finger. She should observe the mucus carefully. Is the mucus white or cloudy? Is the mucus clear? Is the mucus slippery or wet? Is the mucus stringy? She should record these observations on her chart and take the chart to her physician or clinic to discuss it in more detail.

For the first months that she records these observations, it may be a good idea to abstain from sexual intercourse. It is possible to confuse spermicides, vaginal infections, semen, foam, or lubrication from sexual arousal with true mucus secretions. After douching, a woman will be unable to observe normal mucus secretion. The changes (and differences) are subtle and not always easy to detect.

EFFECTIVENESS

The mucus method alone and the mucus method combined with the basal body temperature method are 78% to 80% effective.

BENEFITS

The mucus method may be combined with the basal body temperature and calendar methods to predict the fertile period when pregnancy is desired.

SIDE EFFECTS

Abstinence during mucus secretion may be frustrating.

CONTRAINDICATIONS

Women who are unable to obtain accurate observations of the mucus secretion should not use this method.

COST

Many clinics and physicians will give their patients a chart and a mucus spoon to facilitate observation.

Coitus Interruptus or Withdrawal

HOW IT WORKS

Coitus interruptus, or withdrawal, really means interrupting coitus or intercourse. This form of birth contraception relies on the male removing his penis before ejaculation.

INSTRUCTIONS FOR EFFECTIVE USE

For coitus interruptus to be considered a contraceptive, ejaculation must occur away from the vagina and the external female genitalia. This requires "expert" timing on the male's part.

> They say it's not really effective, but I've been lucky so far. When I feel it coming, I pull out fast. I've had some close calls.

There is still a chance of pregnancy. When a male becomes sexually excited, his penis becomes erect and he secretes a small amount of lubricating fluid from Cowper's (bulbourethral) glands. There may be sperm in the male ducts at this time, especially when intercourse takes place more than one time. So, although the male withdraws, or pulls out, before ejaculation, he may already have deposited sperm in the vagina. He may also ejaculate on the vulva, and some sperm may get into the vagina.

EFFECTIVENESS

If a couple used withdrawal or coitus interruptus every time they had intercourse, it would be about 85% effective. However, most couples who rely on this method do not use it all the time, and its actual rate of effectiveness is 75%.

BENEFITS

There are no noncontraceptive benefits.

SIDE EFFECTS

There are also no medical side effects. However, the male or female or both may experience dissatisfaction with the method. As a technique, withdrawal relies heavily on the male's waiting for signs of ejaculation. Some men feel that they are forced then to focus on performance rather than on excitement. Some women feel that withdrawal shortens the physical contact and intimacy needed for sexual fulfillment.

CONTRAINDICATIONS

Men who experience premature ejaculation (lack of ejaculatory control) should not use coitus interruptus as a birth control method.

COST

There is no cost.

The Douche

HOW IT WORKS

The *douche* is used as a contraceptive method when the woman rinses out her vagina with water or another substance immediately following intercourse in an attempt to rinse out the sperm.

INSTRUCTIONS FOR EFFECTIVE USE

Sperm, however, can be found in the cervical opening as soon as 90 seconds after intercourse. It is highly unlikely that a woman would be able to douche that quickly. The douche may actually help the sperm move into the uterus and increase the likelihood of pregnancy.

EFFECTIVENESS

The douche is about 60% effective and should not be relied upon by those attempting to prevent pregnancy.

BENEFITS

Some women like to douche or "rinse themselves out" after intercourse. They feel fresher or cleaner. However, it should be remembered that a woman using a diaphragm should not douche for at least 6 to 8 hours following intercourse.

SIDE EFFECTS

Some women have read that acidic liquids such as Coca-Cola are effective in immobilizing or killing sperm. Although it is true that acidic liquids may immobilize sperm, it must be remembered that these same liquids may irritate the vagina and cervix.

CONTRAINDICATIONS

Too frequent douching can disrupt vaginal flora.

COST

Other than the cost of a douche bag and douching preparations, there is no cost.

STERILIZATION

Sterilization is any procedure by which an individual is made incapable of reproduction. The federal government requires informed consent of patients prior to the procedure. To meet the guidelines or regulations of informed consent, the patient must be informed of the following (Hatcher et al., 1980):

1. *Benefits:* permanent; effective; repeated decisions or costs unnecessary.
2. *Risks:* surgery has attendant morbidity and mortality; expensive in short run; occasional future pregnancy (that is, not 100% effective).
3. *Alternatives:* all options of reversible contraception and explanation of the possibility of sterilization of the partner.
4. *Inquiries:* patient should be encouraged to ask questions; myths and misinformation should be cleared up.
5. *Decision to change:* patient should always feel he/she can freely decide not to undergo sterilization if he/she wishes — without experiencing clinician's wrath or having the decision affect her/his life in other ways (e.g., welfare benefits).
6. *Explanation:* the entire procedure and its possible side effects should be explained in detail. Clearly emphasize the permanency of the procedure, along with accurate estimates of chances of reversal. Explain the psychological and/or physiological effect of hormones, weight, menses, and sexual response. In addition, it is important that the patient be aware of the costs of the procedure and where the procedure can be performed.
7. *Documentation:* written instructions; written risks; and a written, signed and witnessed consent are important parts of the informed consent process.

Male Sterilization—Vasectomy

HOW IT WORKS

Male sterilization is accomplished by a simple surgical procedure called a *vasectomy* (Figure 7.6). This procedure or surgery can be done in a physician's office. The physician will inject a solution of 1% lidocaine, a local anesthetic, into the scrotum near the vas deferens to numb the area.

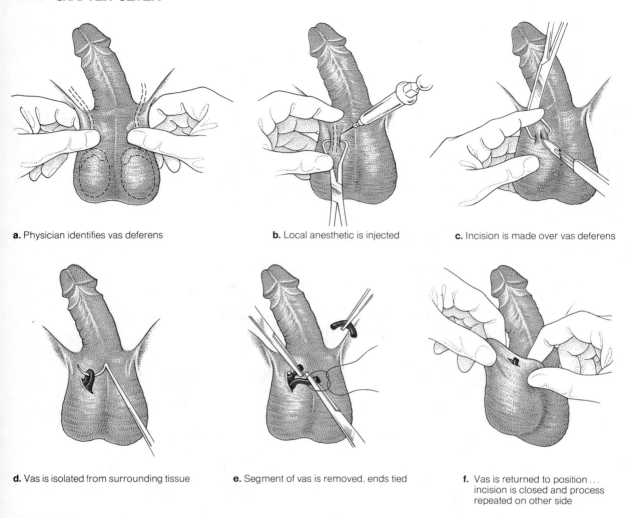

a. Physician identifies vas deferens

b. Local anesthetic is injected

c. Incision is made over vas deferens

d. Vas is isolated from surrounding tissue

e. Segment of vas is removed, ends tied

f. Vas is returned to position . . . incision is closed and process repeated on other side

FIGURE 7.6   Male sterilization by vasectomy.

Then he will make an incision in the scrotum, locate the vasa deferentia, and cut, tie, and coagulate them. The procedure lasts about twenty minutes.

After the procedure, the male is examined to be certain that there are no complications. He can leave shortly, but he should not drive home himself. To aid the healing process, he should keep an ice pack on the scrotum for several hours (4 to 5) and wear a scrotal support for a few days. He should not bathe for a couple of days while the stitches heal. They will dissolve and do not need to be removed.

In 2 to 3 days, a man can participate in his daily routine. It is best to avoid strenuous exercise and intercourse for a week.

INSTRUCTIONS FOR EFFECTIVE USE

In one out of a thousand cases, the vas deferens will rejoin. For this reason and because some sperm may have been further up the vas deferens when the vasectomy was done, it is important to have follow-up sperm counts to be certain that there are no sperm in the ejaculate. The first sperm count is taken two months after the vasectomy. The second sperm count should be taken the third month after the vasectomy. If both counts are negative, the vasectomy was probably successful. To avoid an unwanted pregnancy, a backup method should be used during this three-month period.

EFFECTIVENESS

Vasectomy is theoretically 100% effective. The failure rate is 0.15. Failure may occur because (1) the vasa deferentia rejoin after surgery, (2) the surgery was done incorrectly, or (3) sperm were present and no backup method was used for the first three months and two negative sperm counts after the procedure.

BENEFITS

The main benefit of a vasectomy is the permanence. There is no worry about contraception. Some men collect sperm and have them stored in a sperm bank before having a vasectomy.

SIDE EFFECTS

Few men have side effects from this procedure. A recent study at the Boston University Medical Center disputed earlier reports that vasectomies may cause heart disease or other serious health dangers for the 250,000 American men who undergo the simple sterilization procedure each year. (Jick, JAMA, 1981.) The most likely physical effects would be excessive bleeding, blood clots, and/or infection. Some men develop antibodies to their sperm after a vasectomy.

Psychological effects following a vasectomy are rare. The chances of psychological effects are diminished by the regulations of informed consent, which help to screen those men who might not be certain how they feel about permanent sterility.

CONTRAINDICATIONS

Men who are not certain should not have the vasectomy procedure.

COST

The cost of a vasectomy is approximately 150 dollars.

Female Sterilization—Tubal Ligation and Cauterization

HOW IT WORKS

There are several procedures used to surgically sterilize a woman. These procedures all involve cutting or cauterizing (burning) the oviducts so that the egg and sperm will not meet. These procedures may involve general, spinal, or local anesthesia.

The most common sterilization technique involves cutting the uterine tubes (oviducts), removing a small section of the tubes, and tying off the cut ends. This technique is called a *tubal ligation.* When the incision to locate the tubes is made through the abdomen, the procedure is known as a laparotomy (Figure 7.7). When the incision is made at the end of the vagina, the cul-de-sac, the procedure is called a colpotomy.

Another sterilization procedure involves locating the uterine tubes with a small tube with lights and mirrors in it. The tubes are *cauterized,* or burned. The surgical procedure used is called an endoscopy. If entry is through the vagina, the procedure is called a culdoscopy. If entry is through the abdomen, it is called a laparoscopy. When entry is through the vagina and uterus, it is called a uteroscopy.

After sterilization, the egg cannot move down the oviducts to meet the sperm. The egg disintegrates and is absorbed by the surrounding fluids. There are no other changes to the female cycle. A woman will still have the same circulating hormones and her normal menstrual flow. Sterilization does not bring on menopause, nor does it cause a woman to develop male secondary sex characteristics.

INSTRUCTIONS FOR EFFECTIVE USE

Before the procedure, a woman should have a Pap smear. If she has an IUD, it should be removed to avoid infection. If she has been taking oral contraceptives, she should discontinue them at least 1 month before surgery.

After the procedure, a woman can go home as soon as her blood pressure and temperature have been carefully checked. She will need to rest for about 24 to 48 hours. She can resume her normal activities in a few days. Heavy lifting, strenuous exercise, and intercourse should be avoided for a week. The stitches will dissolve on their own, and a follow-up physical examination should be performed a month later.

The procedure is immediately effective unless ovulation occurred in the 2 days prior to the surgery. For absolute effectiveness, a backup method should be used until the first menstrual perood.

EFFECTIVENESS

Female sterilization is theoretically 100% effective. The actual failure rate is less than 0.2%. Failure may occur if the tubes rejoin or if the surgery is incorrectly done.

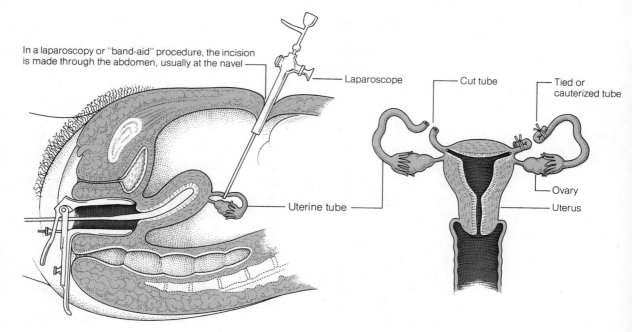

FIGURE 7.7 Female sterilization by laparoscopy.

BENEFITS

Sterilization is one of the most popular means of contraception for women over 30. It is highly effective, is permanent, and is a one-time expense.

SIDE EFFECTS

In addition, only about 2% of women will have complications. The danger signals are bleeding, a fever greater than 100°F, fainting spells, persistent abdominal pain that increases after 12 hours, and/or bleeding from the incision sites (Hatcher, Stewart, et al., 1980). Rarely will a woman die from a sterilization procedure. For example, the death rate for laparoscopy is 1 to 2 per 100,000 (Phillips et al., 1975).

The usual side effects are discomfort and pelvic pain, pain near the incision site, and shoulder and chest pain caused by the gas in the abdomen. A mild pain killer for 24 to 48 hours will relieve these symptoms.

CONTRAINDICATIONS

Obese women or women who have had pelvic inflammatory disease or adhesions may not be good candidates for sterilization. It may be too difficult for the doctor to easily locate the oviducts.

COST

Female sterilization costs at least 200 dollars, and may cost a great deal more, depending on the procedure, hospitalization, and complications.

ABORTION

The Legal Issue

Abortion is not a birth control method in the traditional sense of preventing pregnancy, but rather a fertility control method whereby women terminate pregnancy for medical or personal reasons. Because the pregnancy has already occurred, the abortion issue is debated by the *Right-to-Life* and *Pro-Choice* groups. Right-to-Life advocates believe that life begins at conception, and that at the point of conception the unborn has "rights." One of these "rights" is the right to live. They view abortion as violating this basic human right. The Pro-Choice advocates believe that a woman has the right to make decisions regarding her body and regarding her destiny. One of the choices that the Pro-Choice group supports is the choice to have a full-term pregnancy versus the choice to terminate pregnancy.

On January 22, 1973, the Supreme Court handed down decisions in *Roe* vs. *Wade* (1973) and in *Doe* vs. *Bolton* (1973) that clarified the legality of abortion and the right of a woman to make this decision. The Supreme Court rulings held that (1) during the first trimester of pregnancy, the abortion decision should be left to a woman and her physician; (2) during the second trimester of pregnancy, the state could make necessary regulations that were designed to promote the health of the pregnant woman, and (3) after 24 to 26 weeks the state could deny a woman an abortion in the interest of human life, except in cases where pregnancy endangered the life of the mother. In further court action on July 1, 1976, the Supreme Court held that a state could not make third-party consent necessary for abortion (*Planned Parenthood of Central Missouri* vs. *Danforth*, 1976).

Making a Responsible Decision

When a woman first learns unexpectedly that she is pregnant, she may not know how she thinks or feels or what she wants to do. She may want to examine the possibility of having an abortion. The following questions have been used by counselors to explore these feelings (PreTerm Institute, 1973):

1. When did you learn that you were pregnant?
2. How did you feel when you found out that you were pregnant?
3. Did you expect that you would become pregnant?
4. What did you do first after you learned that you were pregnant?
5. Have you talked with anyone about your pregnancy?

6. When did you first consider abortion?
7. What led you to consider abortion?
8. Have you considered carrying this pregnancy to term?
9. How would continuing this pregnancy affect your life?
10. Is there anything that would make you decide to continue this pregnancy?
11. Have you ever considered having a baby and placing it for adoption?

When a woman has decided to have an abortion, most doctors, clinicians, and counselors will explore the decision further. Here are some questions to think about (PreTerm Institute, 1973):

1. What made you decide to have an abortion?
2. How did you feel about abortion before this pregnancy?
3. How do your parents/boyfriend/husband feel about abortion?
4. Who helped you make this decision?
5. Has this pregnancy affected your relationship with your parents/boyfriend/husband?
6. Do you think having the abortion will affect your relationship?
7. How do you think you will feel about this decision after the abortion?
8. Do you think you will ever tell anyone/your friends/your parents about this abortion?
9. Who can you talk to if you feel the need to discuss your experiences afterward?
10. Do you know other women who have had abortions?

The counseling sessions usually involve four main parts: (1) discussion of the abortion decision and alternatives to abortion, (2) preparation for the abortion procedure, (3) contraceptive counseling afterward, and (4) assistance and support for the woman as an individual.

When I found out that I was pregnant, I was shocked. There was no way that I wanted to continue the pregnancy. I had so many questions and so many fears. I felt everyone was looking at me. The counselor really helped me. She told me exactly what to expect. I sorted through my feelings. When the day came, she was with me through the procedure. I left the clinic feeling very thankful for the kind of people that worked there. I felt that they really cared about me.

Abortion Procedures

Abortion procedures vary, depending on how far along the pregnancy has progressed and the risks involved (Figure 7.8).

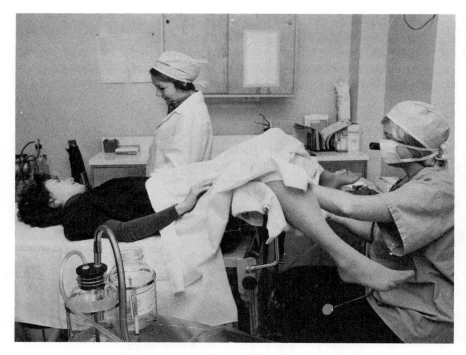

FIGURE 7.8 Woman demonstrating position for first trimester abortion. (Photo by Erika Stone)

VACUUM CURETTAGE

Vacuum curettage has become the most commonly used procedure during the first trimester of pregnancy (Figure 7.9). The vacuum curettage procedure is also known as suction, vacuum aspiration, and dilation and evacuation (D & E).

Vacuum curettage is a 5- to 10-minute procedure that can be performed in a clinic or an office on an outpatient basis up to 20 weeks from the beginning of the last menstrual period. It is seldom performed beyond 16 weeks. The procedure is relatively safe and is actually seven to ten times safer than a term pregnancy.

Prior to the procedure, laboratory tests are done for blood type, blood count, Rh factor, and any gonorrheal infection. A Pap smear is taken. Then the doctor will do a pelvic examination to determine the size and position of the uterus as well as how far the pregnancy has progressed.

Next the doctor will insert a metal or plastic speculum into the vagina. The speculum allows the doctor to spread the vagina and see the cervix. The area around the cervix is cleansed with a cotton swab soaked in Betadine, a solution that contains iodine. The doctor will inject a local anesthetic into the cervix to numb the uterine area. The injection is similar to the Novocain injections given by a dentist. There are few nerve endings in

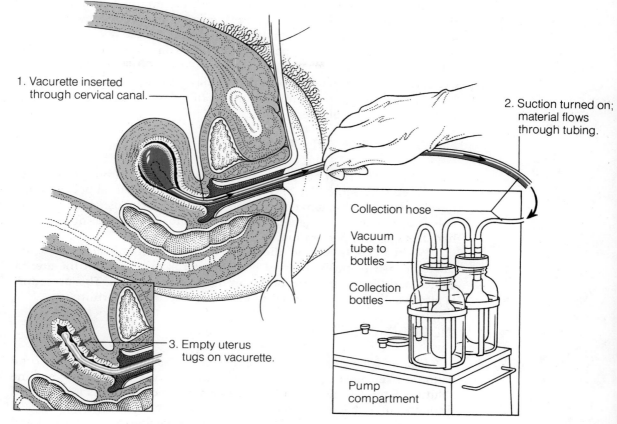

1. Vacurette inserted through cervical canal.

2. Suction turned on; material flows through tubing.

Collection hose

Vacuum tube to bottles

Collection bottles

3. Empty uterus tugs on vacurette.

Pump compartment

FIGURE 7.9   Vacuum curettage (D & E).

the cervix, so the injection will be a pinch or sting that lasts only a few seconds.

The doctor will then widen the cervical opening by using metal dilators. Dilators are used, increasing the size, until the cervical opening is the width of your little finger. While the doctor is dilating the cervix, there may be cramping.

After the cervix is dilated, a sterile tube that is attached to a vacuum aspirator is inserted into the uterus. When the vacuum aspirator is turned on, the fetal tissue and some of the lining of the uterine wall is pulled out. This procedure lasts about a minute.

Two to three hours after a procedure with no complications, the woman may go home (someone else should drive). There may be bleeding for a week and spotting for another two weeks. Sanitary napkins are used to collect the blood, because tampons may be irritating and may cause infection. A woman should not douche or have intercourse for three weeks. Normal activities can be resumed the following day, although strenuous work or exercise should be avoided for a week.

The risks involved in vacuum curettage are minimal. They are infection, uterine perforation, hemorrhaging, and failure to remove all the products of conception (fetal material). A woman should take her temperature (before aspirin or other painkillers) twice a day for a week. She should call her physician if she has (1) a fever over 100.4°F, (2) severe cramping, (3) excessive bleeding (when bleeding for 2 days is heavier than the heaviest flow of a normal period), (4) a foul-smelling vaginal discharge, or (5) a rash of any kind (Founder's Clinic, 1974).

DILATION AND CURETTAGE

Dilation and curettage is usually called a *D & C*. Although it can be performed between 8 and 20 weeks from the last menstrual period, it has been replaced by vacuum curettage as the method of choice because it involves a hospital stay, general anesthesia, and greater risk of infection, hemorrhage, and perforation.

When a D & C is done, the cervix is dilated with metal instruments. Then an instrument is inserted into the uterus to scrape out the uterine contents, ridding the uterus of the products of conception. This procedure is also used to treat menstrual problems and to treat infertility.

INDUCED LABOR AND MISCARRIAGE

Induced labor is a method of abortion that is used late in the second trimester. The most common means of inducing labor is the use of a saline solution. Some of the amniotic fluid that surrounds the fetus is drawn off through a tube that is inserted through the abdomen. The fluid is replaced with a saline, or saltlike, solution that causes fetal circulatory arrest and causes labor to begin within a few hours. The fetus is expelled. Complications can be serious if the saline solution gets into the bloodstream.

Another means of inducing labor is the use of prostaglandins. Prostaglandins can be injected into the amniotic sac, inserted as a vaginal suppository, or given intravenously. Labor begins more quickly than it does when saline is used. However, the potential side effects are greater. There is the possibility of delivering a live fetus or of lacerating the cervix. There is a high incidence of nausea and vomiting.

HYSTEROTOMY

When the induction method cannot be used in the late second trimester and when a woman's health is at risk, a *hysterotomy* is done. The procedure is done in a hospital under general anesthesia. A small cesarean section is performed, and the fetus is removed. There is the chance that the fetus will be alive.

This procedure is serious, since it involves intra-abdominal surgery. The recovery time is longer, and the general risks of major surgery and a general anesthetic exist.

SUMMARY STATEMENTS

- *Several conditions must exist for pregnancy to occur: (1) semen must be deposited in a woman's vagina, (2) the semen must contain healthy sperm, (3) sperm must find conditions conducive, (4) sperm must travel through the woman's uterus to the oviducts, (5) sperm must meet a living egg, (6) the fertilized egg must travel to the uterus and implant itself.*
- *There are three alternatives to consider when pregnancy is not desirable: birth control methods, sterilization, and abortion.*

- *Birth control methods are designed to alter the conditions that are necessary for a pregnancy and/or conception to occur: contraception, the prevention of conception, and interception, the prevention of implantation.*
- *Sterilization is any procedure (usually surgical) by which an individual is made incapable of reproducing.*
- *An abortion is the premature expulsion of the products of conception (fertilized ovum, embryo, or nonviable fetus) from the uterus.*

SUGGESTED READINGS

Barr, Samuel J. *A Woman's Choice*. New York: Rawson Associates, 1977.

Cherniak, Donna, and Allan Feingold. *Birth Control Handbook*. Montreal: Montreal Health Press, 1978.

Fleishman, N., and P. L. Dixon. *Vasectomy, Sex, and Parenthood*. Garden City, New York: Doubleday, 1973.

Francke, Linda. *The Ambivalence of Abortion*. New York: Random House, 1978.

Hatcher, Robert, et al. *Contraceptive Technology: 1980-1981*. New York: Irvington Publishers, 1980.

Levin, Marshall. "Let George Do It: Male Contraception." *Ms.*, January 1976.

Sanford, Wendy Coppedge, and Barbara Bridgman Perkins, "Birth Control," in *Our Bodies, Ourselves*. Boston Women's Health Book Collective. New York: Simon and Schuster, 1979.

Shapiro, Howard. *The Birth Control Book*. New York: Avon, 1978.

A LOOK AT YOUR LIFESTYLE

You and your boyfriend/girlfriend have been dating exclusively for about eight months. You have no marriage plans. Recently you have become sexually involved. It was uncomfortable discussing birth control, so you did not. You had sexual intercourse three times using no means of birth control. You have just returned from a clinic, where a pregnancy test proved positive. You are both flabbergasted.

Write an I-message describing your reaction:

When I learned I/she was pregnant, I _____

_____

_____

_____

_____

_____

BIRTH CONTROL, STERILIZATION, ABORTION

Identify the issue or problem.

_____

_____

Identify five possible solutions or alternatives.

_____

_____

_____

_____

_____

GATHERING INFORMATION
Look at each alternative and identify at least one piece of information you would like to have before making a decision.

_____

_____

_____

_____

EVALUATING THE INFORMATION/ALTERNATIVES
Give at least one pro and one con for each alternative.

_____

_____

_____

_____

_____

_____

_____

_____

_____

MAKING RESPONSIBLE DECISIONS
What alternative best suits your needs?
What are the possible consequences?

_____

_____

_____

_____

EIGHT

Homosexuality and Bisexuality

A LOOK AT YOUR LIFESTYLE

Probably the majority of those reading this book are heterosexual. Yet how many of you have given thought to, or are able to provide answers to, these questions:

- What is *heterosexuality?*
- If one engages in a *heterosexual* act, does that make one a heterosexual?
- Can *heterosexuals* be easily identified?
- Is *heterosexuality* an unnatural way of life?
- What causes one to become *heterosexual?*
- What kinds of professions do *heterosexuals* choose?
- When did you first discover you were *heterosexual?*
- Are *heterosexuals* child molesters?
- Are children seduced into *heterosexuality?*
- Is *heterosexuality* abnormal?

In-depth and widely accepted answers to the above questions, while they appear simple at first, may in fact be quite complex. If we were to substitute the word *homosexual* for *heterosexual,* the responses would

223

remain just as complex. Yet these are the questions that the heterosexual population often asks of homosexuals.

The majority of the heterosexual population have preconceived ideas about homosexuality. Some of these ideas hold credence, but others may be replete with myths. The purpose of this chapter is to provide you with the skills you will need to gain insight into the concept of homosexuality as well as into the often associated lifestyle — bisexuality.

GATHERING INFORMATION

When the concept of homosexuality or bisexuality surfaces, it is important to deal with these and other related issues. In order to understand homosexuality, we must be able to answer the following:

1. What is homosexuality?
2. What are the causes of homosexuality? Since many theories have been espoused, it may be easier to understand the phenomenon of homosexuality if we examine some of its purported causes. Various psychoanalytic and environmental theories have been proposed — none of which is universally accepted.
3. Is homosexuality widespread? Sometimes people become much more accepting of their own and others' lifestyles if they see that what they believe and practice is not so uncommon.

In addition to the above areas, this chapter will provide you with information about homosexuality based upon the research of Kinsey, Hunt, and other significant pioneers in the area of human sexuality.

EVALUATING THE INFORMATION

In this chapter, factual information is provided with the understanding that responsible decision-making is based upon accurate facts. The following information needs to be evaluated in assessing one's knowledge, attitudes and values regarding homosexuality:

1. definition: understanding what it means to be a homosexual
2. causes: what different researchers, analysts, and theoreticians believe cause one to become a homosexual
3. prevalence: the prevalence of homosexuality and homosexual behavior in our society
4. attitudes toward homosexuality: the impact of the attitudes and behaviors of others as a determinant of our own attitudes and behavior toward homosexuality
5. the homosexual lifestyle: what it is like to be a homosexual
6. trends and the homosexual lifestyle: what the future holds

MAKING RESPONSIBLE DECISIONS

Each of us has certain ways of responding to the subject of homosexuality. Regardless of our behavior, we need to assess our actions and determine whether these actions are consistent with our value system. Often we may feel one way about a particular issue with regard to homosexuality but not act upon that feeling. For example, you are at a party and someone tells "fag" jokes that you find particularly offensive. Whether you are homosexual or heterosexual, you may feel embarrassed about telling the person about your displeasure. If you have made a decision that homosexual men and women should be treated in the same way as heterosexual men and women, you may choose to reaffirm your decision by interjecting a simple statement such as, "I believe homosexuals have feelings just like the rest of us," or by just ignoring and not responding to the comment.

Regardless of the position taken on homosexuality, it is important that we feel we have made the best decision possible and that we assess the consequences of this decision. If the consequences of the decision have a negative effect on us, we need to reassess our thinking. Homosexuality is a very sensitive area of concern for both men and women. The decisions we make will have an effect on our lives as well as the lives of others. Evaluating our past as well as present decisions requires that we possess the best information available. The rest of this chapter will provide you with the tools you need to understand homosexuality.

WHAT IS A HOMOSEXUAL?

The word *homosexuality* is derived from the Greek root *homo,* which means "same." Thus, two individuals of the same sex who are involved in sexual activity with each other are engaging in homosexual behavior. This term is applicable to women as well as to men. *Lesbianism* is the term that is more often used to describe female homosexuals. Lesbianism gets its name from the classic Greek poet Sappho, who described sexual relations between women on the island of Lesbos.

However, to limit the word *homosexuality* to "sexual activity between two people of the same sex" is narrow in scope. According to this definition, the following circumstances would label one a homosexual:

1. A man first engages in homosexual acts while in prison.
2. A 13-year-old boy reaches orgasm during mutual masturbation with a peer.
3. A 19-year-old young man performs sexual acts with other men for a fee.

Each of these situations, though constituting a homosexual act, does not mean the man involved is a homosexual. Homosexual activity may occur for any number of reasons: incarceration, leading to restricted choices of sexual partners; curiosity; need for money; as well as a host of other circumstances. Therefore, homosexuality can be more specifically defined as a preference for partners of the same sex who cause arousal in fantasy and in sexual encounter. According to this definition, a person can engage in sexual activities with a person of the opposite sex and be aroused if he or she fantasizes these activities as taking place with a person of the same sex.

CAUSES OF HOMOSEXUALITY

Biological Research and Theory

One of the most common questions asked by heterosexuals of homosexuals is: "What caused you to become a homosexual?" The response to this question is no easier to explain than the response to the question: "Why did you become a heterosexual?" Several theories of the causes of homosexuality have been put forth.

HORMONAL IMBALANCE

Some investigations of the causes of homosexuality have purported to show that an imbalance of sex hormones may be a contributing factor. Since the male homosexual was often seen as effeminate, it was thought he might be deficient in androgens. Likewise, the lesbian, viewed as masculine, might possess an excess of androgens. These theories are outdated and hold no credence today. Although the techniques for measuring hormonal levels are better today than yesterday, there remains the failure to find differences between male homosexuals and male heterosexuals based upon testosterone or gonadotropin levels in the blood or urine (Rose, 1975; Meyer-Bahlburg, 1977).

HORMONE LEVELS DURING THE PRENATAL PERIOD

Another speculation about the cause of homosexuality is an exposure to inappropriate hormones during the prenatal period. This exposure can lead a genetic female to have male genitals or a genetic male to have female genitals (Money and Ehrhardt, 1972). In rare cases a person is born with both male and female genitalia. This is known as *hermaphroditism*. Some studies provide some indirect evidence that abnormal hormone levels during fetal or early postnatal stages may be correlated with sexual orientation. However, this idea remains purely speculative and has not been proven.

Some investigators claim minimal hormonal differences between heterosexual and homosexual men, but these differences may be a *result* of the homosexual lifestyle rather than a *cause* (Masters and Johnson, 1979).

GENETIC FACTORS

During the early part of the 20th century, researchers believed that the cause of homosexuality was direct genetic inheritance. In a study conducted by Franz J. Kallman (1952), 85 pairs of male fraternal and identical twins were followed. One member of each pair was known to be homosexual. Both members of the fraternal twins studied were homosexual in fewer than 50% of the cases studied. However, in the pairs of identical twins studied, both members in every pair were homosexual. Based upon the results of this study, one may come to the conclusion that homosexuality is genetically determined. Yet one year after his famous study, Kallman discounted his own conclusion and instead supported a genetic–environmental interaction. The 100% finding in the identical twin population was considered a "statistical artifact." Among the major criticisms of this study were that identical twins were reared together and therefore shared a common environment, which in turn could explain the results, and since nonidentical twins share approximately half their genes, one would expect a greater number of homosexuals among them than among unrelated people.

Other studies that have replicated Kallman's failed to yield the same results, and today the genetic explanation is not generally supported.

In conclusion, the lack of genetic evidence has prompted most researchers to examine other causes. A few researchers do feel (as Freud did) that a hormonal predisposition toward homosexuality does exist and that the individual's life experiences reinforce or eliminate it. For many, the door remains open for a relationship between the aforementioned biological hypotheses and homosexuality.

Psychoanalytic Theory

After clinical observations of homosexual patients, Sigmund Freud deduced that homosexuality originated in a complex relationship between biological and environmental processes. Freud's theory states that the newborn is bisexual and will therefore respond pleasurably to any erotic stimulation, regardless of the sex of the person providing that stimulation. Accordingly, Freud labeled the infant as *polymorphous perverse*. As the child continues to mature and grow to adulthood, sexual preference becomes directed toward members of the opposite sex while the desire for members of the same sex is repressed. This led Freud to believe that homosexuals are at an arrested state of psychosexual development.

At this point, the theory of the *Oedipus complex* comes into play. Freud concluded that homosexuality was caused by a negative Oedipus complex. That is, the child loves the parent of the same gender but identifies with the parent of the opposite gender. Thus a girl may love her mother but yet identify with her father. During the process of maturation, the negative Oedipus complex will be repressed and the child will become a heterosexual. The person who does not repress the negative Oedipus complex and instead becomes locked into this pattern is a homosexual. Belief in this view leads to the conclusion that the homosexual has a continuing love for the parent of the same sex.

Environmental Theory

Is it possible that homosexuality is caused by environmental as well as other factors? Some evidence of this does exist in the literature (Kinsey et al., 1948, 1953; Coleman, 1972). Among some of these reasons may be an unplanned homosexual experience with a friend during youth, which turned out to be enjoyable, or exposure for a long period of time to peers of the same sex such as that in an out-of-town school.

However, the family environment is often thought of as the major contributor to homosexuality. In one of the more publicized studies, Irving Bieber (1962) examined homosexual and heterosexual males who were undergoing psychoanalysis. Bieber's conclusions led to the often talked about dominant-mother–passive-father syndrome as a cause of male homosexuality. That is, the male homosexual's mother was overprotective and intimate, and the father, emotionally removed and detached. This situation caused the male to develop a fear of heterosexual relations because of the mother's possessiveness. The result is homosexuality due to fear of heterosexuality.

Charlotte Wolff (1971) conducted a study similar to Bieber's, but her subjects were women who were not undergoing psychoanalysis. Her findings were somewhat opposite Bieber's in that those women who were identified as lesbians also came from families who had a distant or removed father (geographically as well as emotionally). However, the mother in this situation was also distant. Result: the female seeks the missing love by entering into lesbian relationships. This situation, compounded by the fact that the female grew up not learning how to relate to men, was a basis for lesbianism.

In a study by Saghir and Robins (1973), the relationships within the family were also given as a cause for homosexuality. More of the male homosexuals than male heterosexuals they surveyed asserted that their mothers were over-dominant and their fathers, passive. This may have resulted in a boy's developing an excessive attachment to the mother—one that was never outgrown.

The "harsh father" syndrome has also been given as a reason for the male to become a homosexual. It is not uncommon to observe father–son interactions in everyday situations that reflect the "be a man" attitude. For example, little Johnny hurts himself sliding into second base during a Little League baseball game. He is physically in pain and tears are falling down his cheeks when all of a sudden his father approaches and in a tone of anger says, "Men don't cry, so get back on the field and be tough." This type of father is, in his own mind, teaching his son "to be a man." But at the same time, this father is creating a barrier whereby a relationship based on love, tenderness, and acceptance is prevented from developing.

At this point, the boy is not given the opportunity to identify with his father and therefore is not learning the masculine role in life. Something as simple as a warm hug from the father would have served a more meaningful purpose.

Other environmental reasons for homosexuality have also been espoused, although not proven. The male who was told by a female that he performed poorly during the sex act may turn to homosexuality to avoid rejection again. Similarly, the female who was rejected by her boyfriend determines that this kind of rejection will not occur again and therefore enters into a lesbian relationship. These examples have led some researchers to conclude that individuals enter into homosexual relationships because of fear of the heterosexual relationship (Marmor, 1965).

Behavioral Theory

Attempts have been made to formulate a behavioral theory about the development of homosexuality in males. These attempts by McGuire et al. (1965), Gagnon and Simon (1973), and Masters and Johnson (1979) have focused upon the role of sexual arousal and masturbation in determining one's sexual orientation. The premise from which assumptions have been made states that ejaculation or orgasm which results from masturbation is the most significant reinforcing event for conditioning stimuli accompanying or preceding masturbation. Thus, sexual preference for a partner of the same sex may be based upon one's initial sexual experience. More specifically, if the initial experience was an enjoyable one, it may be used in fantasy as a means of eliciting sexual arousal. This fantasy can also be used in the act of masturbation. For example, if a male engaged in an initial homosexual experience and found a great deal of enjoyment, this experience may be fantasized frequently and may often or always be accompanied by masturbation. If a second or similar sexual encounter is experienced, the conditioning process may be further strengthened. Believers in this theory feel it is valid as a cause for homosexuality. Of course, the opposite can be applied. An unenjoyable initial homosexual experience can lead toward an aversion to homosexuality and a predisposition to heterosexuality, assuming the first heterosexual encounter is a positive one.

Gagnon and Simon (1973) feel that societal norms play a role in the development of homosexual conditioning in the female. While early adolescence in the male is accompanied by a desire to explore sexual activity, the young female at this age has less desire for similar activities — both in fantasy and practice. Therefore the female is learning patterns of behavior that are only indirectly related to sexual orientation. Society condones sexual experimentation by males and not by females. As a result, the female adolescent's outlet for sexual stimulation is centered on sexual activities which take place in movies, on television, or in books. Therefore, Gagnon and Simon (1973) conclude that while sexual orientation in the male may result from early sexual experiences and fantasies, the development of the female homosexual is more likely to be a result of emotional ties between two women that precede sexual activity.

In this chapter, we have examined several theoretical determinants of homosexuality. Among the characteristics have been a dominant mother, a distant father, a fear of rejection by the opposite sex, the first sexual experience with a member of the same sex, masturbation and fantasy, hormonal imbalance, inheritance, and a negative Oedipal complex. You have probably heard one or more of these given as a cause for homosexuality. How many of these theories are based upon fact?

The only fact we know is that no one etiological theory of homosexuality has been conclusively proven (Eysenck and Rachman, 1966). No single factor has been accepted by a large body of behavioral scientists as the determinant of homosexuality in males and females. For each of the major studies identified, reasons can be given that discount its validity. The truth of the matter may be that homosexuality has many causes, rather than one cause, and that there may exist different types or kinds of homosexuals.

PREVALENCE

Now that we have examined what homosexuality is as well as some possible theories of its cause, we would like to discuss its prevalence. Some of you who are reading this text may say, "Why all of this fuss about homosexuality? So few people lead that kind of lifestyle." The truth is that you probably know someone who is a homosexual, perhaps someone who is a close friend or a person in your class.

In my sociology class in college, my professor said he would have a homosexual from one of the campus groups come to speak to the class. Being a member of the campus Gay Activists Alliance, I asked my professor if it would be permissible for me to speak, and he approved. Meanwhile, no one in the class knew I was gay or that I would be the speaker. Throughout the semester I heard comments like "I can't wait for the sessions with the homos" and "I don't want to miss the fairy." On the day of the big event, the professor said, "And now for our homosexual speaker, I'd like to introduce John." When I got up, there was complete astonishment.

Until the research of Kinsey, it was almost impossible to estimate the number of people in the United States who were either homosexual or had had homosexual experiences. This lack of knowledge, among both the heterosexuals and the homosexuals, led to the inference that homosexuality was rare.

When I was taking a health education class, the teacher said there were probably two or three homosexuals in the room, based upon the norms. To my surprise, when we spoke about homosexuality, two of the students admitted they were gay. They certainly could have fooled me.

However, Kinsey reported in his study, that 37% of the men he interviewed had had a sexual experience including orgasm with someone of the same sex.* If we modify Kinsey's figures (exclude men who were exclusively homosexual and men with no college experience) we would find that 30% of college men have had a homosexual contact with or without orgasm (Gagnon, 1977). These figures are from students in college who are younger than 30 years of age. However, while these figures do not tell us what happens after college, they are a more valid representation of the Kinsey data. Still, these studies do indicate that homosexual activity is not something that only applies to "someone else."

At this point we need to clarify what we really mean by the word *homosexual*. Kinsey and his colleagues (1948) believed that homosexuality and heterosexuality were by no means absolute. That is, a person could be from 100% homosexual to 100% heterosexual. The continuum in Table 8.1 illustrates this concept. According to Gagnon (1977), we can estimate that 3% to 4% of the adult male population is entirely homosexual, as opposed to the 10% figure often cited. The comparable figures for the female are much lower—approximately 2% to 3%. The reasons for the difference are not clear.

Among some of the other noteworthy figures in Kinsey's study concerning females, 2% of the female population had a homosexual experience leading to orgasm by the age of 12. By the age of 20, this figure is 10%.

In another well-publicized and highly regarded study, Morton Hunt (1974) surveyed sexual behaviors and practices. His data on homosexuality closely corresponded to Kinsey's. Among Hunt's findings was that 20% to 25% of males have a homosexual experience during adulthood. In addition, 10% of married women and 20% of single women also have had a homosexual experience.

According to the figures presented, homosexuality is by no means an isolated occurrence. If 3% to 4% of the United States' male population is exclusively homosexual, we are talking about a population of possibly more than four million gay men (based on 1980 census figures). This is a substantial number; yet some feel it is too conservative.

The issue of what a homosexual is needs to be further clarified. Kinsey dealt with this concern by arguing that *homosexual behavior*, as opposed to *homosexuality*, should be the criterion. By ascertaining homosexual behavior, one can make a more accurate judgment about a person's sexual orientation. Accordingly, persons can place themselves on the continuum and label the degree to which they lean toward the poles—either homosexual or heterosexual. While this may seem difficult (i.e., do three or four homosexual experiences place a person in Area 1 or 2?), it may be much easier than labeling a person homosexual or heterosexual.

---

*It is believed that figures are inflated, since the sample included a large number of men who had not gone beyond the 12th grade, had been imprisoned, and had come from poverty-stricken sectors of society. This number was far greater than would be identified in a random sample.

TABLE 8.1   HETEROSEXUAL–HOMOSEXUAL RATING SCALE

0	1	2	3	4	5	6
entirely heterosexual	largely heterosexual with incidental homosexual activity	largely heterosexual but with distinct homosexual activity	equally heterosexual and homosexual	largely homosexual but with distinct heterosexual history	largely homosexual but with incidental heterosexual history	entirely homo-sexual

Source: Kinsey, A. C., Pomeroy, W. B., Martin, E. E., and Gebhard, P. H. *Sexual Behavior in the Human Female*, Philadelphia: Saunders, 1953.

On the basis of the large amount of research on homosexuality, it can be said that 75% of men and 85% of women fall into the "entirely heterosexual" area of the Kinsey continuum. Regardless of how one views these figures, the fact remains that homosexual behavior existed in the past, exists in the present, and will continue to exist in the future.

ATTITUDES TOWARD HOMOSEXUALITY

Contrary to what many individuals believe, homosexuality is not something that exists only among male hairdressers, female cab drivers, female football players, and male artists, to name a few. One of the more significant points about homosexuality is that it exists on all social and educational levels. Homosexuals are found among all age groups and occupations. Their interests are as varied as those of the heterosexuals: they play professional sports and hold political offices, and their feelings and concerns about important issues are as strong as those of their heterosexual counterparts.

Yet most Americans consider homosexuals to be harmful to society. It is not uncommon to hear derogatory terms about homosexuals: "fag," "faggot," "queer," "homo," "fairy," "fruit." Sometimes homosexuals may call each other by these words, but only as a putdown of societal attitudes toward them. If homosexuals prefer to be called anything by the "straight" (heterosexual) society, they prefer *homosexual* or *gay*.

Despite the mass of evidence that indicates homosexuals have personalities as varied as anyone else's, many individuals use misconceptions to validate their discriminating practices: homosexuals seduce young children; close contact with a homosexual can turn you into one; male homosexuals hate females. Unfortunately, these kinds of fears, which are unfounded, cause many to refrain from behavior that would be considered natural. Men, being more fearful of homosexuality than women, show restraint in many ways. They are not as likely to hug another man, much less kiss him. Many men will not look another in the eye when carrying on a conversation. In the locker room, most men will avoid looking at another man's body. A compliment such as "You have a super body" is rarely shared among men, even though the thought is very much there. These are just some examples of behavior that indicates the male's fear of being thought of as homosexual.

George Weinberg, in his book *Society and the Healthy Homosexual* (1972), discusses five reasons he feels prompt individuals to discriminate against homosexuals:

1. The religious motive. Many people condemn homosexuality on biblical admonitions. In Leviticus, the recommendation is made that two men who engage in a homosexual act be stoned. However, individuals exercise considerable judgment over which biblical teachings to accept and which to reject. For example, in Leviticus, it is also stated that it is wrong for a woman to wear a scarlet dress or for anyone to eat shrimp. Yet many shrimp-eating people cite Leviticus as their authority for condemning homosexuality.

2. The secret fear of being homosexual. Some individuals discriminate against homosexuals for fear they may be homosexual themselves. Freud called this *reaction formation.*

3. Repressed envy. Some people will belittle others, denying them the right of competition. The heterosexual man may have worked hard to achieve a precarious masculine identity. Along comes the homosexual, who says, "I did not have to 'work' like you because I have no desire for a woman." According to the heterosexual, this attitude is one of disdain for the basic requirements of manhood.

4. The threat to values. Since homosexuality is not valued positively in our society, it may be seen as undermining the society. Not sharing the interests and goals of society leads to suspicion.

5. Existence without vicarious immortality. The notion of homosexuality distresses some people because the thought of persons without children reawakens their fear of death. Reproduction and children and the promise of an afterlife help some individuals cope with the fear of death.

As has been stated, the phobias mentioned represent prejudice. The understanding of these phobias can be clarified by our considering these phobias as prejudice and uncovering the reasons behind them.

THE HOMOSEXUAL LIFESTYLE

In discussing the lifestyle of the homosexual, we must clarify the different types. A person can be a primary or secondary homosexual or a covert or overt homosexual. *Primary homosexuality* is defined as the state of not having had any heterosexual experience. *Secondary homosexuality* indicates that a person has had one or more heterosexual experiences. The *covert* male homosexual is one who is indistinguishable from most other men. He may be married and have children. However, this person leads a double life. When away from home, he may engage in homosexual behavior. Most male homosexuals are of the covert type. The *overt* homosexual is more open about his lifestyle.

Yet due to pressures exerted against homosexuality by society, most homosexuals will choose to live in the straight sector of society and not reveal their sexual orientation. This is known as staying "in the closet." However, some homosexuals (mostly those who are overt) decide to "come out"—that is, make their homosexuality known to a number of other people: parents, friends, co-workers, or others in the gay community. Although one may be "out," he by no means will remain "out." Depending on environmental circumstances, many homosexuals vacillate between "coming out" and staying "in the closet."

Common Assumptions About Homosexuals

ASSUMPTION 1: homosexuals are easily identifiable   Many persons often indicate they can easily identify a homosexual they see walking down the street. However, what they do not realize is that for every one they can identify, there are at least ten they cannot. This mistaken assumption is based upon the premise that the typical male homosexual is a "swish." That is, he has effeminate characteristics, such as a "girlish" walk or a limp wrist. Correspondingly, the female who has masculine

FIGURE 8.1a   A married gay couple. (Photo by Tony Korody/Sygma)

FIGURE 8.1b Two gay men. (Photo by Joel Gordon 1979)

characteristics (a *dyke*)—short hair, stocky build, "tough look"—is more frequently stereotyped as homosexual. Nothing is further from the truth. According to statistics, only 15% of men with extensive homosexual experience and 5% of lesbians can be recognized by their outward appearance (Pomeroy, 1966).

Today, more than ever before, it is extremely difficult to label many homosexuals on the basis of their appearance.

Another point about femininity and masculinity within the homosexual lifestyle needs to be clarified. The homosexual has a *gender identity* consistent with biological sex. The average male homosexual considers himself masculine and for the most part has a great disdain for the effeminate homosexual, otherwise known as a "queen." Likewise, the typical lesbian considers herself feminine and may dislike the woman who tries to appear masculine. The rationale for these concerns is quite evident. If the male homosexual has a sexual desire for another man, why would he bother with a woman figure? The same is true for the female homosexual. If she desired a woman, she would not want a male image. Instead, she would engage in a heterosexual relationship.

In essence, the gender identity of the homosexual is very clear. The male desires to be a male and the female, a female. It is the preference of *sexual partner* that distinguishes the homosexual from the heterosexual.

ASSUMPTION 2: in the homosexual relationship each partner is expected to play a certain role One of the more common misconceptions about the homosexual relationship is that certain roles are played by each

FIGURE 8.2　Two gay women. (Photo by Peter Gerba)

partner. It is believed by many that in the male homosexual relationship, one person assumes the role of dominator, while the other is submissive. That is, one will perform more "womanly" chores, such as cooking, cleaning the house, staying at home, and shopping (submissive), while the other will make "serious" decisions about the house and hold a full-time job (dominant). In the female homosexual relationship, it is often thought that one plays a "male" role ("butch"), while the other assumes the "female" role ("femme"). The roles of the partners in the homosexual relationship are, in fact, no more distinct, and perhaps less so, than they are in the heterosexual relationship. With the increased acceptance of the women's movement, even the roles in the heterosexual relationship have changed. More women work now than ever before, household duties are more equally shared, and decisions are now, more than in the past, based upon a sharing of ideas and concerns. This concept is also predominant in the homosexual relationship.

In the sex act, role delineation in the homosexual relationship is as varied as the role played by a man and woman in a heterosexual relationship. In actuality, homosexual practices are the same as heterosexual practices, except for penile-vaginal coitus. Otherwise, there are no heterosexual practices that cannot be performed by a homosexual couple.

In the male homosexual relationship, kissing and petting are commonplace in initiating a lovemaking session. As in a heterosexual relationship, petting can be self-limited or be foreplay for additional lovemaking practices. Among these may be mutual masturbation with or without orgasm; oral–genital contact—either singly or mutually; interfemoral intercourse (the man's penis moves between his partner's thighs); and anal intercourse. Although anal intercourse may be thought of as difficult to perform, communication with one's partner, proper technique, and the use of lubricants make this act a simple one. The anus is capable of comfortably accommodating an erect penis. While most male homosexuals will at one time or another engage in all forms of sexual activity, they prefer oral intercourse over anal intercourse (McCary, 1978).

The question often arises as to who is assigned the "active" role in male homosexual lovemaking and who is assigned the "passive" role. Some parallels can be made here. In anal intercourse, the one who inserts is known as the active, dominant, or "masculine" partner. The other is known as the passive, receptive, or "feminine" one. However, such distinctions are not meaningful, since the roles frequently are reversed. As in the heterosexual relationship, sometimes one is in the mood to be loved, and sometimes one is in the mood to give love. Homosexuals, for the most part, will not play a fixed role, but rather change it to accommodate the needs of their partners.

Lesbians also practice sex acts similar to those of heterosexuals. While the imagination can be used by lesbians to formulate numerous sex practices and techniques, we will focus on the three most common: mutual masturbation, cunnilingus, and tribadism.

Performed simultaneously or in turn, *mutual masturbation* among lesbians consists of manipulation of the clitoris, caressing the labia, and/or penetration of the vagina by the fingers.

In cunnilingus, one female will stimulate the clitoris and labia of another female with her tongue. Sometimes the tongue will be used to penetrate the vagina of the partner. This act can be performed in turns or mutually.

Tribadism involves one woman lying on top of another woman. They move up and down rhythmically to stimulate each other's clitoris. This technique may take some time to master, and it can be used in various positions.

While many men believe lesbians use dildos (penis substitutes), the fact is that they are rarely used. First, the female homosexual does not need deep penetration, since the first third of a woman's vagina and the labia and the clitoris contain virtually all the nerve endings that serve for sexual stimulation (Masters and Johnson, 1966). Second, lesbians for the most part have no desire for a penis.

I remembered always listening to my heterosexual girlfriends describe their first experience during sexual intercourse. They said they were scared—they were not sure if they were doing the right things, if their partner enjoyed them, and if they were, in general, good lovers. Well, things were no different for me during my first experience with another woman. Luckily, she sensed where I was at, and we ended up having a good time.

It is interesting to note that many homosexuals, both male and female, consider themselves more fortunate than their heterosexual counterparts in achieving sexual satisfaction. Their rationale is that a male knows a male body, and a female, a female body, better than one of the opposite sex. Therefore, to many homosexuals, sexual gratification in the homosexual relationship can be more easily achieved than sexual gratification in the heterosexual relationship. Masters and Johnson (1979) have found that male and female homosexuals take more time during sex and appear to be more relaxed than married couples.

ASSUMPTION 3: *homosexuals are a threat to a child's sexual orientation, and many are child molesters* A common belief among heterosexuals is that homosexuals can and will influence the heterosexual boy or girl to become homosexual. A homosexual is not a threat to the sexual orientation of others. To believe that a homosexual can influence the sexual orientation of a heterosexual is to believe that a heterosexual can convince a homosexual to change his or her sexual orientation. It is not a workable concept.

Another concern of heterosexuals is that most homosexuals are child molesters. Statistics indicate that most child molesting is done by heterosexuals. All too frequently child molesting occurs among members of a family. In most cases, child molesters are relatives, friends, neighbors, or acquaintances of the child.

HOMOSEXUAL LIFE

Many heterosexuals are curious about the homosexual lifestyle. They desire answers to questions such as:

- Where do homosexuals meet other homosexuals?
- What do homosexuals do for fun?
- How does the homosexual know if a person he or she is trying to pick up is gay or straight?

Not too long ago, there were few places gay people could frequent. Perhaps there was only a gay bar or two, where gay people were given the opportunity to meet other gays. Today in major cities there are numerous gay bars where homosexuals can meet. Gay bars are not the only meeting places gays have available, nor are they the usual places in which they meet. But just what happens in a gay bar? Most heterosexuals are afraid to enter one, because they think they may be thought of as gay or they are fearful of interacting with a gay person. A gay bar can be oriented to male homosexuals, female homosexuals, or both. Basically, the events that occur in a gay bar are similar to those in a bar frequented by straights. Homosexuals may be observed dancing with persons of the same sex and occasionally also with partners of the opposite sex. To a great extent, the objectives of the patrons in gay bars correspond to the objectives of those who patronize a heterosexual pub. The male homosexual may be searching for a short-term sex partner, otherwise known as a "trick." He "makes the rounds" of the people in the bar (or "cruises," in gay jargon). Like the heterosexual, the gay person may be intent upon settling down with one partner, also called a "lover," in a long-term relationship.

Gays do not only frequent bars to meet prospective partners. They may go to dances at universities that are sponsored by the gay organization on campus. They may bathe at certain beaches that are known to attract gay people. Or they may "cruise" other locations that are known homosexual hangouts.

Sometimes I meet guys just walking around campus. When I pass guys on the way to class who, I think, are good-looking, I stare at them. Usually, the heterosexual guy will turn his eyes in another direction, but another gay guy will continue to stare at me. That's the start of a pick-up.

Often, male homosexuals, and to a lesser extent, female homosexuals, are content with quick and anonymous sex. An uncomplicated and direct route to impersonal sex for men is selected public toilets, also known as "tearooms." In a famous study conducted by Laud Humphries (1970), patrons who entered a park restroom that was a popular "tearoom" were observed. In the "tearoom trade," words are rare and communication takes place by gestures and other unspoken understandings. The partners remain anonymous and engage in fellatio as the predominant act. Among the men Humphries observed were those who for the most part were married. The reason given by these men ranged from its being a routine behavior to sexual frustrations with one's wife. Although the acts performed were homosexual, the patrons were "heterosexual."

At this point, a pattern is observable between male and female homosexuals. It appears that male homosexuals have significantly more partners than female homosexuals. In a study funded by the Kinsey Institute, it was found that 40% of gay men had more than 500 partners, while the majority of gay women had fewer than 10 partners over a lifetime (Bell and Weinberg, 1978). This data also support the idea that the male homosexual has more short-term relationships with other males as well as more opportunities to meet partners than gay women.

BISEXUALITY

When the word *bisexual* is brought up during a conversation among heterosexuals, they often envision a person engaging in homosexual behavior. The fact of the matter is that a *bisexual*, also known as an *ambisexual* (*AC-DC* in slang, meaning "going both ways"), is not necessarily a homosexual. A bisexual is one who engages in both heterosexual and homosexual behavior (Figure 8.3).

In many circles, bisexuality is thought of as being "in vogue." Rock stars and other celebrities have capitalized from the publicity given their

FIGURE 8.3   Bisexual man (foreground) with male friend (left), and with woman (right).

dual lifestyle. There seems to be a mystique to being "bi" (bisexual). It is not uncommon nowadays to find bars for bisexuals as well as a more lax attitude among heterosexuals toward the bisexual population.

It is often assumed that the bisexual male and female have the best of two worlds. They can engage in sexual activities with members of the same sex as well as with members of the opposite sex, thereby adding variety to their sex lives. On the other hand, the bisexual may be ostracized by the gay as well as the straight population. Often, the heterosexual male will discriminate against the bisexual because he may feel this person is really a homosexual. The female homosexual may discriminate against the bisexual female because it is felt she is not helping the lesbian movement. In fact, female homosexuals are often at odds with male homosexuals. Groups such as the Gay Activists Alliance are shunned by many female homosexuals because they feel that the lesbian is doubly discriminated against—she is gay and also a woman. Many lesbians feel that the Gay Activists Alliance deals with only one of the issues, homosexuality, and not with the other, women's rights.

However, the issue of just who or what is a bisexual is a very cloudy one. We have already made the distinction in this chapter between sexual behavior (sexual practices and activities), biological gender (anatomical male or anatomical female), sex role identity (the male identifies with the male role and the female, the female role), and the choice of the sexual partner (heterosexual, homosexual, bisexual). One concept not dealt with but significant to the bisexual is *self-identity*. In other words, does a person have specific criteria he or she uses to categorize himself or herself? What constitutes being labeled heterosexual, homosexual, or bisexual? It appears the criteria are clearer for the homosexual and heterosexual than they are for the bisexual.

If a male is living in a heterosexual relationship and he permits himself to be sexually satisfied by another male because his wife may not engage in a particular sexual act, is this male then assumed to be bisexual?

What about the heterosexual person in prison who engages in homosexual activity with no commitment to any partner? (A person who engages in homosexual activity because of a particular situation such as being placed in prison is called a *situational,* or *deprived,* homosexual). In the two mentioned cases, the individuals may not consider themselves bisexual. Yet the definition of *bisexual* does label them as such. There are many who would consider them homosexuals.

When does one label himself or herself a bisexual? Do we define sexual orientation by sexual activities or sexual preferences? Can an individual avoid indicting himself as having a preference for homosexuality or heterosexuality by engaging in bisexual activities? Why not have the convenience of both worlds (but really have a sexual preference)?

IS HOMOSEXUALITY NORMAL?

In civilizations that existed before the 20th century pronatalism (activities that increase the population) was valued highly (Bullough and Bullough, 1979). It was not difficult to support this concept, since it was necessary to promote increased populations because of numerous wars, epidemic diseases, and crop failures. The promotion of pronatalism by many societies led to its institutionalization into religious practices and laws as evidenced by its incorporation into Judaic and Greek philosophy.

Toward the end of the 18th century, Samuel Tissot, a French physician, argued that the loss of semen through masturbation and other nonprocreative activities led to insanity (Bullough and Bullough, 1979). Thus, we found homosexuality beginning to be diagnosed as a condition that deserved medical intervention. John Harvey Kellogg, a well-known 19th century authority on nonprocreative sex, considered homosexuality a form of masturbation—at that time masturbation was considered evil. This trend of thinking continued, and in the latter part of the 19th century, Richard van Krafft-Ebing became a key figure in the development of the *medical model* as an explanation for homosexuality. Krafft-Ebing believed homosexuality was an illness that should be cured just as other illnesses were cured.

The major findings of Kinsey and his associates in 1948 struck a major blow to the medical model of homosexuality when it was determined that homosexuality did not fit with an illness model. This idea was later reinforced by numerous research studies.

With the realization today that pronatalism is no longer a viable force in society, the medical model is again looked at as less valid. In 1973, the American Psychiatric Association removed homosexuality from its list of mental disorders.

As much as research has indicated that homosexuality is not a disease or disorder, it appears that historical attitudes have had an impact upon todays attitudes toward homosexuality. A majority of Americans still view homosexuality as sexually abnormal or perverted, or as a sign of mental illness (Weinberg and Williams, 1976). However, public attitude has changed, and instead of ostracizing homosexuals, people appear to be able to tolerate them. But there are still problems for the homosexual.

It always bothers me that people say they do not mind associating with homosexuals as long as they do not make passes at them. As far as I'm concerned, these people can't stand homosexuals. Why don't they make that comment about heterosexuals?

If the issue of abnormality or normality is to be settled in the minds of the overwhelming majority of people, it will be settled through scientific methods. However, the majority of evidence indicates that homosexuality is not associated with any other behavior generally believed to indicate an abnormality.

HOMOSEXUALITY AND THERAPY

In the past, the issue of whether or not homosexuals needed therapy was based upon the idea that homosexuality was abnormal. Some studies have shown that homosexuals do have more psychological problems than heterosexuals, but these may be caused by the social pressures placed upon homosexuals (Rosen, 1974). Others feel that the pressures placed upon homosexuals help them become better able to understand their role in society and develop a greater awareness of their individuality (Hopkins, 1969). Still, some feel that homosexuality or any other behavior itself is not a basis for psychological intervention (Sturgis and Adams, 1978). Individuals who seek the aid of psychotherapists can be normally functioning individuals who experience difficulties in certain aspects of their lives. If the homosexual does not experience these difficulties, the need to receive treatment is unnecessary. Therefore, therapy is no more called for among homosexuals than among heterosexuals. The only time treatment for homosexuality would be helpful would be when the individual is uncomfortable in his or her role. To try to use therapy to convert a homosexual into a heterosexual is perhaps an unworkable practice. Can we take the heterosexual and "make" him or her a comfortable homosexual? Therapy exists for those who feel they need it. Homosexuals need therapy no more than heterosexuals.

HOMOSEXUALITY AND THE FUTURE

While the claim has been made by homosexuals that they are a minority like many other groups (often references are made to blacks), they have not been seen as such by society. Homosexuals have been seeking rights that they feel belong to them. The Gay Activists Alliance has been in the forefront of the gay rights movement. The acceptance of homosexuals in our society still meets with great resistance. However, the efforts of gay activists have served to gain them greater rights by making their existence known through the media and by increasing the openness between people with sexual commitment who share the same social, psychological, economic, political, and religious spaces (Gagnon, 1977).

Among the examples of acceptance have been the lifting of restrictions against avowed homosexuals in many major industrial corporations. In fact, in occupations that were once extremely averse to gays, policies are

FIGURE 8.4 Gay San Francisco police officers being sworn in, with other recruits, by Mayor Dianne Feinstein. (Photo by United Press International)

now being reexamined. For example, the San Francisco police actively solicit gays for its force as a means of dealing more effectively with San Francisco's large gay population (Figure 8.4). There are now houses of worship that cater to gay congregations, the Gay Caucus of the National Education Association, and a host of other activity opportunities, and some organizations who were against gays are now tolerant of them.

However, the road to complete acceptance is in the far future. Old laws remain. For example, the Immigration and Naturalization Service of the federal government is required to enforce the exclusion of homosexual aliens, under the 1952 McCarran-Walter Act.

The changes created by the gay movement and a view of things to come are seen in the following excerpt:

> The gay world is succumbing to its own revolution. Once invisible, it is now being publicly examined as a curiosity. But the more it shows itself, the less reason it has to exist, because it was the creation of a people in hiding, a people who had to develop a private language and secret rituals and obscure places to survive. The laws haven't changed yet, but open gays are slowly being accepted into the life of the city.
>
> For those of us who have unscrewed our doors from their hinges, there is no course but to go forward, continuing to sacrifice our privacy in favor of honesty, and to insist in public on our right to freedom of sexual choice. Whether the straight world abandons its marital family structure or resuscitates it, there ought to be enough room for homosexuals to lead their lives openly among the rest. But it means changes for both worlds. Like the gay world, the straight world is defined by whom it excludes, and the borders are blurring already. As the gay world dies, paying the price of its own honesty, the straight world, as the single framework admitted by society, must die as well, and acknowledge the validity of alternate ways of love. Gays may not be understood or loved in spite of themselves, but with enough exposure, they should soon cease to be treated as the pernicious threat to the community they were once thought to be. The memory of the gay world will be absorbed into the history of Western culture, probably with legends more glittering than the actual facts.
>
> (Kantrowitz, 1975)

SUMMARY STATEMENTS

- *There are many theories for the causes of homosexuality.*
- *The Kinsey Continuum provides a good idea of the number of homosexuals in the U.S. population.*
- *Many persons harbor a great deal of animosity toward homosexuals.*
- *People discriminate against homosexuals for many reasons.*
- *There are different types of homosexuals.*
- *People often make false assumptions about homosexuals.*
- *Society places many pressures on homosexuals.*
- *Many people think the homosexual lifestyle has a mystique about it.*
- *Bisexuals are often ostracized by homosexuals and heterosexuals.*
- *Many models have been proposed that label homosexuality abnormal.*

- The APA has removed homosexuality from its list of mental disorders.
- Psychotherapy probably cannot make the homosexual a heterosexual.

- Many homosexuals regard themselves as oppressed.
- Over the past few years, society has become more tolerant of homosexuality.

SUGGESTED READINGS

Batchelor, Edward, ed. *Homosexuality and Ethics.* New York: Pilgrim Press, 1980.

Boswell, John. *Christianity, Social Tolerance and Homosexuality.* Chicago: The University of Chicago Press, 1980.

Chance, Paul. "Facts That Liberated the Gay Community: An Interview With Evelyn Hooker," *Psychology Today,* December, 1975.

Fast, Julius, and Hal Wells. *Bisexual Living.* New York: M. Evans and Company, 1975.

Katz, Jonathan. *Gay American History.* New York: Avon Books, 1976.

Sasha, Alyson, ed. *Young, Gay and Proud.* Boston: Alyson Publications, 1980.

Weinberg, George, *Society and the Healthy Homosexual.* New York: Anchor Books, 1973.

A LOOK AT YOUR LIFESTYLE

You have decided to live in a dormitory for the coming school year. Two different persons have approached you to share a room. One, however, is your favorite. You feel especially close to him/her. It seems you can be very honest, and you are completely accepted. This person approaches you and says, "Before you decide to room with me, I want you to know that I am bisexual."

Write an "I" message describing your reaction:

HOMOSEXUALITY AND BISEXUALITY

When you told me you were bisexual, I _____.

Identify the key issue or problem. _____
Identify three possible solutions or alternatives. _____

_____

_____

GATHERING INFORMATION
What are three things you would like to know about your friend?

_____

_____

EVALUATING THE INFORMATION
Identify at least one reason for and one reason against each alternative you identified. _____

_____

MAKING RESPONSIBLE DECISIONS
What alternative would you select?
Give the most important reason for your choice.

_____

NINE

Variations in Sexual Behavior

Classifying sexual behavior as normal or abnormal is a nearly impossible task. Many of those who are categorized as participating in sexual behavior acceptable by the majority (sexual intercourse in various positions in a heterosexual relationship) occasionally pay for a prostitute or practice adultery, anal intercourse, or group sex. Regardless of the behaviors selected, individuals who practice certain sexual behaviors that are outside the realm of marriage and are not traditional sexual intercourse may be considered by others "perverted" or "sexually deviant." Since identifying an act as "perverted" or "sexually deviant" is a difficult task (as is classifying one as "normal" and "abnormal"), we will use the term *sexual variation,* which is more favorably accepted among psychiatrists and psychologists today. Classifying a behavior as "variant" vis-à-vis "abnormal" or "deviant" appears more acceptable because of the flexibility allowed for many types of behavior.

GATHERING INFORMATION

When becoming involved in sexual experiences that may be thought of as variations, you should consider many things. In this chapter we will

247

look at those practices that most often cause people to take a second look at their own behavior as well as the behavior of others.

EVALUATING THE INFORMATION

In this chapter, the following information will be included to help you evaluate carefully your position with regard to the variations encountered in the complex world of sexual behavior and practices:

1. the typical variations in sexual behavior: a description of each behavior
2. the causes of the various sexual variations: the psychological theories espoused
3. who practices the variations: the kinds of people who fall into the various categories
4. coping: how individuals learn to accept their behavior if, in fact, that behavior is not deemed extremely deviant by society

It could be that exposure to the facts of the many variations in sexual behavior might help us better understand not only our own behavior but also the behavior of others. Seeking help for oneself or others may be a more positive measure than ostracism. Knowing what motivates one to behave in a certain way may provide the insight needed for us to evaluate the outcome of that behavior.

MAKING RESPONSIBLE DECISIONS

When one decides to engage in behaviors that can be detrimental to the health of others, whether physical, emotional, social, or spiritual, then the behavior as well as its motivation should be examined. The key word in sexual practices is *consenting*. Many psychologists and researchers in human sexuality feel that anything consenting adults decide to do with their sexual behavior in privacy is acceptable. For example, if two consenting adults decide to act out a sadomasochistic fantasy at home, then who is to say that they are wrong in doing so? Might not a couple who decide to refrain from acting out their feelings bring anxiety and frustration into a relationship? Unfortunately, many individuals do not act upon their lifestyle choices. Here are some of the reasons:

"It is embarrassing, especially if someone else should find out."
"I was always told that I was not *supposed* to act that way."
"If I told my partner how I felt, I'd be looked down upon."
"I may find that I will enjoy acting out my fantasy, and therefore I may wish to do it again."
"I may be labeled a 'pervert'."

If we fail to act upon our intentions, then we need to ask ourselves why? In order to understand the values we hold, we need to examine the facts upon which values are predicated. Many forms of sexual behavior are not acceptable by society; yet many individuals unknowingly offend other people. For example, people who expose themselves in public may think they are making people laugh when, in fact, the rights of others are being infringed upon. They need to know the limits of the behavior they select and respect the rights of others.

TOWARD A CLARIFICATION OF NORMAL AND ABNORMAL BEHAVIOR

The sexual lifestyle of today's man and woman has many facets. If we were to list the many departures from standard coital practices, we might find that many practices fall into the category of *sexually deviant behavior*. According to this classification, a person whose sexual interests are directed toward objects other than people of the opposite sex or whose sexual acts are not usually associated with coitus may be considered as engaging in sexually deviant behavior (American Psychiatric Association, 1978). Variance in sexual behavior can range from the flagrantly bizarre, practiced among a very few, to common heterosexual practices, engaged in by many. While many of the activities that will be discussed in this chapter may appear outright pathological, others may actually be variations of sexual behaviors. For example, during the act of sexual intercourse, a man may restrain a woman's movement by holding her wrists down against the bed. During passionate lovemaking, the woman may try to "force" herself free from the man's grasp, yet at the same time find the situation a "turn-on." In this example, the man may be playing a sadistic role and the woman, a masochistic role. Yet is this deviant behavior? Perhaps, a classification of "variation" may be more appropriate.

Freud stated that any form of sexual behavior in adults that took precedence over heterosexual intercourse signified a defect in psychosexual development. Freud used the terms "sexual object" and "sexual aim" to label sexual behavior. The sexual object is the person from whom sexual attraction emanates, whereas the sexual aim is what one wishes to do with the object. According to Freud, a healthy sexual relationship involves a person of the opposite sex (sexual object) and sexual intercourse (sexual aim). Deviations from this situation can therefore take two forms. Homosexuality might be an example of a deviation with regard to the "object" (discussed in Chapter 8), and exhibitionism (exposing one's own genitals) might be a deviation with regard to the "aim." However, if one uses Freud's logic, even widely accepted practices such as oral—genital contact are deviant. Using Freud's logic hinders the objectification or categorization of deviant behavior, since the majority of Americans would have to be labeled deviant, by his definition.

Before I was married, I was always told that oral–genital sex was dirty. During our honeymoon my husband requested that we go "69." Not only did the thought repulse me, but the fact that my husband suggested it made me feel like a prostitute. For the first two years of our marriage, we did not have oral sex. But during these two years, I discovered that most of our friends were engaging in oral–genital contacts. My husband took me to see one of those porno films in which a woman and a man were having oral sex. We were both drinking and so I felt "loose." After that movie, we tried oral sex. It wasn't so bad. Gradually I got rid of my hangups and today, oral sex is an integral part of our sexual relationship. Needless to say, I missed out during the first two years of marriage.

In trying to classify sexual behavior as normal or abnormal, other researchers have used statistical significance (Pomeroy, 1966). They feel that a sexual behavior is deviant if it is practiced by only a few. This concept may be easy to accept if one assesses a bizarre practice such as necrophilia (sex with a dead body), which is rare. However, the spontaneous desire of a heterosexual couple to engage in sexual intercourse on top of a television set is also rare. Yet this behavior might not be considered deviant.

In defining what is deviant and what is not, one must examine one's culture and society. For example, some cultures forbid a husband to engage in sexual intercourse with his wife for months after childbirth. Failure to adhere to this practice would constitute deviant sexual behavior.

FETISHISM

Fetishism is defined as a state of being erotically aroused by objects, commonly by articles of clothing while they are being worn, when they are separated from their owner's body, or when they are depicted in the media (Gagnon, 1977). Thus, a man may be aroused by a woman's leg that has a black nylon stocking on it, by the stocking alone, or by a drawing of the stocking.

One can have a fetish for a sexual part of the body, such as breasts, buttocks, or legs. It is an intensification of a normal tendency that exists in most men and women. For example, men are often heard discussing their preferences in women by indicating that they are "leg men" or "breast men." Women often indicate similar preferences by stating that they are aroused by men who have hairy chests, broad shoulders, or blue eyes. In these cases, the fetish objects are parts of the body and the fetish may therefore be difficult to detect.

When a fetish is an inanimate object, it is much easier to detect. Usually the fetish is substituted for the real love object. Articles such as stockings, shoes, gloves, and women's panties are sometimes fondled, looked at, or used as a part of masturbation. In most cases, the one who has the fetish is male (Karpman, 1954). However, fixation upon inanimate objects does not necessarily indicate that a person is abnormal.

FIGURE 9.1 Articles of clothing, such as black nylon stockings, may be sexually arousing. (Photos, left, by Joel Gordon 1981; right, by Teri Leigh Stratford)

The Gebhard Continuum

Paul Gebhard developed a practical continuum to classify fetishistic behavior (Gebhard, 1976). He classified fetishes as follows (examples are given with each):

1. Slight preference: A man prefers that his wife wear black nylon stockings before sexual intercourse because he finds the stockings to be arousing. However, the nylon stockings are not a prerequisite for sexual intercourse or, for that matter, arousal.

2. Strong preference: A man demands that his wife wear black nylon stockings before sexual intercourse to intensify his feelings of arousal. He feels strongly that these stockings add a desired dimension of arousal.

3. Necessity: A man will not be able to perform unless his wife wears black nylon stockings.

4. Substitution for a human partner: A man satisfies himself by wearing his wife's black nylon stockings and masturbating.

According to Gebhard, normality ends and fetishistic deviance starts at the stage of strong preference. In extreme cases of fetishism, burglaries may take place. In many police investigations of burglarized homes, women's panties containing semen are found. Occasionally the burglar may take women's undergarments and masturbate to achieve erotic stimulation. In such cases, theft is often the secondary motive for entering the house (Coleman, 1972).

Pyromania, or compulsive fire-setting, is another example of a fetishistic pattern. Fire has sexual connotations. A pyromaniac receives gratification by setting a fire, watching it, and then masturbating (Robbins et al., 1969). On occasion, police will look for individuals who are masturbating in a crowd while watching a fire being extinguished.

Causes of Fetishism

The causes of fetishism are not known, although two theories have been described in the literature. The first theory is based upon the research of Freud (1928). He regarded the fetish object as a substitute for the penis that, as a young child, the person with the fetish believed his mother had. As this young child grows older, his perception of the mother's penis is modified, and thus a penis in a true anatomical sense is correctly denied. The child subconsciously believes that his mother does possess a penis, and the fetish becomes a substitute.

The second theory given for the cause of fetishism is based upon a learned experience between the fetish and sexual arousal. For example, if a man's first sexual encounter, in which he achieved orgasm, involved having sexual intercourse with a woman who wore sunglasses, he might begin to associate sexual arousal with sunglasses. As a result, in subsequent encounters he might require that his partner wear sunglasses.

TRANSVESTISM

Transvestism is often defined as the wearing of clothes of the opposite sex in order to achieve sexual gratification. In this respect, it is difficult to distinguish between having a clothes fetish and being a transvestite (Yales, 1970). For the purpose of simplicity within this chapter, transvestism will be considered a separate sexual deviation.

A person who cross-dresses is not necessarily a transvestite. Many adolescent boys will try on clothes of the opposite sex simply to identify with a sex drive or to act out some frustrations (Green, 1975). Some female impersonators perform on stage to make money. Other men may cross-dress so they can pretend they are female prostitutes and thus make money by "turning tricks" on "johns" (their male customers). Since many of the sex acts performed by prostitutes are fellatio, the threat of being discovered as a cross-dressed male is minimal. In addition, if the customer discovered the cross-dressing, chances are he would continue in his quest for sexual

FIGURE 9.2 A man dressed in man's clothing, and in women's clothing. (Photos by Jason Laure' 1981)

gratification, since it is the female image that sparks his arousal. Some, however, would become angry and attack the prostitute.

The Transvestite Lifestyle

Reported data indicate that the "average" transvestite is married, has children, is heterosexual, and does not get into trouble with the law (Bruckner, 1970; Prince and Bentler, 1972). Although accurate figures are not available, it is estimated that there are more than one million males who achieve sexual arousal by wearing women's clothing (Pomeroy, 1975).

I have been cross-dressing ever since I got out of high school. I still live at home, but I think my parents just deny that their son is a "T.V." I'm sure they have looked in my closet and have seen the clothes I've been buying. I also have make-up on my table. Could my parents be that dumb?

Transvestism is almost exclusively a male phenomenon, for reasons not easily identifiable. The most accepted theory is that transvestism is an attempt to overcome the fear of castration, and therefore the male creates an imaginary phallic woman and identifies with her (Tollison and Adams, 1979).

Contrary to what most people believe, the transvestite usually is not a homosexual. In fact, the gay world despises transvestites, since cross-dressing promotes the image in most persons' minds that the male homosexual is effeminate. The gay community is trying to rid society of this stereotype.

The kinds of clothing a transvestite wears are usually ordinary-looking—unlike those of the female impersonator, who wears flamboyant clothing. Many transvestites will shop for their own clothing with the overt pretense of buying clothes for their wives or girlfriends. Often the transvestite is not sure of the corresponding sizes from female to male. As a result, they frequently return items after purchasing the wrong size.

Whether or not transvestism is a problem is something that can only be determined by the individual's behavior. The overwhelming majority of transvestites (86%) indicate that their interest in females is normal or above average, and most of these individuals remain secretive about their behavior (Prince and Bentler, 1972). Thus, privacy appears to be the norm in cross-dressing.

TRANSSEXUALISM

A *transsexual* is a person who wishes to be or sincerely believes that he or she is a member of the opposite sex. A biological male who is a transsexual often feels that he is a woman who is trapped in the body of a man. In each case, we find that the transsexual exhibits a condition in which the individual's anatomy and *gender identity* (sex role orientation) are incompatible.

The transsexual is often confused with the transvestite and the homosexual. The transsexual and the transvestite both have conflicts of gender identity; however, the conflicts of the transsexual are more profound. The homosexual has no gender identity conflict but simply is psychosexually attracted to a person of the same sex. Benjamin and Ihlenfeld (1973), two of the early pioneers in the study of transsexualism, developed a continuum of tranvestism to transsexualism (Table 9.1). According to this continuum, the transvestite and transsexual are distinguishable by the degree of gender discomfort and the measures that are taken to alleviate that discomfort. That is, the higher one is on the continuum toward transsexualism, the greater the frequency and intensity of playing the role of the opposite biological sex. Since homosexuality involves no gender identity conflict, there was no need for us to place this category on the continuum.

Perhaps the major reason people confuse the transsexual and the homosexual lies in the sexual relationship each has. Although the transsexual cross-dresses and engages in sexual relations with persons of the same sex, the idea that a homosexual relationship is taking place is nonexistent in the mind of the transsexual. If the transsexual feels he is a member of the opposite sex (i.e., if "he" feels as if he is a "she"), the natural tendency for a heterosexual relationship would be to take a male partner.

FIGURE 9.3 Dr. Richard Raskind (left), who underwent a sex-change operation to become Dr. Renee Richards (right). (Photos by World Wide Photos, left, and Tony Korody, Sygma, right)

TABLE 9.1 TRANSVESTITE–TRANSSEXUAL CONTINUUM IN MALES*

Type 1	Type 2	Type 3	Type 4	Type 5	Type 6
Pseudo-transvestite. Occasionally cross-dresses; low degree of gender identity conflict.	Fetishistic transvestite. Cross-dresses more often; has low degree of gender identity conflict.	True transvestite. Cross-dresses as often as possible; gender identity still masculine but less than Types 1 and 2.	Nonsurgical transsexual. A true transsexual who is willing to live without surgery; cross-dresses often; gender identity uncertain.	Moderate intensity true transsexual. Lives as a woman when possible; gender identity feminine.	High intensity true transsexual. Usually lives as a woman; gender identity feminine.

*Adapted from Benjamin, Harry, and Charles L. Ihlenfeld. "Transsexualism," *American Journal of Nursing*, March 1973, 73(3): 458–459.

Causes of Transsexualism

Perhaps the most accepted explanation for the causes of transsexualism comes from the work of several researchers (Lukianowicz, 1959; Driscoll, 1971; Green, 1975). Studies of the histories of transsexuals of both sexes indicate that many of their experiences up to age 6 differed from the accepted norm. In the case of the male, it was found that the mother kept the infant very close to herself and gratified his wishes as soon as possible. All of the child's actions that kept child and mother close were encouraged by the mother, while actions which separated child and mother were discouraged. As the child grew, the mother found that she might not be capable of handling aggressive behavior and as a result directed the child to quieter activities and play with girls, causing the child to believe that feminine actions would bring positive responses from the mother. As a result, the child might begin to dress in female clothing so as to receive further positive reinforcement. In families of this nature, the father is often absent or is timid, which leads the child to believe he is weak. Accordingly, the child sees the mother as strong and authoritarian. This kind of child begins to learn that being a girl is much more natural than being a boy.

In the case of the anatomic female transsexual, the cause may differ. In this instance, the mother of the infant girl is not active in the mothering role, perhaps because of an emotional or physical illness. Concurrently, the father may not provide the mother with the emotional support needed. The young girl is then raised as a surrogate husband who is rewarded for behavior that is assertive and independent. The child may be encouraged to care for her mother as much as possible, in a role similar to the role the father might play. Along with this role, the father might encourage the child to be his companion in sports, games, and hobbies. Thus, the young girl, as she is reinforced by her actions, finds it more rewarding and natural to be a boy than a girl.

Behavioral theories frequently suggest that there are four instances in the male's early development that may cause transsexualism:

1. Many males dressed in girl's clothing and performed activities that women did around the house.
2. Many male transsexuals reported that they were dressed in clothing of the opposite sex as punishment.
3. Many male transsexuals received the favored status of a "little girl."
4. Many male transsexuals had no male around the house as a model for behavior (Lukianowicz, 1959).

The causes of these patterns cannot be explained definitively.

CHANGING SEXES

Males seeking a sex change outnumber females by eight to one (Ihlenfeld, 1972). The process of gender reassignment usually is divided into four stages.

The first stage is psychotherapy. During this stage, the person must ascertain whether or not he is a true transsexual.

The second stage consists of hormone treatments that give the male female characteristics.

In the third, or preoperative, stage, the person lives the life of the opposite sex. Once the person is comfortable with these stages, the fourth stage, surgery is undertaken (Figure 9.4).

In male-to-female surgery, the penis and testicles are removed. The skin of the penis is then used to create labia and an artificial vagina. Nerve endings in the skin will still provide sexual excitement. Part of the artificial vagina is made of a plastic pouch to prevent the vagina from growing together.

The female-to-male sex change requires several stages that take about six months. First, a mastectomy (removal of the breasts) is performed. Later, the ovaries and uterus are removed. Last, external genitalia can be made by the forming of a scrotum from labial tissue and testicles from a silicone prosthesis. A penis may be created with skin from the abdominal wall. A tube is extended into the urethra. The "penis," however, is made of nonerectile tissue that functions only during urination.

SADISM AND MASOCHISM

Sadism is a sexual variance in which a person receives sexual pleasure by inflicting physical or psychological pain on the sexual partner. The word "sadism" comes from the Marquis de Sade (1740–1814), a French nobleman and writer who lived during the period of the French Revolution.

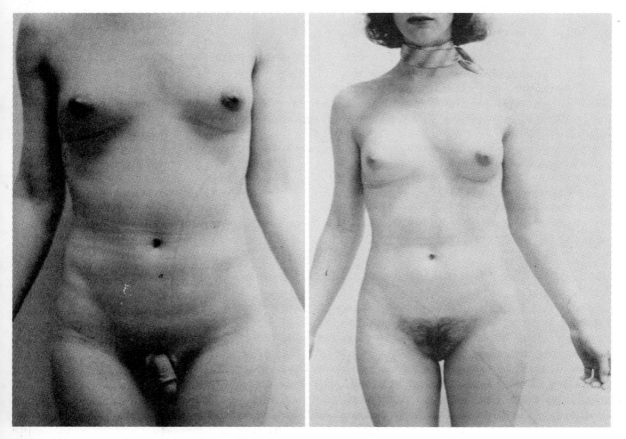

FIGURE 9.4 Result of the conversion of a transsexual male. The breasts have developed naturally as a result of hormone therapy, and the external genitalia have an overall natural feminine appearance. (Reproduced with permission from the *Journal of Plastic and Reconstructive Surgery* 64:311, 1979.)

Masochism, the opposite of sadism, is a sexual variance in which a person receives sexual pleasure from being physically or psychologically hurt by the sexual partner. This variance is named after the German novelist Leopold Sacher-Masoch (1836–1895), who wrote novels that focused on the theme of erotic degradation of a man by a woman.

Besides their sexual connotations, the terms sadism and masochism are often used to mean giving and receiving pain, respectively. However, in this text, these terms will connote sex-related behaviors.

Sadomasochistic behavior can take many forms. In a sexual encounter, the sadist, who may also be known as the *dominant* partner, may engage in behavior such as whipping, biting, or pinching, defecating on, or yelling and swearing at his mate, who, as the recipient, is known as the masochist, or *submissive* partner. Sadomasochistic behaviors appear to be prevalent in the general population to a large extent. Two best-selling books, *The Joy of Sex* (Comfort, 1972) and *More Joy* (Comfort, 1973), advise mild forms of sadistic behaviors for enhancing sexual pleasure. According to Comfort (1973):

> . . . learning to use the sexual language of muscles is a resource, and it can be highly reinforced by the intensity of the climax it gives. Actual struggle, if it's under control, turns many men on, and it may be because abortive movements are effective and reminiscent of infant sensuality experiences that they often wish the women were the stronger. Bondage (i.e. binding someone so that muscular tension is maximal but they can't move or get loose) is another traditional method, and the only one which maintains the tension right up to and through actual orgasm: you can't have sex while wrestling. Skillfully done it can give a man an orgasm in which nearly every muscle of the body takes part, making him, in one informant's words, "feel like one huge penis"—a psychoanalytic bonus which probably contributes to its popularity.

In the sadomasochistic relationship, the partners need to recognize the acts that are dangerous and that go beyond consent. Assuming that two people are consenting adults, their behavior should be sexually satisfying. The sadist must be able to differentiate between when a partner (masochist) says "No" and means "No" and when that partner says "No" and really means "Give me more." In one form or another, many relationships are sadomasochistic, whether consciously or unconsciously.

In sadomasochistic encounters, the variations of behaviors appear to be endless. Generally, the sadists, or dominants, play a "master" role and the masochists, or submissives, play a "slave" role. *Bondage,* meaning that the masochist has his or her feet and hands tied up by the sadist, is a common practice in which the idea of restricting one's movement during the sex act is used as an erotic stimulus. While some couples practice obvious conscious forms of sadomasochistic behavior, such as enacting rape scenes, handcuffing, whipping, and tickling, by no means does this behavior occur in every sadomasochistic sexual encounter.

Steve and Gail have been married for five years. During this period, they have shared each other's fantasies and on occasion have acted them out. Only one in four sexual encounters would entail a sadomasochistic scene. Typical of one of these scenes, Gail was handcuffed to a chair. She was seated on sandpaper, which was glued to the seat. Steve would tickle the bottom of Gail's feet with a feather, and in turn, Gail would be forced to wiggle in her chair and her buttocks would rub against the sandpaper. She found this to be a sexual turn on in her role as the masochist. Steve, in turn, found that this role as the master was sexually gratifying. They would engage in incidents similar to this about once a week with the possibility of a session lasting for several hours or even a full day.

While it may sound absurd to many people that giving and receiving pain could be sexually gratifying, it is not an uncommon phenomenon. Kinsey et al. (1973) found that 3% of females and 1% of males admitted to having an erotic response to sadistic stories, while Hunt (1974) found that

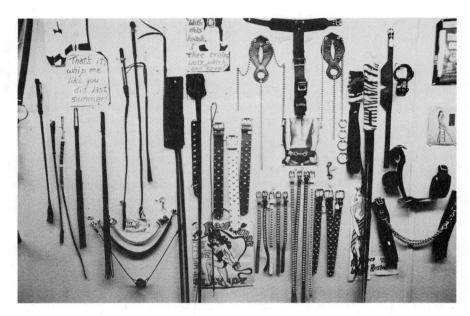

FIGURE 9.5 "Toys" for sadomasochists displayed in a sexual "equipment" store. (Photo by Joel Gordon 1981)

4% to 5% of respondents have obtained sexual pleasure from receiving or inflicting pain. The male is more inclined to inflict pain, while the female is more likely to be the recipient of pain during erotic activities.

The formalization of sadomasochistic aspects of sexuality has taken place in the formation of organizations. One such organization, formed in New York, is called the *Eulenspiegel Society.* This organization supports sexual liberation as a basic requirement of a truly free society. The Eulenspiegel Society, like similar organizations, has a concern for the freedom for sexual minorities and particularly the rights of those whose sexuality embraces sadomasochism.

The examples of sadomasochism discussed thus far reflect its more common forms. On rare occasions, violent and forcible sadistic behavior without consent does occur. These incidents can go to the extreme of involving murder. Some individuals murder for lust. In a *lust murder*, the sadist will mutilate another person's body to achieve sexual gratification. In such cases, the sadist's mental illness is at the psychotic level. John Gacy, convicted of killing 34 young boys and men during the 1970s in the Chicago area, is an example of a homosexual who committed many lust murders.

The Causes of Sadomasochism

The causes of sadism and masochism are not definitely known. Some theorists believe that sadistic behavior develops when a person associates

FIGURE 9.6 Advertising for sadomasochistic relationships. These ads appeared in Prometheus, a publication of the Eulenspiegel Society.

A SPANKING NEW OFFER:
Straight, young, good-looking male, seeks female.
Object: Give and/or take. **Enthusiasm** — Yes! But no way-out scenes.

SUBMISSIVE MALE wishes to serve as a houseboy to a dominant female. I am obedient and require training as a part-time servant.

TURNED ON BY SPANKING? Male, straight, middle aged, dominant, seeks female, straight, submissive, for possible sexual relationship after we get to be friends.

Female/Dominant/Bisexual/30/White — Tall redhead. Interested in meeting all males and females together or separate who are interested in *all* phases of sexual activities.

---

arousal and orgasm with viewing pain or inflicting pain on another individual.

One explanation for the development of masochistic behavior may be a deep fear of abandonment, neglect, or rejection. Often this fear can be traced to an experience during early childhood. For example, a child who feels neglected by her mother may often do things that will cause her mother to punish her. If the child feels that this is the only way she can get her mother to pay attention to her, she will often engage in mischievous behavior. Soon the child begins to equate punishment with love.

Again, theories of the development of sadomasochistic behavior have not been proved. Perhaps the causes of sadism and masochism are as varied as the number of ways these behaviors can be expressed.

PEDOPHILIA

Pedophilia, or child molesting, is a form of sexual variation in which adults derive erotic pleasure from using children as sexual objects. The person who derives the pleasure from the child is known as a *pedophile.* The majority of pedophiles are male. The male pedophile may be interested in either the prepubescent male or the prepubescent female, but not both.

Defining pedophilia is very difficult. Legally, a person can be charged with pedophilia if he has sexual contact with a minor under the age of 18. Thus, an 18-year-old boy can have legal charges brought against him if he has sexual contact with a 17-year-old girl. Obviously, many 18-year-olds would be under arrest if this law were enforced in every instance.

The incidence of child molesting is much higher than most people believe. Kinsey found that 24% of the women in his study had been approached by a male who was at least five years older. The age range of these children was 4 to 13. The girls in this study were reared in a middle-class environment. Girls reared in lower-class environments tend to be the subjects of more frequent adult–child sex acts.

The adult who has committed a sex act with a child is considered by our society to be degenerate. Perhaps no other behavior can generate more social disgust than pedophilia. Even in prison, the convicted pedophile is considered the lowest grade of prisoner by other prisoners. As a result, he is often the object of physical and psychological abuse while confined.

The types of behavior that constitute pedophilia include the following: caressing a child's body, fondling a child's genitals or inducing a child to fondle or manipulate an adult's genitals, partial or complete vaginal or anal penetration, oral–genital contact, or simple touching used to encourage sexual arousal. Pedophilic acts can take the form of homosexual or heterosexual behavior.

Contrary to what many people believe, the typical child molester is not someone who dresses in ragged clothing and lurks in dark alleyways. From 50% to 80% of all child molestations are committed by relatives, friends of the family, or others known by the victim. Only a minority of child molestations are committed by strangers.

A child who is molested is usually only temporarily upset and frightened. If neither violence nor extreme coercion were used, the occurrence is often no more upsetting to the child than being frightened by a dog that growled unexpectedly. However, the effects of child molestation can be long-term. The trauma may be prolonged when parents or other adults involved become hysterical or overreact in other ways. The results of the molestation will be less severe for the child if the parents can deal with it in a controlled manner.

INCEST

The term *incest* (from the Latin word for "impure" or "soiled") is commonly used to indicate sexual relations between people related by birth. It may connote sexual activity between an individual and any close relative, such as a grandparent, uncle, aunt, father, mother, brother, or sister. In some religions, sexual activity between first cousins is considered incest. The Roman Catholic and Greek Orthodox churches prohibit marriage between first cousins. However, marriage between first cousins is accepted by many Protestant churches as well as by Judaism and Islam.

Types of Incest

Studies seem to indicate that father–daughter (or stepdaughter) incest is the most common type reported, whereas mother–son is the least reported (Cavallin, 1973). While the daughter is sometimes a willing participant, the father most often initiates the sexual relationship.

Father–daughter incest seems to appear most in families in which the father is under a great deal of stress from pressures outside the family. Because of the stress caused by these pressures, the wife may withdraw sexual and emotional support from the father. Thus, the father may turn to the daughter for emotional as well as sexual fulfillment. In some families, the father turns his sexual preferences to different daughters. For example, as each daughter grows up and leaves the house, the father may focus his attentions on another, usually younger, daughter.

Sexual activity between brother and sister, although not the most common reported, is considered the most frequent type of incest practiced (Weinberg, 1955). Although this type of relationship is not often discovered by parents, it is usually not treated as a serious problem when it is uncovered. Incest between brother and sister most often occurs in families either when children are given too much sexual freedom or when brothers and sisters share the same bedroom. Females are more likely to engage in sexual relations with a brother than with the father. In some cases, the female may be the aggressor.

The Prevalence of Incest

According to Hunt (1974), 15% of the respondents in his study indicated having some sexual contact with relatives. However, most of this contact was between siblings or cousins, as opposed to parent and child. Seven percent of Hunt's sample reported having been involved in coitus. However, most of these cases involved activity between siblings and their cousins.

The Incest Taboo

Almost all human societies consider incest taboo. It has been suggested that incest prohibitions are instinctive, although this is only a theory. Another reason incest is considered taboo is that it would create situations of intense rivalry within the family structure and this rivalry would lead to the destruction of the family unit (Delora and Warren, 1977).

The third taboo of incest relates to the idea of genetic inbreeding. It is believed that genetic inbreeding causes a deterioration of genetic quality and increases the risk of defective offspring from recessive hereditary diseases (Delora and Warren, 1977).

While there is little information regarding the long-term effects of incest, there is some indication it may be damaging (Gagnon, 1977). A girl who is approached for sex by her father will often run away from home to avoid him. In the process, she may become involved with irresponsible persons. More important, however, is psychological trauma created by her father's behavior that is bound to have a negative effect on the child.

VOYEURISM

Voyeurism generally refers to the act of obtaining sexual gratification from looking at the bodies, sex organs, or sex acts of other persons. While most men and women may at times enjoy looking at the bodies of other men and women, the *voyeur* obtains all of his sexual satisfaction from the act of peeping and the masturbation that accompanies it. Voyeurism is considered a deviation when it is preferred to coitus.

Most voyeurs are male. Often, this type of a person is called a "Peeping Tom." Only 10% of those arrested for voyeurism are female; 90% are male. While most people consider watching others in the sex act as legal (i.e., "peep shows" and pornographic movies), such behavior becomes illegal when the viewing of others takes place surreptitiously in their homes, hotel rooms, or cars. On the other hand, those engaging in sexual acts must make an effort to provide themselves with privacy. For example, a couple who, inside the confines of their home, decided to engage in sexual intercourse in front of the bedroom window with the shades undrawn and in full view of their neighbors could probably be arrested, and the onlookers would not be charged with an illegal act.

Characteristics of Voyeurs

Perhaps the single most common characteristic of voyeurs is a history of deficiency in the quality and quantity of their heterosexual relationships. Most voyeurs are anxious and have great trepidation about forming a heterosexual relationship. As a result, they seek sexual arousal and gratification through peeping. Those voyeurs who are married are only minimally aroused by their wives.

The voyeur will not usually watch a person he knows well. Apparently, there is novelty in viewing strangers. The need to scale fences or balance on window ledges may in itself constitute the very element of danger that the voyeur finds sexually exciting.

While most voyeurs are harmless, some commit rape or burglary. Those who enter dwellings to "peep" or who go out of their way to attract a woman's attention are more likely to commit a rape (Gebhard et al., 1965).

Causes of Voyeurism

The specific causes of voyeurism have, like the causes of other variances, not been isolated. Voyeuristic behavior is probably the result of learning, conditioning, and the reinforcing nature of orgasm. For example, if a voyeuristic sight is positive, in that it causes sexual arousal, the voyeur masturbates at that moment and then recalls it in fantasy and masturbates again. The association becomes strengthened. Repeated voyeuristic behaviors may produce the same effects, which in turn strengthen the desire to "peep."

Another reason given for practicing voyeurism is that the voyeur can guard against personal failure in sexual activity by feeling superior to those being secretly observed. Some theorists believe that this fixation is related to certain events the voyeur witnessed as a child, such as his observing his parents in the act of sexual intercourse.

EXHIBITIONISM

The term *exhibitionism* is defined as the exposure of the sexual organs to the opposite sex in situations in which exposure is socially defined as inappropriate and when the exposure, at least in part, is for the purpose of his or her own sexual arousal and gratification. An *exhibitionist* is a person who participates in such activity.

While a few of the exhibitionists arrested are women, the majority are men. Exhibitionism accounts for 35% of all arrests for sex offenses (Allen, 1969).

In most cases, the exhibitionist will expose himself to strangers. This exposure is usually premeditated. The act can vary. The exhibitionist may expose himself with a flaccid penis, or he may have an erect penis, and this exposure may be accompanied by masturbation.

Studies indicate that the exhibitionist receives satisfaction when a response is elicited from a victim (Ellis and Brancale, 1956). The louder the victim's laugh or scream, or the greater the victim's anger, the greater the joy of the exhibitionist.

Causes of Exhibitionism

The reasons a man exposes himself to females are not known. Some exhibitionists feel that the reaction of others to a large penis is a comment on their virility (Chesster, 1971). In other cases, the exhibitionist considers the shock and fear of the victim as an indication of his masculinity.

The causes of exhibitionism, like the causes of other sexual variances, may be feelings of inadequacy. Some researchers believe that exhibitionism may be due to a fear of castration and that exposure of the genitals, or "flashing," is an attempt to remove this fear (McCary, 1978). Yet other researchers claim that exposing one's genitals in public is a part of narcissism (absorbing self-love).

ANIMAL CONTACTS

Using animals as sex objects is known as *bestiality, zoophilia,* and *bestiosexuality*. While sexual activity between animals and humans has been documented throughout civilization, it is abhorred by societies today. However, many a person has viewed "stag" films that depict various sexual activities between humans and animals. In reality, the occurrence of sexual activity between humans and animals is quite rare, even if films are made that show this behavior.

According to Kinsey (1948), 17% of boys raised on farms had sexual contact with animals that culminated in orgasm. This contact was usually temporary and diminished as the boy became older. The incidence of animal contact for boys who grew up in cities was much less frequent than that of boys on farms because the farm environment has many more animals. The types of sexual activity that may take place are intercourse with an animal or being licked and rubbed in the genital area by an animal.

NECROPHILIA

Necrophilia means using a corpse to obtain sexual gratification. A man who participates in this type of behavior, which is extremely rare, has a profound emotional disturbance. A man who engages in necrophilia can become sexually aroused by either viewing or engaging in sexual intercourse with the corpse. In some cases, mutilation of the dead body follows the sexual activity (Solomon and Patch, 1974).

The *necrophile,* who is almost always male, may go to great extremes to obtain a corpse. Necrophiles have been known to remove corpses from graves and seek employment in funeral homes. Although most necrophiles are not capable of engaging in sexual intercourse with living women, some may be able to if the woman pretends to be dead.

FROTTAGE

Frottage is defined as the act of obtaining sexual pleasure by rubbing or pressing the penis against a person, usually against the buttocks of a fully clothed woman. A person who performs this type of activity is called a *frotteur*. This activity usually goes unnoticed by the person who is being rubbed. Most often it takes place in crowded places, such as elevators or subways. The frotteur will usually seek out a woman and then inconspicuously stand behind her.

I remember riding on the subways in New York during rush hour. Several times a week I would notice guys standing behind women and sharing the same post. These guys would then rub their penis against the woman's buttocks and pretend they were being pushed into that position.

The frotteur is usually, or believes himself to be, unappealing to the opposite sex, impotent, and fearful of engaging in sexual intercourse.

COPROLALIA

Coprolalia is defined as obtaining sexual pleasure from using "dirty" language. The dirty language can be spoken by one's partner or oneself. While slang can be stimulating to many people during the sex act, the use of this terminology does not necessarily constitute coprolalia. Coprolalia refers to persons who can achieve sexual arousal only by using slang words.

Telephone coprolalia, which refers to obscene talking to strangers or known persons on the telephone to achieve sexual gratification, is not uncommon. Often the obscene caller will masturbate while he details a sexual encounter.

> There was this one guy who would call me and always describe what he would do to me sexually. Finally I got wise. The next time he called, I tapped the connection once very quickly and said "Operator, did you trace it?" Of course there was no trace, but it scared the guy so much that he never called back again.

SEXUAL URETHRALISM

A male or female who is sexually aroused by stimulation of the urethra by an object is said to be practicing *sexual urethralism*. Medical problems can result from this practice, since objects that may be inserted into the urethra can damage its lining or enter the bladder. The chances of an object entering the bladder are greater for a female than a male, because the urethra is much longer in the male.

Urophilia, which is sexual arousal from and erotic interest in urine, is closely related to urethralism. Some individuals are sexually aroused by having persons urinate on them. Known as "water sports," this practice is associated with sadomasochistic behavior, since being urinated upon is a type of degradation.

SATYRIASIS AND NYMPHOMANIA

Satyriasis and nymphomania are conditions in which one's appetite for sex is insatiable, so as to interfere with all other concerns or interests. This condition in women is known as *nymphomania* and in men, *satyriasis*.

In our society, it is common for men to label a woman as a nymphomaniac, or "nymph," if she desires frequent sex. However, the true nymphomaniac is a rarity. Just what "wanting too much sex" is, is usually a value judgment, often made by men. True nymphomania is compulsive sexual behavior that causes a woman to engage in irrational and self-defeating activities; the signs and symptoms are those of any compulsion (Ellis and

Sagarin, 1964). Yet as a sexual deviation and disorder, nymphomania is rare.

Often women are given the title of "nymph" by males who are ignorant of female sexual physiology and response. Many sex researchers clearly indicate that the female is capable of multiple orgasms, while most men are sexually fulfilled after one orgasm. This inability by the male to understand a woman's healthy sexuality often leads to his labeling her "oversexed."

In a relationship, a man may use his partner's zeal for sex as a tool for dealing with his inferiority. For example, if the woman wants to engage in sexual intercourse every day and the man desires it only twice a week, he may label her "abnormal." He may do so to preserve his own self-image by covering up what he believes is his inadequacy as a man. Individuals have different sexual needs. It has been ingrained in many people in our society that women are supposed to have a low sex drive and men a high sex drive. To the person not knowledgeable about sex, a strong sex drive in a woman is frequently a problem in a relationship.

The man who desires a great deal of sex is often not branded by society as "abnormal," since it is expected of the man to be able to fulfill his masculine role as a "pleaser of women." However, even though rare, satyriasis does exist. Like the nymphomaniac, the male who has an insatiable sexual appetite is considered to have a problem.

Both satyriasis and nymphomania can be treated successfully with psychotherapy.

PROSTITUTION

A *prostitute* is a person who engages in sexual acts for monetary rewards. Two criteria must be met if one is to be considered a prostitute: (1) that payment for the service is immediate and (2) that the payment is understood by the participants to be limited to the sexual occurrence (Gagnon, 1977). Prostitutes usually are not discriminating in their choice of sexual partners.

Prostitutes in most cases are women, and they are also known as "hookers" or "whores." Male prostitutes are known as "gigolos." Since most prostitutes are women, we will focus our attention on this group in the chapter.

Types of Prostitutes

The female prostitute can conduct business in one of four basic ways: by "streetwalking"; in a brothel; in a massage parlor; as a "call girl." Throughout a career of prostitution, perhaps all of these settings may be used. Each may represent an income level, streetwalking producing the lowest income and being a call girl generating the highest income.

FIGURE 9.7 A streetwalker.
(Photo by Burt Glinn)

STREETWALKERS

The streetwalker is considered the lowest of the prostitutes in terms of income and status on the social scale. As the term implies, she walks the streets to *"turn tricks"* (perform sexual favors). The male who uses her services is called a *john*. The prostitute will sell her wares by walking up to men on the streets or approaching men in cars. Often they will initiate interest by asking, "Are you interested in a good time?" "Would you like to have some fun?" or "Looking to spend some money?" She will then negotiate a fee commensurate with an act. Most acts performed will be either fellatio or sexual intercourse. Once a fee has been accepted by the john and the prostitute, she will take him to either a hotel room or an apartment that usually is used only for turning tricks. Most sexual encounters with a prostitute will be five to ten minutes in length. The john almost always is asked to pay in advance.

PROSTITUTES IN BROTHELS

Some prostitutes may work in brothels, otherwise known as whore-houses. These brothels are usually located in what is known as the "red-

FIGURE 9.8   A legal brothel in Nevada. (Photo by Marvin E. Newman 1981)

light district." Women who work in a brothel turn part of their earnings over to the owner of the brothel, who in turn provides the prostitute with a safe and comfortable place to perform her activities. Different brothels have different methods of operation. Usually the client will enter and select one of the available prostitutes, who in turn will take him to her room after their negotiations have been completed. Some brothels take telephone reservations from clients and negotiate prices and services over the phone. The brothel prostitute is usually considered a step above the streetwalker.

MASSAGE PARLORS

While the number of brothels has declined over the years, the number of massage parlors offering sexual services has increased. While not all massage parlors offer sexual services, the man looking for sexual favors will often be able to distinguish the legitimate from the illegitimate parlor. For example, a massage parlor located next to an adult book store or among a strip of theaters showing pornographic films is most likely not a legitimate one. In a massage parlor, the masseuse (prostitute), while not directly offering sexual services, will make it known to the man that she is available to perform sexual favors (Rasmussen and Kuhn, 1976). The prostitute must be careful that she does not overtly proposition a customer, since that customer could be an undercover vice officer. If the customer does wish to have a service performed, the prostitute will negotiate a fee which she will usually be able to keep and not divide with the owner of the massage parlor. The owner usually keeps 50% of the fee charged for the massage, and the prostitute keeps anything extra.

CALL GIRLS

The call girl is the most prestigious of the prostitutes. She runs her own business and does not depend upon attracting customers by working the streets or massage parlors. She takes on customers she knows or those who are referred by someone she knows. While she does not have the protection from unruly customers that a prostitute working in a massage parlor may have, she does attract a more stable kind of client. Her clients may be executives or professionals, since her rates, which are much higher than the rates of other types of prostitutes, are affordable only to highly paid persons. The call girl may work out of her apartment, or she may go to her client's place. Often she is paid without performing sexual favors. For example, she may be hired to be an escort at a social function or she may be asked by a man to cook dinner and talk with him for the evening. In any event, a successful call girl will increase her business through referrals and eventually be able to produce a large tax-free income.

Why Women Become Prostitutes

The reasons women enter the occupation are quite varied. One motivation, as noted by Laner (1974), is the desire to increase self-esteem and gain financial security. Other possible reasons include the opportunity to do something "different," a glamorous life, and the thrill of doing something illegal. Many streetwalkers are drug addicts who turn to prostitution as a means of earning money to support their drug habits. In rare cases, a woman may have an extremely high sex drive and may turn to prostitution as a means of satisfying this sex drive as well as earning money (Woolston, 1969).

Who Uses Prostitutes

Based upon the data collected by Kinsey, we can see that there has been a shift in the pattern in which men use prostitutes. Kinsey found that in 1948, 69% of white males had sex experience with a prostitute. This figure has declined significantly, for several reasons. First, compared with the 1930s and 1940s, there has been a decline in the proportion of single and never-married men. Second, more sexual opportunities exist for males today than yesterday with the liberalization of sexual attitudes. While the number of single incidents with a prostitute has remained fairly constant, the number of continual contacts with prostitutes by males is relatively low. Only 5% of the sexual activity of 20- to 25-year-olds occurs with prostitutes (Gebhard, 1969).

There are many reasons why men patronize prostitutes.

1. Sex with a prostitute is simple and uncomplicated. Some men do not wish to deal with formalities. They might take a woman out, pay a lot of money for a meal, have to get dressed up, and take the time to travel to pick her up and take her home, all of this with the intent of being repaid by sex. However, the man's date might decide not to cater to his sexual whims, and as a result, the man would be disappointed. In the case of frequenting a prostitute, the objective is clear to both parties, and the man's needs are met without his having to go through any preliminaries.

2. Sex with a prostitute reduces a man's obligation to a woman. The man can have a sexual encounter without the fear that a woman will seek a commitment, i.e., marriage. At any time the man can just walk away from a prostitute, whereas in a relationship he may have guilt feelings.

3. Sex with a prostitute offers a means of variety. Many men see the prostitute as a woman who can perform acts that his wife will not perform. Even if the prostitute performs sexual acts that are the same as he experiences at home, the fact that these acts are performed by a person other than his usual mate adds excitement. At one time, many men frequented prostitutes to receive oral sex. However, since sexual attitudes have changed and many wives will perform fellatio upon their husbands, the need to visit a prostitute strictly for this act is not overwhelming. Some men cannot accept their wives' performing various sexual acts such as fellatio, and therefore they will use the prostitute for the "dirty" things.

Prostitution can offer some men sexual experiences that cannot be expected from conventional women. For many, perhaps *anything* can be done. Thus, if a man wishes to act out a sadomasochistic fantasy, the prostitute may be the person to see.

4. Some men use prostitutes for sociability. With the increase in male escort services, we see men using prostitutes to "show off" or for company. In these cases, sexual favors are not the primary cause of contact.

5. Men use prostitutes when no other women are available. This is the predominant case in the military, where men may be in close quarters with other men only, and the only available women are prostitutes.

6. Some men have sexual encounters with prostitutes because this is the only group that would cater to their needs. For example, people who are handicapped, disfigured, or considered very ugly may not be able to attract a woman. However, some prostitutes are just as repelled by these individuals as others are and will often charge a high fee or not get involved with them.

Regardless of the reason a man frequents a prostitute, the prostitute regards her job as business. Generally, she does not obtain any sexual enjoyment from her encounters and, as a rule, does not become emotionally involved with her clients. Prostitutes have different feelings toward their clients. Those clients who request what the prostitute considers deviant forms of sex are disliked more than the usual client, although prostitutes in general do not like their clients (Jackman et al., 1963).

The Pimp and the Madam

Generally speaking, prostitution is illegal, although it is known as the "world's oldest profession." (Only in Nevada is prostitution legal. In that state, fees are regulated for the profit of the state.) Since prostitution is illegal, the prostitute is vulnerable to arrest by the police. If the prostitute is a streetwalker, she will usually be controlled by her *pimp,* a person who lives directly on the earnings of prostitutes. The pimp, in exchange for his earnings, supplies the prostitute with affection and caring, as well as protection from clients who may physically abuse her. He also bails the prostitute out of jail should she be arrested. Each pimp usually has a "stable" of prostitutes who work a particular area or street. Prostitutes from outside the stable are not permitted to infringe upon the pimp's territory. For his services, which some prostitutes consider quite minimal, the pimp collects most of the fees paid to them. A good number of pimps are wealthy. The stereotypical pimp can often be spotted because of the outrageous clothes he wears or the flashy car he drives.

The *madam,* more obviously known as a manager of brothels, is now making a reappearance. With prostitutes making their operation of business in brothel-type apartments, the madam has resurfaced as a manager

FIGURE 9.9 A street pimp with his fancy car. (Photo by Bob Adelman)

of these operations. The madam is usually better educated than other prostitutes and is therefore better able to handle managerial and fiscal matters. She is often a former prostitute.

Male Heterosexual Prostitutes

Gigolos, or male heterosexual prostitutes, perform sexual services for women. Gigolos are not nearly as common as female prostitutes. Often, the gigolo will seek business by frequenting bars, vacation spots, or resorts that are frequented by wealthy, middle-aged women. Most gigolos are fairly young, handsome, and have athletic-looking bodies. When a gigolo is approached by a woman, he may pretend to become attracted to her. He will provide her with flattery and compliments and then serve as a sexual partner. In return for "keeping" the man, the woman will shower him with gifts and pay him money.

Some male prostitutes work in escort services that operate on the same principle as that of the female escort services. Obviously, unlike the female prostitute, the gigolo cannot entertain woman after woman in a short period of time, since he is not usually capable of achieving many erections within a short time span.

SUMMARY STATEMENTS

- *It is often difficult to label sexual behaviors normal or abnormal.*
- *There are many kinds of sexual variations. Among them are fetishism, transvestism, transsexualism, sadism, masochism, pedophilia, incest, voyeurism, exhibitionism, zoophilia, necrophilia, frottage, coprolalia, sexual urethralism, satyriasis, and nymphomania.*
- *Prostitution is illegal in almost all parts of the United States.*
- *A prostitute conducts business in one of several ways.*
- *Although most prostitutes are women, some are men.*

SUGGESTED READINGS

Bryant, Clifton D. *Sexual Deviancy in Social Context.* New York: Watts, Franklin, Inc., 1980.

Bullough, Vern L. *Sexual Variance in Society and History.* Chicago: University of Chicago Press, 1980.

Comfort, Alex. *The Joy of Sex.* New York: Simon and Schuster, 1972.

Gebhard, Paul, John Gagnon, Wardell Pomeroy, and C. V. Christensen. *Sex Offenders: An Analysis of Types.* New York: Harper & Row, 1965.

Money, John. "Destereotyping Sex Roles," *Society*, July-August, 1977.

Money John. *Love and Sickness: The Science of Sex Gender Difference and Pair Bonding.* Baltimore: Johns Hopkins Press, 1980.

Sheehy, Gail. *Hustling: Prostitution in Our Wide Open Society.* New York: Delacorte Press, 1971.

Weber, Ellen. "Sexual Abuse Begins At Home," *Ms*, April, 1977.

Winer, Julius H., and Stephen D. Bloomberg. 'Transsexual Surgery," *The Humanist*, March-April, 1978.

A LOOK AT YOUR LIFESTYLE

You are marooned on an island with 15 people. Each one has a different sexual variation. The sexual variations are:

1. fetishism
2. transvestism
3. transsexualism
4. sadism and masochism
5. pedophilia
6. incest
7. voyeurism
8. exhibitionism
9. animal contact
10. necrophilia
11. frottage
12. coprolalia
13. sexual urethralism
14. satyriasis and nymphomania
15. prostitution

SEXUAL VARIATIONS

Write an I-message describing your feelings about sexual variations:

When I know someone is sexually variant, I _____

_____

_____

Identify the key issue or problem.
Given:
I am to select one of 15 persons with whom to have a meaningful relationship while I am marooned.

_____

Identify the possible solutions or alternatives.
Given:
The possible solutions or alternatives are the 15 variations listed at the top of the page.

_____

_____

_____

_____

GATHERING INFORMATION
Make one informational statement about each of the behaviors.

1. _____ .

2. _____ .

3. _____ .

4. _____ .

5. _____ .

6. _____ .

7. _____ .

8. _____ .

9. _____ .

10. _____ .

11. _____ .

12. _____ .

13. _____ .

14. _____ .

15. _____ .

EVALUATING THE INFORMATION
Rank-order your preference for a meaningful relationship using "1" as the most acceptable and "15" as the least acceptable.

1. _____	6. _____	11. _____
2. _____	7. _____	12. _____
3. _____	8. _____	13. _____
4. _____	9. _____	14. _____
5. _____	10. _____	15. _____

MAKING RESPONSIBLE DECISIONS

Give at least two reasons for the choice you made for the relationship with the most meaning.

_____

_____

_____

TEN

Psychophysiological Sexual Disorders

A LOOK AT YOUR LIFESTYLE

Sexual difficulties are experienced by many individuals in varying circumstances. Yet some of these difficulties are not considered difficulties. It may be that the individual does not perceive his or her functioning as problematic.

We are beginning to see more and more concern on the part of the male to take responsibility for satisfying his partner.

> I am more concerned about my girlfriend's sexual satisfaction than I am of my own. My attitude is that I can always be satisfied very easily, whereas satisfaction for my girlfriend is much more difficult. However, once I have satisfied her, I know I have accomplished my goal. The rest is all downhill.

However, preoccupation with a partner's sexual satisfaction can be just as detrimental to a relationship as preoccupation with one's own fulfillment.

When sexual difficulty arises, it is often the case that one or both of the partners will not admit that there is a problem. In addition, if the dif-

279

ficulty is acknowledged, one or both partners may be reluctant to do anything about it because they may feel stigmatized as "abnormal." Fortunately, this attitude is changing. Men and women are learning that each has sexual needs and desires and that sometimes these needs and desires cannot be fulfilled.

Individuals who are responsible in their sexual relationships will take the initiative to learn more about the sex-related difficulties that can arise. This responsibility must be shared equally by the male and the female. A part of this responsibility entails knowing the nature, causes, and treatment of sexual difficulties. It also entails knowledge of one's body as well as the nature of sexual response, which has been discussed. Knowledge of sexual difficulties as well as their causes and treatment can help people to understand that no one is immune to having sexual problems; that sex therapy can be a viable solution to a sexual difficulty; and that dealing with sexual difficulties can help improve relationships.

GATHERING INFORMATION

Sexual difficulties are a complex phenomenon. The number of difficulties possessed by males and females are many and varied. The methods used to deal with these difficulties effectively are numerous, as are the approaches and philosophies of sex therapists. As a result, we will present only the major sexual difficulties as well as their causes and treatment. The major difficulties we will examine in the male are impotence, premature ejaculation, and retarded ejaculation. The difficulties of the female that will be covered include orgasmic dysfunction and vaginismus. Among the difficulties of both males and females that we will discuss are painful intercourse (this is much more common in females) and sexual disinterest.

EVALUATING THE INFORMATION

Perhaps each of you has raised questions about your sexual functioning, regardless of your degree of sexual experience. You may have asked:

- Why do most men reach orgasm more rapidly than women?
- Why do some men have difficulty getting erections?
- Is sexual intercourse for a woman sometimes painful, and if so, why?
- What causes the vaginal muscles to tighten up sometimes when sexual intercourse is anticipated?
- Can any of the sexual problems of males and females be treated successfully?
- What causes the sexual difficulties experienced by couples?

The information that is presented in this chapter will need to be evaluated in terms of what it means to you. You must assess the impact that your choices will have upon your lifestyle. Carefully analyzing and assessing information can help you form healthier attitudes toward yourself as well as others.

MAKING RESPONSIBLE DECISIONS

Men and women need to assume responsibility for the decisions they will make about their sexual interaction with others. They need to understand that sexual behavior is learned, and anything that is learned can also be unlearned. The best way to prevent sexual difficulties for you and others is to accept the idea that people change sexually as a result of being exposed to many conditions.

SEXUAL DYSFUNCTION

Sexual dysfunction is an impairment or ineffectiveness in sexual performance. Of the dysfunctions we will discuss, impotence, premature ejaculation and retarded ejaculation are male-related. Orgasmic dysfunction and vaginismus are female-related. Two others, painful intercourse and sexual disinterest, can occur in both men and women.

Male Sexual Dysfunction

IMPOTENCE

Masters and Johnson once said that there is no such thing as an impotent woman. That is, in the absence of anatomic or psychosomatic abnormalities, any woman can have sexual intercourse. However, if a male is impotent, he cannot even fake having sexual intercourse.

Impotence, or *erectile dysfunction,* is the male's inability to produce or maintain an erection sufficient for sexual intercourse in the majority of his sexual contacts. There are two types of impotence — primary and secondary. *Primary impotence* is that in a man who has *never* had the ability to maintain an erection for sexual intercourse. *Secondary impotence* is that in a man who cannot maintain or perhaps achieve an erection but has succeeded at vaginal or rectal intercourse at least once.

Many men often become anxious if during isolated experiences they cannot achieve an erection. A single failure, or even several failures, for that matter, does not indicate impotence. Approximately 50% of all men experience sporadic periods of impotence (Kaplan, 1974). The reasons for this problem can vary. A man may be upset, anxious about a major decision, or intoxicated by alcohol or drugs. However, the reactions to the inability to become erect upon attempting sexual intercourse can be severe. If the man or the woman does not accept the rare occurrence of impotency as normal, anxiety, frustration, and depression can set in, leading to a preoccupation with male erectile competence. Each sexual encounter can then mean meeting the big challenge: "Will he or won't he?" This preoccupation is enough spark for the fire. If both men and women can acknowledge the fact that sporadic failure to become erect is common, and that it is also normal, then the incidence of impotency can probably be reduced.

CAUSES OF IMPOTENCE There are two causes of impotence. *Organic impotence* can be due to physiological and chemical phenomena such as anatomical abnormalities in genital structure, problems of the nervous system such as Parkinson's disease, medications, surgery, spinal cord injuries, and excessive intake of drugs and alcohol. Organic impoence is not common. Only 10% of all cases of impotence are organic. *Psychogenic impotence* results from psychological factors and is the cause of 90% of all cases of impotency. We will therefore discuss this type in greater detail.

Masters and Johnson (1970) and Kaplan (1974) believe that anxiety about a sexual performance is the most common cause of impotence. Only one failure is required for one to make a sporadic case of impotence into a chronic sexual problem. Instead of becoming an active participant in the sexual experience, the man may allow his isolated incident to "get the best of him." In other words, he becomes the overseer of his sexual functioning. He becomes so preoccupied with the degree of penile erection that he becomes a "spectator" instead of a "participant" (Masters and Johnson, 1970). As a result, the spectator's monitoring inhibits the spontaneity of lovemaking. In turn, anxiety, which leads to impotency, is produced.

My wife and I had been married for 15 years. One time I was not able to achieve an erection during our lovemaking. She became very upset. She told me that I did not find her attractive any more. This caused her to react negatively to me. One thing led to another. She thought I was having affairs. All the time this was taking place, I became even more upset at her. After all, I still loved her. But look what happened, all because of one instance during which I could not have an erection.

With the onset of failure comes the need for the man to prove that this one spell of inability to become aroused is a freak occurrence. He may rush into another sexual encounter outside of marriage. One of three things can then result. First, the man may fail at his extramarital encounter and jump into numerous affairs to prove his masculinity via the achievement of an erection. Second, the man may find that he is capable of being aroused by another woman. As a result, he may condition himself to being aroused by another woman or other women and not by his wife. Third, and, we think, the best solution, he may find his experience with his wife to be an isolated occurrence. Regardless of what action is taken, it is important for men and women to understand that incidental erectile failure does not mean that the man will become impotent.

A man's prior experiences can play a role in his becoming impotent. For example, if during his first sexual encounter, a man's partner told him that his penis was too small and that he was a sexual misfit, future sexual encounters might be accompanied by anxiety.

> When I was young, there was a girl in the neighborhood who went to bed with just about everyone — that is, everyone but me. When I tried to make passes at her, she told me that I looked like I had a small penis and she didn't want to waste her time. This got me angry. Even though it was another two years before my first sexual encounter, her comments still had an effect, because I was unable to have an erection. I felt I would be too small.

TREATMENT OF IMPOTENCE   If impotence is due to physiological disorders, surgery may be performed. The surgical procedures most commonly performed include the tightening of the perineal muscles and the insertion of a penile prosthesis. This prosthesis can be pumped up with a tiny pump implanted in the scrotum. When pumped, fluid from a reservoir in the abdomen causes erection.

Since 90% of cases of impotence result from psychological factors, we will emphasize the treatment employed for this condition. The treatment model most widely known today is that of Masters and Johnson, who treat primary and secondary impotence using the same techniques. For this dysfunction and all others that are dealt with in the Masters and Johnson program, the first three days of treatment are similar.

Day 1: During the initial interview, the co-therapists direct the partners not to participate in any sexual activity without specific instructions. This instruction takes the pressure off the male to perform. Information about the partners — their background and sexual functioning — is collected.

Day 2: More sensitive questions are asked during the collection of data. The female therapist interviews the male partner, and the male therapist interviews the female partner.

Day 3: Joint exploration of the couple's marriage relationship is undertaken. The man, woman, and both therapists meet together. A physical examination is also given to rule out the possibility of a physiological factor as a cause of the sexual dysfunction. The couple are also taught about natural sexual response and are given other information that may be relevant to their situation. *Sensate focus* exercises, with the recognition that touch is a communicative way to achieve the fullness of sexual expression, are given. The couples must touch all areas of each other's body except breasts and genitals. They then must communicate to each other what is pleasant or unpleasant.

Day 4: The partners are asked again to touch each other, but this time, they are instructed to touch the genital areas and the breasts. On this day the previous "homework" assignment is discussed.

During Days 5 through 14, the treatment for the specific dysfunction, in this case impotence, is pursued. The impotent man is taught to give himself up to his partner's pleasure and allow himself to be aroused by it.

If erection occurs during one of the initial pleasuring sessions, sexual intercourse will not be permitted. Instead, the partners are told to communicate their pleasures to each other. Feedback is given to the co-therapists at round-table discussions. After about a week, the woman can insert her partner's penis into her vagina while she is astride him. In this position, the man does not have to perform. The position is important, because many impotent men suffer from performance anxiety, and in this position, the woman is the main performer, although the partners are told specifically that pelvic thrusting should not be vigorous. On the following days, the man's attention is turned to the warm, intimate, and sexually satisfying mood of the total situation. Orgasm, if it should occur, should be natural and not planned. When the penis can remain erect in the vagina for 20 minutes during subsequent sessions, there is a good chance of long-term stabilization of the man's response to sexual intercourse.

Masters and Johnson claim that about 75% of impotent patients are successfully treated.

PREMATURE EJACULATION

Defining *premature ejaculation* has become a controversial issue. Generally, premature ejaculation is thought to occur when a man ejaculates "too soon." The issue here is, What is too soon? Some of the answers that have been given are

1. ejaculation within ten seconds after vaginal penetration
2. ejaculation before vaginal penetration
3. ejaculation within one minute after vaginal penetration (Kinsey et al., 1948)

Some people have defined premature ejaculation by the number of pelvic thrusts before ejaculation (Kaplan, 1974). One of the more commonly accepted definitions of premature ejaculation is that put forth by Masters and Johnson (1970). They define premature ejaculation as the inability of the man to delay ejaculation long enough for the woman to achieve orgasm 50% of the time. This definition takes into account the requirements of the sexual partners rather than a period of time. However, the time it may take for a woman to reach orgasm can vary. According to Masters and Johnson's definition, a man would be a premature ejaculator if it took him 75 minutes to ejaculate and it took his partner 80 minutes to achieve orgasm. Is a man a premature ejaculator if he ejaculates in 30 minutes? . . . 45 minutes? . . . an hour? Obviously, this definition is also open to criticism. Kaplan's (1974) definition seems to be the one that makes the most sense. She defines a premature ejaculator as one who has no control over the ejaculatory reflex. This lack of control can take the form of ejaculating in two thrusts, ten minutes, or before or after the female reaches her orgasm. For our purposes, we will use the Kaplan (1974) definition and add that the lack of ejaculatory control causes the male to believe he is performing inadequately or the accompanying detumescence (reduction of erection) causes problems for his partner.

It should be noted that at one time or another, almost every man will ejaculate too quickly for his partner. This is by no means abnormal. However, as we have seen with our discussion of impotency, premature ejaculation can become a problem if the man allows the isolated or rare occurrence to bother him and thus create anxiety.

Premature ejaculation is the most common of all the sexual dysfunctions. To a great extent, cultural and social variables often determine whether or not premature ejaculation is a problem. For example, people from lower socioeconomic classes are not as likely as people from upper socioeconomic classes to perceive premature ejaculation as problematic (Kerchoff, 1974).

CAUSES OF PREMATURE EJACULATION   Many psychologists and psychiatrists believe that a lack of control over ejaculation is a learned response. The major premises purport to show that: 1) premature ejaculation occurs because of conditions that facilitate rapid ejaculation, which in turn results in the inability to control the ejaculatory response; and 2) anxiety facilitates premature ejaculation.

Let us now look at how conditioning can cause the male to become a premature ejaculator. Suppose you are a young man of 19 who is sexually active with one or several partners. You find that the only way you can be alone with your female partners is in the privacy of your car. As a result, you often go to secluded areas to park. While in these secluded areas, you are always fearful that the police may pull up next to your car while you and your partner are in the midst of a torrid lovemaking session. Whether by having sexual intercourse or by "dry humping" (the male's penis is rubbing against the female's vulva while both are fully clothed), your main objective is to achieve a rapid ejaculation. If this type of situation occurs frequently, the male is conditioning himself to become a premature ejaculator. For many young men, this is a typical occurrence. Other examples may be experiences with prostitutes or in a girl's house where there is worry about her mother or father walking in. In all these examples, the rapid ejaculatory response is learned. What has *not* been learned is the male's ability to identify the sensations that immediately precede ejaculation. In order to control ejaculation, a man must be aware of the feelings that arise when he is about to ejaculate.

A premature ejaculator may be burdened with anxiety. He may feel that his masculinity is threatened by his inability to satisfy his partner. As a result, he may resort to all sorts of psychological and physical means of delaying ejaculation. He may count backwards from 100, think about what he will do the next day, or devise a host of other psychological distractions to delay his ejaculation. He may decide to masturbate before sexual intercourse so that subsequent ejaculations will be delayed (although doing so may delay subsequent ejaculations, it may also diminish the intensity of his orgasm). In any event, these anxieties will only make the male more aware of his dysfunction and facilitate its occurrence.

TREATMENT OF PREMATURE EJACULATION Premature ejaculation is almost always caused by psychological factors. Therefore, it is reversible. Since premature ejaculation is learned, it, like other sexual dysfunctions that are learned, can also be unlearned.

In the Masters and Johnson therapy session, the man and woman practice "pleasuring" each other during the sensate focus sessions. After several days, the woman can begin to caress the man's genitals. At this time, the *"squeeze technique"* is introduced. First, the woman must arouse the male to an erection. When the man feels the urge to ejaculate, he signals his partner, who then applies a "squeeze." She holds the penis between her thumb and the first two fingers of the same hand. The thumb is placed on the frenulum and the two fingers are placed on the opposite side. One finger is placed on each side of the coronal ridge, one slightly above it and one just below it. With the fingers in this position, the woman then can apply fairly hard pressure upon the penis when he indicates to her that he feels the urge to ejaculate. While we do not know why, the squeeze does make the man lose his urge to ejaculate. It may also make him partially lose his erection. After about 15 to 30 seconds, the woman stimulates the man again. With repetitions of this procedure, the couple can have 15 to 20 minutes of continuous sex play. The squeeze technique can be repeated three or four times during the first training session.

Once the male becomes accustomed to the squeeze technique (it does not hurt), he is ready for the next step, sexual intercourse in the woman-on-top position. In this position, the woman sits astride the man. First, she applies the squeeze technique two or three times. She then gently inserts the man's penis in her vagina but does not thrust her hips. The man can then become used to the new feeling of penile containment without any immediate urge to ejaculate. If the man signals to the woman that he is about to ejaculate, she raises her body and repeats the squeeze technique. After the man gains ejaculatory control using this technique, he is in-

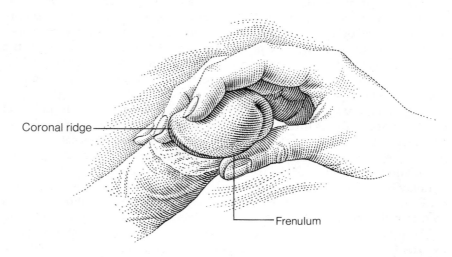

Coronal ridge

Frenulum

FIGURE 10.1 The "squeeze" technique.

structed to thrust just enough to maintain his erection. The man and woman will often find that they can stay in this position for 15 to 20 minutes. When this step is mastered, the couple can begin to change positions by first moving to the side position and then to the man-on-top position. Even though ejaculatory control may be mastered in the clinical setting, the couple must practice the squeeze technique at least once a week for the first six months. It usually takes six to twelve months for complete ejaculatory control to be mastered.

It should be noted that the squeeze technique is only one of several methods that have been used to control premature ejaculation. The Semans start–stop technique (Semans, 1956) is also used by many therapists. This technique requires that the woman stimulate the man until he feels the urge to ejaculate. Upon his signal, she halts contact with the genitals until the urge to ejaculate passes. This sequence can be repeated three or four times. Eventually, the number of pauses required is diminished, and the man soon gains the capacity for penile stimulation of long duration.

Masters and Johnson found that premature ejaculation is the easiest male sexual dysfunction to treat. Of 186 men, 182 (or 97.8%) were successful in overcoming premature ejaculation. While no figures are available for the Semans technique, Kaplan (1974) feels that the start–stop procedure has advantages over the squeeze technique, in that the former is less uncomfortable for the man.

RETARDED EJACULATION

Retarded ejaculation, also known as ejaculatory incompetence, ejaculatory impotence, and delayed ejaculation, is an inability in the man to ejaculate even though he desires to do so. Men with this problem can respond to erotic feelings and maintain an erection. Although most can achieve orgasm through masturbation and some can achieve orgasm through manual or oral–genital stimulation from their partners, they cannot ejaculate in a woman's vagina. Since they can maintain their erection for up to an hour or more, they are capable of helping many women achieve more than one orgasm. However, many women find this condition depressing, since they may interpret the failure to ejaculate to indicate that they are not sexually arousing to their partners.

CAUSES OF RETARDED EJACULATION The causes of retarded ejaculation are not fully known. Most of those in the helping professions believe that retarded ejaculation is due to a past traumatic psychological experience, which resulted in anxiety occurring during sexual activities (LoPiccolo et al., 1972). For example, a man who is discovered by his wife while he is engaging in sexual intercourse with another woman may develop anxieties that in turn may result in retarded ejaculation.

TREATMENT OF RETARDED EJACULATION Retarded ejaculation can lead to impotence. In cases where this condition exists, the impotence is dealt with first and the delayed ejaculation, second. In the Masters and

Johnson program, sensate focus pleasuring techniques are initiated. After five or six days, the woman is instructed to stimulate her partner in whatever way he finds most arousing. The idea here is that ejaculation should occur so that the man can identify his partner with pleasure rather than as a threat. Once ejaculation occurs in the presence of the woman as a result of her efforts, both partners can begin to appreciate the experience as a pleasurable one.

Once the woman is successful at manipulating the man to ejaculation, sexual intercourse can begin. The woman-on-top position in sexual intercourse is used. Sitting astride her partner, the woman is instructed to insert the man's penis into her vagina and begin to thrust demandingly until ejaculation occurs. If ejaculation does not occur, she is instructed to go back to manual stimulation. Once she brings the man close to ejaculation again, she reinserts the penis and begins once more to try to bring the man to ejaculation. Once the man ejaculates in the vagina, regardless of how soon it may be, the anxiety pattern is well on its way to being broken.

After the initial ejaculation occurs, the man and woman are instructed to prolong the amount of time the penis is in the vagina before ejaculation so that the woman can have her orgasm. If the man has trouble ejaculating, the woman can manually stimulate the shaft of the penis while it is still inside the vagina. However, once the male is about to ejaculate, she can remove her hand and allow the ejaculation to occur while the male is penetrating the vagina deeply.

Masters and Johnson reported a success rate of over 82% with the use of this therapeutic approach.

Female Sexual Dysfunction

ORGASMIC DYSFUNCTION

Orgasmic dysfunction, or *anorgasmia,* is the inability of a woman to achieve orgasm. She may be quite capable of sexual arousal and may have stimulation sufficient to produce an orgasm, as determined by sex therapists. The term *frigidity* was previously used to describe orgasmic dysfunction. However, this term means different things to different people. For example, if a woman does not become sexually aroused or if a woman refused a sexual offer, she may be called "frigid" by a man. This ambiguity plus the derogatory connotations associated with this term have prompted its discontinuation in therapeutic circles.

Orgasmic dysfunction can be categorized into two types. A woman with *primary orgasmic dysfunction* has never had an orgasm by any method. The woman who suffers from *secondary orgasmic dysfunction,* also known as *situational orgasmic dysfunction,* has had an orgasm sometime in her life but now cannot, at least with any predictability, in coitus. With this type of dysfunction, the woman can be orgasmic in some situations but not in others. For example, she may be capable of achieving orgasm with masturbation, with partner manipulation of the genitals, or with oral–

genital contact, but not during sexual intercourse. Labeling situational orgasmic dysfunction as a problem is open to interpretation. For example, a woman who can reach orgasm quite readily when she is masturbated by her partner or when he engages in cunnilingus with her, and yet who cannot achieve orgasm during sexual intercourse, may very well be sexually satisfied.

Perhaps what we really need are expanded criteria of secondary orgasmic dysfunction. That is, a woman should be considered as having a situational orgasmic dysfunction when she feels that the lack of orgasm in sexual intercourse is distressful enough that she wishes to further explore her concern with the hope of becoming orgasmic during sexual intercourse.

Orgasmic dysfunction, whether it be primary, secondary, or situational, is the most common type of dysfunction found in the clinical setting, probably because at least 10% of all women have never achieved an orgasm and even more have not had an orgasm within the first year of marriage.

CAUSES OF ORGASMIC DYSFUNCTION Although most of the causes of orgasmic dysfunction are psychological, there are some physiological factors that should be mentioned. Drugs such as alcohol, barbiturates, and narcotics can decrease the sex drive and in turn result in orgasmic dysfunction.

Some of the psychological causes of orgasmic dysfunction result from a physiological condition. For example, situational orgasmic dysfunction can be the result of a girl's losing her virginity. She may then feel anxious during subsequent engagement in sexual intercourse with her first lover but not with someone else. In some cases, orgasmic dysfunctions can be associated with surgical procedures such as an episiotomy or hysterectomy. Congenital abnormalities such as a tight clitoral hood can also be a cause.

According to Masters and Johnson (1970), the most frequent cause of orgasmic dysfunction is the woman's inability to identify with her partner. In such cases, the woman may consider her partner to be a liar, sloppy, an introvert, or an extrovert. Regardless of the man's status, if the woman does not feel he is "for her," she can consciously or unconsciously withhold her sexual response and, in turn, discourage orgasm.

Religious prohibitions can also be a factor in orgasmic dysfunction, in that a woman who is taught that sexual feelings are wrong and should be repressed can have difficulties once she becomes sexually involved with a man.

Many therapists believe that anxiety plays a direct or indirect role in orgasmic dysfunction because the anxiety inhibits the excitement phase of sexual response to the extent that the woman cannot become sufficiently aroused to reach orgasm (Hogan, 1978).

Another very significant reason a woman will maintain a constant state of orgasmic dysfunction is that she may play the role of spectator. In our discussion of male sexual dysfunction, we mentioned that many men become so concerned about their performance that their ability to perform is impaired. The same observation regarding "the spectator role" can be made about the woman; that is, the woman may become so concerned about whether or not she will reach orgasm that her ability to reach this goal becomes severely impaired. Thus, we can safely say that the development and maintenance of orgasmic dysfunction can be a result of ill feelings toward a partner, lack of adequate sexual technique by the partner, religious conflicts, and taking the role of spectator.

TREATMENT OF ORGASMIC DYSFUNCTION The approach of the Masters and Johnson program in dealing with orgasmic dysfunction has proven to be quite successful. In this program, the therapists set as the goal for the couple the removal of barriers that facilitate acting out in hostile ways. After this is done and the objectives of the program are explained, the couple is given instructions in sensate focus. After closeness is developed, the woman is given permission to enjoy her partner's caressing of her genitalia. She is encouraged to help guide him toward those things she finds pleasurable, as opposed to letting him discover them for himself.

The most effective position for teaching genital play is one in which the man is leaning against pillows at the head of the bed. The woman then sits between his legs with her back against his chest. She extends her legs and crosses them over her partner's. In this position, the man has access to any part of the woman's body. The woman is instructed to place her hand over her partner's. She then can press him lightly when she wants to be touched more lightly, and she can also press him harder when she wants to be touched harder—communication without verbalization. When this phase is successfully accomplished, the couple can try stimulative techniques preferred by the man.

The man is then taught by the therapists how to stimulate his partner, especially around the clitoris. He is also taught how to gently stroke and "pleasure" his partner's entire body. All the while this is happening, the couple is aware that there is no demand for the woman to achieve orgasm. The purpose of the stroking is to discover what the woman's preferences are and that these preferences are then to be communicated to the man. If orgasm occurs at this stage, that is acceptable, as is no orgasm. The major purpose here is that the woman understand that nothing is demanded of her.

Once this phase is mastered, the man is allowed to insert his penis into the woman's vagina while she is in the woman-to-top position, astride him. This procedure carries over the excitement from genital play to an experience in which the woman can begin to feel the sensation of the penis in her vagina. She is told to refrain from reaching orgasm so that she can appreciate the pleasurable feeling a penis in the vagina can bring. All the time, the woman is told to think of the penis as something that is hers to enjoy. The man's role is to provide the erect penis for his partner.

Once the woman has become used to this feeling, the man is instructed to initiate slow and nondemanding pelvic thrusting. At the same time, the woman is to communicate to the man the pace she prefers. During this stage, one or both partners may experience orgasm. If the man has not as yet reached orgasm, the woman can be instructed to manipulate him to this point, since he may already be experiencing a great deal of tension.

After the man has developed ejaculatory control and the woman develops vaginal feeling, sexual intercourse with slow thrusting is continued for as long as it remains pleasurable. Afterwards, the couple takes a break. When sexual arousal begins again, they repeat the preceding. Once the woman finds this enjoyable, the couple can switch to the side-to-side position for coitus. Eventually, orgasmic dysfunction disappears — in most cases once the woman discovers, accepts, and shares her partner's sexual stimulation.

Other therapists have dealt with orgasmic dysfunction in different ways. Some treatment modalities involve the woman's first achieving orgasm by masturbation, then through clitoral stimulation by her partner, and then through coitus.

VAGINISMUS

Vaginismus is an intense and involuntary contraction of the muscles near the vaginal entrance that occurs when penetration is attempted. This penetration, whether in the form of a penis, a finger, or a tampon, or during gynecological examination, causes the vaginal introitus to shut tightly. A woman who has vaginismus will have an impossible or very painful time trying to have sexual intercourse.

A definite diagnosis of vaginismus can be made during a gynecological examination. In this situation, the woman who has vaginismus will move away from the doctor and hold her legs tightly together. Some women can tolerate a pelvic examination better than others. It may depend upon who is conducting the exam as well as who is present during the exam. For example, a woman may tolerate a pelvic examination if only a physician is present, whereas vaginismus might occur if her husband were also present.

Since the physical pain associated with penile penetration is extreme, many women feel embarrassed and frustrated. Thus, depression and a negative self-concept can result. As a consequence, many women suffering from vaginismus avoid sexual encounters of any kind (Kaplan, 1974). This avoidance serves only to reinforce the dysfunction. Obviously, vaginismus can take its toll in a relationship. A man may interpret his wife's avoidance of his sexual advances as a lack of interest in him or a threat to his masculinity. If vaginismus is not treated, a relationship may be subject to frustration, controversy, and eventually termination.

CAUSES OF VAGINISMUS On rare occasions, vaginismus can be caused by a disorder of the genital organs. If a woman has pelvic inflammatory disease, a rigid hymen, or disorders resulting from childbirth, intercourse can be painful, and the pain may cause vaginismus. Once the physical condition that produces painful intercourse is treated, the woman can resume her normal sexual practices.

Several psychological factors have been given as reasons for vaginismus. Masters and Johnson (1970) believe that vaginismus can develop in women who are married to men who are impotent. A woman can become frustrated by the repeated failure of her partner to perform adequately and, as a result, subconsciously protect herself from frustration by denying penile penetration.

Another important cause of vaginismus is trauma. A woman who was brutally raped can consequently have an aversion toward having a penis inserted into her vagina. She might also have vaginal lacerations that left scar tissue.

Other causes of vaginismus are strong religious taboos about sex, chronic painful intercourse, and feelings of hostility toward a sexual partner. Generally speaking, vaginismus is a conditioned response that is a result of associating pain with vaginal penetration.

TREATMENT OF VAGINISMUS Since vaginismus is a contraction of the vaginal muscles, some doctors feel that this "tightness" needs to be treated. They may do so by injecting a local anesthetic into the vaginal area before intromission to help reduce the pain associated with sexual intercourse. Some doctors prescribe tranquilizers such as Valium so that the woman can feel more relaxed and be better prepared for sexual intercourse.

Another approach to the treatment of vaginismus is to have the woman overcome her dysfunction by herself. She is told to study her vagina by looking into a mirror while she is in a relaxed and private setting. She is then told to insert a fingertip into her vagina and focus on the sensation this brings. After she can insert a fingertip with comfort, she is instructed to insert her entire finger. Eventually, she works her way up to inserting three fingers in her vagina. Once she can insert three fingers without discomfort, her sexual partner is included in the therapy. He also inserts his fingers into her vagina, beginning with one finger and working up to three. When no muscular spasms occur in the vagina, the woman is ready for penile penetration. If penile penetration at this point can be performed comfortably, subsequent penetrations become easier.

The procedures in the Masters and Johnson (1970) approach differ. The most important part of the treatment in this program is showing both the man and the woman that the vaginal spasm is real. In the examining room, with the man looking on, the doctor inserts his finger into the vaginal canal. The man can see the vaginal spasm, and the woman becomes much more aware of her condition, and the treatment of vaginismus is made easy.

The couple are given Hegar dilators, which they use during treatment. With the woman's assistance, the man inserts the dilator into the vagina. Gradually the size of the dilator is increased. Once a large dilator is inserted without any discomfort, the woman is instructed to leave the dilator in her vagina for several hours during the night. Most of the muscular spasms can disappear in three to five days if the dilators are used daily. After this time, penile penetration is possible. It should be noted that the emotional aspects of vaginismus must also be dealt with.

Dyspareunia

Dyspareunia, or painful intercourse, is a condition that, although a predominantly female dysfunction, can also affect men. The pain associated with dyspareunia in the woman can occur in the vagina, cervix, uterus, or bladder. On the man, pain may occur in the penis, prostate, or seminal vesicles when he ejaculates. For the woman as well as the man, pain may occur before, during, or after sexual intercourse.

CAUSES OF DYSPAREUNIA IN MEN

In men, the causes of painful intercourse can be many. A tight foreskin in the uncircumcised male may cause pain to the glans of the penis. When the foreskin is so tight over the glans that it cannot be pulled back, the man is said to have *phimosis*. Irritation of the glans can also be due to infections beneath the foreskin. Infection can occur if the male does not pull back the foreskin and wash the smegma away. Painful intercourse in men may also be due to infections of the urethra, bladder, prostate, and seminal vesicles that can produce a burning, itching, and painful sensation in the man when he ejaculates.

CAUSES OF DYSPAREUNIA IN WOMEN

Painful intercourse in women can be due to psychological or physiological conditions. One of the most common causes of painful intercourse in the woman is the failure to lubricate. This condition, which indicates a failure to become aroused, can be due to a lack of effective stimulation, inhibition, or relationship difficulties with a partner.

Vaginal infections such as those caused by bacteria (syphilis), protozoa (trichomoniasis), and fungus (moniliasis) may cause painful intercourse. These microorganisms can cause the vaginal walls to become inflamed.

Another frequent cause of painful intercourse is a thinning of the vaginal walls. This thinning occurs most frequently in women over 50 Because of a reduction in female hormones, the vaginal walls may crack, bleed, and become irritated quite easily. Vaginal creams are frequently prescribed in such cases to lubricate the mucous membrane.

Pain near the opening of the vagina can be due to an intact hymen or scar tissue that has resulted from a tear during the birth of a child. Sometimes the clitoris becomes irritated when substances accumulate under the clitoral hood. During sexual intercourse, the clitoral hood may be pulled back and forth, causing a sharp pain to be felt in the vaginal area.

A woman may experience pain in the vaginal muscles. If she engages in sexual intercourse after having abstained from coitus for an extended period of time, she may be sore the very next day. This soreness can make subsequent attempts at sexual intercourse painful.

When my girlfriend and I have sex after about a one-month period of abstention, she complains the very next day that her vagina aches.

Some women experience painful intercourse deep in the pelvis. This pain may be due to tears in the ligaments that support the uterus. These tears may be due to childbirth or a traumatic event such as rape. Women may experience this pain only in certain positions during sexual intercourse.

Sometimes the pain experienced deep inside the pelvic area can be due to infections in the cervix, uterus, and fallopian tubes. This pain may be caused by a condition known as *endometriosis.* In this abnormal condition, the tissue that normally lines the uterus grows in areas other than the uterus. These growths can cause a crowding effect between organs that, in turn, makes intercourse painful.

TREATMENT FOR DYSPAREUNIA   Whenever a woman notices that she experiences pain during sexual intercourse for an extended period of time, she should see her physician. Often this pain is the initial indication that a physical condition that needs attention exists. For example, it is possible that she has a vaginal infection that becomes painful only during sexual intercourse. Without coitus, she might never have known this condition existed.

For the dysfunctions we discussed, there is no doubt that medical and surgical treatment is the most effective intervention. However, the potential benefits of psychotherapy should not be overlooked when dyspareunia has as its foundation emotional anxieties and fears.

Sexual Disinterest

Another sexual disorder is a lack of interest in sex. This lack of interest can be due to a fear of intimacy. In her approach to dealing with this concern, Kaplan (1979) combines Masters and Johnson's techniques of re-learning with psychoanalysis. She feels that the reasons for a lack of interest in sex must be uncovered before a couple can begin to develop insight into their sexual problems. Kaplan believes that if the stresses in a relationship are not resolved, therapy for the overt sexual problems will not be beneficial (Kaplan, 1979).

TYPES OF SEX THERAPY

When a couple or individual believes that a sex-related problem exists, they may decide to opt for sex therapy. Unlike general psychological or psychiatric therapy, sex therapy focuses on the sexual interaction of an individual or couple with the purpose of assisting the couple to overcome a sex-related difficulty. Like psychotherapy, sex therapy can be individual, co-marital, or group in format. The type most appropriate may depend upon factors such as the type of problem, the reputation of the therapist(s), costs, the clients' goals, and intelligence and education, to name a few.

Individual Sex Therapy

Individual therapy is best for persons who either do not have a sex partner or have a sex partner who is not willing to participate. If a couple is married, individual sex therapy might not be the recommended course to follow, since each partner in the marriage is considered an involved partner.

If a person does not have a partner, the sex therapy team may choose to find this person a *surrogate,* or a third member of the therapy team who can serve as a sexual partner for the individual. The use of a surrogate might be effective in the treatment of a sexual dysfunction for some.

Co-Marital Sex Therapy

Perhaps the most well-known example of a co-therapist approach to sexual dysfunction is the Masters and Johnson program. In the co-therapist program, a female therapist and a male therapist work together to help a sexually dysfunctional couple. The advantages of the use of co-therapists are the client's opportunity to identify with the therapist; the client's feeling that there is support because no one is "outnumbered"; and less chance of the client's becoming emotionally and sexually attached to the therapist.

Co-marital sex therapy may sometimes be the quickest and most effective method of dealing with sexual dysfunction.

Group Sex Therapy

Sometimes sex therapists find that group treatment is an effective way to treat an individual with a sexual dysfunction. In this form of therapy, an individual with a specific sexual dysfunction, such as premature ejaculation, is put into a group with others who have a similar problem. These persons meet to discuss their sexual concerns. At the same time, they are assigned "homework" by the therapist. These individuals then meet in the therapist-led group to discuss their "homework" experiences as well as their sex-related concerns. The principal theory behind this type of therapy is that people who have similar problems can identify with each other and thus lend support and give "permission." This approach is no different in principle than other support groups such as Alcoholics Anonymous (AA), except that AA is peer-centered rather than therapist-centered.

While there is evidence that sex therapy is effective in many cases, there is little evidence to indicate *why* it works and *what* types of sex therapy are successful (Hogan, 1978; Ersner-Hershfield and Kopel, 1979).

TECHNIQUES OF SEX THERAPY

Although some techniques of sex therapy have already been described in detail, there are others that need mentioning.

Kegel Exercises

Kegel exercises are techniques that are intended to strengthen the female's pubococcygeal muscle, which runs from the pubic bone to the coccyx. The name is derived from Arnold Kegel (1952), the physician who developed them. Although the pubococcygeal muscles contract involuntarily at orgasm, they can also be "trained" to contract voluntarily. This exercise serves to help women improve the tone of this muscle if it has been stretched during pregnancy. It also is helpful in redeveloping control of urination after childbirth. Many women who practice this exercise report an increase in sensation during intercourse as well as greater sensitivity in the vaginal area.

The steps in the Kegel exercises are simple. The woman must first locate the muscles surrounding the vagina. She can do this by stopping the flow of urine. The muscles that stop the flow of urine are the ones she will focus on. She is instructed to practice tightening and relaxing these muscles several times a day. This practice strengthens these muscles much like other exercises strengthen other muscles. The Kegel exercise is used by many sex therapists to treat orgasmic dysfunctions.

Sensate Focus

Sensate focus exercises are stroking and massage exercises that are used by couples as a form of sexual expression. This technique, developed by Masters and Johnson, is used as a basic treatment of many sexual dysfunctions. These exercises help a couple to experience the sensuality of each other's body without orgasm as an outcome.

In sensate focus, one partner is a "giver" (touches the other) and one is a "receiver" (is touched). The giver massages or fondles the other partner. In turn, the giver is provided feedback about what is and is not pleasurable. After a certain period of time, the couple switch roles.

These exercises encourage people to learn to respond to and focus their attention on the sensuous pleasure they are receiving. The sensate focus exercises train people to enjoy the situation at hand and not drift toward thinking about things like cooking supper or what is going to be playing on television. These exercises can be practiced by any couple who have a meaningful relationship. You don't have to have a sexual dysfunction to benefit from sensate focus.

Masturbation

Since masturbation is the technique that is most likely to produce orgasm in many women, many therapists prescribe using this activity in treatment modalities. It is most likely to be used by women with a primary orgasmic dysfunction. LoPiccolo and Lobitz (1972) developed a nine-step program for female masturbation. In step one, the woman examines her genitals with the aid of a mirror and starts Kegel exercises. In steps two and three, she tactilely explores her genitals for the purpose of locating the pleasure-sensitive areas. In steps four and five, she is encouraged to intensely stimulate these areas while fantasizing or looking at explicit photos. If orgasm is not experienced in step five, vibrator stimulation is used in step six. Steps seven through nine are skill development for the partner. By the seventh step, the woman usually experiences orgasm. In step seven, the woman's partner observes her masturbating. In step eight, he learns how to manipulate her to orgasm. Step nine consists of intercourse paired with manual stimulation.

CHOOSING A SEX THERAPIST

While all states regulate the licensing of individuals to perform psychotherapy, the competence of these psychotherapists in providing adequate sex therapy may be suspect. There are many people who have a shingle outside their offices, proclaiming themselves sex therapists. Many of these persons have little or no ability to handle sexual concerns. Therefore, knowing how to select a sex therapist is important, and selecting an appropriate and well-trained sex therapist is no easy task. With this in mind, the American Association of Sex Educators, Counselors, and Therapists (AASECT) began a licensing procedure for sex therapists. To become certified, certain criteria, such as a minimum number of clinical hours under the guidance of another certified therapist, must be met. While this attempt is only one step in trying to tighten quality control, it is not enough.

According to LoPiccolo (1978), certain steps can be taken by consumers in selecting a competent sex therapist. First, do not respond to paid advertisements, since this practice is against the ethical code of psychotherapists. Second, check with local universities or community agencies. They are often reliable, and some of their staff members serve as good contacts. Third, make sure that a psychotherapist who practices sex therapy has a state license. Fourth, check to see whether the therapist has had special training—e.g., marriage counseling. Finally, don't just assume that a sex therapist recommended by your family doctor or the clergy is qualified.

HEART DISEASE AND MENTAL AND PHYSICAL HANDICAPS: THEIR EFFECT ON SEXUALITY

Sexual needs and desires are the same for everyone. However, our society seems to avoid consideration of the sexuality of people who have physical or mental disorders and handicaps. The need for sexual expression is felt not only by people in good health but also by people who are more limited than the general population. People who suffer chronic illness, physical disabilities, and mental retardation may be either psychologically or physically prohibited from leading the type of sexual life they prefer.

Our purpose in this section of the chapter is to shed light on some of the more common handicaps and look at their implications in sexual function and dysfunction. It is impossible within the confines of this book to describe all or even most of the handicaps that exist. Therefore we will focus our attention on those handicaps we feel may be of interest to the majority of people reading this book.

Mental Retardation

In our society, many people believe that the mentally retarded have no desire for sexual relations and are incapable of engaging in appropriate sexual activities. This assumption could not be further from the truth.

In contemporary society there is a growing acceptance of the idea that people who are mentally retarded can be capable and responsible sexual persons. Of course, we need to clarify our concept of mentally retarded. Some people are mentally retarded to the extent that only their basic needs can be met. For these profoundly retarded individuals, sexual desires usually are not perceived as being a basic need. Yet this population constitutes only 20% of the mentally retarded population. Eighty percent of the mentally retarded are educable. These individuals are capable of academic learning up to the sixth grade level (Hall, 1975). They are also capable of engaging in relationships with other people. The higher the IQ of a mentally retarded person, the greater is his or her probability of forming an intimate relationship with another person. Many retarded individuals do marry and have children.

Today, some administrators of institutions that house the mentally retarded are accepting the fact that these people are sexual human beings. As a result, we have begun to see some changes taking place. For example, comprehensive sex education courses are sometimes available for the mentally retarded. In addition, the rules that govern sexual behavior in institutions are adapting somewhat to the sexual needs of the confined individuals. For example, mentally handicapped people may be taught that certain places in the institution are appropriate for engaging in either solitary sex play or sex play with a partner.

At this point, it appears that society has made progress in dealing with the mentally retarded. However, there is a need for more progress.

Spinal Cord Injury

Men and women who have spinal cord injuries are often seen by society as being unable to perform sexually or become sexually aroused. However, some *are* able. Whether they are able or not depends on their specific physical and psychological condition.

In Chapter 4 we discussed the impact of spinal injury on sexual arousal. The two variables that are important for sexual functioning are the site of the injury and the extent of the injury. Generally, people who have not severed the entire spinal cord have a greater capability for sexual functioning than people who have completely severed spinal cords.

Men who have severed spinal cords are still capable of ejaculating. However, they often do not have an accompanying pleasurable experience; that is, they do not "feel" their orgasm. But many of these men do experience varying degrees of sexual pleasure even when they do not achieve orgasm.

Women who have spinal cord injuries generally experience the same degree of sexual response as men. The clitoris, labia, and breasts can respond to sexual arousal. Some women report that they become vaginally lubricated during sexual arousal (Bergman, 1975). Yet some women say that they have no pleasurable feelings associated with sexual experiences (Money, 1960). The data we have about the effects of spinal cord injury and women's sexual functioning are incomplete at this time. Fewer women than men have spinal cord injuries, and therefore the number of subjects we can study is limited. Women are not usually impaired as severely as men (Hohmann, 1973).

The reproductive capacity of persons whose spinal cord has been injured varies. If a man can retain his ability to ejaculate, he may be able to impregnate his partner. However, his sperm count may be low.

Among women, becoming pregnant after a spinal cord injury may be more difficult than before the injury. After an injury, the menstrual cycle may be irregular, thereby making conception difficult. However, normal menstrual patterns usually return after a year (Comarr, 1966). Furthermore, women whose spinal cord has been injured do ovulate and can become pregnant and have a normal vaginal delivery. A pregnant woman with a spinal cord injury will probably need no anesthetic during labor and delivery, because she will not feel pain. She will probably not be able to push.

Heart Disease

Although heart disease per se is not a sexual dysfunction, it can lead to problems that affect one's sex life. When you consider that over 40 million Americans are afflicted with cardiovascular diseases, which include heart diseases, it is not surprising to find substantial changes in the sexual functioning of these individuals (Bloch et al., 1975). The major reason individuals limit their sexual activity after a heart attack is the fear that sexual activity will cause another coronary accident or death. As a result, about 10% of men who have had heart attacks experience permanent impotence.

The changes in sexual activity among postcoronary individuals are probably based upon myth, fear, and misinformation. Depending upon the extent of damage to the heart and the amount of recovery, most doctors recommend that patients begin to exercise regularly. With regular exercise as well as with a return to the healthy activities engaged in before suffering the heart attack, the patient can begin to return to a normal life. The same regimen relates to sexual activity. The average maximum heart rate for postcoronary men during orgasm is 117 beats per minute (Hellerstein and Friedman, 1970). This is the same stress produced by engaging in many everyday tasks such as climbing stairs. Accordingly, sexual activity should not have to be redirected. However, each individual may have characteristics that require special recommendations. It is best that a coronary patient ask questions of his physician concerning sexual activity.

Based upon the work of various researchers, investigations have shown that while the chance of sustaining another heart attack during coitus is low, it still occurs (Massie et al., 1969). However, when it does occur, it does so often when the man is having an extramarital affair or is engaged in coitus in an unusual setting. So we might ask whether the cause of the heart attack is coitus or anxiety.

SUMMARY STATEMENTS

- *There are two types of impotence — primary and secondary.*
- *Impotence is usually caused by psychological factors.*
- *Premature ejaculation is a common male sexual disorder.*
- *There are several techniques used to treat premature ejaculation.*
- *Retarded ejaculation is another male sexual disorder.*
- *Primary and secondary orgasmic dysfunction can occur in women.*
- *Vaginismus is another female sexual dysfunction.*
- *Dyspareunia is much more common in women than in men.*

- *Most sexual dysfunctions in men and women are due to psychological factors.*
- *Sexual expression is a need for most mentally retarded persons.*
- *Spinal cord injury does not necessarily mean the end of sexual activity.*
- *Heart disease often inhibits sexual activity.*
- *Several types of sex therapy can help people with sex-related problems.*
- *Sex therapists can use different techniques to help people.*
- *Sex therapists should be carefully selected.*

SUGGESTED READINGS

Barbach, Lonnie G. *For Yourself: The Fulfillment of Female Sexuality.* New York: Doubleday, 1975.

Belliveau, Fred, and Lin Richter. *Understanding Human Sexual Inadequacy.* New York: Bantam, 1970.

Kaplan, Helen. *The Illustrated Manual of Sex Therapy.* New York: Quadrangle/New York Times, 1975.

LoPiccolo, Joseph, and Leslie LoPiccolo (eds.). *Handbook of Sex Therapy.* New York: Plenum Press, 1978.

A LOOK AT YOUR LIFESTYLE

As two college students, you are intimately involved and sexually active with each other. However, in this relationship, the male ejaculates prematurely.

Complete the following statements using an I-message:
Whenever we make love and ejaculation occurs before I have the opportunity to reach orgasm I _____

_____

I would tell my partner that _____

_____

**PSYCHO-
PHYSIOLOGICAL
SEXUAL
DISORDERS**

GATHERING INFORMATION

You have decided that you want to deal with this sexual dysfunction in an effective manner. List two courses of action you could possibly take.

_____

_____

EVALUATING THE INFORMATION

Choose the most appropriate course of action you would take in dealing with the sexual dysfunction and list two reasons you chose this course.

_____

_____

_____

MAKING RESPONSIBLE DECISIONS

List the most important criteria you would use in determining whether or not your decision was the proper one.

_____

_____

_____

_____

VD
It
travels in
the best
circles

ELEVEN

Sexually Transmitted Diseases

A LOOK AT YOUR LIFESTYLE

For most people, participation in intimate sexual practices with another person is a safe and enjoyable experience. However, just as many activities in which we take part have healthy outcomes, so they can also have unhealthy outcomes.

Today, sexual behavior without the chance of contracting a sexually transmitted disease (STD) is not a reality for many people. Consider some of the following statistics:

- With over 3 million new cases each year, gonorrhea is the leading reportable sexually communicable disease.
- Young women lose 900,000 schooldays each year because of gonococcal infection.
- Herpes simplex virus Type 2 is not only incurable, but it is estimated by the Center for Disease Control that anywhere from 300,000 to 1 million persons contract this disease each year.
- The majority of STDs occur in the 15-to-24 age group (Yarber, 1978).

303

Our awareness of STDs is not recent. "Love's diseases" were mentioned in the Old Testament. In 400 B.C., Hippocrates said that "excessive indulgence in the pleasures of Venus" caused venereal disease (VD).

Let us now examine why knowledge of STD is something important to us. The increased incidence of these diseases is no doubt due to the fact that a large number of people are sexually active. Whenever sexually active people increase the number of their sexual contacts, so does the likelihood that STD incidence will increase.

Other factors have also played a role in the incidence of STD. Oral contraceptives and IUDs make the chance of becoming pregnant almost nil. If there is a lower risk of pregnancy, there is not as great a hesitation to engage in sexual intercourse. And an increase in the frequency of sexual intercourse with multiple partners increases the chances of contracting an STD.

For many people, contracting a venereal disease can result in drastic changes in lifestyle. Let us look at some examples:

- A man is divorced by his wife because he passed gonorrhea on to her. He had contracted this disease from a partner with whom he had had an extramarital affair.
- A woman goes through days of pain and embarrassment because of the recurring effects of herpes simplex virus Type 2.
- A couple's child is born with a defect because the woman contracted syphilis early in her pregnancy.

Our purpose here is not to scare you into a sense of panic. Rather, it is to focus upon prevention. If you are aware that STDs can be contracted through sexual activity, then you may be one step ahead in making sure you have responsible habits that decrease your susceptibility to these diseases.

GATHERING INFORMATION

We have used two terms thus far that you probably recognized — sexually transmitted diseases and venereal diseases. These two terms are often used interchangeably. However, many people think *VD* refers only to syphilis and gonorrhea. For many, *VD* has become overused. Therefore, we will refer to all sexually contracted diseases as *sexually transmitted diseases* (STDs). However, there are limitations even here. If *any* disease that is transmitted through sexual contact were considered a sexually transmitted disease, then we would have to label such conditions as the common cold, mononucleosis, and chicken pox as STDs if they were transmitted during sexual activity. Therefore, we will discuss those diseases whose mode of transmission is *primarily* through sexual contact. Thus, the common cold, which can be passed through nonsexual contact, is *not* an STD, whereas gonorrhea, which can be passed *only* through sexual contact, *is* an STD. Thus, a sexually transmitted disease is defined as a disease whose mode of transmission is *almost always* by sexual contact (pubic lice, which can be contracted from infected toilet seats or towels is one such exception; thus the phrase "almost always").

In gathering information about STDs, our discussion in this chapter will focus on the following:

- description of the disease
- mode of transmission
- symptoms
- treatment
- complications
- prevention

The most prevalent diseases, and those we will discuss, are gonorrhea, syphilis, nongonococcal urethritis, genital herpes virus, pubic lice, cystitis, genital warts, and the two types of common vaginal infections— trichomoniasis and moniliasis.

EVALUATING THE INFORMATION

This chapter will provide readers with the information needed to answer many of the following types of questions:

- At what point do I suspect that I may have an STD?
- What if I have an STD and I suspect I have infected my partner?
- What methods or techniques can I use to avoid contracting an STD?

People who are responsible about their health as well as the health of those individuals to whom they are close will take precautions against the spread of STDs. We hope that for everyone reading this chapter, the information provided will make your knowledge and behavior, as well as the knowledge and behavior of others, the first line of defense in the prevention of STDs.

MAKING RESPONSIBLE DECISIONS

The decisions you will make about STDs will probably have an effect upon the areas of treatment and prevention. For example, in the area of treatment, let's assume the following occurred. A man wakes up one morning and notices a cloudy discharge from the urethral opening of his penis. He had had sexual intercourse with a woman about five days before. If this man possesses a knowledge of the signs and symptoms of STD, he will probably suspect that he has gonorrhea. However, whether or not this man decides to *accept the fact* that he *may* have the disease is questionable, for several reasons. By denial, he may not have to face embarrassment (i.e., telling his doctor or girlfriend), he may not have to abstain from sexual intercourse (which he would have to do during treatment, or else use a condom), and he may not have to incur expenses for treatment. People often deny the signs and symptoms of a disease, thinking it will go away. For example, most women know about breast cancer. They also know that if they discover a lump in the breast, they should see a physician. Yet some women do nothing about their discovery, in the hope that the lump will disappear, so that the threat of cancer will be eliminated. This same behavior holds true for an STD. Therefore, we need to make sound decisions based upon our interpretation of information.

We also need to make decisions about treatment. For example, if an STD is not treated, it can be spread from person to person. Yet some people may not seek treatment for an STD because they may be asked to name their contacts. Or if they *are* treated, they will not acknowledge to someone with whom they are intimate that they have had contact with someone else. This type of situation often interferes with one's ability to make rational decisions. For example, a woman might say to herself, "I'll get treated for my STD and not tell my husband." While this decision may cure the wife (at least until she contracts the disease again from her husband), it does nothing for the husband. On the other hand, making a decision to tell the husband about his need to be treated could be risky insofar as the marriage is concerned. Therefore, what should the woman do? Most people would say that telling the husband and having him treated is the most responsible decision.

Caring, concerned individuals will be more than likely to base their decisions upon their health and well-being and their partner's. Although some decisions about STDs will be difficult to make, the fact remains that they can be made. If the decision is a difficult one, then the concerned individual should seek assistance from a counselor or a physician about the available options.

GONORRHEA

Gonorrhea, also known as the "clap" and the "drip," is the most widespread of the *reportable* communicable diseases in this country. The common cold is the only communicable disease that has a higher incidence than gonorrhea. So widespread is this disease that it is considered to have reached epidemic proportions. The Center for Disease Control estimated in 1979 that well over a million cases of gonorrhea exist in the United States.

Several reasons have been given for the increased incidence of this disease. First, gonorrhea is often asymptomatic (without symptoms). Therefore, a person may not know the disease is present and thus continue to infect other persons. A second reason for the increased incidence of gonorrhea is what appears to be an increase in the number of young people who have become sexually involved.

Many people today have reservations about using condoms as a method of birth control, a factor to consider when we examine the increase in the number of cases of gonorrhea. Yet the condom is fairly successful in preventing the spread of gonorrhea. The widespread use of oral contraceptives has also contributed to the increase in gonorrhea. Oral contraceptives facilitate the susceptibility of the female to gonorrhea. If a man has gonorrhea and his partner is *not* taking oral contraceptives, his chance of passing this disease to his partner is about 30%. However, if she *is* taking oral contraceptives and he does have gonorrhea, there is over an 80% chance that this disease will be contracted by the female. Oral contraceptives change the vaginal environment. This environment facilitates the growth of the microorganism that causes gonorrhea.

Mode of Transmission

The microorganism responsible for gonorrhea is the bacterium *Neisseria gonorrhoeae.* This microorganism can survive only in the warm mucous membranes that line the genitals, anus, and throat. Therefore, the idea that gonorrhea can be contracted from toilet seats, doorknobs, and other sources is purely myth. The only way that gonorrhea can be contracted is through intimate sexual contact: sexual intercourse, oral–genital contact, and anal–genital contact. It cannot be transmitted by kissing.

Symptoms

IN THE MALE

During sexual intercourse, the gonococcus can enter the male's body through the urethra. *Urethritis,* an inflammation of the urethra, develops. This inflammation, which causes a thick white, yellow, or yellow-green discharge from the urethral opening of the penis, occurs from two to seven days after contact with an infected person. The area around the urethral opening may become tender. When the man urinates, he may feel a burning sensation. In some men, the lymph glands around the groin may swell and become tender to touch. When a man notices these symptoms, he should see a physician. About 90% of males who contract gonorrhea will notice signs and symptoms.

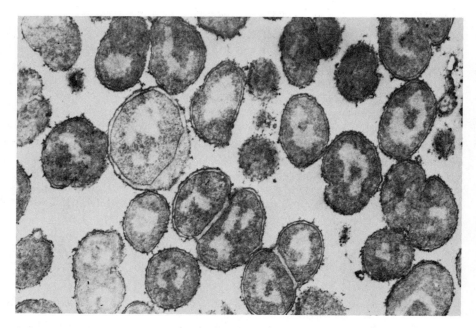

Cross section showing diplococci, **Neisseria gonorrhoeae,** which causes gonorrhea and pelvic inflammatory disease. (Photo, Center for Disease Control, Atlanta)

Sometimes young people are aware of changes that occur in the body and do not know that they indicate gonorrhea. For example, a young man walked up to us after a sex education lecture once and said that he had had sexual intercourse with a girl a week before. He then indicated that he had semen coming out of his penis for several days. We told him that the semen was probably a discharge of pus and a sign of gonorrhea. He was referred to a physician, who, in turn, diagnosed gonorrhea. The young man and his contact were treated.

Many of the early symptoms of gonorrhea may disappear without treatment. Yet if the gonococcus is still present, the man can continue to infect his partners.

As mentioned previously, gonorrhea can also be transmitted through oral–genital contact—more specifically, through fellatio. If fellatio is performed on an infected person, the gonococcus can invade the throat, and the infected person will experience a sore throat. Gonorrhea is not as likely to be spread through cunnilingus.

Rectal gonorrhea can be transmitted through anal intercourse. A person who has gonorrhea in the rectum may experience an itching as well as a slight discharge in the rectal area.

Most cases of gonococcal invasion of the throat and rectum are asymptomatic. These conditions can occur in heterosexual as well as homosexual relationships. However, gonorrhea in the rectum is much more common among homosexuals than heterosexuals.

Gonorrhea can also be contracted in the eyes of newborn infants during birth. For this reason, silver nitrate or another medication is always put in the newborn's eyes. If this precaution were not followed, infected babies would become blind in a period of several days.

IN THE FEMALE

Unlike the male, about 80% of females who have gonorrhea do not have any observable signs and symptoms. The most common site of infection in the female is the cervix. If the woman does have a cervical discharge, it will usually be green or yellow in color. Normal cervical mucus is clear and white. In addition, a discharge due to gonorrhea may spread to the urethra, and if so, the woman will experience a burning sensation during urination. In some cases, the discharge can irritate the vulva. Since the signs and symptoms of gonorrhea can be disguised as other vaginal infections, doctors may overlook the disease during an examination. Also, because half of all women who have gonorrhea also have trichomoniasis, this disease can be overlooked. Thus, the doctor may treat one disease and not the other. It is possible for a woman to have several STDs at the same time. For example, a woman, as well as a man, can have syphilis, trichomoniasis, and gonorrhea. In such a case each disease would need to be treated separately.

Since many women are asymptomatic, they often do not get treatment. It is important that women become aware of any possible vaginal secretions that are out of the ordinary. When this occurs, she should seek medical attention. It may be a good idea for the woman to ask her doctor to examine her for the presence of gonorrhea.

Diagnosis

IN THE MALE

In males, a definite diagnosis can be made one of two ways. After inspecting the genitals, the physician can insert a cotton-tipped swab about a half inch up the urethra. This procedure is minimally painful. Then a smear is made on a slide, which is then examined under a microscope. However, this technique is often inaccurate.

The other way of diagnosing gonorrhea is to wipe the swab's secretions in a special nutrient jelly (culture). Within 48 hours, any bacteria present will multiply, so that a more accurate diagnosis can be made. Since the test for diagnosing gonorrhea requires meticulous care, improper techniques can cause false negative results.

If gonorrhea is suspected in the throat or rectum, swabs are taken from these areas. The same laboratory techniques are then followed.

IN THE FEMALE

A female who is thought to have gonorrhea will have a pelvic examination to check for inflammation. A cotton swab is inserted into her cervix to collect mucus for a culture. The procedures used for the diagnosis of gonorrhea in the male also apply to diagnosis of the disease in the female.

The same procedures used in the male for detection of throat and rectal gonorrhea are also used for detection in the female.

Once a diagnosis of gonorrhea is confirmed, treatment can begin.

Treatment

For both males and females, treatment for gonorrhea consists of a large dose of penicillin, which is injected in the gluteal muscle of the buttocks. Usually, one dose is enough to kill the gonococcus. If a person is allergic to penicillin, tetracycline can be used as a substitute. If a woman is pregnant, tetracyline should not be used. Instead, erythromycin can be substituted.

Some important points should be made concerning treatment for gonorrhea. Both partners should be treated. If they are not, and they continue to engage in intimate sexual contact, gonorrhea will be transmitted back and forth. A cure can definitely be confirmed via a follow-up culture seven to fourteen days after treatment. Ideally, both partners should avoid intercourse until a cure is obtained. If a couple chooses to engage in intimate sexual contact, then a condom should be used.

A person should always contact his or her physician or clinic if he or she has any reactions to the antibiotics used during treatment.

Complications

IN THE MALE

If an infected male is not treated within a couple of weeks, the gonorrhea may spread throughout the genitourinary tract. When this condition occurs, the prostate (prostatitis), seminal vesicles (seminal vesiculitis), and the urinary bladder (cystitis) can become inflamed. These conditions occur only in a small number of men. Sterility will probably not occur in the male even if gonorrhea is left untreated. What may occur is an infection of the epididymis, known as *epididymitis*. In epididymitis, the man may experience painful swelling on the bottom of the testicle. Sometimes its after effect can be a blockage of sperm to that testicle. If this condition were to occur to both testicles, sterility would set in. However, when this condition occurs in only one testicle, the male remains fertile. The reason this condition usually occurs in only one testicle is that almost any man, if he felt the pain of epididymitis, would seek treatment. If the man were able to bear the pain of epididymitis and not seek treatment, then sterility might become a possibility.

IN THE FEMALE

If a woman is not treated for gonorrhea, several complications may set in. First, Bartholin's glands can become infected; they become swollen and produce pus. The infection can also spread to the anus and rectum via menstrual or cervical discharges. The second and more serious of the consequences of untreated gonorrhea is infection of the reproductive organs. In about half of all women who are not treated for gonorrhea for two months, the gonococcus moves into the uterus. This problem usually occurs during the menstrual cycle. Once the gonococcus enters the uterus, it can travel to and infect the oviducts. Once the oviducts are infected, pus will form. The oviducts and the ovaries may become inflamed, leading to a condition known as *pelvic inflammatory disease* (PID). The symptoms of PID (PID can also have causes other than gonorrhea) are pain in the lower abdomen, nausea, vomiting, fever, irregular menstruation, and malaise. PID also poses a great problem, should the woman conceive. A woman who has PID will probably have a slightly blocked oviduct. If a sperm cell gets by the blocked area and fertilizes the egg, an ectopic pregnancy may be likely, since the fertilized egg will have difficulty passing through the oviduct that is blocked. The treatment for an ectopic pregnancy is surgery.

In some cases, the oviducts may be scarred to the extent that neither sperm nor egg can pass through them, and the woman is rendered sterile.

On rare occasions in both the male and female, the gonococcus can invade the bloodstream and produce arthritic pain in the joints, a condition known as *gonococcal arthritis*.

SYPHILIS

Syphilis is not as common as gonorrhea. In 1977, there were 20,362 reported cases, or 9.5 per 100,000 population (DHEW, 1978). However, it continues to be a major concern to public health officials as well as to many men and women, even though its incidence is decreasing. Many theories about the introduction of syphilis to the United States have been espoused; however, no single theory has been accepted.* We also do not have any proof of how and when syphilis originated. One theory, perhaps the most logical, indicates that syphilis originated in a cell mutation. Probably, we will never discover any widely accepted theory for the origin of syphilis.

---

*For a detailed account of how syphilis was introduced to the U.S., read: U.S. Department of Health, Education, and Welfare. *Syphilis: A Synopsis*. Public Health Service Publication No. 1660, January 1968, pp. 1–16.

Mode of Transmission

Syphilis is caused by a corkscrew-shaped bacterium called *Treponema pallidum*. This bacterium is also known as a *spirochete*. The spirochete can enter the body in the same ways as the gonococcus. It is transmitted through the mucous membranes or skin abrasions from the open lesions of an infected partner. A pregnant woman who contracts syphilis can infect her unborn child by transmitting the spirochete to the fetus through the placenta. Spirochetes can cross the placental barrier by the 18th week of pregnancy if no treatment is initiated.

Like gonorrhea, syphilis can be contracted through sexual intercourse as well as through oral–genital and anal–genital contact. The bacteria can also enter any part of the body where there is an open cut if the cut area is brought into contact with a lesion. A person cannot contract syphilis in any way other than close contact with an infected person, since the spirochete needs a warm and moist environment in order to survive. Therefore, contracting syphilis from toilet seats and doorknobs is, again, purely myth.

Symptoms

The progress of syphilis can be broken into four stages: primary, secondary, latent, and late (tertiary) syphilis.

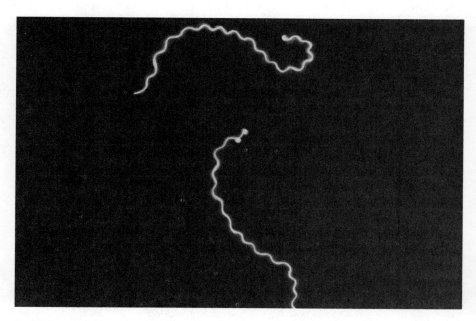

Darkfield microscopy showing **Treponema pallidum,** which causes syphilis. (Photo, Center for Disease Control, Atlanta)

PRIMARY SYPHILIS

Between ten days and three months after sexual contact with an infected person, a *chancre* may appear at the entry site of the spirochete. A chancre is a red bump the size of about a pea. Shortly after the chancre develops, it becomes an open sore covered by a yellow or gray crusty scab. The chancre is painless, and it will not bleed easily. In some cases, the chancre will be surrounded by a thin pink border. Its edges may also be hard and raised.

If the site of invasion of the the spirochete is the male genitalia, the chancre will appear on the glans or shaft of the penis or on the scrotum. In the woman, the chancre will often appear on the cervix or the internal vaginal walls. For this reason, syphilis often goes unnoticed in the woman. On occasion, the chancre may appear on the labia, in which case the woman will stand a better chance of making a diagnosis.

In oral–genital and penile–anal contact, the spirochete can enter the mucous membrane of the throat or anus. In such cases, the chancre can appear on the lips, tongue, and mouth or around the anus. In most cases, only one chancre will appear, although on occasion more than one have been known to surface. After about one to five weeks, the chancre will disappear. When it does, the primary stage has ended. However, the disappearance of the chancre does not indicate the disappearance of syphilis.

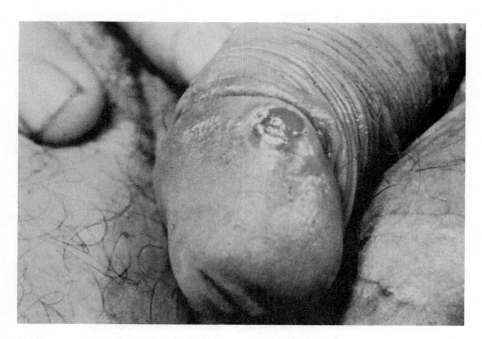

Syphilitic chancre on penis. (Photo, Center for Disease Control, Atlanta)

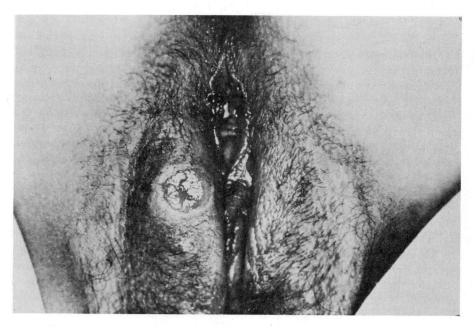

Syphilitic chancre on labia. (Photo, Center for Disease Control, Atlanta)

SECONDARY SYPHILIS

About six weeks (actually, anywhere from two weeks to six months) after the chancre disappears, secondary syphilis begins. During this stage, a rash may appear over the body. This rash may be barely or severely noticeable. It consists of raised bumps that do not hurt or itch. If this rash appears on the soles of the feet or the palms of the hands, it is an indication that syphilis is present. Also, with this rash, the infected person may experience a sore throat, headaches, joint and muscle pain, and a low-grade fever. Syphilis is called "the great imitator," since its signs and symptoms are indicative of a host of other maladies. If treatment is sought at this stage, there will be no permanent damage due to syphilis. Rarely does syphilis go past this stage, since treatment is almost always sought. In earlier times, when treatment was not available, syphilis often advanced beyond the secondary stage.

If by some chance the infected person does not seek treatment during the secondary stage, the signs and symptoms will disappear anyway after two to six weeks. At this point, the infected person will enter the latent stage of syphilis.

LATENT SYPHILIS

During the latent stage of syphilis, an infected person may be asymptomatic. For about a year, the disease is not contagious. Yet if a woman becomes pregnant, she can pass the disease to her fetus. Meanwhile, the spirochete is busy gaining entrance into the central nervous system, the blood, and the bones. Half the people in this stage of syphilis may live the rest of their lives without further complications. However, the other half will enter the tertiary stage.

TERTIARY SYPHILIS

In the tertiary stage of syphilis, infected individuals may develop a *gumma*, or ulceration, of a body organ (three to seven years after infection), major heart and blood vessel damage (ten to forty years after infection), or damage to the central nervous system (ten to twenty years after infection). Ultimately, death can result.

Diagnosis

Since syphilis looks like many other diseases, it is often difficult to diagnose. However, there are several methods that are used to diagnose syphilis. In one method, called the *darkfield examination*, fluid from a chancre is placed on a slide. Since *Treponema pallidum* needs to be seen in a living stage, and since its narrow width does not permit it to be seen under an ordinary light microscope, a darkfield microscope is employed. Usually the spirochete can be seen in this manner and a diagnosis can be made.

Another method of diagnosis is a blood test. The blood test most often used to test for syphilis is called the VDRL (named after the Venereal Disease Research Laboratory of the U.S. Public Health Service). This test is most accurate if it is administered at least four to six weeks after the person was infected.

The test for syphilis that is most recommended today is the *MHA-TP* (microhemagglutination treponemal pallidum) antibody test. The MHA-TP test is considered the most reliable of the diagnostic procedures for syphilis.

Blood tests are required in many states before a marriage license will be issued.

Treatment

The treatment for syphilis is penicillin. A large, short-term dose of penicillin is usually enough to cure syphilis that has been contracted within ten days from exposure. For syphilis in the primary or secondary stages, 2.4 million units of benzathine penicillin (given in two doses of 1.2 million units each) is needed. For latent and tertiary syphilis, 2.4 million units of benzathine penicillin per week for three weeks is administered. It should be noted that treatment for syphilis will cure the disease but not the damage it has caused.

If a person is allergic to penicillin, tetracycline can be used as a substitute treatment.

Further precautions — any sex partner should be treated, and condoms should be used during sexual contact for one month after treatment. A follow-up examination should be given to make sure that syphilis has been cured.

Complications

Most of the complications of syphilis have been discussed with its signs and symptoms. However, one complication needs mentioning here with regard to pregnancy. The longer the duration of untreated syphilis before pregnancy, the less likely it is that the fetus will be stillborn or infected. Thus, a woman who becomes pregnant while she is in the primary or secondary stages of syphilis frequently has a stillbirth. If the woman is in the latent stage of syphilis, the fetus may or may not have the disease. Adequate treatment of the mother before the 18th week of pregnancy will prevent infection of the fetus. Because penicillin crosses the placenta in the amounts necessary to cure the disease, treatment of the mother after the 18th week of pregnancy wil also cure the infected fetus.

GENITAL HERPES

Genital herpes, an STD that is caused by the herpes simplex virus, was rarely seen by physicians in this country until about 1965. Since that time, its incidence has increased dramatically. The Center for Disease Control estimates that there are 300,000 to 1 million new cases of genital herpes each year, and many consider this disease the number one STD problem.

There are two closely related herpes simplex viruses — *Type* 1 and *Type* 2. Most people are somewhat familiar with the herpes simplex virus that manifests itself as cold sores or fever blisters affecting the lips, nose, or mouth. Most oral herpes infections are caused by the Type 1 virus, although about 10% of oral herpes cases are caused by Type 2. Generally, in 90% of the cases, the Type 2 virus causes genital herpes infections.

Mode of Transmission

Genital, or Type 2, herpes can be transmitted from one partner to another when one partner has genital herpes in the active stage. It can be transmitted by penile–vaginal, oral–genital, or anal–penile contact.

In some cases, herpes infections in the mouth can be caused by Type 2 virus. It is in this case that the Type 2 virus can be transmitted through oral–genital contact. In some other cases, Type 1 herpes, manifested by cold sores around the mouth, can be transferred to the genital area. If the partner who has Type 1 performs oral–genital sex on another partner, Type 1 may be transmitted.

Symptoms

About two to eight days after contact with an infected person, minor rashes or itching in the genital area, followed by a cluster of blisters or tiny fluid-filled lesions, appear. These blisters and lesions are painful. Sometimes they open and form sores, or ulcers. In men, these sores are usually found on the glans or shaft of the penis; in women, they can be found on the labia, vaginal walls, and cervix. When genital herpes is contracted by anal intercourse, the symptoms appear in and around the anus. If con-

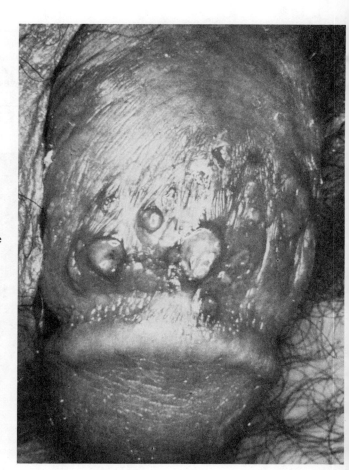

Genital herpes of the penis. (Photo, Center for Disease Control, Atlanta)

tracted by oral–genital contact, the sores can be on the lips, tongue, mouth, and throat.

When the blisters open, the disease is highly contagious. Ten days after the initial appearance of the sore, the healing process begins. This process can take about ten days.

One of the unfortunate outcomes of contracting herpes is that the virus continues to live in the body's cells for the remainder of one's life. While a few people will never have the symptoms of genital herpes again, most will be affected by their reappearance. Some of the factors that contribute to the reactivation of the symptoms of genital herpes are emotional stress, poor nutritional habits, fatigue, and a general state of poor health. Recurring symptoms may not appear until several years after the initial outbreak. For this reason, couples must be very careful, in that one partner can infect another simply because he or she is unaware that the sores or lesions two years later are those of genital herpes.

One year after we were married, I contracted genital herpes from my husband. Initially, I was furious. I thought he had had an extramarital affair. Then our doctor explained to us that my husband could have contracted herpes many years ago and that the signs and symptoms had reappeared. From now on, we will be much more aware of the signs of herpes.

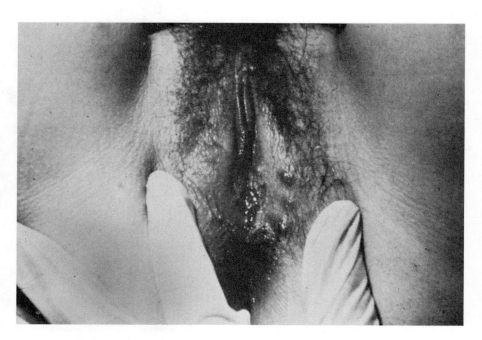

Genital herpes of labia. (Photo, Center for Disease Control, Atlanta)

Diagnosis

The physician can make a definite diagnosis of genital herpes by making a smear of herpes cells taken from lesions and examining these cells under a microscope. Accurate results can be determined within 48 hours. Blood tests can also be used to detect antibodies for herpes. However, this test can indicate only whether herpes was contracted in the past and not whether the patient has an active infection (Kagen, 1978). On rare occasions, herpes can show up on routine Pap smears.

Treatment

Herpes can be treated but not cured. The general treatment consists of sitz baths, compresses, ointments, and antibacterial creams to prevent secondary infections. In cases where extreme pain exists, painkillers may be prescribed.

Other treatment methods for genital herpes are being researched. One such method is called *photoinactivation*. In this treatment, lesions are painted with light-sensitive dye and then exposed to light. The light inactivates the virus and the sores heal. However, this treatment modality is controversial, and its widespread use, questionable. Other researchers are trying to prevent herpes by injecting antibodies into the body, therefore promoting immunity. However, recurrences of herpes persist in the presence of antibodies. For now, there is no known cure for this disease.

Complications

Women who have had genital herpes have an increased chance of contracting cancer of the cervix. However, the overwhelming majority of women who have had genital herpes will not get cervical cancer. If a woman has had herpes, she should have a Pap smear every six months. Cervical cancer, if caught early, is almost 100% curable.

Another second major complication of genital herpes in women occurs during childbirth. If herpes is dormant during the time of delivery, the baby will not be affected. If herpes is in the active stage at the time of delivery, the baby has about a 50% chance of contracting this disease (Blakeslee, 1981). Sixty percent of all newborns who contract herpes die (Kagen, 1978). The disease is transmitted to the baby from the mother's vagina during the delivery. Women who have genital herpes should have smears taken from the vagina as they approach the latter stages of pregnancy. If the physician notices that an active case of herpes does exist, the baby will probably be delivered by cesarean section.

Genital herpes has occasionally been implicated in *keratitis*. Keratitis is an inflammation of the cornea which can lead to blindness (Raber and Blough, 1980).

NONGONOCOCCAL URETHRITIS (NONSPECIFIC URETHRITIS)

Nongonococcal urethritis (NGU), also called *nonspecific urethritis* (NSU), is an inflammation of the urethra not caused by gonococcus bacteria. NGU is the second most common STD. At on time, NGU was only called NSU because this disease was thought to be caused by any number of microorganisms. However, it is now believed that NGU is caused by two microorganisms—Chlamydia and T-strain mycoplasma (Wear and Holmes, 1976). Other factors may also be causative agents in NGU. Among them are allergic reactions and irritations.

Mode of Transmission

Although the symptoms of NGU can disappear after two or three months, it can still be spread during sexual intercourse. Men and women can pass the disease back and forth to each other.

Symptoms

Although NGU is more common among males, the female can also harbor the microorganisms. In males, the symptoms resemble those of gonorrhea. The male may experience a burning sensation during urination. He may also have a thin, clear, or slightly white discharge from his penis. The gonorrhea discharge is usually white or yellowish. However, there is less of the discharge from the penis in NGU than in gonorrhea.

Many women who have NGU are asymptomatic. However, some women may experience a mild discharge of pus from the vagina.

Diagnosis

The physician can make an accurate diagnosis of NGU by taking a swab of the discharge and smearing the microorganism on a culture, where colonies of bacteria will grow.

Treatment

The effective treatment of NGU is dependent upon an accurate diagnosis. Since the symptoms of NGU are similar to those of gonorrhea, doctors may often prescibe penicillin, since they may think the NGU is gonorrhea. Unfortunately, penicillin does not cure NGU. However, tetracycline is successful in the treatment of NGU. If one is allergic to tetracycline, erythromycin can be substituted effectively.

Complications

The only major complication of NGU can occur during childbirth. If the woman houses the NGU microorganism on the cervix, it can enter the baby's eyes and produce an infection. This infection can then scar the cornea.

PUBIC LICE

Pubic lice, also known as "crabs," are yellowish gray insects the size of a pinhead. The louse attaches itself to the pubic hair and sucks the skin. When it is filled with blood, it appears to the eye like a black dot. When these insects are examined under a microscope, they look like crabs—hence their nickname (Figure 11–1).

Mode of Transmission

Pubic lice can be transmitted through close sexual contact when the pubic area of an infected person comes in contact with another person. Since the lice can live away from the body for one day, it is possible for a person to contract them from wearing another person's underclothing, sleeping in infected bedsheets, and sitting on toilets.

Diagnosis and Symptoms

It is rather easy to tell when a person has pubic lice. For one thing, little black spots may be visible on parts of the body that have dense hair growth—usually the pubic area. In addition, most people will feel very itchy where the lice are attached. The infected area may have a rash composed of small blue spots.

Pubic lice can also be found under the armpits, on the scalp, and in eyebrows. If a man has a very hairy chest, the lice can be found there also. Scratching the area only serves to perpetuate the spread of lice over the body, since the fingernails carry the eggs to other sites.

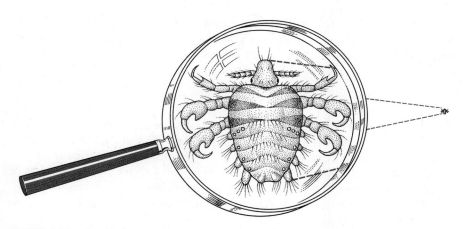

FIGURE 11.1   A pubic louse.

Treatment

Persons who suspect that they have pubic lice can treat the problem themselves. One cure is *A-200 pyrinate,* which is an over-the-counter drug. The most commonly known treatment is *Kwell,* which comes in the form of a cream, shampoo, or lotion. This drug can be purchased only with a prescription (Stewart et al., 1979).

When treating pubic lice, it is important to apply the drug being used to all possibly infected parts of the body. The treatment used should remain in place for several hours. The louse cannot live for more than 24 hours after detachment from the body. However, many doctors recommend disinfecting clothing and bedsheets as a precaution.

Since lice lay eggs that take seven to nine days to hatch, it is important that medication be reapplied throughout this period.

I remember when I had the crabs—I was driven crazy. I had a girlfriend at the time, and I avoided having sex with her. I took hot baths and changed my underwear three times a day. That didn't work.

There are no known major complications associated with pubic lice.

VENEREAL WARTS

Venereal warts, also known as *genital warts,* are dry wartlike growths that are caused by the same virus that produces warts on other parts of the body.

Mode of Transmission

While venereal warts are not as common as some of the other STDs we have discussed thus far, they are not rare. They can be transmitted primarily by sexual, oral, and anal intercourse.

Diagnosis and Symptoms

After contact with an infected person, venereal warts appear anywhere from one to three months later. These warts appear on the labia, vaginal walls, and cervix of the female. In the male, they appear on the glans or shaft of the penis. Sometimes these warts appear in the urethra of both males and females. They are raised, cauliflower-like bumps.

Diagnosis of venereal warts is simple because of their easy-to-spot and distinctive appearance.

Treatment

Most genital warts are treated with podophyllin liquid or ointment. When this ointment is applied, it should remain in place for four to six hours. At the same time, a lubricant jelly should be applied to the surrounding area. This procedure is followed to prevent a possible toxic reaction. Podophyllin ointment should be applied weekly, and the time it is left on increased. It often takes three or more applications to eliminate the wart (Hatcher et al., 1980). For internal warts, treatment with sulfa cream is recommended.

During all cases of treatment, condoms should be used during sexual intercourse.

CYSTITIS

Cystitis is an infection of the urinary bladder that is caused by the bacterium *Escherichia coli.* This bacterium is normally present in the intestines and can spread into the urethra and pass into the bladder upon anal contact. While this disease can strike both men and women, it is much more common in women. It is less likely to occur in males because the urethra, which is much longer in men than women, poses too long a trip for the microorganisms.

Mode of Transmission

The cystitis bacteria are normally present in the large intestine. Sometimes the bacteria from this area can spread to the urethra from the hands or anus as well as from sexual intercourse with an infected person. On other occasions, the urethral opening of the woman can become irritated because of rigorous sexual intercourse. This irritation, in turn, may cause infection. In the past, women often contacted cystitis during their honeymoon. Since the honeymoon was often the initial attempt at sexual intercourse, the experience may have involved poor sexual technique, which may irritate the urethra — hence the nickname "honeymoon cystitis."

Diagnosis and Signs and Symptoms

The diagnosis of cystitis is based upon its signs and symptoms: pain or burning upon urination, the constant urge to urinate, frequent cloudy and foul-smelling urine, pain in the lower abdomen, blood in the urine, pain on manipulation of the urethra, and pain during sexual intercourse. The physician can make an even more accurate diagnosis of cystitis by analyzing a sample of urine.

Treatment

Sulfa and antibiotic drugs are usually successful in the treatment of cystitis. These drugs can cause rust-colored urine, so the patient must be warned not to become alarmed. Along with the drugs, the patient should drink fluids — as much as 10 to 15 glasses of water per day. Coffee, tea, and alcohol should be avoided. After sexual intercourse, the patient should urinate and drink a glass of water.

TRICHOMONIASIS

Many vaginal infections *(vaginitis)* are attributable to a single-celled organism called *Trichomonas vaginalis.* When a male or female contracts this infection, he or she is said to have *trichomoniasis* (or "trich"). The microorganism has four tail-like strands that it uses to propel itself. It survives only in the genitourinary systems.

Mode of Transmission

Trichomoniasis afflicts about 25% of all women, thereby making it the most common STD. Contrary to what many believe, trichomoniasis is transmitted *solely* by sexual intercourse (Hatcher et al., 1980). This point may be controversial, since the organisms can survive outside the body on a moist object for several hours. Therefore, some researchers claim that the infection can be contracted from washcloths, toilet seats, and towels. However, the consensus among most authorities in the field of human sexuality is that this mode of transmission is highly unlikely.

Symptoms

In men, there are rarely any symptoms of trichomoniasis. If symptoms do exist, there is a white discharge from the urethra. On rare occasions, the urethral tract may burn or itch.

The female, on the other hand, may have some overt signs and symptoms. The most common is a frothy, thin, greenish white, and sometimes bubbly vaginal discharge. Sometimes this discharge may cause the vulva to become itchy and painful. An increased frequency of urination may also occur.

Diagnosis

Diagnosis of trichomoniasis is relatively easy. A smear of the discharge is placed under a microscope, and if the infection is trichomoniasis, the motile microorganisms will be evident. Unlike some of the other diagnostic procedures for STDs, the diagnosis for trichomoniasis is immediate.

Treatment

The most effective treatment for trichomoniasis is the drug metronidazole, more commonly known as *Flagyl*. Since this disease can be passed back and forth between partners, it is important that both partners be treated. The drug will usually be prescribed for ten days. During this time, the patient is cautioned not to drink alcohol, because the interaction of the alcohol and Flagyl can have an adverse effect. The patient should also abstain from sexual intercourse to avoid spreading the disease. In addition, Flagyl must not be used during the first trimester of pregnancy.

Some believe that Flagyl may be related to an increased risk of cancer. However, this connection has not been proven. The effects of Flagyl on subsequent offspring are not known. We do know that Flagyl is secreted in breast milk; therefore, this drug should not be prescribed while a woman is nursing.

Complications

The only major complication of trichomoniasis is that it may damage the cells of the cervix and possibly increase the woman's chances of contracting cervical cancer. However, this complication is a danger only if the woman does not seek treatment for her condition.

MONILIASIS

Moniliasis, which is also known as Monilia, Candida, yeast infection, and fungus, is caused by a yeastlike fungus called *Candida albicans*. This organism is present normally in the vagina in many women and can also be found in the mouth and large intestine in many men and women. Candida organisms will begin to multiply in the vagina when the environment is altered. Thus, the long-term use of birth control pills, pregnancy, or diseases such as diabetes can promote the growth of Candida in the vagina. Recurrent growth of Candida can be an indication that diabetes or another condition that requires attention exists. Candida organisms often accompany other organisms that infect the vagina. Although moniliasis can be caused by means other than sexual contact, it can be spread in this manner. Hence the categorization of moniliasis as an STD.

Mode of Transmission

Moniliasis can be transmitted to the vagina through sexual intercourse (if it is under the foreskin of an uncircumsized male) or through cunnilingus. However, these are not the usual routes of transmission. As stated previously, a change in the vaginal environment is the most important factor in the growth of moniliasis organisms.

Signs and Symptoms

The major sign of moniliasis is a thick, white discharge from the vagina that looks like cottage cheese. Accompanying this discharge is itchiness in the vagina as well as the vulva. This condition may lead to painful intercourse as well as a lack of desire for coitus.

Diagnosis

A culture must be grown to diagnose Candida accurately.

Treatment

The best treatment for moniliasis is the use of Mycostatis or Nystatin vaginal suppositories. Monistat vaginal cream is another alternative. This cream will be most effective when it is used nightly for 7 to 14 days. If the woman finds suppositories to be messy, she may use a tampon to keep the suppositories in place. To make sure the treatment of choice will be effective, the patient should complete her prescription. In addition, occasional white vinegar and water douches may help prevent recurrences of yeast infections.

Complications

No major complications of moniliasis are known. However, if a woman has this infection, she can transmit it to her baby during birth. If the yeast gets into the baby's digestive system, the baby can develop a yeast infection called *thrush*. Thrush can also develop in the throat of an infected woman's partner if cunnilingus is performed.

OTHER DISEASES

While other STDs exist, their incidence in the United States is so low that we have excluded detailed descriptions. Among these STDs are chancroid, lymphogranuloma venereum, and granuloma inguinale. In this chapter, we have identified those STDs that we feel you stand a greater chance of encountering in your lifetime.

PREVENTION OF STDs

The responsibility for preventing these diseases lies with the individual. Public health officers have tried to control the spread of STDs by asking infected individuals to identify their contacts. This tactic obviously is not helping to control the spread of many STDs. For a myriad of reasons, people are reluctant to identify their sexual contacts. If the government were able to implement a mass inoculation program to eradicate STDs, such a tactic might be a viable solution. After all, it worked in preventing diseases of epidemic proportions, such as polio. However, there is one problem— there is no known vaccination that can prevent one from contracting an STD.

Comprehensive health and sex education courses in our public schools hold the promise of decreasing the number of cases of STDs. But many communities do not permit schools to teach this important information. Therefore, the onus falls on the individual. If men and women can obtain accurate information, develop healthy attitudes, and make responsible decisions concerning sex, we will be on our way to ridding society of this unnecessary public health problem. Understanding the nature of our society, as well as the behavior of its people, can help to curb the increasing STD statistics.

Using Condoms

The condom, which is considered one of the most effective methods of controlling STD, provides a barrier through which many STD organisms cannot pass. When they are used properly (see Chapter 7), condoms can provide a complete defense* against gonorrhea, nongonococcal urethritis, and trichomoniasis. Condoms are a good safeguard against syphilis, genital herpes, and venereal warts (Darrow, 1976). Condoms are of no value in preventing the transmission of pubic lice.

If it is suspected that a male has a lesion or sore of suspicious nature on the penis, and the couple has not been involved in a long-term relationship, a condom should be required by the partner. Even if oral sex will be performed on the male, a condom should still be worn. Because many males often use as an excuse that the condom destroys spontaneity and interferes with sensitivity, they are often reluctant to use a condom. In this case, the couple may wish to incorporate putting the condom over the penis in foreplay. The condom, in this manner, can be used as a sexual aid.

Contraceptive Foams and Jellies

Common over-the-counter contraceptive foams, jellies, and creams that are used intravaginally do more than help prevent conception. They also provide some protection against the organisms that cause gonorrhea, syphilis, genital herpes, and other sexually transmissible diseases.

Douching

If a woman douches soon after sex (she may use soap and water), she may be able to kill some STD microorganisms. However, she must be sure

---

*We are taking into account that STDs are transmitted mostly through sexual intercourse. These statements do not pertain to oral–genital and penile–anal contact.

not to disturb the chemical balance in her vagina, since she may kill some of the bacteria that help prevent diseases and infections.

Washing

Whether or not washing with soap and water is effective in preventing STDs is controversial. In the male, washing with soap and water will not kill STD microorganisms if they have entered the urethra. If the foreskin in an uncircumcised male is retracted and the penis is washed, many of the microorganisms in this area will be killed. Although this procedure is more effective for the male than for the female, the female can also benefit from washing, since microorganisms that may inhabit the vulva can be killed. The rectal area should be washed if sexual contact occurred there. However, care should be taken not to wash in the direction from the rectum to the vagina.

One school of thought is that washing with soap and water should not occur before sexual contact, since washing can make the skin more susceptible to an STD (Yarber, 1978).

Urination

Urinating after sexual contact may be beneficial, especially to men. Since many STDs enter the male urethra after sexual contact, urinating may serve to flush out the microorganisms. In the female, most STDs are deposited in the vagina; therefore, urination may not serve the same effectiveness as for the male. However, it can help in avoiding infections of the urethra. There is no scientific proof as yet that urination helps reduce the chances of contracting an STD, but its merits are based on logic.

Inspecting the Partner's Genitals

Another way of preventing contraction of an STD is to inspect the genitals of the sex partner. STDs may be easier to detect in the male than in the female, since signs on the male are often external, whereas in the female the symptoms are usually internal. If a person is afraid that his or her partner has an STD, the easiest way to learn the truth is to ask. However, many people feel rather uncomfortable about posing this question. Therefore, one can be inconspicuous in trying to gather information. A shower or bath can be recommended, where the genitals can be inspected. If that is inappropriate, perhaps a nude massage, in which the genitals can be observed, can be tried. If something appears suspicious, such as a lesion on the genitalia, one should be comfortable and assertive in saying, "Thanks, but no thanks until you prove that your sore is not contagious."

Routine Medical Examination

During routine physical examinations, sexually active people should stress that their doctor look carefully to determine whether an STD exists, especially since some STDs in many people are asymptomatic. If a person has an unusually high number of sexual contacts, it would be a good idea to have a physical examination every six months, if not every three months. As we stated previously, the greater the number of partners, the greater the chance of contracting an STD.

Avoiding Indiscriminate Selection of Partners

Persons should be selective about those with whom they engage in sexual contact. A person who is quick to "jump into bed" is most likely the same with others. Their sexual contacts are probably many, and thus their chances of carrying an STD are higher than normal.

SUMMARY STATEMENTS

- *Millions of people are affected by STD each year, thousands suffering irreparable damage.*
- *Gonorrhea is the most widespread of the reportable communicable diseases. It is transmitted by intimate sexual contact.*
- *Untreated syphilis can go through four stages — primary, secondary, latent, and late (tertiary). However, syphilis can be easily treated with penicillin.*
- *There are two types of herpes — Type 1 and Type 2. Type 2 herpes is the more serious of the two and is the one that is contracted through sexual contact.*
- *NGU is an inflammation of the urethra that can be caused by two microorganisms — Chlamydia and T-strain mycoplasma.*
- *Pubic lice, also known as "crabs," can be contracted from contact with an infected person or from infected towels, undergarments, or toilets.*
- *Venereal warts, also known as genital warts, are dry wartlike growths that are caused by the same virus that produces warts on other parts of the body.*
- *Cystitis is an infection of the urinary bladder that is caused by a bacterium. The bacterium is normally present in the intestines.*
- *Trichomoniasis is an STD that survives in the genitourinary system in males and females.*
- *Most men are asymptomatic, whereas women will often know they have this disease because of a frothy, thin, greenish white, and sometimes bubbly vaginal discharge.*
- *Moniliasis is a yeast infection of the vagina that is made noticeable by a discharge that looks like cottage cheese.*
- *Several precautions have been suggested for preventing STD. Among these are using condoms and contraceptive foams and jellies, douching, urinating, inspecting the partner's genitals, having routine medical examinations, and avoiding promiscuity.*

SUGGESTED READINGS

Boston Women's Health Book Collective. *Our Bodies, Ourselves.* New York: Simon and Schuster, 1979.

Kagan, Julia. Herpes: It Can Be Treated, Not Cured, *Ms.,* January 1978.

Montreal Health Press. *VD Handbook.* Montreal: MHP, 1973.

Yarber, William L. Preventing Venereal Disease Infection: Approaches for the Sexually Active, *Health Values: Achieving High Level Wellness,* March-April 1978.

**SEXUALLY
TRANSMITTED
DISEASES**

A LOOK AT YOUR LIFESTYLE

You and your partner have been dating for two years. You are sexually intimate with your partner. One day you notice a lesion in your genital area that you suspect may be a sign of an STD.

Complete the following sentence:
When I first thought that I might have an STD, the first thing that came to my

mind was _____ .

_____

_____

GATHERING INFORMATION

List two STDs to which you believe your lesion may be attributed.

_____

_____

List two facts that support your belief.

_____

_____

List one thing that comes to your mind regarding your partner.

_____

EVALUATING THE INFORMATION

What is the *first* thing you would do after your condition was confirmed as an STD?

_____

_____

_____

What is the *second* thing you would do after your condition was confirmed as an STD?

_____

_____

MAKING RESPONSIBLE DECISIONS
Based upon the given hypothetical situation, list three decisions you would make about your partner or the relationship.

_____

_____

_____

Which decision would be the most important? Why?

_____

_____

TWELVE

Liking, Loving, and Intimacy

We must understand love; we must be able to teach it, to create it, to predict it, or else the world is lost to hostility and suspicion.

–Abraham Maslow, 1970

A LOOK AT YOUR LIFESTYLE

Have you ever stopped to think about how your personal relationships affect your mood? If you have, you have probably realized that some of your relationships lift your spirits, while other relationships leave you feeling down in the dumps.

Relationships that lift your spirits are said to be *inspiriting*. When your spirits are elevated, you experience joy, enthusiasm, passion, hope, and satisfaction. Inspiriting relationships make you feel worthy, important, and high in self-esteem (Jourard, 1971). Relationships that are characterized by a state of low spirits are said to be *dispiriting*. Dispiriting relationships make you feel unimportant, worthless, isolated, and frustrated. They result in low self-esteem (Jourard, 1971).

Of course, most relationships do not have the extreme effect of being dispiriting or inspiriting. Most relationships fall somewhere in between.

Thus, a *spirit-relationship continuum* (Table 12.1) could be developed that contains dispiriting relationships at one end and inspiriting relationships at the other end. The continuum could be marked into units ranging from 0 (dispiriting) to 100 (inspiriting).

Every time you enter into a relationship, you might ask, "Where does this relationship fall on a spirit-relationship continuum? Does this relationship contribute to my sense of well-being? Do I feel enthusiastic and joyful? Or does this relationship contribute to feelings of isolation and frustration?" You might also ask how the relationship affects your partner.

Unfortunately, many people settle for relationships that are not highly inspiriting. They become content with personal relationships that fall between 30 to 60 units on the spirit-relationship continuum. They are unaware or unwilling to acknowledge the effort that is needed to have a high-quality inspiriting relationship.

Herbert Otto, Director of the Human Potentialities Institute, agrees:

> We are all functioning at a small fraction of our capacity to live fully in the total meaning of loving, caring, creating, and adventuring. Consequently, the actualizing of our potential can become the most exciting adventure of our lifetime.

> (Buscaglia, 1972)

The purpose of this chapter is to examine the characteristics of relationships that are inspiriting. The authors recognize that you do not want to settle for an average relationship when you can achieve a high-quality relationship. What are the characteristics of a high-quality, inspiriting relationship, and how can I achieve it?

GATHERING INFORMATION

Gathering information that will answer this question is difficult. Yet the influence that your relationships have on the quality of your life makes

TABLE 12.1 SPIRIT-RELATIONSHIP CONTINUUM*

					Spirit Range					
0	10	20	30	40	50	60	70	80	90	100

Our Usual Range

Dispiriting Relationships		*Inspiriting Relationships*	
unimportant	depressed	joyful	hope
worthless	bored	passionate	satisfied
hopeless	anxious	dedicated	meaningful
isolated	lonely	enthusiastic	important
frustrated	low in self-esteem	worthy	high in self-esteem

Adapted from Sidney Jourard. *Transparent Self*. New York: D. Van Nostrand, 1971.

it necessary for you to seek some answers. Harry Stack Sullivan, a psychiatrist, says that "all personal growth, all personal healing and growth, comes through our relationships with others" (Powell, 1969).

Your authors believe that personal relationships are inspiriting when:

- you like someone
- your relationship is intimate
- you have a mutual understanding of love
- you love someone unconditionally
- you and your partner maintain a sense of autonomy within the relationship
- you and your partner can disclose yourselves freely with one another
- your relationship is growth-producing
- your needs for physical intimacy are mutually satisfied within the relationship
- You and your partner share mutual projects
- You freely commit yourself to one another

EVALUATING THE INFORMATION

This chapter contains information pertaining to each of these ingredients. You will need to evaluate this information to formulate your ideas about relationships. In developing your formula for an inspiriting relationship, ask yourself two questions. First: How will this component of the relationship contribute to my spirit and the spirit of my partner? Keep in mind, an inspiriting relationship fosters a sense of identity, worth, hope, and purpose. Second: What does it mean to have a responsible and caring relationship?

MAKING RESPONSIBLE DECISIONS

It is unlikely that you will meet someone special and that your relationship will proceed smoothly without any effort. Although this happens in the movies and in fairy tales, it is unrealistic. If your expectations parallel those of fairy tales, you might be disillusioned and dispirited when you "fall in love" and your relationship sinks to the middle or lower end of the spirit-relationship continuum. High-quality, inspiriting relationships require attention, care, responsibility, and decisions. You need to take an active role in developing the many facets of an inspiriting relationship.

THE RELATIONSHIP WHEEL

The *Relationship Wheel* in Figure 12.1 symbolizes an inspiriting relationship consisting of ten desirable components: liking, intimacy, love, unconditional acceptance, autonomy, disclosure, growth, physical in-

FIGURE 12.1 The Relationship Wheel identifies ten components of an inspiriting relationship. Each component is inspiriting by itself and has a positive effect on the relationship. Each component affects the other components and the smooth flow of the relationship.

timacy, mutual projects, and commitment. When all ten components are contained in one relationship, the relationship wheel is balanced. It symbolizes a smooth-flowing relationship. Each partner will feel highly inspirited, worthy, and lovable.

Sometimes one of these parts or components is lacking. You might ask, "If my partner and I have most of the components, isn't that enough?" It is enough if you want to be content with a relationship that is not of the highest quality; however, the relationship would be of higher quality with all ten components. Loss of one component can also have an effect on one of the remaining components. For example, a lack of disclosure in a relationship may inhibit physical communication, or a lack of mutual projects may block growth. Thus, attention to each component is important in establishing an inspiriting relationship. A discussion of each of the ten components in the Relationship Wheel follows.

Liking

Each of us has a need to be liked, especially by those who are important to us. *Liking* is composed of affection and respect (Rubin, 1975). *Affection* is a fond or tender feeling that you have toward another person. It is experienced as emotional warmth, or closeness. *Respect* is liking that comes from having esteem for someone's admirable characteristics or actions.

In your relationships you may receive affection, respect, neither, or both.

Affection is based on the way another person relates to you personally, and it is experienced as an emotional warmth and closeness. (Photo, Chester Higgins, Jr.)

I really like him. He's so bright and helpful. I can always count on him for good advice. But I don't feel close to him emotionally. It's hard for him to understand how much I like him and why I won't accept him as a partner.

Being the recipient of affection and respect is inspiriting and will promote your well-being and self-esteem.

Intimacy

Each of us has a need to share our personal and private self with at least one other human being. This personal and private closeness is what we mean by *intimacy*. An intimate relationship goes through several stages (Calderone, 1972):

1. Choice: You meet someone, you like each other, and you try to become closer.
2. Mutual: Your desire for closeness is shared by the other person. You have made the same choice. You cannot be more intimate than your partner for true intimacy to exist.
3. Reciprocity: You give to each other. You grow by confiding in each other. Again, there is an equal sharing of confidences.
4. Trust: You begin to share at deeper levels. You are aware that your deepest feelings and thoughts are accepted.
5. Delight: You have unconditional acceptance of one another. You delight in the relationship.

> In intimacy two people are constantly saying to each other without words, "I delight in you as a whole person and you delight in me, and I can, I want to, I may express this delight in such and such ways."
>
> (Calderone, 1972)

Having an intimate relationship is inspiriting.

Love

The renowned psychoanalyst Erich Fromm says, "Love is the only satisfactory answer to the problem of human existence" (Fromm, 1956). Being the giver and the recipient of love is important in our struggle to overcome our feelings of being alone. Yet what does it mean to love? What does it mean to be loving?

LOVESTYLES

A sociologist named John Alan Lee (1974, 1977) concluded that there are different *lovestyles* and that partners with the same lovestyle are more likely to have an inspiriting, high-quality relationship. The three basic styles of loving are eros, ludus, and storge.

- If you exhibit the *eros* lovestyle, you seek persons to whom you are powerfully attracted. You value physical attraction, sex, and sex technique.
- If you exhibit the *ludus* lovestyle, you view love as a playful encounter. You have a low commitment to your lovers and seek involvement with several persons at a time. Rarely will you work out difficulties in a relationship. You would rather move on to someone new.
- If you exhibit the lovestyle called *storge,* you build your relationships with others slowly. After spending time and effort with someone, you find yourself caring without remembering how it all came to be. You tend to form stable, committed relationships and are willing to iron out difficulties.

You may find that your behavior or your lovestyle is not that of eros, ludus, or storge, but a combination of these three.

- If you exhibit a lovestyle called *mania,* you are a combination of eros and ludus. You are obsessed with love. You have the powerful passion of eros, and you jump from person to person.
- If you exhibit a lovestyle called *pragma,* you combine the game playing of ludus with the practicality of storge. You are likely to jump from person to person, looking for certain qualities. This is a common lovestyle that is symbolized by "dating around" to find someone special.
- If you exhibit a lovestyle called *agape,* you are a combination of eros and storge. You have a powerful attraction to someone you value and to whom you will commit yourself. This is classic, unselfish love.

You can imagine the difficulties that might arise from unmatched lovestyles. You might want to date around with no strings attached and become involved with someone who desires a committed relationship.

I can't understand my partner. I looked around for three years and found the qualities that I wanted in a relationship. I'd like to begin building a future. My partner is only interested in sex. I'm worried that if I don't focus my energies on being attractive, someone new will quickly take over.

It is important that you determine your lovestyle and make it clear to others. Of course, your lovestyle can change.

"I LOVE YOU"

The three words "I love you" have several interpretations. According to Leo Buscaglia, "The difference between saying I love you to a friend and to a lover is that if you said I love you to a friend, the friend would know exactly what you meant" (Buscaglia, 1972).

What do you mean when you say "I love you"? You might have one of many answers: "I need you," "I respect you," "I want to dominate you," "I want to have sex with you," "I want you to take care of me," or "I want to be like you." The list of meanings for "I love you" is endless. However, in an inspiriting relationship *I love you* means "I respect, admire, and love who you are, and want to help you to continue to grow and benefit—to become" (Benson, 1974).

INGREDIENTS IN A LOVING RELATIONSHIP

A *loving relationship* consists of at least four ingredients: labor, responsibility, respect, and understanding (Fromm, 1956). When you labor in a relationship, you are willing to work for and give of yourself for the person that you love. If you accept responsibility, you are constantly evaluating the consequences of your behavior as it relates to others. You are willing to help when needed. Respect in a relationship means that you refrain from exploiting others and you avoid behaviors that benefit you at your partner's expense. You demonstrate understanding in a relationship by putting yourself in your loved one's shoes. A loving relationship requires constant effort, but it has many benefits.

> Like "life" in general, love embodies what appears to be a contradiction: the satisfaction of the self through the satisfaction of the needs and desires of others. . . . Far from being selfless, love provides a double satisfaction—even a triple satisfaction—to the self: once to the self because you can love and are loving; once to the self when love is reciprocated and you are loved; and once to the self because you know that, since you are loving and being loved, you must have a lovable self. When it is all there, you are well and truly "locked in." Nobody wants out.
>
> (Bohannon, 1969)

Unconditional Love

For love to be inspiriting, it must be unconditional. *Unconditional love* means that there are no strings attached. You simply are the giver or the recipient of love as a free gift. Conditional love is dispiriting:

> Unconditional love corresponds to one of the deepest longings, not only of the child, but of every human being; on the other hand, to be loved because of one's merit, because one deserves it, always leaves doubt; maybe I did not please the person whom I want to love me, maybe this, or that—there is always a fear that love could disap-

pear. Furthermore, "deserved" love easily leaves a bitter feeling that one is not loved for oneself, that one is loved only because one pleases, that one is, in the last analysis, not loved at all but used.

(Fromm, 1956)

Autonomy

If you examine your needs, you will discover a contradiction. Although you want to be very close to another person, you will discover that you need time for yourself. Although you want to connect, you still desire a degree of *autonomy* or independence.

Before we started dating, I used to see my friends and my family. I enjoyed painting with watercolors. Things have certainly changed. I don't have a minute for myself anymore.

Many persons have difficulty giving a loved one space. In an inspiriting relationship, you need to preserve your autonomy and independence and to encourage your partner to do the same. Autonomy is necessary for you to develop your full potential, your partner's potential, and the potential of the relationship.

Self-Disclosure

Ralph Waldo Emerson once said, "A friend is someone with whom I may be sincere. Before him I may think aloud." In an inspiriting relationship, you are able to discuss your feelings and thoughts without feeling judged.

I just can't talk to him. He wouldn't understand how I feel. I'm afraid that if I told him the truth it would ruin the relationship.

Self-disclosure is the act of making yourself known. It may carry with it much risk or fear. After all, if you share who you are and how you feel with someone and that person does not like or accept you, there is no place to go. If you hide yourself, you may be able to keep the relationship going.

But in the words of Hugh Prather, "the only way to be is me, then those who like me, like me" (Prather, 1970). Unless you are yourself and you are able to discuss your thoughts openly, you will not receive feedback that is directed at you. You will feel that something is missing in the relationship. Talking and listening may provide the thermometer that measures the wellness or illness of a relationship. When you are in a healthy relationship, you should be able to say, ''My partner is so easy to talk to. (S)he listens to me. I want to hear what (s)he has to say, too.''

Growth

To be alive and well, you need to be growing. For a relationship to be alive and well, it must be growing. There are two main roadblocks to growth (Herdegger, 1969). The first roadblock is a complacent satisfaction with what is. In a complacent relationship, you say, ''Things are going OK the way they are; why rock the boat?'' You settle into a routine without looking for fresh approaches to living and loving in your relationship.

The second roadblock to growth is restless activity from one distraction to the next. In a relationship that involves restless activity you might say, ''There are needs that I have that are not being met in this relationship, but I'd rather move from one thing to another (or one relationship to another) to avoid doing much about it. I'm so busy with school and. . . .'' Bouncing back and forth from one thing to another inhibits growth as much as avoiding the issue altogether.

A good relationship keeps developing new dimensions. You feel you are learning and discovering. During the painful growing stages, when you are not certain what will happen, you are willing to take risks. You and your partner are willing to experiment within a good relationship.

For a relationship to be inspiriting you will need to be able to discuss your feelings and thoughts without feeling judged. (Photo, Robert DeGast)

Physical Intimacy

Physical intimacy is a special type of communication involving physical contact. This contact may include a variety of behaviors: touching, hugging, kissing, caressing, and having sexual intercourse.

The purpose of physical intimacy is at least twofold. First, being touched, held, cuddled, and fondled is pleasurable. When you are in physical contact with someone, you feel more closely connected. Your being is affirmed. Second, physical intimacy is closely related to trust and self-disclosure. Physical intimacy is a way of acting out how you feel. It is a form of expression.

Sometimes I feel like the world is closing in on me. Like I can't pull myself together to go on. Then he holds me in his arms and gives me strength.

Our nakedness in physical intimacy is symbolic of a good relationship. It may say, "Here I am naked, with no masks, nothing to cover me, and you accept me as I am. You find me desirable." This type of relationship is affirming and inspiriting.

Talking and listening may provide the thermometer that measures the wellness or illness in your relationships. (Photo, Joel Gordon 1980)

Mutual Projects

When you share mutual projects within a relationship, your medium of sharing goes beyond discussion and emotional response. You reveal yourself "while working." Without discussion, your talents or lack of talents become apparent as you make contributions to the collective effort (Burt, 1977). In mutual projects a closeness called *creative intimacy* is created.

In a healthy inspiriting relationship, you will feel that you are growing, your partner is growing, and the relationship is growing. (Photo, Joel Gordon 1980)

When two people share mutual projects within a relationship, their medium of sharing goes beyond discussion and emotional response. This develops a closeness called creative intimacy. (Photos, Mimi Forsyth)

For many, creative intimacy is highlighted in the occupational setting but is not included in a loving relationship. How often have you learned that a relationship has terminated because one of the two partners became interested in someone at work? Sometimes at work two people begin to build a relationship together during a joint venture. They learn to communicate in fresh ways, and they change together as they are involved on a daily basis.

Creative intimacy should be a part of any significant relationship. Mutual projects will blend your self-expression and your partner's and will serve as building blocks that may provide the foundation for added growth. These projects may include taking a class together, designing a coffee table or clock, playing in a tennis or racquetball league, painting a picture, building a house, having and rearing a child. You may want to develop your own list of possibilities.

When you complete a mutual task, you will have a good feeling, a feeling that, when shared with someone special, will affirm you and the relationship.

Commitment

A *commitment* can be defined as (1) a pledge to do something or (2) a state of being bound emotionally or intellectually to some course of action (American Heritage Dictionary, 1969). You have the greatest chance of having an inspiriting relationship when you make a commitment to another human being.

To work, a commitment must be mutual. You and your partner each need to have "everything to lose and everything to gain." If not, the partner who has a lower level of commitment usually sets the terms and controls the relationship. This leads to a "one-upsmanship" relationship rather than a relationship where you and your partner are mutually concerned about each other's needs and growth. In an unequal relationship, the one who dominates or who is least committed frequently becomes bored. The other partner, who struggles desperately, becomes resentful. As time passes, neither partner is inspirited.

A commitment must be freely chosen. You will not be able to force someone to love you or to accept you. It is possible to have an external commitment without an internal commitment. You probably know of partners who have made pledges without ever expecting to honor them. When thinking about the potential of commitment, ask yourself: (1) Do I freely commit myself to my partner without outside pressures? (2) Does (s)he freely choose me above all others without outside pressures?

Mutual projects are like building blocks that may support the foundation for added growth in a relationship. (Photo, Michael Kagan)

When you commit yourself to someone, you choose total intimacy or fusion into one relationship over a variety of other encounters:

> Making a commitment to permanent, unconditional love will mean for one that certain experiences, which might otherwise have been mine, are now impossible for me. The man who chooses one woman for his wife and life partner by his very choice has eliminated all other women as possible wives and life partners. It is this very elimination that frightens us on the brink of commitment. Every commitment is like every moment of life: there is a birth and a death in every moment. Something is and something else can never be again. There is a choice and a surrender, a "yes" and a "no." To love is indeed costly. To love unconditionally is a life wager. In love we put ourselves on the line and there is no going back. It is at this brink that so many seem to collapse. Within arms' reach of greatness, they faint at the thought of never returning. It is the less travelled road.

(Powell, 1978)

SUMMARY STATEMENTS

- *Relationships may be inspiring and elevate your spirit, sense of joy, and self-esteem; or they may be dispiriting, creating a feeling of frustration, isolation, and loneliness.*
- *Most people settle for relationships that fall somewhere in the middle range (30 to 60) of the Spirit-Relationship Continuum and thus never achieve their full capacity for an intimate relationship.*
- *The authors believe that you are more likely to be in an inspiring relationship when: (1) you like someone, (2) your relationship is intimate, (3) you have a mutual understanding of love, (4) you love someone unconditionally, (5) you and your partner maintain a sense of autonomy within the relationship, (6) you and your partner disclose yourselves freely with one another, (7) your relationship is growth-producing, (8) your needs for physical intimacy are mutually satisfied within the relationship, (9) you and your partner share mutual projects, and (10) you freely commit yourselves to one another.*

SUGGESTED READINGS

Berne, Eric. *Sex in Human Loving*. New York: Pocket Books, 1970.

Brandon, Nathaniel. *The Psychology of Romantic Love*. Los Angeles: J. P. Tarcher, 1980.

Colgrove, Melba, Harold Bloomfield, and Peter McWilliams. *How to Survive the Loss of a Love*. New York: Bantam, 1976.

Derlega, Valerian, and Alan L. Chaikin. *Sharing Intimacy*. Englewood Cliffs, New Jersey: Prentice Hall, 1975.

Fromm, Erich. *The Art of Loving*. New York: Harper & Row, 1963.

Lasswell, Marcia, and Norman Lobsenz. *Styles of Loving*. New York: Doubleday, 1980.

Peele, Stanton, and Archie Brodsky. *Love and Addiction*. New York: New American Library, 1975.

Rubin, Zick. *Liking and Loving: An Invitation to Social Psychology*. New York: Holt, 1973.

Seligson, Marsha. *Options*. New York: Charter, 1978.

Shain, Merle. *When Lovers Are Friends*. New York: Bantam, 1978.

Singer, June. *Androgyny*. New York: Anchor Books, 1977.

Walster, Elaine, and G. William Walster. *A New Look At Love*. Massachusetts: Addison Wesley, 1978.

LIKING, LOVING, AND INTIMACY

A LOOK AT YOUR LIFESTYLE

Lately you have been feeling lonely. You have seen many different persons you enjoy, but no one is of special interest to you. You recognize that in each relationship some of your needs for liking, loving, and intimacy are met. You are trying to sort through your feelings and to decide what really counts to you in a relationship.

Write an I-message describing your feelings:
When I think about my relationships, I _____.

_____

1. Identify the key issue or problem.
Given:
I would like to examine what I value in a relationship.

_____

_____

2. Identify three relationships that you have had and give one need that was met through each relationship.

_____

_____

_____

_____

_____

GATHERING INFORMATION

List ten components that *you* feel are included in a satisfying relationship.

_____   _____

_____   _____

_____   _____

_____   _____

_____   _____

EVALUATING THE INFORMATION

Rank-order these ten components, using the number 1 for the most valued.

MAKING RESPONSIBLE DECISIONS

Now that you have identified the components that you would include in a satisfying relationship and ranked them by importance, discuss how you would experience these components with a potential partner. How would you and a partner make a responsible decision about entering into or continuing a relationship?

_____

_____

_____

_____

THIRTEEN

Marriage and the Family

Marriage is one of the most important institutions in our society. It has a profound impact upon one's lifestyle. Why do people marry? There are a variety of rather inadequate reasons: fear of living alone, unresolved rebellion against the family, identity crises in the teenage years, unwanted pregnancy (1/6 of marriages), pressure from family and friends, a feeling that "everybody's doing it" (Reed, 1976). In addition, some sexually active partners marry because they believe marriage to be a natural outcome of physical intimacy. Most express concern for the partner as one of the reasons for marriage. Yet when the question, Why did you marry? is asked, many stumble for an answer.

> I finished college, and we had been dating for three years. It just seemed like the time to get married. Our families kind of expected it, and all of our friends were doing it, too. We had the same problems then that we do now. I thought that they would go away. If only I had thought about my decision.

The funny thing is that marriage was the best decision that I have made. Our relationship has worked out great. But to be honest, neither one of us sat down and thought about what it would mean.

Isn't it ironic, the carelessness with which many persons view and enter into the most serious of our institutions? Even more ironic is the fact that it is easier to marry in a legal sense than it is to separate or divorce. Americans concentrate more effort on designing laws to protect us and to spell out fairness for breaking our marriage commitment than for making it.

I wish it had been as difficult for me to say "I do" as it is for me to say "I don't." I have spent hours thinking about the long-term effects on the kids, my finances, my sex life, and my family. Before I married, I didn't plan a day ahead of time.

To understand more about contemporary marriage, you might examine why people divorce or separate. There are a variety of reasons committed relationships terminate. Three reasons frequently cited are (1) lack of companionship and communication, (2) sexual difficulty (usually infidelity), and (3) financial disagreements.

Each of these reasons is closely related to changes in contemporary living that were not considered part of the traditional institution of marriage. Traditional marriage, with its rules and expectations, has changed for several reasons: a longer lifespan, more education and employment for women, greater mobility, rapid communication, and technological advances (O'Neill, 1976).

Thus, the traditional marriage with the husband as breadwinner and the wife as homemaker has been threatened. Replacing the concept of traditional marriage is the concept of the companionship marriage. In a *companionship marriage,* the purpose of marriage is not the fulfillment of certain socially accepted roles but a working together for mutual satisfaction and pleasure. Companionship exists when two partners can accomplish more personal and interpersonal growth together than they could separately—without the loss of individual identity (Maslow, 1964).

The traditional marriage can be contrasted with the contemporary companionship marriage (Sargent, 1972):

Traditional Marriage	Companionship Marriage
1. contracts set by tradition	1. contracts developed by and for the persons involved
2. role-to-role relating	2. person-to-person relating
3. fighting over issues	3. fighting for mutual growth
4. compromise (sacrifice)	4. synergy, or union, of differences
5. security based on rules	5. security based on trust

Occupational roles for women are changing. Left, This woman is a New York telephone installation worker. Right, A surveyor at work on a construction site. (Photo, left, Ellen Pines Sheffield 1980; right, Bruce Roberts)

One can deduce that the companionship marriage is developed by the persons involved, concentrates on their needs, and is concerned with mutual growth. By contrast, *traditional marriage* has rules that are set by society, concentrates on role expectations, and is concerned with social approval. In a rapidly changing society it is difficult for the traditional marriage to be maintained without many external threats and pressures. Role expectations are no longer black and white, nor is social approval. We are not saying that couples who select traditional roles do not have a companionship marriage. If a couple decides to assume traditional roles (husband as breadwinner, wife at home with children) after developing a mutual contract for the satisfaction and pleasure of both partners, the marriage is a companionship marriage. If a couple assumes traditional roles because of family and social pressures and without careful consideration of the satisfaction and pleasure of both partners, the marriage is a traditional marriage.

We don't have a traditional marriage by definition. My husband and I developed our own contract. He wants to work to provide for me and the kids, and I prefer to stay at home. We are both pleased with the arrangement. It meets our needs. (companionship marriage)

She wants to work, but that is not the way it is supposed to be. My parents would be embarrassed, and I just wouldn't feel like a man. (traditional marriage)

We are going to take turns going to graduate school. She is going to go first while I work to support us, and then she will work while I complete my schooling. We decided that we would switch back and forth so that we could both meet our professional goals. I think we are closer from having to listen carefully to one another's needs. (companionship marriage)

A companionship marriage is developed by the persons involved, concentrates on their needs, and is concerned with mutual growth. This husband and wife work together as jewelry makers. (Photo, Mimi Forsyth)

If you were entering a joint venture with someone else, you would probably give it some serious thought, especially if it were going to be a long-term commitment. Then you would make some agreements. In most cases, the agreements would be finalized legally. Marriage necessitates some serious discussion and planning. It is a joint venture requiring communication and negotiation. One way to enter a marriage is to form a mutually acceptable contract for the satisfaction and pleasure of both partners. This contract is an agreement about certain behavior, a division of tasks according to your particular situation, background, and needs, rather than an acceptance without question of the predetermined role behavior outlined by marriage as we now know it (O'Neill, 1976).

If you were to form a business partnership, you would certainly set some guidelines before signing your name. Does not marriage deserve the same consideration?

GATHERING INFORMATION

Before you form a long-term committed partnership, you need to gather certain information. For example, when forming a business partnership, most men and women carefully gather information regarding (1) goals, (2) definition of roles, (3) assets, (4) liabilities, (5) budget, (6) investments, (7) expansion, (8) competition, and (9) growth. These nine projections make it easier for you to decide whether or not the partnership will be a success. To build a successful marriage, you would be wise to gather information based on these nine components — a relationship projection.

EVALUATING THE INFORMATION

These nine areas could be the basis for a marriage contract. Then each partner could evaluate the contract to decide whether or not the terms were agreeable. An "I do" would be a commitment to a mutually acceptable, person-to-person contract.

MAKING RESPONSIBLE DECISIONS

Your decision to marry, not to marry, or to divorce is personal. No one else can force you to examine your decisions or commitment. A partnership can be a tremendous source of joy. It can also be devastatingly painful. You can influence the quality of the partnership you form by examining different components. Whether or not you want to use the suggested contract, you will want nevertheless to make a responsible and caring decision about marriage.

A successful marriage takes work, careful planning, evaluating, and reevaluating. A successful marriage includes mutual agreements in the nine areas mentioned. Each of these components are examined in the discussion that follows.

GOALS

A *goal* is a statement of aim or purpose. Goals are the most important consideration in the formation of a partnership.

> If you have a goal in life
> that takes a lot of energy,
> that incurs a great deal of interest,
> and that is a challenge to you,
> you will always look
> forward to waking up to
> see what the new day brings.
>
> If you find a person in your life
> that understands you completely,
> that shares your ideas,
> and that believes in everything you do,
> you will always look
> forward to the night,
> because you will never be lonely.

(Susan Polis Schutz, 1974)

Each partner should answer the following questions openly and honestly:

1. What are my personal goals?
2. How do I plan to reach these goals?
3. What are my partner's goals?
4. How does my partner plan to reach his or her goals?
5. What are my goals for our marriage?
6. What are my partner's goals for our marriage?
7. How will conflicting goals be handled?

DEFINITION OF ROLES

My dad made all of the decisions about money. Of course, Mom didn't earn money. She worked in the home. I never felt that their arrangement was fair. I couldn't sit back and let my husband make all of the economic decisions. I want some say.

A *role* is a function assumed by someone. In traditional marriage, the roles that a man and a woman assume are more clearly defined than in companionship marriage. The traditional husband has an instrumental role. He is expected to achieve, to work, to perform in his career, and to bring prestige and success to the family. The traditional wife is expected to nurture and feed and to "feel more than to do" (Reed, 1976).

In a companionship marriage, the partners assume roles that are designed from their personal needs and their needs as a couple. It is important to clarify these roles. Role perceptions are at the root of communication in marital relations (Reed, 1976). According to Vincent (1968), most communication problems treated in marital therapy are rooted in perceptual distortions. A summary of the overlap of perceptual distortions is shown in Table 13.1.

Each partner has three perceptions of the roles that are operating in the relationship. The self's view of the self (S–S) is the perception we have of our role. The self's view of the other (S–O) is the way that we perceive the role of the spouse. The self's view of how the other perceives the self (S–O–S) is the way that we believe our spouse perceives our role (Vincent, 1968). With these several perceptions of the roles that each partner plays, there is a need for direct communication.

Each partner answers the following questions openly and honestly:

1. What is my role in the married relationship?
2. What is my partner's role in the married relationship?
3. What role does my partner expect me to assume?
4. How will we resolve a conflict in roles?

The roles that are assumed in a relationship are closely related to how decisions are made and how work schedules and conflicts are dealt with. Further questions for consideration include:

5. Which decisions will I make alone?
6. Which decisions will my partner make alone?
7. Which decisions will we share?
8. How will duties be shared?
9. What if one partner's job requires a transfer?
10. What adjustments are made for irregular working hours?

ASSETS

An *asset* is a strength or a desirable possession. Research into relationships and marriage indicates that there is an interpersonal marketplace where assets are closely examined. According to Rubin (1973), the rules of the marketplace imply that whom you marry is closely related to how

TABLE 13.1 PERCEPTIONS OF ROLE*

Husband	Wife
S–S	S–S
S–O	S–O
S–O–S	S–O–S

* Adapted from C. E. Vincent, *Human Sexuality in Medical Education and Practice.* Springfield, Ill., Charles C Thomas, 1968.

The roles of marriage partners are changing. (Photo, Mimi Forsyth)

many assets you think you have to offer and how many assets you can get in return.

Although this bartering of assets sounds somewhat callous, it has been documented in research studies. Findings indicate that favorable occupational status and higher income are important male assets. Attractiveness is an important female asset. Attractive women are much more likely than other women to marry men with higher status (Elder, 1969).

Both men and women prefer mates who are similar. Thus, it is an asset to a partnership to have a similar family background, a similar economic and social status, and a similar education. It is also an asset to have similar attitudes and opinions (Byrne, 1971).

The notion of trading assets in an interpersonal marketplace is related to ego development. In a successful marital partnership, each partner's ego must expand pertaining to his or her view of self, of the partner, and of the marriage itself.

Each partner can examine his or her personal assets, the assets of the partner, and the assets of the relationship:

1. What assets do I have to offer?
2. What assets does my partner have?

3. What assets does my partner think I have?
4. What assets do we have together, as partners?

LIABILITIES

A *liability* is a weak point, something that works to disadvantage. A sad commentary is that sometimes people try to hide or cover up these weaknesses when they are involved in a relationship that really counts. They may be fearful of losing a loved one if they disclose their liabilities. Yet at the same time, each person needs a partner who will accept him or her and who will help him or her to overcome human liabilities.

I'm very uncomfortable when my wife talks to someone attractive. I have a jealous streak that I try to hide. Rather than telling her, I usually begin to flirt with someone. Then when my wife gets hurt, I know she cares.

I can't chit-chat, so I try to avoid large parties. He likes to mix and is really comfortable in a group. I plan other activities to avoid his parties. I haven't told him why.

A mutual disclosure of liabilities is helpful:

1. What are my weaknesses?
2. How might my partner help me to overcome these weaknesses?
3. What are my partner's weaknesses?
4. How will I help my partner overcome these weaknesses?
5. What liabilities do we have as a couple?
6. How can we overcome the weaknesses in our partnership?

BUDGET

When two people merge their economic resources, they should make some mutual agreements about their finances. They should design and live within a carefully planned budget. A *budget* is a plan or schedule adjusting expenses during a certain period to the estimated or fixed income for that period. A budget would alleviate marital difficulties due to financial pressure.

In planning a budget, you and your partner might want to consider the following questions:

1. What is our income?
2. What are our fixed expenditures?
3. What other necessary expenses do we have?
4. What are some ways that we can cut back on our expenses?
5. How will we spend extra money?
6. Who is responsible for paying the bills?

A budget is a plan or schedule adjusting expenses during a certain period to the estimated or fixed income for that period. A budget helps to alleviate marital difficulties caused by financial pressure. (Photo, Teri Leigh Stratford)

7. What financial decisions are personal?
8. What financial decisions are mutual?
9. How will we resolve a conflict regarding money?

We are very similar except when it comes to money. His family had more money than mine. He's used to buying whatever he wants whenever he wants it. My family had to follow a careful budget. We've talked it over and decided that I'll pay the bills. We will have only so much extra money each month. That's all we can spend. I think it will be hard for him at first.

INVESTMENTS

In addition to a carefully planned budget, you and your partner may want to examine your investments. An *investment* is putting effort and/or money into a venture that will make a profit. Your relationship or partnership can be viewed as an investment. You are involved in your relationship today and at the same time building for tomorrow.

We want a three-bedroom house with a huge fireplace in the family room. We both feel that family life centers around an open fire. Of course, we can't afford our dream home for a few years. But it gives us something to build for.

In building or investing in your future together, you may want to consider:

1. What things do I want most?
2. What things does my partner want?
3. What investments do we mutually agree upon?
4. What decisions will I make about investments?
5. What decisions will my partner make about investments?
6. How will we resolve a conflict over investments?
7. Will our investments be joint or individual?

Each of us holds some beliefs and feelings about our lifestyle. You may have heard, "I don't care if I have a shirt on my back if I can travel." And yet another person would rather invest all capital in a home. The values that you hold regarding investments affect the quality of your relationship. Persons who agree on a budget and on investments have alleviated a major source of marital conflict.

EXPANSION—ADDING TO THE FAMILY

Expansion refers to enlarging the size of the family. Each of us was raised in some type of family setting. This family setting has influenced our feelings about the type of family that we want. For some, a partnership of two constitutes an ideal relationship. Children are not desired and may be viewed as an inconvenience or as a threat to the couple's perceived goals. Others marry to have children. Some delight in children as a shared responsibility, while others maintain that childrearing is the sole responsibility of one of the partners. A more thorough discussion of parenthood is included in Chapter 15.

Whether or not you have children will certainly influence other parts of your contract—goals, budget, investments. Questions you might discuss with your partner include these:

1. Do I want to have children?
2. Does my partner want to have children?
3. If we do not agree, how will we decide?
4. How many children will we have?
5. If we are infertile, how does each of us feel about adoption?
6. How will we space the children if we have more than one?
7. What will my role be in raising the children?
8. What will my partner's role be in raising the children?
9. What effect will children have on our individual and mutual goals?

COMPETITION—OUR VIEWS TOWARD SEX

I wouldn't tolerate an affair. If she ever cheated on me, I'd divorce her immediately.

Almost everyone tries something new now and then. I'd like to be able to discuss our outside sexual relationships with one another. I think that we'd be closer this way. The thought of her sneaking around would bother me much more than simple honesty.

We've made the decision to marry, but my partner knows that I plan to have an occasional homosexual experience. I've known for a long time that I was bisexual, but I still want a marriage to a man and children.

Competition is part of a marriage when one or both partners seek out someone else for sexual gratification. *Fidelity* is a pledge or a promise to have sex only with one's spouse. *Infidelity* is the breaking of this pledge or promise.

Many couples do not discuss their sexual lifestyle with one another. There are several reasons for this lack of communication. They may feel that their sexual commitment to one another is implied. In this case, each partner assumes that the other expects certain behavior. In other relationships, the partners assume the attitude, "What I don't know won't hurt me." They view an open discussion of expected sexual behaviors as unnecessary.

Other couples want to share their views with one another. Some want a "forsaking all others" promise, while others want to have and discuss sexual relationships outside the marriage.

Discuss the following questions with your partner:

1. What are my feelings about the following sexual attitudes and behaviors: sexual fidelity, extramarital sex, swinging?
2. What are my partner's feelings about sexual fidelity, extramarital sex, and swinging?
3. Do I expect the same behavior from myself as I do my partner?
4. Does my partner expect us to have similar sexual behavior?
5. How will we resolve any conflicts that arise regarding our sexual behavior?

Each of the sexual behaviors mentioned is discussed in more detail in Chapter 16.

GROWTH—KEEPING IN TOUCH

A marriage is not static but dynamic—marriage is constantly changing. A *growing relationship* is developing and maturing. Sidney Jourard (1971), a psychologist, suggests that instead of divorcing or terminating a marriage, one terminate the marriage as it exists and redefine the marriage in new ways. Jourard advocates several different marriages to the same person.

The concept of many marriages to the same person is compatible with a mutually acceptable marriage contract. When the marriage becomes stale or threatened, the partners are challenged to reexamine their goals, roles, assets, liabilities, budget, and investments and formulate a new contract. Many couples are threatened by the idea of an annual review where partners sit down and discuss their needs. But this type of working together has more of a constructive than a destructive effect on a relationship.

> My parents set aside Sunday evenings for themselves. They would pour a drink and sit by the fireplace and talk. We weren't allowed in the living room. I liked the idea that they had a special time to build their relationship.

You and your partner may want to discuss these questions:

1. How will we know when we need to reexamine our commitments to each other?
2. How will we initiate a discussion of our commitments?
3. How will we resolve a conflict that arises?
4. What are some ways that we can break long-standing habits and reinvent our relationship?

SUMMARY STATEMENTS

- *There are a variety of rather inadequate reasons for marriage: fear of living alone, unresolved rebellion against the family, identity crises in the teenage years, unwanted pregnancy, pressure from family and friends, and a feeling that "everybody's doing it" (Reed, 1976).*
- *Common reasons for terminating marriage are a lack of companionship or communication, sexual difficulty, and financial problems.*
- *A companionship marriage is developed by the persons involved, concentrates on their needs, and is concerned with mutual growth.*
- *A traditional marriage has rules that are set by society, concentrates on role expectations, and is concerned with social approval.*
- *It is the opinion of the authors that successful marriages include mutual agreements in nine areas: (1) goals, (2) definition of roles, (3) assets, (4) liabilities, (5) budget, (6) investments, (7) expansion, (8) competition, and (9) growth.*

SUGGESTED READINGS

Bach, George, and Peter Wyden. *The Intimate Enemy.* New York: William Morrow, 1976.

Bach, George, and Ronald Deutsch. *Pairing.* New York: Avon, 1970.

Bird, Caroline. *The Two Paycheck Marriage.* New York: Pocket Books, 1980.

Braudy, Susan. *Between Marriage and Divorce: A Woman's Diary.* New York: William Morrow, 1975.

Cuber, C. F., and P. B. Haroff. *The Significant American.* New York: Appleton-Century-Crofts, 1965.

Jackson, Don, and William Lederer. *The Mirage of Marriage.* New York: W. W. Norton, 1968.

Masters, William, and Virginia Masters. *Pleasure Bond.* Boston: Little, Brown, 1974.

O'Neill, George, and Nina O'Neill. *Open Marriage.* Philadelphia: J. B. Lippincott, 1971.

Otto, Herbert, Ed. *The Family In Search of a Future.* New York: Appleton-Century-Crofts, 1970.

Rogers, Carl. *Becoming Partners.* New York: Delta, 1972.

Slater, P. *Pursuit of Loneliness.* Boston: Beacon Press, 1970.

Sussman, M. B., Ed. *Non-traditional Family Forms in the 1970's.* National Council of Family Relations, Minneapolis, 1972.

Udry, R. J. *The Social Context of Marriage.* Philadelphia: J. B. Lippincott, 1971.

Wallerstein, Judith, and Joan Berlin Kelly. *Surviving the Breakup.* New York: Basic Books, 1980.

Willison, Marilyn Murray. *Diary of a Divorced Mother.* New York: Wyden, 1980.

**MARRIAGE
AND THE FAMILY**

A LOOK AT YOUR LIFESTYLE

We have focused on nine areas to be examined when you are building a successful marriage. A personal examination of each of these nine areas will tell you a great deal about your lifestyle. Sharing your findings with a significant other will also be a valuable learning experience. Select someone with whom you can do this exercise.

Write an I-message concerning marriage:
When I think about marriage, I _____

_____

_____

_____

GATHERING INFORMATION

For each of the following areas, write a statement concerning marriage:

1. Goals: _____

_____

2. Definition of roles: _____

_____

3. Assets: _____

_____

4. Liabilities: _____

_____

5. Budget: _____

_____

6. Investments: _____

_____

7. Expansion: _____

_____

8. Competition: _____

_____

9. Growth: _____

_____

EVALUATING THE INFORMATION

Share your statements with each other. In which areas did you agree? In which areas did you disagree? To build a successful marriage, which areas would need to be negotiated?

_____

_____

_____

MAKING RESPONSIBLE DECISIONS

Reexamine the areas that need negotiation. Brainstorm and discuss your conflict until you are able to make a mutually agreeable statement about each of these areas.

_____

_____

FOURTEEN

The Single Lifestyle

A LOOK AT YOUR LIFESTYLE

There are more than 52 million single adults in the United States. Some have never been married; others are divorced or widowed. Sexual preference varies. A single person may be heterosexual, homosexual, or bisexual. A single person may live alone, may live with a friend or with family, or may cohabitate.

The attitude toward single living has an effect on emotional health and behavior. John Powell, author of *Fully Human, Fully Alive*, says that "one's perception or vision is the key to one's emotional health. All change in the quality of a person's life must grow out of a change in his or her vision of reality. There cannot be any real and permanent change unless the vision is changed" (Powell, 1977).

> I came to college to get a degree in elementary education and to find a husband. I know that sounds really corny and traditional in 1980, but it's true. I have to face up to it now. Here I am, a senior. I'll get my degree in June, but there's no man in the picture. I've got to face the single life. I don't know what that means yet. I've got some soul-searching to do.

Those who view single living positively make the best adjustment. Those who view single living negatively often block their growth. They are likely to believe one or more of the following myths: (1) all single women want to get married; (2) all confirmed bachelors (single men) are afraid of responsibility; (3) single women need to wait for a man to ask them out; (4) singles are terribly lonely; (5) singles have no one to help out when they are sick; (6) singles get sick and depressed more often than those who are married (Edwards, 1974).

Myths About the Single Lifestyle

Our visions affect our behavior and attitudes. For example, do you believe that single living is hazardous to your health? Many believe that singles suffer greater health problems because of a stressful existence. This is not necessarily true. A study begun in 1970 by the United States Department of Public Health, called "Selected Symptoms of Psychological Stress," contains data that do not support this belief. With three years' worth of data collected, the findings indicate that (1) never-married persons suffer less than marrieds from headaches, dizziness, heart palpitations, insomnia, nightmares, nervousness, psychological inertia, feelings of impending nervous breakdown, and actual reported nervous breakdown; (2) the widowed and divorced have the same frequency of these problems as marrieds; and (3) never-married women suffer least (Edwards, 1974).

Another faulty vision is that our society is "coupled," singles being outcasts, or misfits. Although more adults are married than not, singles can hardly consider themselves a minority. More than a third of the adult population is single. There are 5 million divorced singles, 4 million separated singles, and 12 million widowed singles. In some parts of the United States, children are almost as likely to live with a single parent as with married parents.

GATHERING INFORMATION

Each of us, married or single, can examine this growing lifestyle.

> Someone who really cares about himself/herself says "Everything is filtered through me, and so the greater I am, the more I have to give. The greater the knowledge I have, the more I'm going to have to give. The greater the understanding I have, the greater is my understanding to teach others and to make myself the most fantastic, the most beautiful, the most wondrous, the most tender human being in the world."

> (Buscaglia, 1972)

Single living affords you an opportunity to experience a commitment to yourself. This focus on self may be what has created some negative visions of the single lifestyle. Many believe that the mature person focuses on others and that a focus on self is immature and unloving. Yet knowing yourself is an important prerequisite to appreciating and loving others.

This chapter focuses on seven areas of self-development. These areas are (1) developing autonomous adulthood; (2) developing balance; (3) developing goals; (4) developing a healthy lifestyle; (5) developing a support network of friends; (6) developing dating skills; and (7) developing sexuality. A current single lifestyle, cohabitation, or living together, is also discussed.

EVALUATING THE INFORMATION

You are responsible for evaluating this information and for selecting what you can use. If you are single, you have the opportunity for growth if you make a commitment to yourself. If you are married, you can examine this information carefully with two points in mind. First, did you develop these skills while you were single? If not, you and your spouse can discuss these seven areas and formulate a plan for mutual self-development. Second, if you believe in these seven areas, how will you assist your single friends? If you are a parent or are planning to be a parent, how will you assist your children in their development? How will you influence their attitudes about single living?

I almost didn't go to lecture on Friday. Here I am returning to school at 23, married, with a child and you want to talk about the single life! But I learned a great deal about myself and my need to grow in some areas. I talked with my husband about developing autonomous adulthood. We can see some areas that needed growth when we were single that we overlooked. I think we'll work hard at them.

MAKING RESPONSIBLE DECISIONS

The period of one's life when there is no commitment to another can be described as a "single space." A space can be further described as an empty place, a void. Some people are so uncomfortable with single space that they fill it with anything. They run from distraction to distraction to keep their "single space" full, never experiencing a positive single life. Others are desperate when confronted with "single space." They grab a partner who fills the space but may or may not provide a quality relationship. Others choose meaningful experiences to fill their "single space." They experience personal fulfillment and self-development. The decision is a personal one. Each of us takes responsibility for the direction and quality of our lifestyle.

DEVELOPING AUTONOMOUS ADULTHOOD

An important task of adulthood is to become *autonomous,* to learn to meet your needs in a way that makes sense to you. Dr. Stephen Johnson, a clinical psychologist, has developed an inventory to measure your skills and attributes for autonomous adulthood (Johnson, 1977). These skills are grouped into three categories. The first category, autonomous functioning skills, deals with skills necessary for independent living. The second category, social attributes and skills for friendship maintenance, deals with skills pertaining to a network of support. The third category, social attributes and skills for dating, sex, and amative (loving) relationships, deals with connections with other people on an intimate level.

Developing Skills and Attributes

When you have completed this inventory, Table 14.1, you will have assessed your ability to live comfortably as an independent person. You will have identified skills and attributes that need to be developed. Johnson suggests the following guidelines for the self-discipline necessary to attain a skill or attribute (Johnson, 1977):

1. *Goal setting:* Break the skill into smaller goals. For example, if you are uncomfortable "finding ways to meet the opposite sex," you might begin with the smaller goal of making a list of places you go where there are members of the opposite sex.
2. *Graded assignments:* Make a contract with yourself for something you are going to do. For example, you might decide to introduce yourself to someone new each day for a week.
3. *Self-observation and planning:* Develop a systematic way of recording whether or not and how successfully you completed your assignments. For example, you might check off on your calendar whether or not you introduced yourself to someone new. You might write down what comment you used to initiate the conversation.
4. *Self-imposed consequences:* Decide how to reward yourself for completing an assignment or how to punish yourself for not completing an assignment. For example, you might buy yourself a new shirt or blouse after you have introduced yourself to five new people.
5. *Environmental planning:* If you need to change unwanted behavior, you may have to alter your environment. For example, you might be in a rut. It may be impossible to introduce yourself to someone new because of your daily routine. You will need to alter your routine.

Achieving autonomous adulthood is an important step in being single. When these skills and attributes are lacking, you may be unsuccessful living by yourself and you may ruin relationships that you enter by heaping your unmet needs onto a partner.

> We can picture the autonomous person as a competent man or woman who is not afraid of his or her individuality and who relates to the environment freely, enjoying the interaction rather than being intimidated by it. Such persons, secure in their worth, welcome feedback from the outside world, even when it is critical, rather than suppressing it or blocking it out. They see this information not as an assault on their self-esteem, but as an aid in becoming a better person. For example, when rejected by a lover, the autonomous person can consider seriously the lover's critical observations, not simply to get back in the other's good graces, but to learn how to deal better with people.

> (Stanton Peele, *Love and Addiction*, 1975)

TABLE 14.1 SKILLS AND ATTRIBUTES FOR AUTONOMOUS ADULTHOOD*

DIRECTIONS: To take this inventory, you need a large sheet of paper (standard typewriter or legal size) and a pen or pencil. Using the longest side of the sheet as the top, start five columns across it with headings, under which you will rate your own competence: *Excellent, Good, Adequate, Fair, Poor.* Now consider each item on the list and enter it in the appropriate column. If, for example, your cooking skills are excellent, enter "Cooking" under that heading. Or, if you are unable to enjoy being alone, you'd enter two items under *Poor:* "Tolerating/enjoying aloneness" and "Enjoying solitary activities."

1. Autonomous Functioning Skills
   Cooking
   Housekeeping
   Providing own transportation
   Automobile maintenance
   Money management
   Wardrobe management
   Caring for children (if applicable)
   Tolerating/enjoying aloneness
   Enjoying solitary activities
   Providing adequate income
   Pursuing satisfying career
   Pursuing satisfying interests or hobbies

2. Social Attributes and Skills for Friendship Maintenance
   Making and keeping friends of the same sex
   Making and keeping friends of the opposite sex
   Developing depth of friendship
   Communicating with friends
   Being with friends regularly
   Initiating outside activities with friends
   Entertaining friends at home
   Finding ways to meet friends

3. Social Attributes and Skills for Dating, Sex, and Amative Relationships
   Initiating conversations with other sex
   Finding ways to meet other sex

TABLE 14.1 (continued)

Attracting members of other sex
Ease in asking for dates
Ease in refusing dates
Dating regularly or often
Knowledge of and comfort with dating etiquette
Ease in communicating with other sex in early contacts and dating
General ease in dating
Ease in being affectionate
Ease in receiving and reciprocating affection
Ease in rejecting affection
Ease in making sexual advances
Ease in receiving and reciprocating sexual advances
Ease in rejecting sexual advances
General sexual ability
Ease in sexual interaction
Communicating about affectionate and sexual behavior
Communicating in love–sex relationships
Quality of love–sex relationships

FURTHER DIRECTIONS: To take the next step, get another sheet of paper, divide it in half, and list at the top those skills or attributes you have entered under "Fair"; list on the lower half those you entered under "Poor." Then classify each item on the list according to its importance to you. Give an "A" priority to those problems you see as most critical to you in attaining autonomous adulthood, a "B" to those of moderate importance, and a "C" to those of least importance. Also, rate each item on how easy it would be to remedy the problem. Thus, give an "A" priority to the things that would be easiest to improve or learn, a "B" to more difficult items, and a "C" to the really difficult items. When completed, think about your list and the priorities you have attached to each item. You may wish to use this list to choose aspects on which to work. Obviously, those skills you have rated high in both categories would give you the best starting points in your self-change program.

Stephen M. Johnson, Ph.D. First Person Singular: Living the Good Life Alone. New York: J. B. Lippincott, 1977. Dr. Johnson is an associate professor of clinical psychology at the University of Oregon. He has a private practice and conducts weekend workshops on Autonomous Adulthood.

DEVELOPING BALANCE

Another investment is to balance your inner and outer lives. Kenneth Wydro, author of *Flying Solo: Being Happy Being Single* (1978), identifies six elements to be balanced: (1) the personal self, (2) the physical self, (3) the spiritual self, (4) the social self, (5) the communal self, and (6) the financial self. These elements can be placed on a wheel Wydro calls "The Wheel of Fortune," depicted in Figure 14.1.*

The *personal self* is your relationship with yourself and how you feel about your past, present, and future. To keep the personal self tuned, Wydro suggests keeping a personal inventory journal where you record and review your perceptions each day. The *physical self* is the condition of

---

* Adapted from Kenneth Wydro. *Flying Solo: Being Happy Being Single.* New York: Berkeley Books, 1978.

your body and how you feel about your appearance. Physical tuning in-volves both vigorous exercise and relaxation.

The *spiritual self* houses your mysterious center; it is the element that guides your behavior unconsciously. Wydro suggests that each person needs to spend time finding his or her center. He suggests meditation and the study of astrology as well as a careful piecing together of a jigsaw puzzle.

The *social self* is concerned with emotional relationships—family, friends, and lovers. Wydro suggests paying close attention to relation-ships, keeping in touch and reaching out via telephone calls, letters, and visits. The *communal self* is also socially oriented. It is an association with a cause or group. Wydro suggests joining special-interest groups such as tennis clubs, theatre groups, and art associations.

The *financial self* focuses on your means of making money. Wydro suggests combining your moneymaking activity with another element in the Wheel of Fortune. He says, "When you know who you are, and de-velop your talent, and act on what you want, the financial self falls in place. When people do what they want to, money comes" (Wydro, 1978).

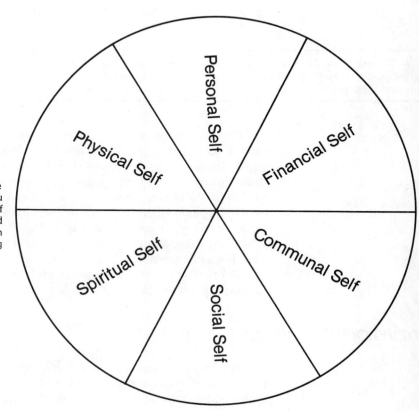

FIGURE 14.1 During your "single space," one of the best investments you can make is to align your own Wheel of Fortune. Seek to balance your inner and outer lives. (Adapted from Kenneth Wydro, Flying Solo: Being Happy Being Single)

Examine these six elements carefully. If you are neglecting any of the elements, you may want to try one of Wydro's suggestions.

DEVELOPING GOALS

The happiest singles have meaning and purpose in their lives. They give their life direction by identifying goals. Goal-oriented singles differ considerably from singles who fill their time with one distraction or another. They also differ from the single whose primary goal is to find a one-and-only. Singles with a marriage goal may feel that life is empty when there is no one "special" in their lives. This attitude is a frequent cause of depression. Unfortunately, this problem has a merry-go-round effect. As a single becomes more and more depressed and further removed from establishing personal goals, he or she becomes less attractive to others. He or she becomes less likely to connect with someone, and life becomes meaningless.

Research indicates that if you associate with persons who are depressed and who feel empty inside, you are more likely to begin to feel depressed yourself. People are drawn toward people who have goals and direction. Goal-oriented people feel good, alive, and energetic, and we experience these feelings in their presence.

There is something about her that is contagious. She picks up my spirits. I feel good about myself, good about school, and good about my family when she's around. She seems to know what she wants, and she goes after it.

Goals are important. *Long-term goals* shape our lives and give us direction. Graduation or deciding upon a major are examples of long-term goals. *Short-term goals* give us something to look forward to in the immediate future. Short-term goals are psychological stepping stones. You decide to study two hours a day this week for a test on Friday. You set a goal of 30 pages of review each night. This short-term goal assists you in a larger goal—your grade for the course and eventually graduation. By designing these stepping stones, you can feel immediate achievement and positive self-esteem.

People who have short-term and long-term goals have a happier, healthier lifestyle. Set a time each week to review your goals.

DEVELOPING A HEALTHY LIFESTYLE

When you assume personal responsibility for your health, you are more attractive to others. A healthy single announces to the world, "I care enough about myself to give myself the care and attention I deserve, to be at my best." Singles who abuse their health send out negative messages about themselves to others.

> Whenever we are together, he chain-smokes. It's one cigarette after another. It bothers me to see him abusing himself. It also hurts our relationship. He smells and tastes like smoke. I wonder why he needs to rely so much on cigarettes.

Dr. John Burt designed a Taxonomy of Lifestyles.* Depicted in Figure 14.2, the Taxonomy of Lifestyles contains 12 components needed to make a plan for healthy living:

1. *Coping style:* Develop a plan for dealing with stress.
2. *Relating style:* Develop a plan for relating to family, friends, and lovers.
3. *Risk-taking style:* Develop a plan for your health that examines trade-offs between present goals and long-range health risks.
4. *Decision-making style:* Develop a plan for your health, using observation, reasoning, and judgment when you make decisions.
5. *Working — creating — producing style:* Develop a plan for your life that enables you to be creative and productive.
6. *Self-conservation style:* Develop a plan for your health in which you reduce the risk of degenerative diseases by choosing behaviors that positively affect the heart, arteries, pancreas, teeth, liver, and so on.
7. *Environmental conservative style:* Develop a lifestyle in which you make a conscientious effort to maintain a healthy environment — land, water, air.
8. *Rest and relaxation style:* Develop a daily plan that includes time for rest and relaxation.
9. *Nutritional style:* Develop a healthy, well-balanced diet to maintain your desired weight.
10. *Pleasure-seeking style:* Develop a lifestyle that includes healthy means of pleasure-seeking rather than temporary, abusive highs such as those from drugs.
11. *Consumer style:* Develop a lifestyle that includes the careful evaluation of the potential health and safety risks of products and services.
12. *Grooming style:* Develop a plan for daily attention to skin, hair, teeth, mouth, gums, and general body cleanliness.

---

*Burt, John, Linda Meeks, and Sharon Pottebaum. *Toward A Healthy Lifestyle Through Elementary Health Education.* California: Wadsworth Publishing Company, 1980.

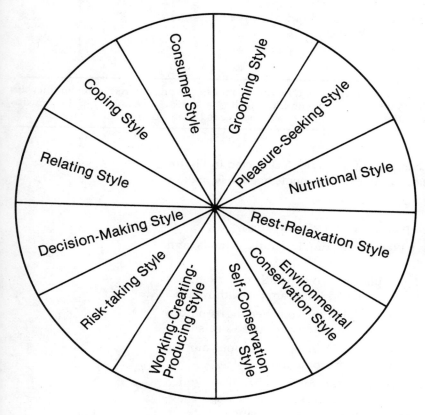

FIGURE 14.2 A healthy lifestyle involves the assumption of responsibility for positive, healthy behaviors in each of the 12 components identified. (Designed by Dr. John Burt. From John Burt, Linda Meeks and Sharon Pottebaum. Toward a Healthy Lifestyle Through Elementary Health Education)

I like a date to be well groomed. It tells me a lot about her. She feels good about herself and wants to take care of her body. She also conveys to me that I am important. She wants to look her best for me. Someone once told me to always meet a girl's mother to see if she was healthy and well-groomed. I like people who take care of themselves. There's no reason to let yourself go.

DEVELOPING A SUPPORT NETWORK OF FRIENDS

Good friendships are a network of support for singles. Here are five guidelines for friendship (Johnson, 1977):

1. Have more than one best friend.
2. Work at developing close friendships.
3. Value the time spent with friends as much as the time spent with potential lovers.
4. Have married as well as single friends.
5. Cultivate the friendship of both sexes.

Good friendships are the backbone or the network of support for singles. (Photo, Susan Lapidus, Design Conceptions)

When you are single (or married!), you should be busy developing the skills and attributes needed for autonomous adulthood. You should be working on balancing the six areas in your Wheel of Fortune. Time is at a premium. You need to pick and choose wisely. You might select one best friend and rely heavily on this person for advice, comfort, companionship, and support. But one trusting friendship is not enough. What happens when your "one and only friend" is not available? A house built on one support beam has a shaky foundation. If your support network consists of one friend, you are cheating yourself. *If you have more than one close friend, you multiply your opportunity for intimacy, contact, advice, comfort, companionship, and support.*

Work at developing close friendships. Set aside a special time to keep in touch. During this special time, share and discuss your life with your friend(s). Spend time listening to their concerns. Sometimes singles turn

Singles who have more than one close friend multiply their opportunity for intimacy, contact, advice, comfort, companionship, and support. (Photo, Peter Vandermark, Stock, Boston)

to their friends only in times of crisis. Although this reliance is very important in a friendship, it is not enough. Relationships need constant nurturing.

Your friends need to know that you value them when you are in the midst of an important relationship with a lover or a potential lover. Some singles forget this important guideline to good friendship. When a new relationship is developing, the old stand-by friendships are neglected. There is truth to the saying: "Make new friends but keep the old; one is silver but the other gold."

I feel used at times. When things are going well for him, he never calls. It's like I don't exist. Then when he has an argument with her, he calls. I'm supposed to drop everything and help him with his problems.

It is good to have both married and single friends. Sometimes singles drop their friends who marry, or married friends quit calling. Relationships between singles and marrieds offer terrific opportunities. There is the opportunity to share what your lifestyle is like and how you feel about it. Often singles view marriage unrealistically. Through contact and sharing, a more realistic perspective is gained. The basic needs of friends, single or married, are the same — intimacy, contact, advice, comfort, companionship, and support.

These special needs exist in both same-sex friendships and opposite-sex friendships. *Cultivate the friendship of both sexes.* A friend of the opposite sex offers some unique attributes that are beneficial to your support system. Opposite-sex friends are important whether you are homosexual or heterosexual. First, if you are heterosexual, a friend of the opposite sex may help you abandon your search for a one-and-only. When you desire the company of the opposite sex, you can call your friend. Second, a friend of the opposite sex can help you learn another point of view. You can sort out ideas without the confusion that may arise in a love relationship. Third, it is easier to hear constructive criticism from a longtime friend than it is in a new relationship. Perhaps you are too pushy or demanding in a relationship, and your partner is trying to tell you. You are not getting the message. But when your friend shares this observation, you begin to accept this new information and to examine your behavior. Fourth, a friend

It is important to cultivate the friendship of both sexes. An opposite sex friend offers some unique attributes which are beneficial to your support system. (Photo, Paul S. Conklin)

of the opposite sex can be a bonus socially. You may need a partner for a social obligation. Your friend can accompany you. Fifth, a friend of the opposite sex is helpful in making contact with other desirable singles. Together you may go to a singles party. You may introduce each other to more people.

DEVELOPING DATING SKILLS

Most singles want to date. Heterosexual singles date members of the opposite sex, while homosexual singles date members of the same sex. Dating skills and feelings about dating are nearly the same for both groups. Venturing out is risky, and extending yourself in relationships may seem uncomfortable at first.

> Nobody is emotionally or socially confident from the start, so extending ourselves personally will not be any more natural at first than stretching muscles that have been unused for years.

> (Stanton Peele, *Love and Addiction*, 1975)

Dating success requires effort. To increase your emotional and social confidence and your dating skills, you need to make contact. You need to be in social situations to practice your skills.

Set Time Aside for Social Contacts

Several recommendations may work for you. *First, set at least one or two nights aside (minimum) each month to practice dating skills.* Call someone and ask him or her to join you for some event that is not too demanding or intimate. Before you call, remind yourself that you have a task at hand. Your task is to make the effort. Reward yourself for effort, *not* performance. If you make the plans and the person you call is unavailable, do not set yourself up for rejection. You are a worthy person. The other person may be busy or may not choose your company. That is OK.

The important point is to make the effort to practice dating skills. You have learned to tell someone else that he or she is desirable. It is important to learn how to express your feelings. When someone says "no," you are still to be rewarded for expressing your needs.

If your date says "yes," you have an additional reward. You have the opportunity to get to know someone. If you are a woman, do not worry about making contact. Men are no more interested in a woman who plays hard-to-get than a woman who expresses an interest (Walster, 1973).

Examine Your Skills Frequently

After you have made your two contacts, stop for a moment to examine your skills. Did you state specifically what you wanted? Could you have

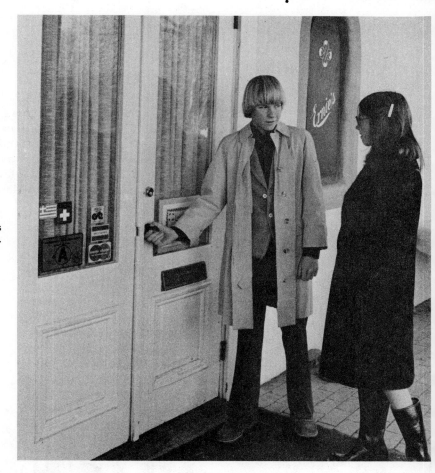

Extending yourself in relationships may seem uncomfortable at first. (Photo, Mimi Forsyth)

handled the conversation in a more direct or positive manner? Were you comfortable with the reply? How did you respond to a "yes"? How did you respond to a "no"?

Examine the skills you have when accepting or refusing a date. Are you comfortable saying "no" when you would rather not be with someone or go somewhere? Do you handle a "no" gently but firmly? It is important not to accept dates that you will begrudge and unfair to both someone else and you. However, you should be gentle with another's ego. The other person should be rewarded for taking a risk. He or she has expressed an interest in you that should be acknowledged. You might respond, "I am pleased that you would enjoy my company, but I am unable to go out now."

Dating Expectations Should Be Realistic

When you are out on a date, you have a further opportunity to learn and to interact with someone else. Make a simple task. *Share two things about yourself and learn two things about your date. When you set a realistic task, every evening will be rewarding.*

Avoid Looking for a One-and-Only

Unrealistic expectations can ruin dating relationships. Try to avoid falling into the "one-and-only" pitfall. This is a "snap" judgment about whether or not a relationship could be permanent. If you spend a few minutes with a date, decide there is no future, and make no further effort, the date will be a disappointment. The goal was unrealistic. If a "one-and-only" did not emerge, then the date was a failure. Singles with this goal lower their self-esteem. Singles who view dating relationships with realistic expectations gain confidence.

When you are out on a date, you have a further opportunity to learn and to interact with someone else. (Photo, Mimi Forsyth)

> I used to go out to find that someone special. I was miserable. Every time I had a date that didn't "send" me, I came home early and depressed. I wondered if I'd ever meet someone. I thought something was wrong with me. I had a date with this one girl my roommate knew. When I came home early, he said, "Isn't she terrific to be with?" I fumbled for an answer. I didn't get to know her. I realized how narrow I had been in my dating.

How to Know Whether You Have a Good Relationship

Good relationships evolve when you are realistic in your expectations and when you are honest about the interaction that is occurring. You accept and affirm what is strong in a relationship while questioning and repairing its weaknesses (Peele, 1975).

When you think you are in love, how do you know whether the relationship promotes growth or whether you've simply become dependent upon or used to your partner? Stanton Peele, author of *Love and Addiction* (1975), contends that many love relationships are as addicting as drugs. They develop out of a need for dependency rather than mutual growth. He suggests examining a love relationship by asking yourself (and your partner) the following questions: Can you bear to be without the person you love when it is necessary or desirable for him or her to be away? Have you maintained the interests and associations you had before you met your lover? Have you developed new ones? How would you feel toward your lover if he or she went off on his or her own? Can you imagine still being friends with this person if you were no longer lovers? Are you a better person and is your lover a better person as a result of the relationship?

Breaking Off a Relationship

When you are involved in a stunted relationship, you will need to change the relationship or break it off. Change is difficult for addictive, dependent personalities. If you feel "anyone is better than no one," you need to examine your feelings about yourself. Begin by listing all of the good characteristics you have. Look at your list and pick out three reasons someone would want your company. Examine your monthly calendar and set at least one or two nights aside to explore new relationships. Make at least two contacts. You will be surprised to learn how soon you can become actively dating new people.

Meeting New People

A common concern of singles is meeting other singles. Meeting people takes effort. Two important factors in meeting others are (1) developing a plan to meet others and (2) having an open attitude and being willing to take a risk.

Some singles have the attitude "if I am meant to meet someone, I will chance upon him (or her)." Although many meetings are by chance, you can multiply your opportunity for contact by making yourself available. Make a list of your interests. What things do you like to do? Brainstorm. Look at your list. What interests do you have that other singles would have on their lists? Plan to pursue one of your interests. Ask yourself what new activity you would like to try. Make a plan. Singles meet other singles pursuing their interests.

> . . . 65–70% of meaningful, long lasting relationships grow out of attending a class, meetings at work or participating in neighborhood situations. People meet each other while engaged in an activity where they can come into contact with others on more than one occasion.
>
> (Kenneth Wydro, *Flying Solo*, 1978)

Have an open attitude, and take risks. If you are comfortable with yourself, you can attempt many new experiences. Join a singles club, go to a singles bar, or place an ad in a singles magazine. When you make yourself available, you are not announcing that you have low standards or that you will be sexually involved. You are announcing that you are open to meeting new people. This is perfectly acceptable.

At first, going to a singles party or venturing alone to the tennis courts may be uncomfortable for you. Set a realistic task for your venture. Learn the names of five people at a party. Reward yourself if you learn five names. You have ventured out to meet people. Finding a "one-and-only" is an unrealistic goal.

Avoid the saying, "I'll never meet anyone who is my type at _____." This statement is usually an excuse. You are at a function to meet people, not to meet "your type." If you are at a party or in an unlikely situation, someone else has the same feeling.

I hated to go to parties by myself. I tried your suggestion anyway and went. I decided to meet two people. I was scared at first. I told this one girl that I had never been to a party by myself before but I wanted to meet at least two people. She smiled with relief and told me that she had had reservations about coming, too. We realized that others probably shared the same feelings. I guess we all need some polish on our skills!

DEVELOPING SEXUALITY

Sex is sure full of contradictions! Sometimes I think it's the most important part of a relationship; other times it's the least. Sometimes my opportunities for sex are abundant and at other times there is a complete void. I'd sure like to balance this thing called sex!

Our culture is obsessed with sex. Sex is everywhere—the newspapers, radio, TV, advertisements. You learn that being sexual is important. You

A singles bar. (Photo, Will McIntyre Photography)

want to be sexual, but you may not know what that means. You learn to judge sexual behavior, particularly your own. The standards you use for judgment evolve from peers, parents, society, religion, and experience. These standards often lack clarity. You end up confused.

Deciding to Have Sex

Leo Buscaglia, author of *Love,* remarks, "In the last analysis each man [and woman] stands alone." *You* are responsible for deciding when to have sex, with whom, how often, and under what circumstances.

The most pressing issue centers on "when to have sex." The Puritan–Permissiveness Continuum (Burt, 1975) offers a list of behaviors to help heterosexuals answer this question. A homosexual may use this continuum by substituting "genital sex" for "sexual intercourse." Which number best describes your sexual standard?

1. sexual conversation with other "nice people"
2. nonsexual contact with special persons

3. sexual contact above the waist with a person you love
4. sexual contact below the waist with a person you love
5. sexual intercourse with a person to whom you are married
6. nonmarital intercourse with a person you love
7. nonmarital intercourse with a person for whom you have deep affection
8. nonmarital intercourse with a person who "turns you on"
9. nonmarital intercourse for profit

In a survey of over 500 college students per year from 1970 to 1975, Burt found that heterosexual college students consistently located themselves between steps six and seven on the Puritan–Permissiveness Continuum. (Burt did not study homosexual behavior.) He found that heterosexual college women usually started at step six or seven. If they moved up or down the continuum, their decision was closely related to how they were treated in the interpersonal relationship. As a consequence of being hurt, college women tended to become either more puritanical or more permissive (Burt, 1975).

Heterosexual college men gave opportunity as the reason for becoming more permissive. They gave "falling in love with a girl that I really care for" as the reason for a more puritanical position.

Burt's findings suggest that you need to decide what ethical standard you have for your behavior *and* what factors will cause you to deviate from this position. You and a potential sexual partner need to share this information. Burt suggests that partners might agree to the following five criteria prior to participation in heterosexual intercourse:

Criterion 1: Both partners in sexual intercourse must be certain that they are not infected with one of the venereal diseases. The best way to achieve this certainty is through regular medical examinations, including blood tests.

Criterion 2: Prior to participation in sexual intercourse, both partners must recognize their responsibility to love and care for any offspring that may result, or carefully evaluate the effect of an abortion.

Criterion 3: Prior to participation in sexual intercourse the two people involved should have some notion of direction and goals in life.

Criterion 4: One person must not exploit another. To counter exploitation they must agree that sexual intercourse is for the mutual improvement of both people involved.

Criterion 5: Prior to participation in sexual intercourse, both partners should agree upon whether they want or do not want children. If children are not wanted, a mutually acceptable and effective form of contraception should be planned.

Making Contact

It is less difficult to make sexual contacts when you have decided on appropriate sexual behavior. You know what message you want to give someone and what response to give someone when you are approached.

Seduction is a three-step process in which you attempt to make sexual contact with another. You (1) reach out, (2) notice the reaction of your partner, and (3) move forward, stop, or back up (Johnson, 1978).

The quality of your relationships is enhanced by the actions you take during seduction. It is helpful to give your partner indirect information. Discuss what sex means to you in a relationship.

The last relationship I had ended abruptly when my boyfriend wanted to have sex and he wouldn't use anything. I prefer that a man use something.

I very much enjoy the closeness of physical intimacy. I have sex with people I care about and will see again. Sex doesn't mean marriage, though.

When you reach out and discuss sex indirectly, notice the reaction of your partner before moving forward, stopping, or backing up. Here are two possible responses to the comment made in the second example from the authors' files:

> "I know what you mean. I'm not ready for a commitment either but I like to express myself sexually when I've dated someone for a month or so."
>
> "For me sex means commitment. I'd feel too guilty having sex for pleasure alone. I've always felt this way."

These messages convey ego-sparing information. This indirect interchange allows both partners the opportunity to retreat, back up, or move forward. The best way to convey "no" is to state what it means as soon as a partner reaches out. The first example conveys "No, but maybe in a month." The second says "Not without commitment."

A "yes" can be followed with more indirect moves or a direct conversation. Regardless, partners should clarify the meaning of sex. The topics of sexually transmissible diseases and contraception are necessary.

Sexual Performance

Both men and women worry about sexual performance. A discussion before sexual activity can alleviate anxiety.

The first time I have sex with a girl I come quickly. It's not that I don't care; it's just that I'm anxious. Then I wonder if she'll compare me with other guys. It makes the first time difficult.

I need a lot of foreplay to enjoy sex. I don't feel comfortable telling my partner this until I've become relaxed. It take three times or so.

Provide positive feedback to your partner during sex play. This feedback helps your partner discover your wants and needs. A moan or a groan may convey what you need and want. A comment such as "I like that" is helpful. All of us want to be satisfied as well as to satisfy. When you provide feedback, your partner feels that he or she is able to satisfy you.

She's great in bed. She'll do anything that I like. I want to please her, too, though. It would make sex even better. I try different things, hoping to find out what makes it for her. Should I ask her?

When sex is dissatisfying, indirectly signal your feelings to your partner. Gently say, "Not so hard," or "Let's slow down." Move your partner's hands or lips to another area of your body. If you remember that most of us want to satisfy, you will teach your partner about yourself.

Feedback is often important to both partners after sex play. Men and women often wonder what their partners think. Reassure your partner that he or she is worthy as a person. This reassurance relieves any feelings of having been used or having been inadequate. With rare exception, check back with a sexual partner. You need not continue the relationship, but acknowledge your partner's worth.

I worried after we had sex. What did he think of me? Was I just another one-night stand? I felt cheap. My roommates kept saying that I was OK, but I needed to hear it from him. Then he called. What a relief! I'm not really serious about him, but I needed that call.

The last time I had sex, the girl dropped me like a hot potato. Whenever I saw her she ignored me. Since then I've worried. Last night I stayed up thinking about the sex I'd had. I walked into class today, and my partner gave me a big smile. It made my day. I knew I was OK.

COHABITATION, OR LIVING TOGETHER

Many singles choose to live together with sexual involvement, or cohabitate. The U.S. Bureau of the Census reported that 1.1 million unmarried persons lived together in 1977, an 83% increase over 1976 (Mitchell, 1979). In seven out of ten couples, both partners were under 45. Some 236,000 couples were under 25. A fourth of the couples had one or more children living with them (Flanagan, 1979).

Cohabitation, or living together, appears to be the lifestyle of choice for many college students. The estimates of its popularity vary from 10% at small liberal arts colleges to 35% at large universities where students can live off campus. At Pennsylvania State University 1000 students were asked if they were living with someone or had lived with someone. One third said they were currently doing so or had done so (Macklin, 1974).

Reasons for Cohabitation

In a study at Cornell, students were asked why they cohabitated. The primary reason given was strong emotional attachment to someone and the desire to be together more often. Other reasons given were sexual fulfillment, loneliness on a large campus, dissatisfaction with "dating around," the desire for a meaningful relationship, the desire for security, a lack of readiness for marriage, doubt about the institution of marriage, and the opportunity to learn about the other before making a marital commitment (Macklin, 1976).

I got tired of trying to meet new people and form a good relationship. We dated long enough to get a good sexual relationship going. She would spend the night. Soon it became more often. Finally, I asked her to move in.

Eighty percent of the cohabitants indicated a strong emotional attachment for their partner but no marriage plans. Ten percent moved in together with future marriage plans established. Another 10% began a relationship with the understanding that it would be temporary (Macklin, 1976).

Cohabitation Versus Marriage

Dr. Robert Ravich, Associate Professor of Psychiatry at Cornell University Medical School, says that cohabitation and marriage differ in several ways. Successful cohabitation is not necessarily a good predictor of future marital success. First, society does not have the same set of expectations for cohabitants as it does for marriage partners. Second, marriage is seen as an indoctrination into a family. Living together does not qualify a partner as a family member. Third, a married couple is more discriminating about time spent apart. Fourth, partners seem to have different expectations of each other when a marital commitment is made. For example, many male cohabitants stop sharing housework (Ravich, 1980).

According to Marion E. Dunn, Assistant Clinical Professor of Psychiatry at Downstate Medical Center in Brooklyn, New York, "People are more indulgent of one another when they're living together. They tend to let things slide, and not work them out. Part of it may be the fear that they'll break up if they don't squelch their anger" (Dunn, 1980).

Legal Implications

When cohabitation does not lead to marriage, the partners may face the difficult problem of dividing property. The courts have not provided the legal protection to cohabitants that has been provided for those in the legal institution of marriage. Different states and different judges vary in their feelings about cohabitation and the law. For example, Henry W. Foster, former Chairman of the American Bar Association Family Law Section, says:

> I won't lift a finger to disturb unmarried couples but at the same time I'm opposed to giving them everything that a husband or wife would receive by way of legal status when they have deliberately refused to acquire that legal status. Just because we're against discrimination doesn't mean we're going to give cohabitants Brownie Points, or the Good Housekeeping Seal of Approval.
>
> (Abrams, 1978)

The courts' view of cohabitation is best described as one of tolerance. There are so many new and varied cases that lawyers have invented several names for use in trials: *cohabitation, pseudomarriage, domestic partnership, surrogate marriage, LTA* ("living together arrangements") and *new marriage* (Abrams, 1978).

Society has mixed feelings about cohabitation and the rights of each partner. The famous Marvin case was carried by the media and evoked a variety of emotional responses:

> Lee Marvin lived with a woman named Michelle Triola. Michelle changed her name to Michelle Triola Marvin even though the couple never married. They lived together for seven years. Lee wanted to terminate the relationship. He agreed to pay Michelle alimony for five years but he quit after a year and a half. Michelle sued for $1.8 million. She was awarded $104,000 by a California judge. The case is now being appealed.
>
> ("The Trials of Unmarriage," *Newsweek,* 1979)

Public reaction confirmed the confusion over what is fair and moral in settlements between cohabitants. Out of this confusion came several news articles, legal briefs, and television commentaries on how to protect yourself while engaged in cohabitation. In *New York* magazine, an article entitled "How to Sue Your Live-In Lover" (Abrams, 1978) gave tips for holding on to your property:

1. In New York, the courts award property to the person who paid for it. Therefore, keep a record of which purchases each partner made, and record all bills of sale.
2. Joint checking and savings accounts or credit cards spell trouble because of the difficulty in tracing the funds. The less combining of assets, the fewer the problems at the end of a relationship.
3. When making big purchases, try to alternate buying. If you must split the tab, keep separate records.
4. The person whose name is on the lease of an apartment retains occupancy unless otherwise stated in the contract.

5. To protect property interest, put both names on the deed so that one partner can have the option of buying out the other if he or she leaves. You don't have to split purchase or maintenance costs in half to have your name on the deed but can contribute according to your capital and get back what you put in. If you don't want a partnership, agree on who should retain the title to the property.

6. If one party agrees to provide support to another when the affair is over, that promise should be in writing.

The contractual idea is advised for both heterosexual and homosexual cohabitation. "In gay relationships a contract is almost a must where there is any property of substance," says attorney Robert S. Cohen, who speculates that more contracts are written in New York for homosexuals than for heterosexuals. Cohen says "The failure to draft one could create a very costly, possibly notorious lawsuit, which would be in the best interest of no one."

Implications

Cohabitation offers the single a unique opportunity to explore the intimacy of living with someone without a legal commitment. Many view this opportunity as a chance to learn and grow in new ways. The relationship can be terminated without a divorce.

There are ambiguities to cohabitation, however. There is no guarantee that those who live together will have a happy marriage. The legal implications of cohabitation are not clarified, and cohabitants may be faced in the courtroom with the same troublesome problems as married persons desiring a divorce.

SUMMARY STATEMENTS

- *Single living affords one the opportunity to enhance one's lifestyle by developing (1) autonomous adulthood, (2) balance, (3) goals, (4) a healthy lifestyle, (5) a support network of friends, (6) dating skills, and (7) sexuality.*
- *Important aspects involved in autonomous adulthood include goal setting, graded assignments, self-observation and planning, self-imposed consequences, and environmental planning (Johnson, 1977).*
- *Balance can be divided into six areas: the personal self, the physical self, the spiritual self, the social self, the communal self, and the financial self (Wydro, 1978).*

- *Well-adjusted singles establish long-term and short-term goals to give their life meaning and purpose, and they assume personal responsibility for their health.*
- *Good friendships form a network of support for singles.*
- *Singles should frequently assess their dating skills and set realistic expectations for relationships.*
- *Each person is responsible for deciding when to have sex, with whom, how often, and under what circumstances.*
- *Cohabitation, or living together with sexual activity, may have legal implications.*

SUGGESTED READINGS

Edwards, Marie, and Eleanor Hoover. *The Challenge of Being Single*. New York: Hawthorn Books, 1974.

Colgrove, Melba, Harold H. Bloomfield, and Peter McWilliams. *How to Survive the Loss of a Love*. New York: Bantam Books, 1976.

Gaylin, Willard. *Feelings*. New York: Ballantine Books, 1979.

Johnson, Stephen. *First Person Singular: Living the Good Life Alone*. New York: The New American Library, 1978.

Seligson, Marcia. *Options*. New York: Charter Communications, 1978.

Wassmer, Arthur. *Making Contact*. New York: Fawcett Popular Library, 1978.

Wydro, Kenneth. *Flying Solo*. New York: Berkeley Publishing Company, 1978.

Zunin, Leonard, and Natalie Zunin. *Contact: An Intimate Guide to First Counters*. New York: Ballantine Books, 1972.

A LOOK AT YOUR LIFESTYLE

How much of an effort do you make to meet other people who are available? Meeting people requires an effort on your part. You need to plan to meet others if you are in a rut. In the space provided, list ten ways that you could meet people.

THE SINGLE LIFESTYLE

Ways to Meet People	#1	#2	#3
1.			
2.			
3.			
4.			
5.			
6.			
7.			
8.			
9. ·			
10.			

GATHERING INFORMATION

There are three columns to complete to give you some insight into the likelihood of meeting someone. Complete these columns using a five-point scale. A "5" is a positive response; lower numbers are less positive.

Column 1: *What is the likelihood of my meeting someone in this way?* (Very likely is a "5," not likely is a "1.")

Column 2: *What is the likelihood of my meeting an interesting person in this manner?*

Column 3: *Am I willing to try to meet someone this way?*

EVALUATING THE INFORMATION

Examine your responses. Rank-order these responses giving the most desirable means of meeting someone a "1" and the least desirable means a "10." What is the best way for you to meet someone? Why? What is the second-best way? In the next two weeks, try to meet someone new in either of these ways.

_____

_____

MAKING RESPONSIBLE DECISIONS

Remember, you can take responsibility for meeting new people. What have you learned by completing this exercise?

_____

_____

FIFTEEN

The Parenthood Option

In our society we define parenthood as a biological act instead of a behavioral process. We equate family planning with contraception instead of contemplation. We become parents without knowing what parents do. We have children without knowing what children are like. And we make mistakes without knowing why.

—Arthur Ulene, M.D. Today Show Family Physician, 1978

A LOOK AT YOUR LIFESTYLE

A study of the marriage and parenthood expectations of 400 under-graduate women at York University was conducted in 1971. More than 95% of the women studied indicated that they expected to marry. Of these, more than 95% wanted to have at least one child. Most indicated that they would be "very disappointed" if they never had any children (Simmons, 1971).

The feelings of these York students were not very different from the feelings of other women during the late 1960s and early 1970s. Several other researchers gathered data that indicated a similar desire for children.

These are some of the concluding remarks from these studies: "There is a universal desire for children" (Martinson, 1970); "The vast majority have high positive values about having children" (Bell, 1971); "Few women completely reject the idea of having one or more children" (Williamson, 1966).

As the 1970s progressed, there was a change of attitude, and the birthrate in the United States began to decline steadily. There are three factors that might explain this shift in attitude and the resulting change in behavior. First, the cost of living steadily increased. In the late 1970s, it cost an average middle-class family about $100,000 to raise a child (Morrow, 1979). At the current rate of inflation, this figure will have doubled by the late 1980s. Many couples decided that their pocketbooks could not withstand the financial burden.

A second reason for the declining birthrate may have been the increasing divorce rate. In some areas of the country as many couples were divorced as were married in the same given year. Statistics indicated that childless marriages had a better chance of surviving (Maynard, 1978). Children were no longer viewed as the cement that held a marriage together. And for those that divorced and waited a few years to remarry, there was simply less time to have children.

The third reason for the declining birthrate was the return of many women to the work force. Many women chose a career other than one as a traditional housewife and mother. These women saw no need to be a mother when their adult role was filled with an occupation. Many women who combined motherhood and a career reduced the number of children that they planned to have.

> . . . A woman who has a high level of energy and ability may be able to do everything. But most of us aren't super women, which means that if you say yes to motherhood, you're saying no to other things, just as if you say yes to becoming a lawyer, you're saying no to becoming a doctor. You devalue motherhood and parenting if you believe you can bring children into your life without making some very important changes.
>
> (Carole Baker, Executive Director, The National Alliance for Optional Parenthood, 1979)

Although there is still social pressure to become a parent, the decision to remain childless is becoming more popular. Parenthood is no longer inevitable. To make a responsible decision, you should examine the options of parenthood and the consequences of each.

GATHERING INFORMATION

There are at least three options to parenthood available. The first option is to become a parent by means of childbearing or adoption. The second option is to remain childless. The third option is to remain childless but to select an alternative experience, such as Big Brothers or teaching, that allows you to use parenting skills in a broader context. The advantages and disadvantages of each of these options are described in this chapter.

EVALUATING THE INFORMATION

Traditional discussions of parenthood have been *pro-natalist*. The pro-natalist viewpoint is pro-birth and encourages reproduction and parent-hood (Peck, 1974). You are led to believe that this option is the *natural* and *correct* option for you to select. It is not the purpose of this chapter to en-courage or to discourage parenthood. The purpose is to present informa-tion for you to examine carefully. You can evaluate the consequences that each option will have on the type of lifestyle that you desire.

MAKING RESPONSIBLE DECISIONS

You are the one who will make the final decision and stand account-able for the consequences. The decision to become a parent should be made carefully. Children have a permanent effect on lifestyle. Remember that there are options. Appreciate and accept the right of others to select the option of their choice.

CHOOSING PARENTHOOD

The motivation for parenthood is closely related to success and satis-faction with the task. Consider the following motivations:

Motivation 1: I've never doubted for a minute that I'd want my wife to have a child. I want a boy to take over the family business and to carry on the family name. He'd be John III.

Motivation 2: A baby makes a marriage. It cements you together. It gives you a reason to be alive and something to do. I don't think I'll really be a woman until I'm a mother.

Motivation 3: Children are a natural part of life if you want to be a part of the middle class. Everybody has them! I'd feel left out without children.

Motivation 4: I've always liked kids. I like to watch them play in the sand and smash their fingers in their food. I can't wait to have my own. I want to help a child grow and discover something new.

Reasons for Parenthood

The previously stated quotations from the authors' files are examples of the four major categories of motives for parenthood — egoistic, compen-satory, conforming, and affectionate. These categories were identified by Peck and Granzig (1978). They include the following components:

Egoistic reasons focus on the self.
— to have a child who will look like me
— to have a child who will carry on my admirable traits
— to have a child who will be successful
— to have someone who will carry on my name
— to inherit family money or property
— to have someone who will regard me as the greatest
— to do something I know I could do well
— to feel the pride of creation
— to keep me young at heart
— to help me feel fulfilled

Compensatory reasons involve having children to make up for something or to add to something.
— to make my marriage happier
— to make up for my own unhappy background
— to make up for lack of satisfaction in my job
— to make up for social isolation, lack of friends
— to make me feel more secure about my masculinity or femininity

Conforming motives involve being like everyone else.
— to be like most other people
— to please my parents
— to forestall social criticism

Affectionate reasons involve caring and giving.
— to have a real opportunity to make someone happy
— to teach someone about all the beautiful things in life
— to have the satisfaction of giving myself to someone else
— to help someone grow and develop

Successful parents have a mutual understanding of their roles. (Photos, left, Suzanne Szasz; right, Jim Anderson)

Egoistic, compensatory, and conforming motives can lead to problems. The desire to have children is not related to the reality of dealing with them. Peck and Granzig found that parents motivated by "affectionate" reasons were more likely to be successful, satisfied parents.

Characteristics of Successful, Satisfied Parents

What other characteristics are related to successful, satisfying parenthood? What traits do successful, satisfied parents have that are lacking in those who deem themselves and are viewed by others as unsuccessful, dissatisfied parents?

Peck and Granzig devised a Parent Test to give to two groups of parents to examine these differences. The successful, satisfied parent group were rated as such by themselves, their children, two professionals, and acquaintances such as neighbors, co-workers, and relatives. All of the couples were happily married, and at least one of their children had reached adolescence.

This group was compared with a group of unsuccessful, dissatisfied parents. Conclusions about parental success can be made from the comparisons. Table 15.1 summarizes the conclusions of Peck and Granzig. The authors suggest taking the detailed test in their excellent book *The Parent Test* (New York: G. P. Putnam's Sons, 1978). The Parent Test and the characteristics indicated in Table 15.1 provide insight into the likelihood of being a good parent.

Advantages and Disadvantages of Children

You may also gain insight by making a list of the advantages and disadvantages of having children. Brainstorm until you have made a

complete list. Your list may help you identify potential problem areas. Comparisons can be made with national studies examining advantages and disadvantages.

TABLE 15.1 CHARACTERISTICS OF SUCCESSFUL, SATISFIED PARENTS*

Successful, satisfied parents:

1. interact with children when they encounter them.
2. are willing to see children integrated into the social world of adults.
3. have an innately high energy level.
4. are at least 25 years of age.
5. like to hold infants and small children.
6. allow children to progress at their own rate rather than pushing them.
7. tolerate early forms of sexual curiosity and experimentation among children.
8. understand the compelling nature of children's play.
9. deal forcefully with the "bratty" behavior of 6- to 12-year-olds.
10. are concerned about the popularity and peer group acceptance of their children.
11. communicate through talk rather than action with teenagers.
12. accept teenage sexuality.
13. are needed by someone or something other than their children.
14. have low ego needs and are willing to accept a child for whatever he or she might become.
15. like and enjoy other children as well as their own.
16. do not count on having a physically perfect child.
17. assume that they will not be able to go out as much after the birth of their children.
18. make many recreational choices with their children in mind.
19. plan many social activities in conjunction with parents of their children's friends.
20. value companionship over sex in their marriage.
21. agree with the spouse on issues relating to parents and child raising.
22. have the same desire as the spouse for a child.
23. have a realistic advance assessment of the adjustment needed after the birth of a child.
24. do not expect their children to support them when they are old.
25. tend to be nurturers.
26. frequently have other people on their minds.
27. are apt to be tactile — "touching" — people.
28. would send an encouraging note.
29. are empathetic, able to put themselves in another's place.
30. view teaching courtesy and kindness as important as teaching the alphabet and reading skills.
31. create conditions favorable for learning.
32. believe that teaching occurs when a child is ready to learn, even if it is inconvenient.
33. are willing to admit they are wrong.
34. are consistent in their personal behavior.
35. demonstrate self-discipline.
36. do not worry about being liked.
37. are good managers.
38. have tolerance for repetitious and routine activities.
39. are able to defer personal gratification.
40. have a high tolerance for frustration.
41. do not place time and money at the top of a personal priority list.

42. prefer doing volunteer work to developing a personal priority list.
43. usually were involved in a community drive when they had to disappoint a child who wanted to play.
44. do not separate their children's needs from needs of other children.
45. respond to the idea of adopting children positively.
46. are flexible about their own lives.
47. indicate a tolerance for diversity of ideas.
48. have interests outside the home.
49. seem content with the present.
50. are willing to plan modest adventures in advance.

---

*Excerpts adapted with permission from Ellen Peck and Dr. William Granzig. *The Parent Test.* New York: G. P. Putnam's Sons, 1978.

In one U.S. study, 1569 married women between the ages of 15 and 39 were interviewed for the purpose of examining the advantages and disadvantages of children (Hoffman, Manis, 1978). One-third of their husbands were interviewed. The primary advantage of children identified was "giving and receiving love and affection" and "having a family feeling." This was mentioned first by 66% of the women and 60% of the men who were parents. Of the nonparents, 64% of the women and 51% of the men thought that this feeling was the major advantage.

"Stimulation and fun" was rated second by both parents and nonparents. Some of the accompanying reasons were "Children bring liveliness to our lives," "We love playing with them," and "We like having new growth and learning experiences."

One-tenth of the respondents felt that children were an economic advantage. Black respondents mentioned this advantage more often than white respondents with a more than average education.

Women with traditional values, who did not think women should work outside the home, were more likely to feel that being a mother provided a woman with an adult role. Women who were working were less likely to see children as a source of stimulation in their lives.

The major disadvantages of children given were loss of freedom and financial burden. Of the parent group, 53% of the mothers and 49% of the fathers mentioned loss of freedom. Of the nonparents, most of the women mentioned loss of freedom first, while the men mentioned the financial burden.

You are more likely to be a satisfied parent if the advantages that you identify clearly outweigh the disadvantages.

Myths About Parenthood

Carole Baker, Executive Director of the National Alliance for Optional Parenthood (Baker, 1979) identifies four myths about parenthood. These myths focus on work, personal relationships, feelings about children, and self-growth.

Myth 1: "Quality time is much more important than the quantity of time I spend with my children." Baker suggests that children need both. If you plan to have other people raise your children, she says, don't have them.

Myth 2: "Children will save a marriage." The reverse is more likely. Children place stress on a relationship. If a relationship is already stressful, it is better to wait to have children.

Myth 3: "I love cuddly babies; so I will enjoy raising children." Children require 18 years of nurturing; during most of this time they are not cuddly babies. It would be more realistic to examine the developmental tasks of children from birth to age 18. If nurturing children through these stages appears exciting, parenthood is a realistic goal.

Myth 4: "How will I know if I'll like parenthood till I've tried?" There are ways to predict success that should not be overlooked. It would be better to examine the characteristics of satisfied parents and the advantages and disadvantages of children, in your case, than to "try" parenthood to see.

Would I Be Happy As a Parent?

I am confused about the effects of parenthood on me and my partner. We like the idea of making money and being free to travel. We also like the idea of working together to establish values for our children. How do we know what will make us the happiest?

More American women than ever in history now have a choice about whether or not to give birth and how often (Morrow, 1979). The National Alliance for Optional Parenthood (NAOP) is an organization that deals specifically with this choice. This is the most important point that can be made. There is a choice. Whenever there is a choice, a rational decision should be made, a decision that follows an examination of the consequences on one's lifestyle. Table 15.2 contains a test called "Would I Be Happy As a Parent?" It has been developed by the NAOP, and it focuses on choice. Such a choice should be followed by a firm commitment.

A CHILDLESS LIFESTYLE

There are two kinds of childless singles and couples: voluntary and involuntary. *Voluntarily* childless singles and couples are assumed to be fertile but not inclined toward parenthood. *Involuntarily* childless singles and couples are assumed to want children but to be unable to have them.

TABLE 15.2 "WOULD I BE HAPPY AS A PARENT?"

Nobody can answer that question for sure. But we can be sure that many people have become parents without really thinking about it. And we can be sure that people are more likely to be happy as parents if they know in advance that it won't be easy. Remember, it is your life that will be affected.

Here are some of the reasons people decide to have children. Rate each reason according to its importance to you; see the scale below. A reason that hardly influences you at all rates 1, while a very important reason rates 8.

This is not a scientific test. There is no score that tells you whether or not you should have children. It is an exercise to help you think about your reasons for becoming a parent or not becoming one.

1	2	3	4	5	6	7	8
Unimportant							Important

REASONS FOR HAVING CHILDREN:
—So I won't have to cope with people wondering why I didn't have children _____
—To experience the sheer entertainment that children can provide _____
—To nurture in someone characteristics that I believe are important _____
—To have someone to stand by me when I'm old _____
—To make my partner happy _____
—To be needed _____
—To have a feeling of accomplishment _____
—To carry on the family business _____
—To have the satisfaction of giving myself to someone else _____
—To add interest to my home life _____
—Because my life wouldn't be complete without a child _____

REASONS FOR REMAINING CHILD-FREE:
—My partner and I will have a more satisfactory relationship without children _____
—I want to concentrate on my own growth and development _____
—My partner wants to remain child-free _____
—I want to be free from the responsibility of child-rearing _____
—I want to travel freely _____
—My partner and I want to continue to enjoy our leisure time _____
—My partner and I want to put our full energies into our careers _____
—I want to be able to use my income for things I want to do _____
—I want to do my part to control population growth _____
—I'd prefer to use my talents in other ways _____
—My partner and I want to maintain our privacy _____

Take a look at the reasons you rated with high numbers. Are there more high-numbered reasons for remaining child-free or for having children?

Perhaps the reasons you marked as important will show you something about how you really feel about having children or about not having them. Everyone has reasons pulling both ways. When you know what your reasons are, you'll have a better chance of making the right choice.

Research shows that having a child will not necessarily make you happier or make your marriage more satisfying. Like other decisions in life, having a child has both joys and sorrows, rewards and costs. It will be right for some people and wrong for others; for many, it will be in-between. Whatever you decide, make sure it is your choice.

Often decisions are easier to make if you talk about them with someone else. You may want to talk to:
   —a school guidance counselor
   —a parent and a child-free adult
   —a close friend whom you can confide in easily
   —a counselor at a family-planning clinic
   —and, most important, your partner

For more information: The NAOP offers a number of leaflets, including "Am I Parent Material?" and "Children, Why Not?" Write to: National Alliance for Optional Parenthood, 2010 Massachusetts Avenue NW, Washington, DC 20036.

The many possible causes of childlessness are classified into two main groups: (1) physiological factors, and (2) psychological factors (Veevers, 1974). *Physiological* factors are those that contribute to a physical malfunction or abnormality that leads to sterility of the male or female. These factors include congenital defects, traumatic injuries, disruptive diseases such as gonorrhea or mumps, and impairment due to surgery. About 10% of all couples are sterile for these reasons.

Sometimes, despite the absence of apparent physical reasons, people remain infertile. In these cases, the problem is attributed to *psychological* factors. These factors include psychosomatic infertility and voluntary childlessness. *Psychosomatic infertility* may result from tension, strain, or the intense desire to avoid parenthood (Veevers, 1974).

Voluntary childlessness involves a deliberate decision by a male or female not to have children and to use contraception, sterilization, and/or induced abortion to prevent any live births (Veevers, 1974). The following discussion focuses on voluntary childlessness.

Incidence of Childlessness

Childlessness is not randomly distributed throughout the population (Veevers, 1971). It is more common among those with a college education than those with only a high school education. This is particularly the case among women who have a degree that has led to a career. It is more common among women who marry for the first time relatively late than among women who marry relatively early.

Childlessness is less common among Catholic women than among non-Catholic women and less common among religious women than among nonreligious women. It is also less common among women who have been married only once and who are living with their husbands than it is among women who have been married more than once and who are widowed, separated, or divorced (Bogue, 1969).

Reasons for Childlessness

The child-free lifestyle can be selected due to *reactive* factors or *attrahent* factors (Veevers, 1974). Factors that are reactive involve reactions to the disadvantages of having children. Reactive factors include unhappy parental marriages, atypical experiences with siblings, and financial burden.

My parents argued all the time. I never knew what to expect or if I could bring my friends home. I wondered if it would have been better for them without children. Many of the arguments centered around what my brother and I should or should not have been doing. No children for me!

The attrahent factors involve attractions toward the advantages of the adult-centered lifestyle (Veevers, 1974). A couple might decide that children would involve quantitative and qualitative changes in their relationship. The child-free lifestyle allows one the freedom to change jobs and is more compatible with professional aspirations.

Men and women who wish to avoid routine and experience novelty and newness may see children as a factor. Those who value the childless lifestyle also mention traveling and leisure time as attrahent factors.

We like children, but it boils down to making a difficult choice. It's either children or high-quality living. We want to earn enough to have a nice home with antiques. We'd also like to travel and to join a recreational club. I'd like to go back to school now and then. Something doesn't fit the plan—children!

Pressures to Have Children

We aren't even married yet, and the pressure has started. We go over to his house, and his mom says they can't wait to baby-sit. My mom and dad tell me what nice-looking children we'll have. There is so much pressure! Don't they understand it's *our* decision?

Men and women who are childless or who openly discuss the desire for a childless lifestyle are frequently pressured to change their minds. Janet Griffith (1973) surveyed men and women aged 18 to 39 to study the social pressure on family size intentions. She found that the most likely alternative selected by Americans is the two-, three-, or four-child family. This alternative affords the least social pressure from others.

Of the childless men and women in her study, 78% expected pressure to have a child from parents or close relatives. Sixty-nine percent of the women and 62% of the men said that friends would urge them to have a child. Among the college-educated, more women than men expect pressure from friends to have a first child. Well-educated men do not expect the same social pressure. They feel that their occupational status confirms their standing as a successful adult whether or not they have children.

Stereotypes of the Childless

If a couple can explain that although they dearly love children, they are unable to have them because of the wife's heart condition, or because of an unfortunate genetic background or because they are poverty-stricken and could not give a child the advantages all children deserve, the couple can in varying degrees be defined as unfortunate. However, if the reasons given are in terms of career aspirations, freedom, lack of responsibility, or worst of all, materialistic comfort, the character is blemished and the couple are considered selfish.

(Veevers, 1971)

Parents usually stereotype, or attribute certain traits to, childless couples. One stereotypical assertion is that childless couples are abnormal. Although childless couples are in the minority (approximately 15%), there are no data that suggest they are abnormal. The opinion that those who are childless by choice are emotionally unstable or maladjusted has not been proven (Pohlman, 1970).

The second stereotypical assertion is that the childless by choice are unnatural. This opinion arises from a belief that there is a natural instinct to reproduce. It is more likely to be attributed to women than men, because of the maternal instinct.

A third stereotype, the immature adult, arises from the belief that children confirm adulthood (LeMasters, 1957). If one is a parent, one can no longer be a child. In addition, without parental status one has missed a stage of life. Thus one is rendered immature and not ready for the next stage.

A fourth stereotype holds that the childless are sexually inadequate. The assumption is made that the reason for not having children is failure to perform the sex act adequately or frequently enough for conception to occur (Veevers, 1971). The childless may be viewed as lacking moral standards, since sex is not linked to conception.

The fifth stereotype attributes unhappiness and instability to childless marriages. This stereotype results from the inaccurate assumption that children increase marital happiness. There is no evidence that children add to stability. The divorce rate is not higher among childless couples.

These five examples of stereotyping add to the pressure to have children that is felt by childless couples. The message is clear: "If you have children like we do, you are OK; if not, there is something wrong with you."

Strategies to Deal with Voluntary Childlessness

According to Veevers, one of the leading researchers on the childless lifestyle, couples will adopt one of several strategies to deal with these pressures. These strategies involve selective perception, differential association, structuring of social situations, and societal ambivalence (Veevers, 1974).

Selected perception (Veevers, 1974) occurs when a couple focuses on the disadvantages of having children without acknowledging any advantages. They are "selective" in what they see or "perceive." This focusing is reflected in the choice of reading material or television viewing. The couple would not read *Parents Talk* or *Family Circle*, nor would they watch children's shows. They are more likely to notice an article on child abuse than one on the joys of parenthood. They are more likely to notice a parent spanking a child than kissing a child.

Differential association (Veevers, 1974) refers to associating with persons who reinforce the beliefs of the childless. The childless choose friends who are single or childless or parents who resent their children. The support group fosters attitudes that reinforce behavior. The group reinforces the insignificance of motherhood. A mother is sometimes described as a "baby machine" or a "breeder."

Childless couples can also *structure social situations* (Veevers, 1974). They set up undesirable situations with children. For example, they might babysit for a child for a weekend without being prepared. The weekend is a disaster, and the couple says, "It sure is good we don't have children. We would be miserable!"

Another strategy allows the childless couple to capitalize on *societal ambivalence* (Veevers, 1974). Those who use this strategy believe that parents envy them. They see attacks on them as rationalizations by parents who feel ambivalent about their role as parents. Rather than be questioned about their childless lifestyle, they shift the question back to the others.

I'm tired of being asked why we don't have a baby. Our friends just envy Bill and me. Rather than diapers, we have a down payment for a house. I ask them why they have a baby and not a down payment. Why do they want to bring a child into the world when the cost of living is so outrageous!

These strategies have developed as a result of social pressure. It is unfortunate that people pressure or stereotype the childless. Each of you should carefully make the choice. It would be best if those who became parents made the choice *willingly*.

Our closest friends don't want children. We used to think they were selfish. I have a different idea after talking about this in our sex class. I don't think so much about our being right and their being wrong. Now I think about our both being right. What is more important, I think about the child. We will be able to tell our child that we gave him or her a great deal of thought.

ALTERNATIVES TO PARENTHOOD

I'm majoring in elementary education because I love kids. I guess I should clarify what I mean. I like other people's kids. It turns me on to teach them to read. Then at three o'clock I'm free to send them home to their parents. The best of both worlds is what I want.

The preceding comment from the authors' files describes someone who wants to enjoy and guide children, but not through the role of parenthood. This can be accomplished by selecting an occupation that focuses on children or by becoming involved with children through a volunteer effort. It can also be accomplished by a work that guides the next generation.

Many occupations provide the framework for directing the lives of children. Teaching and counseling are examples. (Photos, left, Sepp Seitz 1981; right, Paul Fortin, Stock, Boston)

Occupations That Focus on Children

Many occupations provide the framework for directing the lives of children. Teaching and counseling are examples. In these instances, an adult can "parent" by teaching, guiding, and disciplining. These occupations offer the unique opportunity to gain training in needed tasks. The teacher or counselor can interact with a variety of youngsters and can learn from each interaction. No mistake is weighed too heavily. To some degree, success can be measured—often a difficult situation for parents.

Who says I'm childless! I have 30 kids, and I love every one of them. I can watch their progress. A part of me will be with them the rest of their lives.

Volunteer Opportunities

Numerous community activities are available to adults who want to assist parents in their role. Two obvious opportunities are Big Brothers

The Big Brother program allows this single man to play a role in guiding this young boy's life. (Photo, Harvey Stein)

and Big Sisters and foster parenting. The adult's influence supplements the influence of the child's home.

> I came from a broken home. My dad was an alcoholic, and it was tough on me. One of our neighbors became my second father. I learned that a man could be strong and responsible. I want to be a Big Brother. Reaching out to some boy in need is more important to me than having my own.

The list of community activities where adults are needed is endless—churches, camps, Little League, juvenile homes, Boy Scouts, Girls Scouts, Brownies, Camp Fire Girls, halfway houses, drug-counseling centers. In addition, regular baby-sitting for children with special needs can be rewarding. Parents of handicapped children may welcome the helping hand of an adult who will assume responsibility on a regular basis.

Children at any age benefit from the care, concern, and love of adults. When an adult adds his or her love to that of a parent, it heightens the self-esteem of the child. All who are involved benefit.

Projects That Focus on Children

The third alternative approaches parenthood from a different perspective. Rather than interacting with children, a project is selected that will influence the lives of children. You could make children's records, write a book, design a game, build a playground, raise funds—the list is endless. A commitment to guide the next generation by means of a project will affect greater numbers. The feeling that you have had an impact on children is received indirectly.

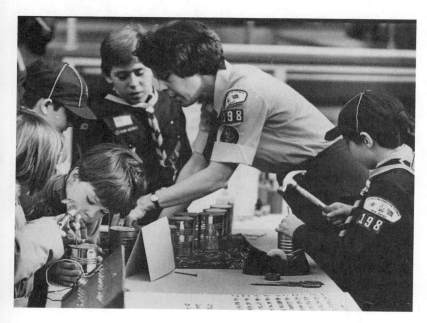

Numerous community activities are available to adults who want to assist parents in their role. (Photo, Joel Gordon 1981)

SUMMARY STATEMENTS

- *There are at least three options of parenthood: (1) to become a parent via childbearing or adoption, (2) to remain childless, and (3) to select an alternative that provides a parent role in a broader context.*
- *One means of predicting potential parental success and satisfaction is to compare your characteristics with those of successful, satisfied parents.*
- *The National Alliance for Optional Parenthood is a national organization that deals specifically with the options available to those contemplating parenthood.*
- *There are two kinds of childless singles and couples: voluntary and involuntary. Voluntarily childless singles*

and couples are assumed to be fertile but not inclined toward parenthood. Involuntarily childless singles and couples are assumed to want children but to be unable to have them.
- *People who hold stereotypes of the childless see them as unnatural, abnormal, immature, sexually inadequate, unhappy, and unstable in their marriages.*
- *An alternative to parenthood is to enjoy and guide children but not in the role of parent. One can do so by selecting an occupation that focuses on children, or by becoming involved with children through a volunteer effort.*

SUGGESTED READINGS

Jaffe, Sandra Sohn, and Jack Viertel. *Becoming Parents.* New York: Atheneum, 1979.

National Alliance for Optional Parenthood. "Am I Parent Material?" and "Children, Why Not?" National Alliance for Optional Parenthood, 2010 Massachusetts Avenue NW, Washington, D.C. 20036

Peck, Ellen, and Judith Senderwitz. *Pronatalism: The Myth of Mom and Apple Pie.* New York: Thomas Y. Crowell, 1974.

Peck, Ellen, and William Granzig. *The Parent Test: How to Measure and Develop Your Talent for Parenthood.* New York: G. P. Putnam's Sons, 1978.

A LOOK AT YOUR LIFESTYLE

If you were to have an ideal living situation with a partner of your choice, what would it be? (Your partner may be homosexual or heterosexual.) Describe your lifestyle in the space provided. Include such things as where you would live, your potential income, how you'd spend money, travel and recreation plans, occupational aspirations.

THE PARENTHOOD OPTION

_____

_____

_____

GATHERING INFORMATION

Now let us suppose that you and your partner have two small children to raise. In what five ways will your lifestyle be changed?

_____

_____

_____

_____

EVALUATING THE INFORMATION

1. Identify the greatest advantage of raising children.

_____

2. Identify the greatest disadvantage of raising children.

_____

MAKING RESPONSIBLE DECISIONS

I have examined the impact of children on my lifestyle, and the parenthood op-

tion I am most comfortable with is _____

because _____ .

SIXTEEN

Sexuality and the Life Cycle

The sexual instincts of man do not suddenly awaken between the thirteenth and fifteenth year, i.e., at puberty, but operate from the outset of the child's development, change gradually from one form to another, progress from one state to another, until at last adult sexual life is achieved as the final result from this long series of developments.

–(Group for the Advancement of Psychiatry, 1965)

A LOOK AT YOUR LIFESTYLE

We express this sexuality in many ways, among which may be by our attitudes, values, and behaviors. Sexual development is an ongoing process that begins at birth and ends upon death. In between a myriad of phenomena are taking place. At each stage of our lives we are sexually alive, whether in conscious activities or in unconscious behaviors. As soon as we are born, we have the ability to respond sexually. As we grow older, we continue to engage in sex-related behavior, but in different forms. Throughout the life cycle, physical, emotional, social, and cultural

413

forces condition our sexuality in intricate and important ways. As we grow through the life cycle, we begin to develop a wide range of sexual attitudes and expressions.

If you can, think of the very first sexual experience you ever had. For some of you, this experience may have been masturbation; for others, it may have been holding hands with your playmate when you were five years of age. Now think about the ways your sexuality has developed. When did you become aware of the physical attractiveness of another person? When was the first time you wanted to have sex with someone? At what age do you remember first becoming sexually aroused?

One of the ways we can develop a clear understanding of our own sexuality is to ascertain what kinds of activities take place with others. Science and research have provided us with a great deal of empirical data that can help us clarify and rationalize our behavior patterns.

GATHERING INFORMATION

In order to understand the dramatic changes that take place throughout each phase of the life cycle, it is important that we examine those behaviors and occurrences that make that part of the life cycle unique.

To help identify the special characteristics of each stage in life, we identified some of the major research projects that have provided us data about human sexual behavior. We looked very closely at the *Morton Hunt Survey* (1974), the *Kinsey Report* (1948, 1953), and the *Redbook Report on Female Sexuality* (1974). However, we would be less than honest if we did not acknowledge that these surveys have shortcomings in their research design and methodology.

To best identify the many facets of human sexual behavior throughout the life cycle, the chapter is divided into separate parts: infancy through early childhood; preadolescence; adolescence; adulthood; and late adulthood. Within each of these areas, those sex-related issues and behaviors unique to them are discussed.

EVALUATING THE INFORMATION

Examining the information that applies to sexual behavior in each of the stages of the life cycle can affect your sexual lifestyle.

Consider some of the following facts:

1. Extramarital sex has not increased significantly over the past 20 years.
2. Most young men and women who are married masturbate.
3. Older persons have a need for sexual expression.
4. Infants can respond sexually.
5. More than half the adolescents in the United States have had premarital sexual intercourse.

The information in this chapter is provided for you to evaluate. Sometimes knowing what occurs can serve to relieve the burden of guilt that one may carry.

When I accidentally walked into my parents' room and saw them having sex, I became angry. After all, why should older people have sex? They are not supposed to.

MAKING RESPONSIBLE DECISIONS

One important part of accepting your own sexual behavior is to acknowledge that others may have behaviors that differ from or are the same as yours. For example, most adolescent males masturbate. Of the adolescents who do masturbate, most enjoy the experience (Sorensen, 1973). Yet about half of these adolescents experience feelings of guilt about their behavior.

Every time I masturbate, I feel as if I'm doing something wrong. I always wonder if my friends do it. They never mention that they do.

Perhaps if adolescents were aware that masturbation is normal, they would not experience the guilt that usually accompanies it. The same can be said to be true of other behaviors. People need to make decisions about the "rightness" or "wrongness" of their own behavior.

INFANCY THROUGH EARLY CHILDHOOD (BIRTH TO AGE 7)

As soon as a child is born, the capacity to exhibit a sexual response is present. This response is more evident among males than among females. The male infant, even at the time of birth, can be observed with an erection. While female sexual response differs somewhat from male sexual response, we do know that similarities exist. Masters and Johnson (1970) have found that female infants have vaginal secretions. Of course, assumptions about sexual response must be based upon observation and scientific correlations, since infants do not have the capacity to verbalize their sexual feelings.

What constitutes sexual behavior during infancy and early childhood is something that may be difficult to interpret. For example, if a child manipulates his or her genitalia, this action may be indicative of curiosity, as opposed to self-stimulation. On the other hand, a child may engage in an act that, according to an adult, is not sexual in nature but may be sexually arousing to the child. For example, a two-year-old child who decides to sit on an adult with her legs straddling the adult's thigh, moving back and forth, may be masturbating. To the adult, this behavior may not appear as such. Therefore, to objectify activities in infants and young children as sexual behavior, we need to identify physical changes that are common indicators of sexual arousal.

Masturbation

The most common sexual activity among children in infancy and early childhood is masturbation. By masturbation, we mean deliberate self-stimulation that leads to sexual arousal. Sometimes this arousal can terminate in orgasm.

While many people may think otherwise, masturbation among children is quite possible, and in many cases, probable. According to Kinsey et al. (1948), masturbation is a normal and quite frequent phenomenon among female and male children. In fact, Kinsey found that some females under one year of age were able to achieve orgasm. One male, in the Kinsey study, at age five months, had three orgasms within an unspecified time frame.

Although the data on the incidence of prepubescent masturbation are minimal, we do have some data about its incidence. According to Elias and Gebhard (1969), 56% of the males and 30% of the females in their study reported they had masturbated. The techniques children use to masturbate are similar to those of adults. Most children masturbate by lying face-down on the bed and pressing and rubbing their genitals against the bed or an object such as a rolled up blanket or a pillow. Most children will first discover masturbation by accident. When they find this discovery to be pleasurable, they may then decide to continue in this behavior.

It is often difficult to categorize sexual activity among children during early childhood and infancy. For example, breast-feeding could possibly be a sensuous experience for an infant (we have already mentioned that it can be a sensuous experience for the mother). We do know that infants enjoy having something to suck on, whether a thumb or a nipple.

Many studies are being conducted now regarding the impact of bonding. There are some indications that a child who is held in close physical contact with its parents is less likely to refuse being held in years ahead. The intimate encounters during the early years of life may influence one's receptivity in later years.

Changes in the 3 to 4 Age Group

Based upon Freudian theory, several things occur during the ages of 3 to 4. First the child enters what is known as the *Oedipal period.* At this age, children are capable of experiencing romantic feelings even though their thinking is still immature. They may become attracted to a parent of the opposite sex. These attractions will be manifested not by sexual acts but by wishes and fantasies. Thus, a young boy may flirt with his mother and

During the ages of 3 to 4 children are capable of experiencing romantic feelings even though their thinking is still immature. Young children may become attracted to a parent of the opposite sex. (Photo, Sherry Davis)

think about marrying her. Within the confines of a loving family, these feelings will eventually disappear. The boy will learn to identify more with his father and begin to engage in enjoyable activities with him, and the girl, likewise with her mother.

At this age comes an awareness of the genital differences between males and females. The child often asks why mommy differs from daddy. Children may be fascinated now by how each sex urinates, and they may often ask to accompany their mothers and fathers to the bathroom.

Also at this age children experience affection toward others. They will often hug, kiss, and stand next to others to whom they feel close. At the same time, they may also cry when the baby-sitter comes to the house because they know their parents are leaving.

Changes in the 5 to 7 Age Group

At this age children become more social. Since children usually begin school by age 5, they are forced to interact with the same and the opposite

This little girl is anticipating how her body will change when she becomes an adult. (Photo, Joann Leonard 1981)

sex. They play the usual games of "doctor" and "house" and thus begin to develop sexual roles in their social activities. For example, it's not uncommon to hear a 5-year-old girl say to her male playmate, "You be the daddy, and I'll be the mommy."

At this age children acknowledge that they and their friends have genitalia. They may play "doctor" and examine each other's genitalia as well as their own.

They become more modest now. They may seek privacy when they are getting dressed and lock the bedroom door. Also, they may resent another person's walking into the bathroom when they are defecating or urinating.

PREADOLESCENCE (AGES 8 to 12)

Preadolescence, also known as *middle childhood* or the *"latency age,"* occurs from about age 8 to age 12. This age period was labeled "latent" by Freud because he believed that the sex drive during this period was dormant. However, it is not. Children do express an avid interest in sex during this age. They cannot help but become aware of their sexuality,

Young children are frequently curious about sex. (Photo, Fredrik D. Bodin, Stock, Boston)

because of the many changes that occur with the onset of puberty (see Chapters 2 and 3).

Masturbation

During preadolescence, the incidence of the number of children who begin to masturbate increases. In the Kinsey (1948, 1953) studies, as well as in the studies of Hunt (1974), it is evident that masturbation during preadolescence is not at all uncommon (see Table 16.1). In the Hunt study, it was found that children are now masturbating at an earlier age than in the past. Generally, boys begin to masturbate at an earlier age than girls.

TABLE 16.1 COMPARISON OF MALES AND FEMALES WHO HAD
MASTURBATED BY AGE 13 BASED UPON KINSEY AND HUNT

	Kinsey (1948, 1953) (%)	Hunt (1974) (%)
Males	45	63
Females	15	33

In his analysis of preadolescent masturbation, Sorensen (1973) found
that most girls who masturbated began masturbating before the age of
13; the majority of boys who masturbated first masturbated before the age
of 14 (see Table 16.2). More boys reported masturbating than girls.

TABLE 16.2 AGE AT WHICH BOYS AND GIRLS WITH MASTURBATION
EXPERIENCE FIRST MASTURBATED

Age	Boys (%)	Girls (%)
10 or younger	12	33
11	11	8
12	14	13
13	27	18
14	18	19
15–19	8	9
TOTAL	100	100

Source: Robert Sorenson, *Adolescent Sexuality in Contemporary America*. New York: World Publishing,
1973.

Homosexual Activity

During preadolescence, boys and girls often have a preference for
playmates of the same sex. As a result, homosexual activity may not be at
all uncommon. Kinsey (1948) found that 52% of males and 35% of females
have engaged in homosexual activity by the age of 14. The most common
type of homosexual activity at this age is genital exhibition, followed in
frequency by touching each other's genitals.

Most boys and girls who engage in homosexual behavior during
preadolescence are not aware that it is "bad." In most cases, it is easier for
preadolescents to engage in homosexual contact than in heterosexual contact, since parents are more apt to chaperone heterosexual play. In most
cases, homosexual contact and play during preadolescence is quickly
forgotten in the years that follow.

Heterosexual Activitity

Just as there is homosexual play, there is also heterosexual contact
during preadolescence. According to Kinsey (1948), about one-third of
males and females engage in heterosexual contact. As in homosexual
expression, genital exhibition is the most frequent activity, followed by
manual manipulation of the genitalia.

During this age, many romantic activities may also take place. Usually, boys will be rough and chase after and wrestle with girls as a means of expressing sexual affection. Girls, however, will usually be much more subdued in their behavior.

Boys and girls may begin to date during preadolescence. However, dating often begins as a group activity. Parties are popular, and during these parties boys and girls may try to "outpopularize"each other. Being popular is often associated with being more appealing to members of the opposite sex. The interest in making sexual contact with a member of the opposite sex at parties is evident. Boys and girls play games such as "spin the bottle" and "post office" — two varieties of kissing games. They may also pair off and have "make-out" sessions. These episodes usually entail nothing more than kissing.

As the preadolescent nears the age of 13, attitudes, values, and behavior begin to take new forms.

ADOLESCENCE (AGES 13 to 19)

Adolescence is a period during which one "rehearses" or prepares for adulthood. During this age period, one moves from dependence to independence. With this independence comes a complex myriad of psychological, physiological, and sociological changes. We have already focused on the physiological changes that occur during puberty (see Chapters 2 and 3); so at this point we will examine the psychological and sociological dynamics of adolescence.

Both of these pictures show typical pre-adolescent behavior! (Photos, left, Stephen Sharnes, 1980; right, Joel Gordon, 1974)

Masturbation

During adolescence, masturbation increases in frequency. By the time adolescence ends, almost all males and two-thirds of females will have masturbated to orgasm (Hunt, 1974; Kinsey, 1948). Even though masturbation is the primary means of sexual expression among adolescents, its degree of acceptance among adolescents varies. In one study, about half the adolescents who masturbated had guilt feelings (Sorensen, 1973); whereas in another study, attitudes about masturbation were much more accepting (Hunt, 1974). The statistics more than indicate that masturbation during adolescence is a natural and normal part of sexuality.

Male adolescents who masturbate learned how from friends—usually by observation. Some males have masturbation contests. In an activity called "circle jerk," a group of male adolescents masturbate together. The first to ejaculate wins.

Females, on the other hand, usually do not learn about masturbation from their friends. Most discover masturbation from reading books. Sometimes a heterosexual petting experience can serve to enlighten the female about the pleasure of genital manipulation. Afterward, she may

During early adolescence, sexuality is frequently expressed in playful ways. (Photo, Hella Hammid)

decide to transfer her knowledge to self-stimulation and thus practice masturbation.

Homosexuality

Homosexual, or same sex, physical contact during adolescence varies between the male and the female. About 20% of males have had a homosexual experience leading to orgasm by the end of adolescence. For females, the incidence is less than 10% (Sorensen, 1973). Most homosexual encounters in this age group take place with another in the same age group. Even though we are witnessing a greater tolerance of homosexuality, Sorensen (1973) found that three-quarters of the adolescents he surveyed found homosexuality among members of their age group to be abnormal or unnatural.

It should be noted that same-sex contact during adolescence does not mean one is homosexual, nor that homosexuality will be the choice in adult life. At this age, young people may be confused about their sexual orientation. Unfortunately, for youngsters in the 13- to 19-year-old age brackets, guidance and counseling for sex-related concerns is inadequate in many situations. Adolescents who believe they are homosexual will probably not be offered the conveniences that university students have— i.e., gay clubs and other organizations. Therefore, support for their lifestyle selection is frequently lacking. In one recent incident, a gay male wanted to take another gay male to his high school prom. After much debate and change in the decision, he was permitted to do so. However, extra police guards were hired to prevent the carrying out of bodily harm by other students.

Just as we have indicated that adolescent homosexual practices do not always carry into adult life, so must the opposite be true. Engaging in heterosexual contacts during adolescence does not prevent one from becoming a homosexual during adulthood. In fact, most homosexuals experience heterosexual contact before becoming homosexual.

Petting

Petting, also known as *"necking"* or *"making out,"* consists of erotic physical contact that goes beyond kissing but stops short of sexual intercourse. This term usually relates to adolescent behavior. Very rarely is the term used to express adult sexual activities. Among the acts that constitute petting are breast fondling, and genital contact—either manual or oral.

Today, petting is an integral part of adolescent sexual expression. The degree of petting among adolescents can be used to indicate emotional commitment. Boys may use petting as a "stepping stone" to status among their peers. It is not uncommon to hear one boy ask another "how far" he got.

When I was young, my friends and I would always ask each other, "How far did you go?" Each act would be placed on a scale that would indicate light petting to heavy petting. The scale would progress as follows: rubbing the breasts clothed, rubbing the breasts unclothed, sucking the breasts, dry humping, rubbing the vagina clothed, then unclothed, having the penis rubbed while clothed and then unclothed, cunnilingus, fellatio, and then sexual intercourse. It was very systematic.

The incidence of petting among young people appears to have been increasing. Kinsey et al. (1953) found that 23% of young females had experienced petting to orgasm; for males, the figure was 25%. Yet, according to Hunt (1974), the comparable figures are over half of females and two-thirds of males.

Sexual Intercourse

Often, when surveys about the incidence of sexual intercourse are conducted, the words *premarital sex* are used. Premarital sex has vague connotations, however. When this term is used, it is meant to indicate that sex in marriage is the norm for sexual intercourse. Obviously, not everyone today chooses to marry. Many people consider "premarital sex" to be an outdated term. The following example can be used to illustrate this point:

John and I are in our thirties. We have been living together for over five years, but we are not married. Recently, we received a survey to complete which asked if either of us had engaged in premarital intercourse. We found it very difficult to relate to this terminology.

It appears that "premarital sex" has become an overused term. In addition, it can be misleading. While a person may never have experienced premarital sex, he or she is not necessarily sexually inexperienced. A person could still be a virgin and yet exhibit indiscriminate sexual behavior.

We had one girl in our neighborhood who said she would be a virgin until she married. However, she was quick to perform oral sex on almost any guy she met.

INCIDENCE OF PREMARITAL SEX

Whenever one wants to look at changes in behavior, one must often look at attitudinal changes. Often, the behavior shifts with the attitude. Therefore, if we examine previous attitudes in premarital sexual behavior, we can see certain trends. In 1937 and 1939, the Roper Agency conducted a study in which they asked men and women the following: "Do you think it is all right for either or both parties to a marriage to have had previous sexual intercourse?" (Hunt, 1974). Over half of the respondents felt it was *not* all right. In 1963, Ira L. Reiss, a noted sociologist, showed an even more conservative estimate. However, in the mid-1960s attitudes began to shift, and by 1973 90% of college women approved of premarital sex for women "in love, but not engaged" (Hunt, 1974).

Along with attitudinal changes came changes in sexual behavior. Table 16.3 indicates this shift.

TABLE 16.3 CHANGES IN PREMARITAL SEXUAL BEHAVIOR BY AGE 25 ACCORDING TO KINSEY AND HUNT

	Kinsey (1948, 1953) (%)	Hunt (1974) (%)
Males	71	97
Females	33	67

As we can see, the increase in sexual behavior is significant. The ages of the persons in the studies summarized in Table 16.3 go up to 25 years. The actual incidence of premarital sexual behavior lowers with age. However, according to the latest figures published, *Newsweek* (1980) quoted Zelnik and Kanter as saying that 50% of the nation's 10.3 million young women between the ages of 15 and 19 have had premarital sexual intercourse. This is nearly double what Zelnik and Kanter found in 1971. The Zelnik and Kanter studies are less conservative than Sorensen's figures (1973), which showed that 72% of males and 57% of females in the 16- to 19-year-old age bracket had premarital sexual intercourse.

While young people may engage in premarital sexual intercourse quite frequently, their experience was not necessarily enjoyable. As would probably be expected, Sorensen (1973) showed that boys were "excited," "happy," satisfied," and "thrilled" two to three times as frequently as girls at the time of their initial experience of sexual intercourse. About two-thirds of females reported a feeling of regret after their first experience of sexual intercourse (Hunt, 1974). This difference is most likely due to fear of pregnancy, moral conflicts, and social conditioning.

Not only has the incidence of reported premarital sexual intercourse increased over the last several decades, but so has the reported incidence of premarital oral–genital contact. Table 16.4 offers a good comparison of these behaviors in 1948 versus 1974.

TABLE 16.4 CHANGES IN ORAL–GENITAL PREMARITAL BEHAVIOR ACCORDING TO KINSEY AND HUNT (%)

Behavior	Kinsey (1948) (ADOLESCENT to 25) %	Hunt (18-24) %
Fellatio	33	72
Cunnilingus	14	69

It appears that oral–genital contact is becoming more and more an integral part of the sexual behavior of young people.

WHY ADOLESCENTS ENGAGE IN PREMARITAL SEX

In his well-researched book on adolescent sexuality, Sorensen (1973) pointed out several reasons adolescents engaged in premarital sex. They had curiosity about a new experience; they saw it as a means of expressing themselves; they saw it as a sign of maturity; and, last but not least, they saw it as taboo—"It was such a forbidden topic around the house." The fact that premarital sex is receiving so much publicity today is perhaps one reason young people need to experience what the "excitement" is all about.

WHY ADOLESCENTS DO NOT ENGAGE IN PREMARITAL SEX

Just as there has been a great deal of emphasis placed on why adolescents wish to engage in premarital sex, there also needs to be equal time given to why adolescents do *not* wish to engage in this behavior. The major reason for remaining a virgin is that sex is considered by many adolescents to be *unnecessary* rather than *unwanted*. Many adolescents may choose not to have sexual intercourse because they have a relationship that is intimate without it. Another reason may be that they are sexually satisfied in their relationship without sexual intercourse. For example, we saw in Table 16.4 that adolescents are engaging more frequently in oral–genital contact than in past years. The advantages of oral–genital contact are (1) that pregnancy cannot occur and (2) in many relationships the male is better able to satisfy his partner through cunnilingus than sexual intercourse, since he can "last" longer this way.

Sorensen (1973) found three major reasons adolescents choose to remain virgins. (1) The majority of adolescents felt that they had never had sex because they had not found a person with whom they wanted to have sex. (2) About half of the adolescents surveyed felt they were not ready for sex. (3) A small percentage of adolescents said there was no one who wanted to have sex with them.

Adolescent Contraception and Pregnancy

With the increased incidence of premarital sexual intercourse have come related problems. Most noteworthy is the increased rate of out-of-wedlock pregnancies. In the United States, at least one out of every ten females under the age of 18 becomes pregnant at least once. Several reasons can be given:

1. More young people engage in premarital sex than ever before.
2. Coupled with this increase in premarital sex is the average age of menarche, which now is 12, as compared with 17 one hundred years ago.
3. Birth control is not used. Eighty percent of couples use no form of contraception during their first sexual intercourse. Most studies indicate that the younger a couple is, the less likely it is that they will use contraception (Cvetkovich et al., 1978).

While the process of pregnancy and childbirth is relatively safe for mothers in their twenties, it poses hazards for the teenage mother and her child. Compared with children born to mothers in the prime childbearing years (20 to 24), children of teens have a death rate of two to three times higher. Babies born to teenagers are also more likely to be premature.

The teenage mother faces a death risk 60% higher than that of mothers in their twenties. Miscarriages, hemorrhages, anemia, and toxemia are also more prevalent among teens. The following excerpt perhaps best explains the reasons for some of the maladies that afflict the pregnant adolescent:

> Obtaining adequate health care is a real problem for young people. Not only do they face the problems of the adult population—lack of access to primary health care and preventive medical services, quality of health care, fragmentation of care, inflated health care costs —but they are also confronted with barriers unique to them, such as requirement of parental consent for treatment, difficulty in obtaining and maintaining confidentiality and anonymity if their problems conflict with community morality.
>
> (Needle, 1978)

SEXUALITY AND ADULTHOOD

We have thus far covered sexual behavior from infancy through adolescence. In several other chapters we have discussed marriage and the single lifestyle. In this part of the chapter, we will examine sexual behavior within marriage as well as sexual behavior and functioning in the later years of adulthood.

Marital Coitus

Although not everyone in the United States marries, the fact remains that most do. Many of the standards established and used as comparisons for sexual behavior are based upon what married people do, because most sexual expression for adults takes place within marriage.

The two major studies concerning marital coitus show that there is greater frequency of marital intercourse today than a generation ago (see Table 16.5). In looking at this table, we can see that there has been an increase in the frequency of coitus in every age group. It is interesting to note that this frequency declines with age. Yet Hunt shows that the frequency in the 55-and-over age category is twice as high as in Kinsey's population. This is the greatest increase for any age group. That "older people do not have sex" is obviously a myth. Hunt showed that older people (55 and over) have coitus once a week. The biggest changes in marital sexuality from Kinsey to Hunt are that couples use more sexual techniques and spend more time in their typical sexual act.

TABLE 16.5 MARITAL COITUS: FREQUENCY PER WEEK MALE AND FEMALE ESTIMATES COMBINED, 1938-1946/9 AND 1972

1938–1946/9 (Kinsey)		1972 (Hunt)	
AGE	MEDIAN	AGE	MEDIAN
16–25	2.45	18–24	3.25
26–35	1.95	25–34	2.55
36–45	1.40	35–44	2.00
46–55	0.85	45–54	1.00
56–60	0.50	55 and over	1.00

Source: Morton Hunt. *Sexual Behavior in the 1970's*. Chicago: Playboy Press, 1974, p. 191.

In the *Redbook Report on Female Sexuality*, it was found that coital frequency tends to decline with a woman's age and length of marriage (see Table 16.6). Unlike the figures of Kinsey and Hunt, the figures for Redbook were not broken down by age group. The *Redbook* survey found that one fourth of the newly married wives said they had sex more than four times a week; that proportion dropped to 12% of the women married one to four years, 7% of those married five to seven years, and 5% of those married eight years or longer.

TABLE 16.6 FREQUENCY OF INTERCOURSE PER MONTH AS REPORTED BY FEMALES — 1974

Times Per Month	Percent Reporting Coitus
0	2
1–5	26
6–10	32
11–15	21
16–20	11
20+	8

Source: Carole Tavris and Susan Sadd: *The Redbook Report on Female Sexuality*. New York: Dell Publishing Co., Inc., 1975, p. 101.

It should be noted that each of the previously mentioned studies has some flaws in research methodology. The Kinsey research has been criticized for its lack of a random sample. Only 20% of the people in the Hunt survey responded to questionnaires. Thus, the data might be highly biased. The criticism leveled against the *Redbook* report is that only those people who read *Redbook* were exposed to the questionnaire. We cannot make the assumption that the sexual behavior of American women who read *Redbook* is typical of the majority of the female population. However, while the frequency of coitus that is reported may be overstated, the trend toward a more increased frequency of coitus in marriage is probably *not* overstated, according to another study conducted by Westoff (1974).

Other Aspects of Marital Sex

All forms of foreplay are used in today's marriages to a larger degree than years ago. Perhaps the most significant changes have occurred in oral–genital acts. Yet the figures in the Kinsey (1948) and Hunt (1974) studies appear small when compared with the responses in the *Redbook* survey. In this survey, 90% of all wives under the age of 25 reported experimenting with fellatio and cunnilingus. The majority of these women reported that they engaged in these behaviors "occasionally" to "often." As we have stated previously, the higher the educational level of a person, the greater the likelihood of his or her engaging in oral–genital contact as well as other sexual variations.

In addition to the frequency of marital coitus and oral–genital contact, there has also been an increase in the regularity of orgasm for married women. Table 16.7 examines the frequency of coital orgasm during marriage. In Hunt's survey, a marked increase in coital orgasm can be observed when compared with the Kinsey data. Kinsey showed that 45% of wives reached orgasm almost all the time, compared with 53% of Hunt's population. The *Redbook* survey showed that 63% of married women reached orgasm during coitus all or most of the time.

In addition to the increased incidence in oral–genital contact and coital orgasm over the past number of years, there has also been an increase in the duration of marital foreplay. This increase may be due somewhat to each partner's awareness of the other's needs. Even the variation in coital positions has increased dramatically over the past number of years. Anal intercourse is also practiced more frequently than before. According to Hunt (1974), 6% of people under 35 have anal intercourse sometimes or often, and one-fourth had tried it at one time during their lives. The *Redbook* (1974) survey found that 43% of its respondents had tried anal intercourse at least once.

Masturbation during marriage is not at all uncommon. According to Hunt (1974), 74% of young husbands masturbate with a median frequency of 24 times per year, whereas 68% of young wives do so about 10 times per year. The *Redbook* survey indicated that 68% of its females surveyed masturbated often or occasionally.

In summary, it appears that masturbation in marriage can serve to meet sexual needs. This frequency can be the basis of a well-supported retort to people who say that when one marries, there is no need to masturbate, since the partner is supposed to take care of sexual desires. However, there are many reasons that people masturbate while they are married.

Among these are an absent partner, relief of tension, unsatisfying coitus, sexual fulfillment of a fantasy, and habit before marriage.

TABLE 16.7 PROPORTION OF MARITAL COITUS RESULTING IN ORGASM

1938-1949 (Kinsey)		1972 (Hunt)		1974 (*Redbook*)	
ORGASM FREQUENCY	*% OF WIVES*	*ORGASM FREQUENCY*	*% OF WIVES*	*ORGASM FREQUENCY*	*% OF WIVES*
90–100% of the time	45	All or almost all of the time	53	All of the time or most of the time	63
30–89% of the time	27	About ¾ to ½ of the time	32	Sometimes	19
1–29% of the time	16	About ¼ of the time	8	Once in a while	11
None of the time	12	Almost none or none of the time	7	Never	7

Sources: Morton Hunt, *Sexual Behavior in the 1970's.* Chicago: Playboy Press, 1974, p. 212, and Carol Tarvis and Susan Sadd: *The Redbook Report on Female Sexuality.* New York: Dell Publishing Company, 1975, p. 110).

> I still do it when the man I live with is away and I feel the need. I enjoy sex with him a great deal more than I do masturbating, but it's a substitute, and it gives me satisfaction and peace, and it keeps me from wanting to go looking for someone else.
>
> (Hunt, 1974)

Satisfaction in Marital Sex

It appears that people experience a greater satisfaction in marital sexual relations today than ever before. The current openness about sex has enabled people to experience joys they ordinarily would not experience. As a result, people today are not as inhibited about communicating their sexual needs to their partners. In the Hunt (1974) sample, most married men and women reported sex to be "very pleasurable" during the past year (Table 16.8). Although women express slightly less satisfaction than men in marital sex, both groups are generally satisfied. The majority of women in the *Redbook* study (1974) also indicated that sex in marriage was "good to very good."

It appears that a cause-and-effect relationship exists between sexual pleasure in marriage and the overall success of a marriage. But it is not known whether sex creates emotional closeness or whether emotional closeness promotes good sex. If a marriage is poor, then so is the sex in most cases. The reverse is also true.

Extramarital Sexual Relationships

The term *extramarital sex,* sometimes called adultery, means sexual interaction between a married person and someone other than that married

TABLE 16.8 SEXUAL PLEASURE BY MARITAL CLOSENESS

Marital Sex Life in Past Year Was:	Marital Relationship		
	VERY CLOSE	FAIRLY CLOSE	NOT TOO CLOSE OR VERY DISTANT
Married males			
Very pleasurable	79%	45%	12%
Mostly pleasurable	20%	50%	47%
Neither pleasurable nor unpleasurable	1%	2%	17%
Mostly or very nonpleasurable	—	3%	24%
Married females			
Very pleasurable	70%	30%	10%
Mostly pleasurable	26%	58%	28%
Neither pleasurable nor unpleasurable	1%	8%	45%
Mostly or very nonpleasurable	3%	4%	17%

Source: Morton Hunt. *Sexual Behavior in the 1970's.* Chicago: Playboy Press, 1974, p. 231.

person's spouse. Extramarital sex can take one of two forms—secretive or nonsecretive. If the extramarital affair is secretive, it is *nonconsensual* or *clandestine*. That is, the extramarital relationship is kept from the spouse. It is assumed that if the spouse knew about the extramarital relationship, there would be disapproval. In *consensual extramarital sex*, the husband and wife both know and approve of one or both engaging in extramarital sex. Often a partner may know that the other partner may be having extramarital sex but would not choose to confront the participant, a situation known as *ambiguous extramarital sex*. In our society, most extramarital affairs are either ambiguous or clandestine, and consensual extramarital sex is relatively uncommon.

INCIDENCE OF EXTRAMARITAL SEX

In 1948, Kinsey found that about half of all married men and one fourth of all married women engaged in extramarital sex. When one looks at these figures today, the tendency may be for many to say, "Those figures are outdated. It must be at least twice the number today." After all, when the mass media profess that traditional marriage is "out" and that sexual freedom is "in," it stands to reason that one would expect extramarital sex to be rampant today when compared with the Kinsey days. But such is not the case. Morton Hunt's study in the 1970s surprised many people when it was found that the rate of extramarital sex for men older than 25 years of age was about the same as the rate in the Kinsey era.

The results of the *Redbook* survey (1974) support Hunt's findings. Of the wives surveyed, it was found that 29% had had extramarital sex. In both studies, it was found that a large number of those who had extramarital sex did so earlier in their marriages. Hunt found a large increase in the number of women under 25 who had had an extramarital affair—the major difference between the Kinsey and Hunt surveys. As the length of the marriage increases, one becomes less reluctant about engaging in an extramarital affair.

While little difference exists between the incidence of extramarital sex during the Kinsey days, when compared with the 1970s, it may very well be that future surveys will show significant increases. The number of women who choose to join the work force has increased and this increases the opportunity for sexual contacts. Also, more sophisticated forms of birth control help remove the fear of pregnancy.

On the other hand, a decrease in the incidence of extramarital sex may occur. People may have reached the point where they feel the need for some part of the old morality, and it is possible that society may shift toward a more conservative stance.

WHY PEOPLE HAVE EXTRAMARITAL SEX

The reasons people choose to have extramarital sex are many and varied. The best predictor of whether or not a person will have an extramarital affair is the quality of the marriage. Bell et al. (1975) found that most women who had extramarital sex rated their marriages "fair to bad." It appears that unhappiness in a marriage can indeed become a factor in whether or not a person will choose to have extramarital sex.

> My husband and I do not enjoy a particularly good relationship, but he won't consider a divorce. We have never been able to communicate freely, and if I suggest something new in sexual activity, he immediately wants to know where and how I found out about it. He is jealous in the extreme and very rigid in his approach to life. As a result, I have had lovers before. My present lover is very special to me, and since I met him nearly a year ago, I have had no interest in other men. We are well matched mentally and sexually and have many more things in common than my husband and I do. I have no feelings of guilt or wrong-doing. I have tried to end my marriage, but when one partner is violently opposed, the obstacles are endless. So I made the best of the situation.
>
> (Tavris and Sadd, 1975)

Many individuals who have extramarital sex have no complaints about their marriage. Sometimes excitement and variety are enough motivation. In other instances, people may have extramarital sex if they are separated for a period of time. If the chance of getting caught is low and the opportunity prime, there are many people who engage in extramarital sex who might otherwise never do so.

CONSENSUAL EXTRAMARITAL SEX

Consensual extramarital sex can be an integral part of the marriage lifestyle for couples who choose this alternative. In this section, we discuss the most predominant forms of consensual marital sex—open marriage, "swinging," and group marriage.

OPEN MARRIAGE The term *open marriage* became widely known in 1972 with the publication of the book *Open Marriage* by George and Nena O'Neill. While we are including the concept of open marriage within the framework of consensual extramarital sex, we by no means intend to imply that open marriage is solely a sexual concept. The O'Neills believed that two people who were married would not be able to fulfill all the intimate needs of the spouse throughout the marriage. Therefore, in an open marriage, both spouses are permitted to develop close relationships with persons outside of the marriage. Some couples agree that these extramarital relationships may include intimate sexual and emotional involvement. Other couples may agree that extramarital relationships will consist of transitory sex only.

Proponents of open marriage claim that if individuals are permitted to explore relationships outside of marriage, the marriage relationship will become one of greater mutual trust and support.

SWINGING *Swinging* is a form of consensual extramarital sex in which married couples exchange spouses with other married couples. Swinging differs from open marriage in that the husband and wife participate simultaneously, usually in the same place, but not in the same room. Some people refer to swinging as "wife swapping." However, this term insinuates that the wife is property and such a concept is looked upon by many people as demeaning to the woman. Another term that can be substituted for swinging is *mate swapping*—a nonsexist term.

Just who are the people who swing? They are of various ages, 18 and up, and the couples stay within a ten-year range of each other (Bartell, 1970; Varni, 1972). For the most part, they are middle to upper-middle class with fairly traditional backgrounds (Rosen, 1971). That is, they do not deviate from the middle American lifestyle except for their swinging.

Swingers can find other swinging couples in various manners. They can go to bars that cater to swingers; they can be invited to a swinger's party by another couple they may know; they can advertise or respond to an advertisement in a newspaper or magazine; or they can be referred by other couples. In most cases, the wife is initiated into swinging at the husband's suggestion (Rosen, 1971; Smith and Smith, 1970).

The basic reason people choose to swap partners is the idea that sexual variety can be brought into the relationship without threatening what is usually a conventional marriage. Some couples swap because it reinforces the feeling of sexual attractiveness of the partner who needs reassurance that "someone finds me sexy." Regardless of how contact is made for swapping, the fact is always emphasized that no one has to have sexual relations with another person if her or she does not wish to do so.

Mate-swapping parties can look just like any other party. People can be observed making conversation over cocktails. Later this socializing may be interrupted by a sexual interlude in another part of the house, and the partners may then again return to socializing. This type of mate-swapping party is known as "closed." Sometimes a mate-swapping party can be "open"—more commonly known as an *orgy*. In this type of party, everyone is nude in one room. They engage in touching as well as various kinds of sexual acts with anyone who is around. Sometimes "closed" and "open" swapping can occur simultaneously at one party.

Swinging appears to be a rare form of sexual activity among couples. Estimates are that only 1% to 2% of couples have ever engaged in this behavior (Bartell, 1970; Hunt, 1974). The consequences of swinging do not differ very much from the consequences of nonconsensual extramarital sex. Like those who have nonconsensual extramarital sex, swingers range from those who desire no social or emotional relationships with their partners to those who seek close, lasting relationships (Gilmartin, 1975).

> I was married 11 years and had three children. I am now separated, in the process of divorce, and have been living with another man whom I will marry when the divorce is final. Sex was totally unsatisfactory with my former husband and he threw me into a "swapping" situation. The one I swapped with is the one I intend to marry! I discovered with him that I am not frigid and now at age 34, I am finally fulfilled sexually.
>
> (Tavris and Sadd, 1974)

GROUP MARRIAGE *Group marriage,* also known as multilateral marriage, is a voluntary family group of three or more persons that is committed to and maintains an ongoing relationship with more than one person in what is regarded by the participants as "being married" (Constantine et al., 1972). Group marriage is a restructuring of the conventional marriage in that it may involve bringing people together in a multilateral sexual relationship. It is not bigamy (being married while still with a spouse) or polygamy (a spouse with several other mates), since it does not involve deception.

Multilateral marriages can take many forms. The greater the number of people, especially if children are involved, the more complex the relationship. People can enter a multilateral marriage for the same reasons they enter any other marital relationship. They may love more than one partner, or they may feel that additional people make for greater personal growth. In the multilateral marriage, people can have multiple sexual partners, rear others' children, give and receive love with more than one person, and, in general, experience what they feel are close human relationships that might ordinarily be experienced in a monogamous marriage.

However, difficulties regarding child-rearing practices, financial arrangements and budget, privacy, and division of work do arise, not to mention the criticism that is rendered by neighbors, friends, and relatives. Putting it another way, the high divorce rate in the United States today indicates that many people are having a great deal of trouble surviving in a two-person relationship. Adding more people can compound the problem. Because of the increased complexity of group marriages, their survival rate is rather short, lasting from several months to a few years (Constantine et al., 1972).

THE OLDER ADULT AND SEX

It is generally thought that people who are older (over 50) have no need or desire for sexual expression. Young people, when asked if they can imagine their parents engaging in sexual behavior, often respond with a "No." The idea that many of the young people in society think that older people lack the desire for sexual expression only reinforces negative feelings among older adults about their own sexuality. However, a decrease in sexual functioning is not a necessary accompaniment of aging.

Sexual Behavior Among the Elderly

Although sexual behavior may decline somewhat with age, research indicates that interest in sexual activity continues well into old age. In one study, it was shown that one out of every six persons has an increased interest in sex as they get older (Lobsenz, 1975). It should be noted that sexual activity does not have to be thought of only in terms of sexual intercourse. Large numbers of older people masturbate, and many continue to engage in sexual intercourse while they are in their nineties. To a large degree, the extent of sexual activity is dependent upon being healthy and having a sex partner. Many elderly people cannot engage in sexual activity because they are in such ill health that they have a difficult time simply taking care of their basic needs, and in many cases, the husband or the wife has died.

FIGURE 16.1 Older couple engaged in sexual intercourse.

Physical Changes in the Female

As the female ages, many changes begin to take place in her body. A decline in the production of estrogen may cause the walls of the vagina to become thin and lose their elasticity (the vagina of the younger woman has thick, elastic walls). Since the walls of the vagina become thinner, sexual intercourse may become uncomfortable. Sometimes the bladder and urethra can also become irritated. Since the width and depth of the vagina also decrease with age, sexual intercourse may prove to be difficult. The diminished production of vaginal lubrication also can make sexual intercourse painful. In younger women, vaginal lubrication takes place 15 to 30 seconds after the onset of excitement, whereas in older women, lubrication may not occur for 4 or 5 minutes. Although the clitoris may shrink with age, it will still respond to sexual stimulation. Prolonged and appropriate clitoral stimulation can serve to produce vaginal lubrication adequate for sexual intercourse. If sexual intercourse is desired and lubrication is not adequate, a water-soluble jelly can be used in the vagina for intromission.

Masters and Johnson (1966) found that those women who maintain a sexually active life will have fewer physiological sex-related problems as they get older. For this reason, Masters and Johnson recommend frequent sexual activity as a means of increasing a woman's ability to engage in more comfortable sexual intercourse with age.

Although sexual behavior may decline somewhat with age, research indicates that interest in sexual activity continues well into old age. (Photo, Elizabeth Crews)

Like younger women, the older woman undergoes the four phases of the sexual response cycle, but with some changes. As we mentioned, vaginal lubrication may diminish with age; however, it will occur during the excitement phase. In the plateau phase, there is much less elevation of the uterus and, therefore, a shortened vaginal canal. At the orgasmic platform, the young woman may experience eight to twelve vaginal contractions, whereas the older woman will have only four or five. In some older women, orgasm may cause painful contractions of the uterus. This effect usually means that hormone levels are low. However, the problem can be alleviated with hormone replacement therapy (HRT). The resolution phase in women is more rapid as she gets older.

Physical Changes in the Male

In the aging male, just as in the aging female, many physiological changes occur during sexual response. To best understand these changes, we will examine them within the framework of the sexual response cycle.

EXCITEMENT PHASE

During this phase, it may take longer for a male to experience an erection than it did when he was younger. While the speed with which an erection can occur has diminished, his capacity to have an erection does not.

PLATEAU PHASE

This phase is where many older men have an advantage over their younger counterparts. During the plateau phase, the male can maintain an erection for a long time after he reaches a pleasurable level of sexual tension. Younger men usually have a stronger drive to ejaculate more rapidly than older men.

EJACULATORY PHASE

There are two changes that occur during this phase. First, there is an "inevitability stage," in which the man feels he is going to ejaculate and can no longer hold back. The second is the "expulsion stage," in which the ejaculate is expelled. After the age of 50, the inevitability stage is shortened from 4 to 7 seconds to 2 to 4 seconds. Sometimes it may not occur. For some men, a one-stage ejaculation is common. In older men, the expulsion of semen during ejaculation is less forceful than in younger men. In addition, the amount of semen is less.

RESOLUTION PHASE

In this phase, the man can lose his erection within seconds after ejaculating. He also may have a longer refractory period—he may not be capable of having another erection for several hours. This is usually not the case with younger men. Although younger men may not be able to maintain an erection for as long a time period as an older man, they may be able to attain another erection shortly after ejaculating.

If older people understand the differences in response cycles between them, they can take steps that will insure that sexual activity will remain pleasurable. In cases where sexual activity is inhibited due to changes in hormone production, injections of the needed hormones can often serve to help the elderly couple maintain their sexual sharing.

There is no doubt that sex education and counseling for the elderly can help alleviate many of the physiological concerns they may have regarding sexual functioning.

Psychosexual Changes in Men and Women

As men and women age, various psychological phenomena occur. Middle-age women, after menopause, may go through a period of depression. One cause given for the onset of depression is the "empty nest syndrome" (Bart, 1971), caused by the grown-up child's leaving home. Sometimes the loss of a child leaves the husband or wife with a void, without the role of father or mother. Yet other researchers feel that there is no such thing as an "empty nest syndrome." When children leave home, some couples find that they can have more time for each other and they can share and give support to each other in their new roles.

Many of the psychological problems related to sex and aging can be the result of physiological health problems. For example, a person who has had a heart attack or stroke may refrain from sexual activity even though this activity may not be harmful. Many women who have a *hysterectomy* (surgical removal of the uterus and sometimes the ovaries) erroneously believe that their sex life is over. If the ovaries are removed, the woman will be deprived of the hormones estrogen and progesterone. A lack of these hormones may cause the symptoms of menopause, and the woman may lose interest in sex. However, injections of supplemental hormones can help the woman regain her capacity for sexual expression.

Removal of the prostate gland in men (prostatectomy) may cause psychological problems. The prostatectomy will cause a decrease in the amount of semen ejaculated. If retrograde ejaculation has occurred, no semen will be ejaculated. While physiologically the male can still enjoy sex, the psychological barriers that may be incurred by a prostatectomy can have long-term implications. Sometimes impotence is one implication.

Regardless of whether or not elderly people are male or female, married or unmarried, they still need to have the same outlets to express their sexuality as any other age group in society. (Photo, Victor Friedman)

As we have stated before, the old adage that "sex in the older years is taboo" can serve as a deterrent to older people's sexual interplay. Often it is the younger children in the family as well as friends who reinforce the myth that sex is not as necessary as one ages. As a result, many older people accept this viewpoint. They feel guilty or morally decadent if they have sexual desires. As a result, they may refrain from sexual activity. As Masters and Johnson (1966) so succinctly emphasize, the best way to have healthy sexual relations during the older years of life is to engage frequently in sexual relations with one's partner.

Perhaps one of the institutions that has served to perpetuate the "double standard" of sex for the aging (young people can, old people cannot) is the nursing or senior citizen's home. Although some of society's views appear to be changing regarding the propensity of older adults for sexual expression, many homes segregate their residents by sex. They have different recreation rooms, dining areas, and residential wings. In an age where people are living longer, it is safe to assume that the population living in nursing homes is increasing. Yet they continue to be deprived of the right to express themselves sexually, even though there is an abundance of research that indicates that both male and female elderly persons have sexual desires.

Some of the desexualized settings in nursing homes are a result of the ignorance of the administrators of these homes as well as the children of the parents confined. Most people, if they walked into a nursing home, would probably be upset if they saw two elderly people kissing or holding hands. Their initial instinct might be to believe that the home perpetuated something "abnormal" or "unnatural." Yet if these same people walked into a friend's home and noticed their friend's daughter and her boyfriend holding hands and giving each other a kiss, they would probably not get as upset. What is even more hypocritical is the fact that in many nursing homes, a husband and wife must be separated. The fact of the matter remains that most nursing home supervisors would find it less troublesome to let their residents take care of their sexual needs.

Older women, more than older men in our society, have two double standards with which to contend. The first we mentioned — sex among older people is immoral, whereas sex among younger people is moral. The second — because she is a woman, she therefore must be much more careful than the man in what she decides to do sexually. For many single, older women, the only alternative to societal acceptance of her sexual behavior is to remarry. Remarrying, however, presents a great problem. There are relatively fewer men than women in the older age group alive, and only a small number who would choose to marry. Many couples decide to live together without marriage, since they might have a greater income single than married, because of present Social Security laws.

Regardless of whether or not elderly persons are male or female, married or unmarried, they have the same need to express their sexuality as any other age group in society.

SUMMARY STATEMENTS

- *Children exhibit a sexual response as soon as they are born.*
- *Masturbation is common among young children.*
- *Children are capable of romantic love by age 3 or 4.*
- *By ages 8 to 12, one-third of males and females have heterosexual contact.*
- *During adolescence, young people "rehearse" for adulthood.*
- *Many adolescents engage in petting.*
- *Half of all teenagers 15 to 19 years old have had sexual intercourse.*
- *One out of ten teenage girls becomes pregnant out-of-wedlock before age 18.*

- *Every form of foreplay is used in today's marriages more so than years ago.*
- *Masturbation is common among married people.*
- *Marital sex is more satisfying today than in the past.*
- *There are several types of marriages as well as types of extramarital sex.*
- *Older people have a need and desire for sexual expression.*
- *The characteristics of the sexual response cycle change with age.*
- *Many sex-related problems of older people are psychological, not physical.*

SUGGESTED READINGS

Butler, Robert, and Myrna Lewis. *Sex After Sixty: A Guide for Men and Women for Their Later Years*. New York: Harper and Row, 1976.

Rubin, Isadore. *Sexual Life After Sixty*. New York: Basic Books, 1965.

Sontag, Susan. "The Double Standard of Aging," *Saturday Review*, September 23, 1972, pp. 23–25.

Tavris, Carol, and Susan Sadd. *The Redbook Report on Female Sexuality*. New York: Dell Publishing Company, 1975.

A LOOK AT YOUR LIFESTYLE

You discover that while your spouse is out of town on a business trip, he or she has an extramarital affair. What is the first thing that would enter your mind? _____

_____

SEXUALITY AND THE LIFE CYCLE

GATHERING INFORMATION

List two reasons it would be conceivable that someone married to you would engage in extramarital sex. _____

_____

List two reasons it would be conceivable that someone married to you would *not* engage in extramarital sex. _____

_____

EVALUATING THE INFORMATION

List three criteria you would examine in determining whether or not you would engage in extramarital sex. _____

_____

Which criterion would be the most important and why?

_____

MAKING RESPONSIBLE DECISIONS

In a process of three to five steps, identify how you would make a decision about the future of your relationship if your spouse engaged in extramarital sex. The last step should indicate your final decision about your relationship. _____

_____

_____

_____

SEVENTEEN

Sex and the Law

You may be surprised to learn that many people in your state are breaking the law when they engage in one of the following sex acts: premarital sex, oral–genital sex, homosexual contact, anal intercourse, coitus with a prostitute, extramarital coitus, and cohabitation, to name a few. Yet most people usually ignore laws of sexual ethics. Since they probably will not be put in jail for practicing these behaviors unless they were committed in public, they are not a public issue.

Two aspects of sex and the law are major issues — rape and pornography. You probably know someone fairly well who has been raped. Perhaps a rape or an attempted rape has been perpetrated upon you (of course, this is less likely if you are a male). Or perhaps you travel with friends when you go out at night because of the fear you may have about being raped. There is no doubt that the lifestyle of many of today's women is affected by the possibility that a rape can occur at any time and in almost any area of the country.

443

I refuse to walk out of my dorm when it gets dark outside. Several girls have been raped on campus this year, and I do not want to be another statistic. Could you believe that? I'm afraid to walk on my college campus for fear of being raped. I even have one of the guys in my evening class walk me back to the dorm — that's how scared I am.

One of the ways of preventing rape is to become aware of the severity of this crime as well as the options that are available to women who find themselves confronted by this problem. The information in this chapter will, we hope, be a valuable tool for both men and women.

One other aspect of sex and the law that we will touch upon involves pornography. Specifically, we are in the midst of a controversy between what is and what is not allowable under the First Amendment of the U.S. Constitution. The decisions that are made by communities and the government regarding what we can and cannot view and hear certainly can have an impact upon how we choose to lead our sexual lifestyle. Should *someone else* have the right to dictate laws that may deny you the opportunity to view erotic material? Should *you* have the right to determine for *others* what *they* should and should not view? These are only a few of the issues that are examined in this chapter. Each of the areas we have mentioned can have a direct influence on your sexual lifestyle.

GATHERING INFORMATION

Sex and the law is a very complex phenomenon. One of the reasons for this complexity is that different people hold different views regarding what is appropriate. For example, there are various theories regarding the causes of rape. The theory you believe can be a deciding factor in how far you would go in seeing that a rapist is prosecuted. For example, if you believe a man rapes because he suffers from a negligent upbringing, you may be more lenient toward him than if you believed his only motive was to degrade women.

Other issues arise in other areas related to sex and the law. Therefore, we focus on three aspects of sex and the law in this chapter. We look at the causes, incidence, theory, prevention, and treatment of rape. We also examine the laws that pertain to the activities in which we can and cannot take part, both within and outside of marriage. Finally, we examine one of the more controversial areas of human sexuality, pornography. We examine the difficulties involved in determining whether or not something is obscene. We also examine the difficulties others have had trying to ascertain what obscenity is as well as its implications for human behavior.

EVALUATING THE INFORMATION

An examination of the information in this chapter will help you to clarify the issues as they relate to your sexuality. We hope you will consider the following questions:

1. What is obscenity?
2. What criteria would I use in considering whether or not something is obscene?
3. Does the government or anyone else have the right to dictate what is appropriate for me?
4. Should some of the laws regarding sexual behavior during marriage bother me?
5. How can I prevent a rape from occurring?
6. What should I do if I am in a rape situation?
7. Who is the typical rapist?
8. Is pornography harmful?

Since some of the information in this chapter is predicated upon your own beliefs, you cannot be considered right or wrong concerning the opinion you hold. You are to evaluate this information and clarify your beliefs. Some of the information in this chapter is very clear-cut. We hope you can incorporate this knowledge and use it in the development of healthy sexuality.

MAKING RESPONSIBLE DECISIONS

In this chapter on sex and the law are what we consider to be some of the "basics." Regardless of what decisions you decide to make, it is important that you have a good foundation for your decisions. For example, you may have to vote on whether or not a certain theater in your neighborhood should be permitted to show X-rated films. Perhaps you will have to educate your child about what to do or not to do when a stranger approaches. Or you may become a proponent of reforming societal sex laws. Regardless of the decisions you need to make about issues related to sexuality and the law, you will need to know the basic facts. We hope the facts in this chapter will help you to become a responsible and rational decisionmaker.

RAPE

The sexual offense that has received the most publicity over the past few years is rape. A clear definition of rape is often difficult to determine, because the legal definition varies from state to state. However, most definitions consider rape to be sexual intercourse with a person without the consent of that person. Sexual intercourse that occurs by force or deception or because another person is too incompetent to give consent (under the influence of alcohol or drugs, mentally deficient, or unconscious) can also be considered rape.

Statutory rape is sexual intercourse with a girl who is under the age of consent—regardless of whether consent has or has not been granted. The age of consent varies in most states. The state with the youngest age of consent (12 years) is Mississippi. For most states, the average age of consent for sexual intercourse is 18 (Poor, 1976). A man can be imprisoned on statutory rape charges even if a girl seems much older than she really is or if she lied about her age.

Recently the California state statutory rape law was challenged because it was felt that this law, as it currently exists, discriminates against men. Women and girls cannot be charged with statutory rape for having sex with boys not yet 18. However, on March 23, 1981, the Supreme Court, by a five-to-four vote, upheld the law that makes it a crime for men or boys in California to have sexual intercourse with consenting females under the age of 18.

It is possible for a woman to be convicted of rape if she is an accessory in forcing coitus on another woman. She can also be convicted and imprisoned for rape if she forces a man (older or younger) to engage in sexual intercourse with her. Such a rape is very rarely reported. After all, in our culture, a man is considered "macho" if he has sexual intercourse with a woman; so why would he want to jeopardize his masculinity? Yet a man who is forced to engage in sexual intercourse with a woman probably would not be in the appropriate frame of mind to enjoy himself.

Men can also be raped by other men. Homosexual rape occurs commonly in prisons.

The definition of rape has gone through some changes over the past few years. At one time, almost all definitions of rape indicated that forced sexual intercourse with one's wife did not constitute rape. However, the famous *Rideout* v. *Rideout* case (1979) changed the way society began to look at what is now termed "marital rape." The Rideout case provided the first significant test of Oregon's revised rape statute, which recognizes that neither marriage nor cohabitation is a defense against rape (Bonventre, 1979). Although John Rideout was not convicted of rape, much to the dismay of many feminist groups, the publicity created has brought attitudinal changes in society toward marital rape. Since the changes in the Oregon law, other states such as Iowa, Delaware, and New Jersey have revised their marital rape laws.

Incidence of Rape

Since most of the research about rape indicates that its incidence is highly underreported (as much as 80%), it is difficult to ascertain the actual number of rapes that occur in the United States each year (Amir, 1971). However, some estimates indicate that as many as 100,000 to 500,000 women are raped each year (Offir, 1975). According to these statistics, rape is one of the most frequently committed violent crimes in America today.

Characteristics of the Rapist

The typical male rapist is 20 to 24 years old, comes from a low-income, culturally deprived background, and has a lower IQ than those convicted of other violent crimes (Ruff et al., 1976). In many cases, the rapist comes from a broken home in which very little supervision was given. Interestingly, most rapists are or have been married (Rada, 1977).

Contrary to what many believe, the rapist's victim can be anyone from small infants to elderly persons. However, the majority of the victims of rape are between 15 and 25 years of age.

Patterns of Rape

When many people think of rape, they often picture a man lurking in a dark alley, waiting to attack his intended victim violently. While this type of example may be accurate in some cases, it does not describe the typical rape scene. Paul Wilson (1978), in his systematic study of unreported rape, identified patterns of rape that are generally considered typical. These patterns are described as follows:

RANDOM BLITZ RAPE

This type of rape was described in the above paragraph and is a reflection of the public stereotype of rape. In this type of rape, there is typically no interaction between the victim and the offender. The rapist suddenly and suprisingly attacks his victim—usually outdoors in parks and in streets. In some cases, the random blitz rape can occur in the victim's home.

SPECIFIC BLITZ RAPE

This type of rape is similar to the random blitz rape, but the rapist observes his victim over a period of time and carefully calculates his moves before attempting rape.

WHITE COLLAR RAPE

Typically this type of rapist is a professional or semiprofessional who uses his position to gain the confidence of a client or colleague. Usually, this type of rapist establishes a relationship with his intended victim, so that this victim will be raped by deceit. In other words, the rapist will lure the victim to a setting to commit a rape on the pretext of discussing some nonpersonal issues.

POWER WITH TRICKERY RAPE

This pattern of rape occurs when the victim does not have the ability to consent or deny, because of her stage of personality or emotional development. Often, this type of victim is a child. For example, in some cases of incest, the father may tell his daughter that she is at an age where she should know about sex, so he proceeds to perform sexual intercourse with her as a means of educating her.

FAMILY RAPE

This pattern of rape differs from power with trickery rape in that deliberate force is used by one family member against another—husband against wife, father against daughter, brother against sister, uncle against niece. Generally, the offender uses his familial role to catch the victim off guard in a situation that is isolated from other people.

CEREMONIAL RAPE

Ritualism and mysticism usually provide the setting for ceremonial rape. For example, to become a street gang member, a boy may be required to provide a girl to have sexual intercourse with fellow gang members. In most cases, females state that they are unwilling victims who are powerless to prevent the act.

FRIENDSHIP RAPE

In friendship rape, the victim and the offender have been friends for a period of time. The offender then uses the friendship position an an opportunity for and justification of the attack. Force rather than trickery is most often used to achieve sexual gratification.

SITUATIONAL RAPE

In situational rape careful arrangements are made by the rapist to lure his victim to him. Usually the rapist has known his victim for several hours before his attack. In this type of rape, people may often be used in collusion with the rapist to entice the victim to a particular place.

It appears that in rape culturally prescribed norms are used to define role expectancies for males and females. These role expectancies establish patterns of behavior that are then used by the offender against the victim.

Theories of Rape

Several theories have been espoused concerning the causes of rape. The traditional psychiatric position views the rapist as having a disturbed personality probably resulting from a disturbed family life during childhood. In contrast, many feminists as well as nonfeminists view rape as a crime against the woman herself and do not view the man as a victim. In this view, the sexual aspect of rape is deemphasized and the need for power and dominance by men is emphasized. The structure of society is such that men are placed in the position in which they are supposed to be dominant sexually. In this position, the woman is supposed to resist and control the situation, and the man is to initiate it and move forward. However, miscommunication is often a factor in this process that can lead to rape. A woman's "no" or "maybe" or even "yes" often leads a man to be forceful. Even in ongoing relationships, this miscommunication can cause the man to use force. In another view of rape the act is seen as an expression of nonconformist values. Thus, for some individuals, rape may be used as a rationale against a society that practices discrimination. In essence, the rapist says, "If it's OK to show prejudice in one setting, it can be shown in another."

Whether or not one or another theory of the cause of rape can be accepted as valid is open to a great deal of debate. If most men are exposed to the influences discussed above, it would seem logical that most men would be rapists. Yet, of course, the majority are not.

The Rape Victim

Rape trauma syndrome was a term first used by Burgess and Holmstrom (1974) to describe the immediate phase of disorganization and the long-term process of reorganization resulting from both attempted and successful forcible rape. The *acute* reactions of rape can last for a few weeks. This phase is marked by feelings of anger, fear, depression, and tension. The woman may spend countless hours crying. In many cases, she may be very quiet and keep her feelings held inside. Physical reactions may occur in the acute phase that can develop into long-term effects. Among some of these effects are bruises and cuts that were received when the victim was fighting off the attacker. Genitourinary disturbance is the most common type of complaint. If anal sex was attempted, the woman may complain about bruises and tissue damage to the rectum. Sometimes bruises are common in the throat if oral sex was forced. Many women will complain about headaches and sleep pattern disturbances, and the majority of women will complain about vaginal discharge, itching, and problems urinating.

Many effects of rape can be long-term. For example, if a woman was raped inside of a car, she may have a fear of getting into cars and, as a result, may never enter one again.

Generally, a common response is avoidance of all men. In one of our classes, a young man spoke to us of a great concern he had about his wife. She was accosted one night on her way home from work and was forced to perform oral sex. After she had come home, she vomited because she found the thought of oral sex, especially with a stranger, to be repulsive. For the next week, she did not allow her husband to touch her. This reaction is very typical of most victims of sexual abuse. We referred the victim to counseling, and after several sessions, she again responded sexually to her husband.

For many rape victims, sexuality is not the only aspect of life that changes. If a victim is raped in her home, she may become fearful of living alone. She may go to great lengths not to divulge her telephone number or address to anyone. She might spend large sums of money on elaborate devices such as locks and alarm systems to prevent anyone from breaking into her home. In essence, her lifestyle could begin to become an extreme form of self-preservation, and a once gregarious person could be prevented from interacting with others as she used to do.

Many rape victims tend to become cynical and somewhat paranoid about society. In many cases, the victim may begin to view all men as cold and cruel. She may view society as a jungle. Many rape victims find great comfort in becoming involved in politics. They may become active in feminist groups as a means of rectifying what they believe are unjust policies and practices perpetrated upon women by society (Wilson, 1978).

At one time, I felt that all feminists were a group of women who joined other women and became activists because they were too ugly or harsh to be attractive to men. Did my mind change quickly after I was raped. I found the rights women are fighting for to be very justified. Rape is a political act which is carried out by men on women. The best way to deal with this crime is to attack it politically.

Unreported Rape

As we mentioned previously, most rapes go unreported. They go unreported for some of the following reasons: a desire to forget about the rape; fear of relatives' reactions; a desire to avoid creating a scene in which the victim's sexual history is uncovered and made public; the social stigma of rape; the insensitivity of the police; and the fear of a partner's reaction. Throughout the past several years, programs on television have shown that a woman who follows through, trying to convict an alleged rapist, is subject to demeaning cross-examination in the courts. As a result, many women who have been raped have subsequently been reticent about pursuing court action against a rapist.

However, the rape laws are changing to accommodate women. For example, many states are now changing their laws so that a woman's sexual history cannot be brought up in the trial. In the past, the offender was the only one whose sexual history could be held secret. Today, more and more, rape is being looked at as an act of violence and coercion as opposed to an act of passion. If a woman was robbed of her money while she was on her way to the grocery store, the courts would not ask her to explain why she was walking alone nor would they ask her if she tried to resist her attacker. But if she were raped, these points might be brought up. Today, many courts are coming to the realization that rape, like many other crimes, is a form of assault and can be treated as a felony. It is to be hoped that this change in attitude will lead more women to report rapes and increase the conviction rate for men who have committed this crime.

Another procedure that may help to increase the rate of reporting rape is the opening of rape crisis centers. In cities that have these centers, a woman is often told to call the center first, before she calls the police. She is then given directions about legal procedures and can also use the rape crisis center for follow-up counseling.

Protection against Rape

Rape can have an impact upon many facets of a woman's lifestyle. Popular magazines are replete with articles about little things a woman can do to minimize attacks. For example, some articles may indicate the vulnerable spots on a male's body where he is very sensitive to a blow or provide hints about how to minimize the chances of getting raped (i.e., if you live alone, place only your first initial on your mailbox so that an intended rapist cannot tell if you are male or female). While these articles are helpful to women, there are other areas that should also be covered. For example, the fact that women are becoming more open to sexuality in nonmarital relationships has created more problems in the case of sexual force. The capacity to communicate sexual interest accurately and clearly by women and the capacity to receive it in the same spirit by men have not been equal (Gagnon, 1977).

With new kinds of sociosexual relationships, there are three types of protection that seem feasible (Gagnon, 1977). First, a clear-cut decision must be made about sexual intent in a relationship. More specifically, the promise of sex should not be used by a woman to hang on to a partner, since changes in a relationship are bound to occur. As a second protection, a man should abandon his role as initiator in a sexual encounter when the woman indicates that she is not interested in his advances. After all, sex with a member of the "same team" will be much more enjoyable than sex with a member of the "opposing team." The third protection we mentioned previously. That is, the importance of rape as a sex act should be reduced, and the significance of rape as an act of violence should be increased. This view of rape can help to remove the stigma that a woman who is raped is "naughty" and "impure," and we can begin to focus on rape as violence.

Male Victims of Rape

Although a man has very little chance of being raped by a woman, he may be raped by another man, desirous of anal intercourse. These situations most often occur inside prisons. Like men who rape women, men who rape other men in prison do so as a means of showing aggression and power. In many prisons, homosexuality is coercive. The stronger and more "con-wise" inmates often band together in what are known as "pressure cliques" in order to extort sexual favors from weaker peers (Kirkham, 1972). Coercive homosexual exploitation in prisons is almost impossible to control because of the impossibility of providing sufficient custodial supervision. Most prison staff usually deal with this problem by transferring sexually aggressive "wolves" and trying to isolate weaker inmates for their own protection (Kirkham, 1972).

Myths about Rape

Despite the information that has been presented by the media, there exist several myths among the public regarding rape.

"Rape is impossible." Many people feel that rape is impossible without willing consent. Nothing could be further from the truth. A woman in a rape situation might—and possibly *should*—give unwilling consent when she is aware of the danger of resistance.

"Some women invite rape." This myth is perpetuated by the idea that a woman who is "wined and dined" by a man must expect to reciprocate at the end of an evening. Another false idea is the notion that a woman who dresses in revealing clothing is tempting a rapist. However, most rapists do not rape for sexual release. Their sexual motive is intimidation.

"Women like to be treated with violence." This idea stems from the rape fantasies that many women have. However, there is a great distinction between fantasy and reality. In reality, the woman does not control the setting, the situation, and the selection of the rapist.

These are some of the kinds of myths that instill fear in women, which, in turn, causes them to "colonize" (Brownmiller, 1975). For example, it is not as safe for women as it is for men to walk the streets alone at night or to hitch-hike. Many activities often take place in groups, and group activities are, in essence, restricting.

Protection and Prevention of Rape

While a great deal has been written about rape, much controversy exists regarding what to do and what not to do in a threatening situation. Among the "stock" responses to a threatening situation are (1) resist if the assailant has a weapon; (2) use self-defense tactics, vomit, defecate, or act out an epileptic seizure; and (3) always plan your next move. However, these tactics are difficult. There are many different types of rapists. A woman cannot know what the reaction of her rapist will be. While one rapist might brutally beat a woman who resists his attempts, another might be scared and permit the woman to escape. In one study, it was found that of women who resist rape, half successfully avoid it, and the other half are brutally beaten.

The best way to avoid rape is to minimize conditions associated with rape. Plan when and how night travels will occur, look into the back seat of a car before getting in, keep car doors locked while traveling, have keys out and ready to be placed in house or car doors, and do not allow strangers to enter the home. While it is nearly impossible to stop rape, proper precautions will reduce its frequency.

If You Have Been Raped

If a rape has occurred, the following steps should be taken:

1. Call the police *immediately*. The longer you wait, the greater the chance to forget clues.

2. Get medical attention.

3. Do not shower or wash. Sometimes traces of the rapist's skin or hair can be found underneath the fingernails. Do not douche. Clues may be

A range of actions from running to self-defense can be taken by a woman to prevent rape. (Photo by Les Mahon)

found on your person that may be helpful in the identification and conviction of the rapist.

4. Provide the police with *any* details that can be remembered.

Rape can be a traumatic experience with long-term psychological effects. For those women who need help, support groups of other women, psychologists, and other professionals can at least help the victim recover, if not make her stronger than before the rape.

Sexual Harassment

Tied in very closely with rape is sexual harassment in business as well as in college. Numerous suits have been filed recently by women charging that they have been denied job promotions or better grades in school because they refused to submit to the sexual advances of their employers or professors. In one poll at a California college, one fourth of the faculty said they had been sexually active with students and another fourth said they would like to be (*Time Magazine*, 1980).

Many feminists have focused on the issue of sexual harassment on

At a NOW meeting, a demonstration of defense against a rapist is given. (Photo by Bettye Lane)

college campuses. They argue that females are being exploited because professors have crucial power over a coed's grades and career. In one of the more famous cases, a Yale professor was accused by an undergraduate of sexual harassment because he offered her an A in exchange for sexual favors (Munich, 1978). However, the suit, filed against Yale for lack of protection against sexual harassment, did not hold up in court. Yet another professor in California was fired from his position because he was accused of embracing, fondling, and propositioning five of his female students.

It appears that today many women are becoming less reticent about reporting sexual harassment. The increased awareness of sexual pressures imposed by people in traditional positions of power is finally being challenged—and those who do not hold these positions are finally realizing that they also have power.

SEXUAL BEHAVIOR AND THE LAW

Throughout history laws have been established that have dictated what people could and could not do sexually. Many of our present-day laws are based upon what were beliefs in the Judeo-Christian tradition of sexual ethics. If these laws were enforced in all cases, the overwhelming

Another procedure which may help to increase the rate of reporting rape is the opening of rape crisis centers. In cities which have this center, a woman is often told to call there first before she calls the police if she has been raped. She is then given directions and can also use the rape crisis center for follow-up counseling. This photograph shows a simulated rape counseling situation at a New York Women Against Rape Clinic. (Photo by Michal Heron 1981)

majority of adults in the United States would be in jail. Many of these laws do not coincide with the personal sexual standards and values held by most people today.

Marriage Laws

Perhaps our most restrictive rules pertaining to sex and the law exist in marriage. Most people assume that what two married people decide to do within the confines of their own home is legal. This assumption is incorrect. If a husband and wife engage in sexual activity other than kissing, caressing, and sexual intercourse, they have broken the law in many states. Acts such as cunnilingus, fellatio, and anal intercourse are considered felonies, and people who perform them can be sentenced to 15 years in prison in California, to 30 years in Connecticut. And in Georgia, such a "crime against nature" could condemn the practitioner to life imprisonment at hard labor. Interestingly someone who engages in a sexual act with an animal in Georgia, can be imprisoned for only 5 years (Talese, 1980).

Premarital and postmarital sex is restricted in many states. *Fornication* (sex between unmarried people), cohabitation, and extramarital sex are practices that some states still ban. However, these laws, for the most part, are not enforced. If, on the other hand, two persons engage in an illegal act in public, these laws can then be used against them. For example, even within the confines of one's home, privacy must be maintained. If a husband and wife attract a crowd outside their house while they are engaging in oral–genital sex near the front window with the shades up, they can be arrested.

Kinship Laws and Sex

In all states, it is illegal for sexual intercourse to occur between parents and children, brothers and sisters, and uncles or aunts and nieces or nephews. In some states first cousins can marry; in other states they cannot. Most states restrict sexual contact between stepparents and stepchildren.

Homosexuality and the Law

While it may come as a surprise to many people, homosexuality in itself is legal in all states. The *acts* in which homosexuals engage are, however, considered crimes. Therefore, when one hears of a homosexual arrest, the person is being arrested because of participation in an illegal act (oral–genital or anal–genital sex) and not because of homosexuality. Since people are protected by the search-and-seizure provisions of the U.S. Constitution, it is very difficult to arrest a homosexual for engaging in sexual activities unless these activities occur in public.

There is no doubt that laws regarding both heterosexual and homosexual behavior need to be reexamined and rewritten to reflect contemporary values, attitudes, and practices. The Wolfenden Commission in England and the American Law Institute are study groups that were commissioned to review the status of sex laws and recommend appropriate changes. However, many of our local and state legislatures have remained opposed to reforming our sex laws. As a result, various individuals have challenged these laws, claiming that they are unconstitutional. Several states have been forced to reform some of their sex laws.

PORNOGRAPHY

One of the most controversial concerns affecting human sexuality and societal values revolves around pornography. Issues related to pornography have been examined from the community level through the Supreme Court. Even the Congress of the United States and a Presidential Commission have spent numerous hours trying to objectify rules and regulations by which pornography can be governed. Many of the problems related to pornography are difficult, if not impossible, to resolve.

One of the most controversial concerns affecting sexuality and societal values revolves around pornography. This photograph shows an anti-pornography demonstration in Times Square, New York City. (Photo by Bill Anderson)

Defining Pornography

Establishing a clear-cut definition of pornography has been attempted many times throughout history. However, many facets of society have their own views about what is and what is not pornographic.

As a cornerstone to any discussion about pornography, we need to identify the laws governing the rights of an individual to express his or her ideas. Accordingly, the First Amendment of the U.S. Constitution states:

> Congress shall make no law respecting an establishment of religion, or prohibiting the free exercise thereof; or abridging the freedom of speech, or of the press; or the right of the people peaceably to assemble, and to petition the Government for a redress of grievances.

Although this amendment refers only to "speech," it is taken by many to include nonverbal conduct that could serve as a means of expression (*Thornhill* v. *Alabama,* 1940). Hence, writings, photographs, movies, paintings, and other symbolic conduct are recognized as being within the purview of its intended scope.

Yet the courts have held that *obscenity* is not protected by the First Amendment (*Roth* v. *United States,* 1957). It is here that the controversy over pornography lies. In the famous *Roth* v. *United States* (1957) case, an attempt was made to ascertain what was "obscene" according to the Constitution. Thus, the following definition of obscenity, which is considered law today, has three elements:

1. The dominant theme of the material taken as a whole appeals to a prurient interest in sex.
2. The material is patently offensive because it affronts contemporary community standards relating to the description or representation of sexual matters.
3. The material is utterly without redeeming social value.

Each of these three elements of obscenity carries some sort of ambiguity—specifically the terms "prurient interest," "community standards," and "redeeming social value."

Prurient interest is difficult to define in a way that is acceptable to all people. The California Legislature (1970) has construed *prurient* to mean "shameful" or "morbid." But the question arises of "shameful" and "morbid" to whom.

Community standards implies that we know what a community is, assuming we can come to an understanding about what is obscene. Is it a county, city, housing subdivision, state? So we have another problem. Is a "standard" something that will be acceptable to all within a "community"? Is it not possible that several sets of "standards" could exist in a "community"? Should something be suppressed just because it is looked upon unfavorably by a community? On the other hand, should something that is undesirable be sanctioned? Again, we are left with a matter that is open to interpretation.

Redeeming social value. Even if we assume we can come to agreement about the first two terms, this term still needs to be interpreted.

> Although court decisions following *Roth* have virtually erased any viability from the word "redeeming," it strangely remains in the formula and in the instructions the judge must give the jury. And the issue is also very unclear as to how far the trial judge must go in making an independent determination of the existence of social value.
>
> The concept additionally snags upon the question of "social value to whom?" This is frequently raised when psychiatrists testify that exposure to pornography is helpful in the treatment of certain patients, thereby implying that obscenity has some intrinsic social value. Is this enough to give protection to materials which have no such value to the rest of the population? If not, how large must the benefitted group be before the material or conduct becomes constitutionally acceptable?
>
> (Warren, 1970)

The fact remains that it is difficult to determine what is considered obscene. The result has been that cases of alleged obscenity are difficult to prosecute. This leaves us with the dilemma of trying to define *obscene* and *pornograply* — words we will use throughout the remainder of this chapter. For the purpose of clarifying further discussion, the following definitions will be used:

Obscene will refer to material that is either sexual or nonsexual that is abhorrent to one's accepted standards of morality.

Pornography will refer to material in literature, art, motion pictures, or other means of communication and expression that has been developed with the intention of evoking sexual interest and arousal.

The Commission on Obscenity and Pornography

In 1967, the Commission on Obscenity and Pornography was established by Congress to study the effects of pornography upon behavior as well as to recommend a means by which pornography and obscenity traffic could be dealt with effectively. This commission was composed of judges, attorneys, sociologists, psychologists, educators, and representatives of the Catholic, Protestant, and Jewish faiths.

After a careful review of the research and materials that were collected, the Commission (1970) made the following conclusions:

- There is no evidence that exposure to or use of explicit sexual materials plays a significant role in the causation of social or individual harm such as crime, delinquency, sexual or nonsexual deviancy, or severe emotional disturbances.
- Explicit sexual materials are sought as a source of entertainment and information by substantial numbers of American adults.
- Present laws that attempt to legislate for adults in the area of obscenity have not been successful.
- The American public does not support the imposition of legal prohibitions upon the right of adults to read or see explicit sexual materials.
- There is a lack of consensus among Americans as to whether or not explicit sexual materials should be available to adults in our society, and the significant number of adults who wish to have access to such materials pose serious problems for the enforcement of legal prohibitions.
- Since obscenity laws are in the realm of speech and communication and since Americans deeply value the right to determine what to read and see, it would seem that the government should not interfere with these rights unless there is a clear threat of harm.
- The government should not seek to prohibit consensual distribution of sexual materials to adults.
- There is no reason to believe that eliminating government prohibitions upon the sexual materials that may be made available to adults would adversely affect the availability to the public of other books, magazines, and films.

- The Commission recognized the concern of many people that the lawful distribution of explicit sexual materials to adults might have a negative effect upon the individual morality of American citizens.

While these conclusions were based upon the recommendation of the majority of members of the Commission, there were some who wrote dissenting views. One dissenter wrote that obscenity corrupts and that this viewpoint lay within common sense, regardless of what the research indicated (Commission on Obscenity and Pornography, 1970). While the results of the Commission's findings are used today to judge issues related to pornography, there are many people who disagree with its conclusions. In fact, President Nixon is known to have rejected the Commission's findings because he felt his common sense held greater validity (Zurcher and Kirkpatrick, 1976). In addition to Nixon, the U.S. Senate rejected the Commission's findings.

The Effects of Pornography

One of the issues related to pornography is whether or not its effects can be detrimental or helpful to the people who are exposed to it. Therefore, we will examine some of the "pros" and "cons" of pornography.

THE "PROS" OF PORNOGRAPHY.

A surprising decision of the Commission on Obscenity and Pornography (1970) was that pornography could be educational if it helped break down inhibited attitudes toward sex and presented accurate factual information. However, if a person is knowledgeable about sexuality, little valuable information can be gained. In one study, it was found that over half of the adult viewers of pornographic films were searching for information (Winick, 1970).

For some who have a lackluster sex life, pornography can serve to increase coital behavior (Commission on Obscenity, 1970). Many people feel that exposure to pornography can be satisfying, in that they enjoy viewing erotic films (Primean, 1977).

THE "CONS" OF PORNOGRAPHY

Several "cons" exist regarding pornography. Many people who view pornographic movies often obtain false information. For example, a young man who views pornographic films may notice that the male actors are often "well-endowed." He may then think that a sexually competent male must have a large penis to be a good lover, and he may unjustly question his sexual competence. (However, exposure to a good sex education program can prevent this problem.)

One of the greater criticisms of pornography comes from many feminists' groups. These groups feel that pornographic materials degrade women in that they portray them as sex objects only, as well as the property of men. Gloria Steinem (1978) clarifies this point by stating:

> . . . its message is violence, dominance, and conquest. It is sex being used to reinforce some inequality, or to create one, or to tell us the lie that pain and humiliation (ours or someone else's) are really the same as pleasure. If we are to feel anything, we must identify with conqueror or victim. That means we can only experience pleasure through the adoption of some degree of sadism or masochism. It also means that we may feel diminished by the role of conqueror, or enraged, humiliated, and vengeful by sharing identity with the victim.

It should be noted in the above quotation, "we" and "us" refer to women.

While we have discussed the pros and cons of pornography, we have by no means shared all of its effects, simply because most of its effects are neither pro nor con. Specifically, some of the other implications of pornography are the following:

- Exposure to erotic materials is not a factor in the causation of sex crime or sex delinquency (Commission on Obscenity, 1970).
- In general, sexual behavior is not altered substantially by exposure to pornography. When sexual activity took place following the viewing or reading of pornographic materials, it constituted only a temporary activation of individuals' preexisting patterns of sexual behavior.
- Male and female college students do not differ in their reactions to erotica or the degree of arousal (Heiman, 1975).
- In one study, most men and women reported sexual arousal when exposed to explicit sexual visuals (Schmidt and Sigusch, 1970).

Regardless of what laws and mandates are put forth, it is clear that there is no agreement on what obscenity is, whether or not it is harmful, and what steps should be taken in the future. Any consensus regarding future positions on pornography needs to be based upon research that is valid and conclusive. That this consensus will be reached in the near future is highly unlikely.

SUMMARY STATEMENTS

- *Rape is sexual intercourse that occurs by force or deception, or because another person may be too incompetent to give consent.*
- *Several theories of rape have been given. One is the traditional psychiatric position that a disturbed family life is a deciding factor. The feminist view is that rape is committed to show power. The third theory views*

- *the motive for rape as rebellion against a society that practices discrimination.*
- *Rape trauma syndrome is an immediate state of disorganization that results from an attempted or successful rape.*
- *Many women are speaking up today against sexual harassment from their bosses and professors.*

- *Some of the most restrictive rules pertaining to sex and the law exist in marriage.*
- *Pornography, although it is difficult to define, often refers to material in literature, art, motion pictures, or other means of communication and expression that has been developed with the intention of evoking sexual interest and arousal.*

- *The President's Commission on Obscenity and Pornography was formed in 1967 to study the effects of pornography upon behavior as well as to recommend a means by which pornography and obscenity traffic could be dealt with effectively.*

SUGGESTED READINGS

Steinem, Gloria. "Erotica and Pornography: A Clear and Present Difference," *Ms.*, November 1978.

Talese, Gay. *Thy Neighbor's Wife.* New York: Doubleday and Company, 1980.

The Report of the Commission on Obscenity and Pornography. New York: Bantam Books, 1970.

Tschirhart, Linda S., and Ann Fetter. *In Defense of Ourselves: A Rape Prevention Handbook for Women.* New York: Doubleday and Company, 1979.

SEX AND THE LAW

A LOOK AT YOUR LIFESTYLE

You notice that the local theater in your neighborhood is changing the types of movies it shows from the family entertainment (G-rated) to X-rated. The manager claims that his theater cannot generate a profit with its present entertainment.

In one sentence, describe how you would feel about the change in format.

_____

_____

_____

GATHERING INFORMATION

You have been asked by a neighbor to sign a petition stating that the theater should close if it begins to show X-rated movies. Would you sign this petition? _____

List three reasons to support your response.

_____

_____

_____

_____

_____

EVALUATING THE INFORMATION
Of the reasons you listed, which do you feel is most important, and why?

_____

_____

MAKING RESPONSIBLE DECISIONS
If you had the opportunity to write the law regarding the showing of X-rated movies, what would you say? (Answer briefly and specifically.)

_____

_____

_____

_____

Bibliography

Abrams, Sally. "How to Sue Your Live-In Lover." *New York,* November 13, 1978, p. 118.

Allen, Clifford. *A Textbook of Psychosexual Disorders.* London: Oxford University Press, 1969.

American Heritage Dictionary. New York: Houghton-Mifflin, 1969.

American Psychiatric Association. *Diagnostic and Statistical Manual of Mental Disorders.* Third edition. Washington, DC: American Psychiatric Association, 1978.

Amir, Mecacheri. *Patterns in Forcible Rape.* Chicago: University of Chicago Press, 1971.

Athanasiou, R., P. Shaver, and C. Tavris. *Sexual Psychology Today,* July 1979, pp. 39–52.

Baker, Carole. "Should I Have a Baby?" by Terri Schults in *Working Woman.* November, 1979, p. 36.

Ball, J. *Journal of Comparative Psychology* 24:135, 1935.

Bart, P. B. Depression in Middle-Aged Women. In V. Gornick and B. K. Moran (Eds.), *Women in Sexist Society.* New York: Signet, 1971.

Bartell, Gilbert D. *Group Sex.* New York: Peter H. Wyden Co., 1971.

Beach, F. (Ed.), *Human Sexuality in Four Perspectives.* Baltimore: Johns Hopkins Press, 1978.

Bell, Robert. *Marriage and Family Interaction.* Illinois: The Dorsey Press, 1971.

Bell, Robert R., Stanley Turner, and Lawrence Rosen. A Multivariate Analysis of Female Extramarital Coitus. *Journal of Marriage and the Family* 37: 375–384, 1975.

Bell, A. P., and M. S. Weinberg. *Homosexualities.* New York: Simon and Schuster, 1978.

Benjamin, Harry, and Charles L. Ihlenfeld. Transsexualism. *American Journal of Nursing* 3:458–459, 1973.

Benson, L. *Images, Heroes and Self Perceptions.* New York: Prentice Hall, 1974.

Bergler, E., and W. S. Kroger. *Kinsey's Myth of Female Sexuality.* New York: Grune and Stratton, 1954.

Bieber, I. *Homosexuality: A Psychoanalytic Study of Male Homosexuals.* New York: Basic Books, 1962.

Blakelee, Alton. Hunt Down: the Herpes Gang. *Perspective,* Summer 1981, p. 22.

Block, A., J. Maeder, and J. Hassily. Sexual Problems After Myocardial Infarction. *American Heart Journal* 90:536–537, 1975.

Bohannan, Paul. *Love, Sex, and Being Human.* New York: Doubleday and Company, 1969, p. 85.

Bonaparte, Marie. *Female Sexuality.* New York: International Universities Press, 1953.

Bonventre, Peter. Was it Rape? *Newsweek,* January 1, 1979.

Boston Women's Health Book Collective (The). *Our Bodies, Ourselves.* New York: Simon and Schuster, 1979, pp. 13, 129, 131–132.

Bregman, S. *Sexuality and the Spinal Cord Injured Woman.* Minneapolis: Sister Kenny Institute, 1975.

Brehm, H., and W. Haase. The Alternative to Hormonal Contraception. Importance and Reliability of a Foam Ovoid for Vaginal Contraception. *Med. Welt* 26:1610–1617, 1975.

Bremes, J. *Asexualization.* New York: Macmillan, 1959.

Brown, Gabrielle. *The New Celibacy.* New York: McGraw-Hill, 1980.

Brownmiller, Susan. *Against Our Will: Men, Women and Rape.* New York: Simon and Schuster, 1975.

Bruckner, H. T. The Transvestic Career Path. *Psychiatry* 33:381–389, 1970.

Bullough, B., and V. Bullough. The History and Present States of the Medical Model as an Explanation for Homosexuality. *Health Values: Achieving High Level Wellness* 3:256, 1979.

Burgess, A. W., and L. L. Holmstrom. Rape Trauma Syndrome. *American Journal of Psychiatry* 31:9, 1974, pp. 981–986.

Burt, John. "On Intimacy," unpublished essay. College Park: University of Maryland, 1977.

Burt, John, and Linda Meeks. *Education for Sexuality.* Philadelphia: W. B. Saunders Co., 1975, pp. 35–36, 33.

Burt, John, Linda Meeks, and Sharon Pottebaum. *Toward a Healthy Lifestyle Through Elementary Health Education,* Belmont, California: Wadsworth, 1980.

Buscaglia, Leo. *Love.* New Jersey: Charles B. Slack, 1972.

Byrne, Donn. *The Attraction Paradigm.* New York: Academic Press, 1971.

Calderone, Mary S. Love, Sex, Intimacy and Aging as a Life Style. *Sex, Love, Intimacy—Whose Life Styles?* New York: Siecus, 1972.

California Penal Code Section 311 (a), West, 1970.

Caprio, F. S. *Variations in Sexual Behavior.* New York: Grove, 1955.

Cavallen, H. Incest. *Sexual Behavior* 3:19–21, 1973.

Center for Disease Control. Gonorrhea—United States. *Morbidity and Mortality Weekly Report* 28 (45): 533–534, 1979.

Center for Science in the Public Interest. *Citizen Petition.* November 15, 1979.

Chesser, E. *Human Aspects of Sexual Deviations.* London: Jerrolds Publishing, 1971.

Coleman, J. C. *Abnormal Psychology and Modern Life.* Fourth edition. Chicago: Scott, 1972.

Comarr, A. E. Sexual functioning among patients with spinal cord injury. *Urologia Internationalis* 25:134–168, 1970.

Comfort, Alex. *More Joy.* New York: Crown Publishers, 1974.

Comfort, Alex. *The Joy of Sex.* New York: Simon and Schuster, 1972.

Connell, Elizabeth. Prostaglandins: A New Wonder Drug? *Redbook Magazine,* January, 1972, p. 11.

Constantine, Larry L., Joan M. Constantine, and Sheldon K. Edelman. Counseling Implications of Comarital and Multilateral Relating. *Family Coordinator,* 1972, pp. 267–273.

Consumer Reports. The Medicine Show. New York: Consumer's Union, 1976.

Cvetkovich, G., B. Grote, J. Lieberman, and W. Miller. Sex role development and teenage fertility-related behavior. *Adolescence* 13:231–236, 1978.

Dalton, Katherina. *The Menstrual Cycle.* New York: Pantheon, 1969, pp. 60–64.

Darrow, W. W. Approaches to the Problem of Venereal Disease Prevention. *Preventive Medicine* 5:165–175, 1976.

Delora, J. S., and C. A. Warren. *Understanding Sexual Interaction.* Boston: Houghton-Mifflin, 1977.

de Moya, A., and D. de Moya. Viewpoints: What is the Basis for the Distinction Many Patients Make Between Vaginal and Clitoral Orgasms? *Medical Aspects of Human Sexuality,* November, 1973, pp. 84–103.

Deutsch, Helen. *The Psychology of Women.* Vols I and II. New York: Grune and Stratton, 1945.

Doe et al. v. Bolton, Attorney General of Georgia, et al, Supreme Court of the United States, Opinion Number 70-40, January 22, 1973.

Driscoll, James P. Transsexuals. *Transaction,* March–April, 1971, pp. 28–31.

Dunn, Marian E. In "Living Together or Being Married" by Jennifer Kintzing. *Mademoiselle,* June, 1980, p. 153.

Dusek, D., and D. Girdano. *Drugs: A Factual Account.* Reading: Massachusetts: Addison-Wesley Publishing Co., 1980, p. 53.

Eastman, N. J., and L. M. Hellman. *Williams Obstetrics.* 12th Edition. New York: Appleton, 1961.

Edwards, Marie, and Eleanor Hoover. *The Challenges of Being Single.* New York: Hawthorn Books, Inc., 1974.

Elder, Glen. Appearance and Education in Marriage Mobility. *American Sociological Review* 34:519–533, 1969.

Elias, James, and Paul Gebhard. "Sexuality and Sexual Learning in Childhood." *Phi Delta Kappan* 50:401–405, 1969.

Ellis, A., and R. Brancale. *The Psychology of Sex Of-*

fenders. Springfield, Illinois: Charles C Thomas, 1956.

Ellis, A., and E. Sagarin. *Nymphomania.* New York: Gilbert Press, 1964.

Ellison, C. Vaginismus. *Medical Aspects of Human Sexuality* 6:34–54, 1972.

Ersner-Hershfield, R., and S. Kopel. Group Treatment of Pre-orgasmic Women: Evaluation of Partner Involvement and Spacing of Sessions. *Journal of Consulting and Clinical Psychology* 47:750–759, 1979.

Eysenck, H. J., and S. Rachman. *The Causes and Cures of Neurosis.* San Diego: R. Knapp, 1966.

Feder, H., and R. E. Whalen. Feminine behavior in castrated male rats. *Science* 147:306–307, 1965.

Flanagan, William. Unmarried and the Law. *Personal Finance,* September, 1979, p. 12.

Founder's Clinic. *Patient Information.* Columbus: Founder's Clinic, Inc., 1974.

Francoeur, Robert T. The technologies of Man-made Sex. In R. T. Francoeur and A. K. Francoeur (Eds.), *The Future of Sexual Relations.* Englewood Cliffs: Prentice-Hall, 1974.

Freud, S. Fetishism. *International Journal of Psychoanalysis* 9:161–166, 1928.

Freud, S. *Three Essays on the Theory of Sexuality.* James Strackey (Ed.), New York: Basic Books, 1963.

Friday, Nancy. *My Secret Garden.* New York: Trident Press, 1977, p. 77.

Fromm, Eric. *The Art of Loving.* New York: Bantam Books, 1963.

Gagnon, V. *Human Sexualities.* Glenview, Illinois: Scott, Foresman and Co., 1977, p. 253.

Gagnon, J. H., and W. Simon. *Sexual Conduct: The Social Resources of Human Sexuality.* Chicago: Aldine, 1973.

Gebhard, Paul H., John H. Gagnon, Wardell B. Pomeroy, and Cornelia V. Christenson. *Sex Offenders.* New York: Harper and Row, 1965.

Gebhard, P. H. Fetishism and Sadomachochism. In *Sex Research: Studies from the Kinsey Institute,* M. S. Weinberg (Ed.). New York: Oxford University Press, 1976.

Gelder, M. G., and I. M. Marks. Aversion Treatment in Transvestism and Transsexualism. In R. Green and J. Money (Eds.), *Transsexualism and Sex Reassignment.* Baltimore: Johns Hopkins University Press, 1969.

Gilmartin, Brian G. That Swinging Couple Down the Block. *Psychology Today,* February 8, 1975, pp. 55–58.

Gordon, Thomas. *Parent Effectiveness Training.* New York: New American Library, 1970.

Green, Richard. Adults Who Want to Change Sex; Adolescents Who Cross-dress; and Children Called "Sissy" and "Tomboy." In R. Green (Ed.), *Human Sexuality: A Health Practitioner's Text.* Baltimore: Williams and Wilkins, 1975.

Green, R., and J. Money (Eds.), *Transsexualism and Sex Reassignment.* Baltimore: Johns Hopkins University Press, 1969.

Griffith, Janet. Social Pressure on Family Size Intentions. *Family Planning Perspective* 5:4, Fall 1973.

Group for the Advancement of Psychiatry. *Sex and the College Student.* New York: Mental Health Materials Center, 1965, p. 18.

Guttmacher, Alan F. *Pregnancy and Birth.* New York: Viking Press, 1962.

Hall, J. Sexuality and the Mentally Retarded. In R. Green (Ed.), *Human Sexuality: A Health Practitioner's Text.* Baltimore: Williams and Wilkins, 1975.

Hamilton, J. Demonstrable Ability of Penile Erection in Castrate Men with Markedly Low Titers of Urinary Androgen. *Proceedings of the Society of Experimental Biology and Medicine* 54:309, 1943.

Hariton, Barbara E. The Sexual Fantasies of Women. *Psychology Today* 6(10):39–44, 1973.

Harlow, H. F., and M. K. Harlow. The Effect of Rearing Conditions on Behavior. In *Sex Research: New Developments.* J. Money (Ed.). New York: Holt, 1968.

Hastings, D. W. *Impotence and Frigidity.* Boston: Little, Brown, 1963.

Hatcher, R. F., G. Stewart, F. Stewart, F. Guest, D. Scwartz, and S. Jones. *Contraceptive Technology: 1980-1981.* New York: Irvington Publishers, Inc., 1980, p. 222.

Heiman, J. R. The Physiology of Erotica: Women's Sexual Arousal. *Psychology Today,* April, 1975 pp. 91–94.

Hellerstein, H., and E. J. Friedman. Sexual Activity and the Postcoronary Patient. *Archives of Internal Medicine* 125:987, 1970.

Hellman, L. M., and J. A. Pritchard. *Williams Obstetrics.* 14th Edition. New York: Appleton-Century Crofts, 1971.

Herbst, A. Clear Cell Adenocarcinoma of the Genital Tract in Young Females. *New England Journal of Medicine* 287 (25):1259–1264, 1972.

Hite, Shere. *The Hite Report: A Nationwide Study of Female Sexuality.* New York: Macmillan Publishing Co., 1976.

Hoffman, Lois, and Jean Manis. *ISR Newsletter* published by the Institute of Social Research at the University of Michigan, Autumn, 1978.

Hogan, D. R. The Effectiveness of Sex Therapy: A Review of the Literature. In J. LoPiccolo and L. LoPiccolo (Eds.), *Handbook of Sex Therapy*. New York: Plenum Press, 1978.

Hokmann, G. Sex and the Spinal Cord Injured Male. *Paraplegin News,* February 1973, p. 16.

Hoover, R., L. Gray, and P. Cole. Menopausal Estrogens and Breast Cancer. *New England Journal of Medicine* 295:401–405, 1976.

Hopkins, June H. The Lesbian Personality. *Britain Journal of Psychiatry* 115:1433–1436, 1969.

Humphries, L. *Tearoom Trade.* Chicago: Aldine, 1970.

Hunt, Morton. *Sexual Behavior in the 1970's.* Chicago: Playboy Press, 1974.

Hyde, J. S. *Understanding Human Sexuality.* New York: McGraw-Hill, 1979.

Ihlenfeld, Charles L. When a Woman Becomes a Man. *Sexology Magazine,* June 1972.

"J." *The Sensuous Woman.* New York: Dell Publishing Company, 1969.

Jackman, N. R., R. O'Toole, and G. Geis. The Self Image of the Prostitute. *Sociological Quarterly* 4:150–161, 1963.

Jick, H., A. M. Walker, et al. Hospitalization Rates in Vasectomized Men. *JAMA* 245(22): 2315–2317, 1981.

Johnson, Stephen. *First Person Singular: Living the Good Life Alone.* New York: The New American Library, 1978.

Jourard, Sidney. *The Transparent Self.* New York: D. Van Nostrand Company, 1971.

Kagen, J. Herpes: It Can Be Treated—But Not Cured. *Ms.,* January, 1978, pp. 38–40.

Kallman, F. J. Twin and Sibship Study of Overt Male Homosexuality. *American Journal of Human Genetics* 115:283–298, 1952.

Kantrowitz, A. A Gay Struggles with the New Acceptance. *The Village Voice,* November 17, 1975, pp. 39–40.

Kaplan, Helen Singer. *Disorders of Sexual Desire.* New York: Simon and Schuster, 1979.

Kaplan, Helen Singer. *The New Sex Therapy: Active Treatment of Sexual Dysfunctions.* New York: Quadrangle, 1974.

Karacan, I. Clinical Value of Nocturnal Erection in the Prognosis and Diagnosis of Impotence. *Aspects of Human Sexuality* 4:27–34, 1970.

Karpman, B. *The Sexual Offender and His Offenses.* New York: Julian Press, 1954.

Katchadourian, H. A., and Donald T. Lunde. *Fundamentals of Human Sexuality.* New York: Holt, Rinehart and Winston, Inc., 1972.

Kegal, A. Sexual Function of the Pubococcygeus Muscle. *Western Journal of Surgery* 60:521–524, 1952.

Kerchoff, A. Social Class Differences in Sexual Attitudes and Behavior. *Medical Aspects of Human Sexuality* 8:10–25, 1974.

Kinsey, A. C., W. B. Pomeroy, and C. E. Martin. *Sexual Behavior in the Human Male.* Philadelphia: W. B. Saunders Co., 1948.

Kinsey, A. C., W. B. Pomeroy, C. E. Martin, and P. H. Gebhard. *Sexual Behavior in the Human Female.* Philadelphia: W. B. Saunders Co., 1953, pp. 730–731.

Kirkham, George L. Violence Accompanies Sex. *Sexual Behavior,* January, 1972, p. 42.

Kiser, C. V., W. H. Grabill, and A. A. Campbell. *Trends and Variations in Fertility in the United States.* Cambridge: Harvard University Press, 1968.

Klaus, M., and J. Kennel. *Maternal Infant Bonding.* St. Louis: C. V. Mosby, 1976.

Kun, H. *Endocrinology* 13:311, 1934.

Laner, Mary Riege. Prostitution as an Illegal Vocation: A Sociological Overview. In *Deviant Behavior: Occupational and Organizational Basis.* Clifton D. Bryant (Ed.). Chicago: Rand-McNally, 1974.

LeBoyer, Frederick. *Birth without Violence.* New York: Alfred A. Knopf, 1975.

Lee, John Alan. A Typology of Styles of Loving. *Personality and Social Psychology Bulletin* 3:173–182, 1972.

Lee, John Alan. Styles of Loving. *Psychology Today* 8(5):43–51, 1974.

LeMasters, E. *Parents in Modern America.* Illinois: Dorsey Press, 1970.

Lobsenz, N. M. *Sex after Sixty-five.* New York: Public Affairs Committee, Inc., 1975.

London, L. S. *Mental Therapy: Studies in Fifty Cases.* New York: Covici-Friede, 1957.

LoPiccolo, J., and C. Lobitz. The Role of Masturbation in the Treatment of Orgasmic Dysfunction. *Archives of Sexual Behavior* 2:163–171, 1972.

LoPiccolo, J. The Professionalization of Sex Therapy: Issues and Problems. In J. LoPiccolo and L. LoPiccolo (Eds.), *Handbook of Sex Therapy.* New York: Plenum Press, 1978.

LoPiccolo, J., R. Stewart, and B. Watkins. Treatment of Erectile Failure and Ejaculatory Incompetence of Homosexual Etiology. *Journal of Behavior*

Therapy and Experimental Psychology 3:233–236, 1972.

Lukianowicz, N. Transvestism. *Journal of Nervous and Mental Disease* 128:36–64, 1959.

MacDougald, D., Jr. Aphrodisiacs and Anophrodisiacs. In *The Encyclopedia of Sexual Behavior.* Vol. I. A. Ellis and A. Abarbanel (Eds.). New York: Hawthorn Books, 1961.

Macklin, Eleanor. Cohabitation in College: Going Very Steady. *Psychology Today* 8(6):53–59, 1974.

Macklin, Eleanor D. Unmarried Heterosexual Cohabitation on the University Campus. In J. Wiseman (Ed.), *The Social Psychology of Sex.* New York: Harper and Row, 1976.

Marmor, J. (Ed.). *Sexual Inversion.* New York: Basic Books, 1965.

Martinson, F. M. *Family in Society.* New York: Dodd, Mead, and Co., 1970.

Marvin, M. T., E. Keerdoga, and J. B. Copeland. Trials of Unmarriages. *Newsweek* 94:14, October 8, 1979.

Maslow, A. H. Synergy in the Society and in the Individual. *Journal of Individual Psychology* 20:153, 1964.

Massie, E., E. Rose, J. Rupp, and R. Whelton. Sudden Death During Coitus—Fact or Fiction? *Medical Aspects of Human Sexuality,* March, 1969, pp. 22–26

Masters, William, and Virginia Johnson. *Human Sexual Inadequacy.* Boston: Little, Brown, 1970.

Masters, W. H., and V. E. Johnson. *Issues in Homosexuality.* Boston: Little, Brown, 1979.

Masters, W. H., and V. Johnson. *Human Sexual Response.* Boston: Little, Brown, 1966.

Masters, W. H., and V. E. Johnson. *Homosexuality in Perspective.* Boston: Little, Brown, 1979.

Maynard, Joyce. How a First Baby Changes a Marriage. *Ladies Home Journal,* May, 1978, p. 162.

McCaghy, C. H. Child Molesting. *Sexual Behavior,* August, 1971, pp. 16–24.

McCary, J. *Human Sexuality.* New York: D. Van Nostrand Co., 1978, 340.

McGuire, R. J., J. M. Carlisle, and B. A. Young. Sexual Deviation as Conditioned Behavior: An Hypothesis. *Behavior Research and Therapy* 2:185–190, 1965.

Meaghes, John F. *A Study of Masturbation and the Psychosexual Life.* New York: William Wood and Co., 1929, pp. 115–116.

Meyer-Bahlburg, H. F. L. Sex Hormones and Male Homosexuality in Comparative Perspective. *Archives of Sexual Behavior* 6:297–325, 1977.

Mishell, D. R., Jr. Current Status of Contraceptive Steroids and the Intrauterine Device. *Clinical Obstetrics and Gynecology* 17(1):35–51, March, 1974.

Mitchell, Cathy. It's Not Easy to be a Woman Today. *Ladies Home Journal,* May, 1979, p. 18.

Mohr, J., E. R. Turner, and M. Jerry. *Pedophilia and Exhibitionism.* Toronto: Toronto University Press, 1964.

Money, John. Components of Eroticism in Man. The Hormones in Relation to Sexual Morphology and Sexual Desire. *Journal of Nervous and Mental Disease* 132:239–248, 1961.

Money, J. Phantom Orgasm in the Dreams of Paraplegic Men and Women. *Archives of General Psychiatry* 3:373–382, 1960.

Money, J., and A. A. Ehrhardt. *Man and Woman: Boy and Girl.* Baltimore: Johns Hopkins Press, 1972.

Money, J., and R. Yankowitz. The Sympathetic-inhibiting Effects of the Drug Ismelin on Human Male Eroticism, with a Note on Mellaril. *Journal of Sexual Research,* January, 1970, pp. 90–97.

Morrow, Lance. Wondering If Children Are Necessary. *Time,* March 5, 1979, p. 42.

Munich, Adrienne. Seduction in Academe. *Psychology Today,* February, 1978.

National Institute on Drug Abuse, Marijuana and Health, Washington, DC: DHEW, Publication No. (ADM) 80–945, 1980.

Needle, Richard H. College Women's Use of Gynecological Health Services: Implication for Consumer Health Education. *Health Education* 9:2, March/April, 1978, pp. 10–11.

Newton, Niles A. Childbearing in Broad Perspective. In Boston Children's Medical Center, *Pregnancy, Birth and the Newborn Baby.* New York: Delacorte Press, 1972.

NIAAA Information and Feature Service, National Clearinghouse for Alcohol Information of the National Institute on Alcohol Abuse and Alcoholism, April 1, 1981, p. 2.

Offir, Carol W. Don't Take it Lying Down. *Psychology Today,* January, 1975, pp. 70–76.

O'Neill, Nena, and George O'Neill. Marriage: A Contemporary Model. In *The Sexual Experience* by Benjamin Sadock, et al. Baltimore: Williams and Wilkins Co., 1976, pp. 231–237.

O'Neill, N., and G. O'Neill. *Open Marriage.* New York: M. Evans, 1972.

Pauley, I. B. Male Psychosexual Inversion: Transsexualism, A Review of 100 Cases. *Archives of General Psychiatry* 13:172–181, 1965.

Peck, Ellen, and Williiam Granzig. *The Parent Test.* New York: G. P. Putnam's Sons, 1978.

Peck, Ellen, and Judith Senderowitz (Eds.). *Pronatalism: The Myth of Mom and Apple Pie.* New York: Thomas Y. Crowell, 1974.

Peele, Stanton, and Archie Brodsky. *Love and Addiction.* New York: New American Library, 1975.

Perls, Frederick S. *Gestalt Therapy Verbation.* New York: Bantam Books, 1969.

Persky, Harold, et al. Plasma Testosterone Level and Sexual Behavior of Couples. *Archives of Sexual Behavior* 7:3, May 1978, pp. 157–173.

Phillips, J. M., et al. Laparoscopic Procedures: A National Survey for 1975. *Journal of Reproductive Medicine* 18:219–226, 1975.

Phoenix, C. H., et al. Organizing Activity of Prenatally-Administered Testosterone. *Endocrinology* 65:369, 1959.

Planned Parenthood of Central Missouri v. Danforth, Supreme Court of the United States, Opinion Number 74-1151 and 74-1419, July 1, 1976.

Pohlman, Edward. Childlessness, Intentional and Unintentional: Psychological and Social Aspects. *The Journal of Nervous and Mental Disease* (151) 1970, pp. 2–12.

Pomeroy, W. B. Why We Tolerate Lesbians. *Sexology,* May 1965.

Pomeroy, Wardell B. Normal vs. Abnormal Sex. *Sexology,* 1966, p. 32.

Pomeroy, Wardell B. The Diagnosis and Treatment of Transvestites and Transsexuals. *Journal of Sex and Marital Therapy* 1:215–224, 1975.

Poor, Henry V. *You and the Law.* New York: The Reader's Digest Association, 1976, pp. 153–155.

Population Reports. Intrauterine Devices. Series B, Number 3, May, 1979.

Population Reports. Oral Contraceptives. Series A, Number 4, May, 1977, A-91.

Population Reports. Oral Contraceptives. Series A, Number 5, January, 1979, A-133.

Population Reports, Periodic Abstinence, Series I, Number 1, June, 1974, I-5.

Powell, John. *Fully Human, Fully Alive.* Niles, Iowa: Argus Communications, 1977.

Powell, John. *Unconditional Love.* Illinois: Argus Communications, 1978.

Powell, John. *Why Am I Afraid To Tell You Who I Am?* Illinois: Argus Communications, 1969.

Prather, Hugh. *Notes to Myself.* Utah: Real People Press, 1970.

Pregnant Women and Smoking. *Forum,* February, 1980, pp. 9–10.

Pre Term Institute. *Counselor's Manual: Individual and Group Techniques.* Newton, Massachusetts: Pre Term Institute, 1973.

Primeau, C. Intercorrelations of Sex Variables Among a Selected Group of Psychologists. Doctoral dissertation, University of Houston, 1977.

Prince, Virginia, and P. M. Bentler. Survey of 504 Cases of Transvestism. *Psychological Reports* 31:903–917, 1972.

Proctor, E. B., N. N. Wagner, and Julius C. Butter. The Differentiation of Male and Female Orgasm: An Experimental Study. Nathaniel N. Wagner (Ed.). New York: Human Sciences Press, 1974.

Raber, Irving, and Herbert A. Blough. Ocular Herpes. *The Helper,* Vol. 2, No. 2, June 1980.

Rada, R. T. Commonly Asked Questions about the Rapist. *Medical Aspects of Human Sexuality,* January, 1977, pp. 47–56.

Ramussen, P. K., and L. H. Kuhn. The New Masseuse: Play for Pay. *Urban Life.* Special issue on sexuality: Encounter, Identification, and Relationships. October 1976.

Raths, Louis E., Merrill Harmon, and Sidney B. Simon. *Values and Teaching.* Columbus, Ohio: Charles Merrill Publishing Co., 1966, pp. 51–82.

Ravich, Robert. In "Living Together or Being Married" by Jennifer Kintzing. *Mademoiselle,* June 1980, p. 152.

Reckless, J., and N. Geiger. Impotence as a Practical Problem. In H. F. Dowling (Ed.), *Disease-a-Month.* Chicago: Year Book Medical Publishers, 1975.

Reed, David. Traditional Marriage. In *The Sexual Experience* by Benjamin J. Sadock, et al. Baltimore: Williams and Wilkins Co., 1976, pp. 217–231.

Riess, Albert J. The Social Integration of Queers and Peers. In *The Other Side.* Howard S. Becker (Ed.). New York: Free Press, 1964.

Riedman, S. R. Change of Life. *Sexology,* August 1968, pp. 64–67.

Robbins, E. S., M. Herman, and L. Robbins. Sex and Arson: Is There a Relationship? *Medical Aspects of Human Sexuality,* October, 1969, pp. 57–64.

Roe, Jane, et al. v. Henry Wade, Supreme Court of the United States, Opinion Number 70-18, January 22, 1973.

Rogel, M. J. A Critical Evaluation of the Possibility of Higher Primate Reproductive and Sexual Pheromones. *Psychological Bulletin* 85(4):810–830, 1978.

Rose, R. M. Testosterone, Aggression, and Homosexuality: A Review of the Literature and Implications for Future Research. In E. J. Sackar (Ed.),

Topics in Pseudoendocrinology. New York: Grune and Stratton, 1975.

Rosen, David H. *Lesbianism: A Study of Female Homosexuality.* Springfield, Illinois: Charles C Thomas. 1974.

Rosenberg, Meriam. The Biologic Basis for Sex Role Stereotypes. *Contemporary Psychoanalysis* 9(3): 374–391, May 1973.

Roth v. United States, 354 U.S. 476, 481, 485, 1957.

Rubin, Zick. *Liking and Loving: An Invitation to Social Psychology.* New York: Holt, Rinehart, and Winston, 1973.

Ruff, C. F., D. I. Templer, and J. L. Ayres. The Intelligence of Rapists. *Archives of Sexual Behavior* 5:327–329, 1976.

Sadok, Benjamin J., and Virginia A. Sadok. Techniques of Coitus. In B. J. Sadok, et al. (Eds.), *The Sexual Experience.* Baltimore: Williams and Wilkins Co., 1976.

Saghir, M. T., and E. Robins. *Male and Female Homosexuality: A Comprehensive Investigation.* Baltimore: Williams and Wilkins Co., 1973.

Salomon, W., and W. Haase. Intravaginal Contraception. Results of a Prospective Long-Term Study of the Foam Ovid. *Sexual Medizin* 6(1):198–202, 1977.

Sargent. Comparison of Closed and Open Marriage. Personal communication with Nena and George O'Neill cited in Marriage A Contemporary Model. In *The Sexual Experience* by Benjamin Sadok, et al. Baltimore: Williams and Wilkins Co., 1976, pp. 231–237.

Schmidt, G., and J. Segusch. Sex Differences in Response to Psychosexual Stimulation by Films and Slides. *Journal of Sex Research* 6:268–283, 1970.

Schutz, Susan Polis. Thoughts of Life. *Blue Mountain Arts.* Boulder, Colorado: Continental Publications, 1974.

Scott, Ann Crittenden. Closing the Muscle Gap. *Ms,* September, 1974, p. 55.

Simans, J. H. Premature Ejaculation: A New Approach. *Journal of Southern Medicine* 49:353–361, 1956.

Sheehy, Gail. *Passages: Predictable Crises in Adult Life.* New York: E. P. Dutton, Inc., 1974.

Shettles, Landrum B. Predetermining Children's Sex. *Medical Aspects of Human Sexuality,* June 1972, p. 172.

Simmons, Alan. Motives for Childbearing and Family Limitation: Some Conceptual and Empirical Observations. Paper given at Canadian Sociological and Anthropological Association, St. Johns, Newfoundland, 1971.

Singer, Josephine, and Irving Singer. Types of Female Orgasm. *Journal of Sex Research* 1:78–79, 1971.

Smith, James R., and Lynn G. Smith. Co-marital Sex and the Sexual Freedom Movement. *Journal of Sex Research* 6:131-142, 1970.

Snyder, Craig W. (Ed.), Proclamation for National Family Sex Education Week. *Journal of the Institute for Family Research and Education,* October 1980, p. 14.

Solomon, P., and J. D. Patch. *Handbook of Psychiatry.* Los Altos, California: Lange Medical Publications, 1974.

Sorensen, Robert C. *Adolescent Sexuality in Contemporary America.* New York: World Publishing, 1973.

Steinem, Gloria. Erotica and Pornography: A Clear and Present Difference. *Ms.,* November 1978.

Steinmann, Anne, and Elinor Lenz. The Man in Your Life: Personal Commitment in a Changing World. In *New Life Options* by Herbert Otto and Rosalind K. Loring. New York: McGraw-Hill, 1976, pp. 287–306.

Stewart, F., F. Guest, G. Steward, and R. Hatcher. *My Body, my Health: the Concerned Woman's Guide to Gynecology.* New York: John Wiley & Sons, Inc., 1979.

Sturgis, E. T., and H. E. Adams. The Right to Treatment: Issues in the Treatment of Homosexuality. *Journal of Consulting and Clinical Psychology* 46:165–169, 1978.

Talese, Gay. *Thy Neighbor's Wife.* New York: Doubleday and Co., 1980.

Terman, L. M. Correlates of Orgasm Adequacy in a Group of 556 Wives. *Journal of Psychology* 32:115–172, 1951.

Test Yourself for Pregnancy. *Consumer Reports,* November 1978, pp. 644–645.

The Report of the Commission on Obscenity and Pornography. Washington, DC: U.S. Government Printing Office, 1970.

Thornhill v. Alabama, 310 U.S. 88, 1940.

Thorpe, L. P., B. Katz, and R. T. Lewis. *Psychology of Abnormal Behavior.* New York: Ronald Press, 1961.

Tietze, C., and S. Lewitt. Evaluation of Intrauterine Devices: Ninth Process Report of the Cooperative Statistical Program. *Studies in Family Planning* 55:1–40, July 1970.

Time Magazine Report. Fighting Lechery on Campus. *Time,* February 4, 1980, p. 84.

Tollison, C. D., and H. Adams. *Sexual Disorders: Treatment, Theory, and Research.* New York: Sardner Press, Inc., 1979, p. 230.

Trials of Unmarriage. *Newsweek,* October 8, 1979, p. 4.

Ulene, Arthur . Forward. In *The Parent Test* by Ellen Peck and William Granzig. New York: G. P. Putnam's Sons, 1978.

United States Department of Health, Education, and Welfare, Public Health Service, Center for Disease Control. *Sexually Transmitted Disease.* (Statistical Letter No. 127), May, 1978.

Varni, Charles H. An Exploratory Study of Spouse-swapping. *Pacific Sociological Review* 15:507–522, 1972.

Veevers, J. E. The Moral Careers of Voluntarily Childless Wives: Notes On The Defense of A Variant World View. *Marriage and the Family in Canada.* S. Parvez Wakil (Ed.). Toronto: Copp-Clark, 1974.

Veevers, J. E. The Life Style of Voluntarily Childless Couples. *The Canadian Family in Comparative Perspective.* Lyle Larson (Ed.). Toronto: Prentice-Hall, 1974.

Veevers, J. E. The Violation of Fertility Mores: Voluntary Childlessness as Deviant Behavior. Reprinted from *Deviant Behavior and Societal Reaction.* Craig Boydell, Carl Grindstaf, and Paul Whitehead (Eds.). Toronto: Holt, Rinehart, and Winston, 1971, pp. 571–592.

Vetter, H. J. *Psychology of Abnormal Behavior.* New York: Ronald Press, 1972.

Vincent, C. E. (Ed.), *Human Sexuality in Medical Education and Practice.* Springfield, Illinois: Charles C Thomas, 1968.

Walker, K. Erection Disorders. *Sexology,* May 1963, pp. 696–698.

Warren, Earl. Obscenity Laws—A Shift to Reality. *Santa Clara Lawyer,* Vol. II, No. 1, Fall, 1970, p. 1–19.

Wear, J., and K. Holmes. *How to Have Intercourse Without Getting Screwed.* Seattle: Madrona, 1976.

Weideger, P. *Menstruation and Menopause.* New York: Alfred A. Knopf, 1976.

Weinberg, G. *Society and the Healthy Homosexual.* New York: St. Martin's Press, 1972.

Weinberg, M. S., and C. Williams. *Male Homosexuals: Their Problems and Adaptations.* New York: Oxford University Press, 1974.

Weinberg, M. S., and C. J. Williams. Male Homsexuals: The Problems and Adaptations. In *Sex Research: Studies from the Kinsey Institute.* M. S. Weinberg (Ed.). New York: Oxford University Press, 1976.

Weinberg, Samuel K. *Incest Behavior.* New York: Citadel Press, 1955.

Westoff, Charles. Coital Frequency and Contraception. *Family Planning Prospectives* 6(3):136–141, 1974.

Whalen, R. E. *Journal of Comparative Psychology* 57:175, 1964.

Wiener, D. N. Sexual Problems in Clinical Experience. In *The Individual, Sex and Society.* C. B. Broderick and J. Bernard (Eds.). Baltimore: Johns Hopkins Press, 1969.

Williamson, R. *Marriage and Family Relations.* New York: John Wiley & Sons, Inc., 1966.

Wilson, Paul. *The Other Side of Rape.* St. Lucia: University of Queensland Press, 1978, pp. 34–43.

Winich, C. A Study of Consumers of Explicitly Sexual Materials: Some Functions Served by Adult Movies. *Technical Reports of the Commission of Obscenity and Pornography.* Vol. 4, Washington, DC: U.S. Government Printing Office, 1970.

Wolff, Charlotte. *Love Between Women.* New York: Harper and Row, 1971.

Woods, N. F. *Human Sexuality in Health and Illness.* St. Louis: C. V. Mosby, 1979.

Woolston, Howard B. *Prostitution in the United States.* New Jersey: Patterson Smith, 1969.

Wydro, Kenneth. *Flying Solo.* New York: Berkeley Publishing Co., 1978.

Yarber, W. L. Preventing Venereal Disease Infection: Approaches for the Sexually Active. *Health Values: Achieving High Level Wellness.* Vol. 2, No. 2, March/April, 1978.

Yates, A. *Behavior Therapy.* New York: John Wiley, 1970.

Zehv, W. Trying New Positions in Intercourse. *Sexology,* January 1969, pp. 364–367.

Zurcher, L. A., and R. G. Kirkpatrick. *Citizens for Decency: Antipornography Crusades as Status Defense.* Austin: University of Texas Press, 1976.

Glossary

abortion The premature expulsion of the product of conception (fertilized ovum, embryo, or nonviable fetus) from the uterus.

AC–DC A slang term for a person who has sexual relations with members of either sex. Also known as bisexual or ambisexual.

active listening A process of feeding back what is heard to the person sending the message.

adultery See *extramarital sex*.

afterbirth The placenta and amniotic sac that is expelled from the uterus after childbirth.

agape A lovestyle characterized by classic, unselfish love, combining powerful passion and a stable, committed relationship.

ambiguous extramarital sex A situation in which a partner chooses not to confront the partner who is engaging in extramarital sex.

ambisexual See *bisexual*.

amenorrhea The absence of menstruation. Primary amenorrhea is the term used when there has not been a menstrual period by age 18; secondary amenorrhea occurs when menstruation ceases after at least one menstrual period.

amniocentesis A procedure in which amniotic fluid is drawn from the amniotic sac and analyzed for possible genetic defects in the fetus.

amnion A thin membrane that forms a sac or "bag of waters" around the fetus and contains amniotic fluid, in which the child floats.

amniotic fluid The liquid in which the fetus floats within the amnion; it acts as a protective cushion and maintains a constant temperature for the child.

amyl nitrite A drug used as an aphrodisiac, popularly known as "snappers" or "poppers." It relaxes the smooth muscles of the body, resulting in vasodilation.

anaphrodisiacs Substances that supposedly inhibit sexual desire.

androgens Male sex hormones produced in the testes and influencing body and bone growth and the sex drive.

anorgasmia See *orgasmic dysfunction*.

Apgar score A health status rating given to babies immediately after birth which scores weight, color, alertness, and posture.

aphrodisiacs Substances that supposedly increase sexual desire, such as foods, drugs, and perfumes.

areola The darkened circular area surrounding the nipple of the breast.

artificial insemination A technique by which

473

semen is introduced into the vagina or uterus of a woman by means other than coitus to induce conception.

asset   An asset is a strength or a desired possession.

attrahent factors   A term for persons who choose not to have children because of the advantages of an adult-centered lifestyle.

autonomous adulthood   A state of knowing how to meet your needs in a way that makes sense to you by setting goals, graded assignments, self-observation and planning.

Bartholin's glands   A pair of bean-shaped glands which secrete a few drops of fluid near the labia minora during sexual arousal; the fluid provides the genital scent that contributes to arousal.

basal body temperature (BBT)   This method of birth control predicts the postovulatory safe period for intercourse. It is based on the slight rise in body temperature that can be recorded 24 to 72 hours after ovulation has begun. It can also be used to time intercourse for couples who desire to conceive.

basal body temperature chart   A graph on which a woman records her temperature to determine when she is ovulating; her temperature will rise slightly after ovulation has begun.

bestiality   Using animals as sex objects. Also known as zoophilia and bestiosexuality.

bestiosexuality   See *bestiality*.

bigamy   Being married while still legally married to another spouse.

birth control   Methods designed to alter the conditions that are necessary for a conception and/or pregnancy to occur.

bisexual   A person who engages in both heterosexual and homosexual behavior. Also known as ambisexual or AC–DC.

blastocyst   A small mass of cells that results after several days of cell division by the fertilized egg.

blended orgasm   The third type of female orgasm experience described by Singer and Singer. It is characterized by both the breath-holding response of the uterine orgasm and the contractions of the vulval orgasm.

body   See *shaft*.

bondage   A common practice in which movement is restricted during the sex act for erotic stimulus.

bonding   The development of closeness between the baby and its parents soon after birth.

Braxton-Hicks contractions   Irregular, painless contractions of the uterus that many women mistake for the onset of labor.

breasts   Organs consisting of fatty tissue and mammary gland tissue. Women have variations in breast size due to the fatty tissue but have nearly the same amount of mammary gland tissue to produce milk.

breech presentation   A position that indicates the baby will be born buttocks-first. If the doctor is aware of the position, he or she may try to manipulate the baby's position so that it is born head-first.

budget   A plan or schedule adjusting expenses during a certain period to the estimated or fixed income for that period.

bulbourethral (Cowper's) glands   Two small pea-sized glands located on either side of the urethra that secrete a slippery precoital fluid that can be noticed on the tip of the penis when a man is sexually aroused.

calendar method   A birth control method based on predicting the time of ovulation by keeping a record of the number of days in each menstrual cycle for at least a year. During the unsafe days, a woman abstains from intercourse or uses another contraceptive method.

Candida   See *moniliasis*.

Candida albicans   A yeastlike fungus that can multiply in the vagina to cause a yeast infection, or moniliasis.

chancre   A red bump about the size of a pea that may appear between 10 days and three months after a person contracts syphilis. It may become an open sore covered by a crusty scab or be surrounded by a thin pink border.

cantharides   A drug commonly known as "Spanish fly," that has been called an aphrodisiac. It irritates the lining of the bladder and urethra and this irritation can stimulate the genitals. Depending on the dosage, cantharides can be dangerous or lethal.

castration   Removal of the gonads—testicles in men, ovaries in women.

celibacy   Abstention from sexual activity.

cephalic presentation   A position that indicates the baby will be born head-first with its face rotated to the side.

cervical cancer   Cancer of the cervix which is most prevalent among women who begin to have intercourse at an early age, who have intercourse frequently, have many sexual partners, or whose mothers took diethylstilbestrol (DES) during pregnancy to prevent miscarriage.

cervix The lowest part of the uterus, which keeps the growing embryo inside the womb during pregnancy.

cesarean section (C section) The surgical removal of the baby through an incision made in the abdomen and uterus.

child molesting See *pedophilia*.

cilia Hairlike projections found on the inner surface of the oviducts; their beating action creates a constant current that directs the ovum into the uterus.

circumcision The removal of the foreskin from the penis for a variety of ritual, religious, or hygienic reasons.

clandestine extramarital sex See *nonconsensual extramarital sex*.

(the) "clap" See *gonorrhea*.

clarifying response A response that can be used to obtain more information or to help one person understand what another is saying.

clitoral orgasm Orgasm achieved after clitoral stimulation; it does not mean that the clitoris experiences orgasm. According to Masters and Johnson, there is no difference between a clitoral and vaginal orgasm.

clitoris A small cylindrical structure projecting between the labia minora, the only purpose of which is sexual pleasure.

cohabitation Living together with sexual activity, also known as pseudomarriage, domestic partnership, surrogate marriage, LTA (living together arrangements), and new marriage.

coitus Sexual intercourse; the insertion of the man's penis into the woman's vagina.

coitus interruptus A birth control method in which the male removes his penis from the female's vagina before he ejaculates.

colostrum A thin, yellowish fluid secreted from the breasts during pregnancy and the first few days after delivery.

co-marital sex therapy A therapy program in which male and female co-therapists work together to help a sexually dysfunctional couple.

combination birth control pill The most widely used oral contraception in the United States. It contains estrogen and progestin, a synthetic progesterone; together they alter the menstrual cycle to prevent ovulation.

companionship marriage A marriage that is developed by the persons involved, concentrates on their needs, and is concerned with mutual growth.

complete celibacy Abstention from any voluntary sexual activity, including self-stimulation.

complete hysterectomy Surgical removal of the uterus including the cervix and sometimes the ovaries and oviducts, in which case estrogen replacement therapy may be needed.

condom A thin contraceptive sheath that is placed over the penis to collect the man's semen so that it does not enter the vagina.

congestive dysmenorrhea "Premenstrual tension" caused by too much estrogen in relation to progesterone. Symptoms include fluid retention, irritability, depression, headache, fatigue, and the urge for simple carbohydrates.

consensual extramarital sex Extramarital sex in which the husband and wife both know and approve of one or both engaging in extramarital sex.

consenting A key word in sexual practices. Many psychologists and researchers in human sexuality feel that anything consenting adults decide to do with their sexual behavior in privacy is acceptable.

contraception The prevention of conception by a variety of chemical, physical, and surgical means or by abstention from intercourse during the fertile period.

contraindications Reasons for not using a certain medical or surgical method or procedure.

controlled breathing An important component of the Lamaze technique of prepared childbirth; it helps a woman to dissociate herself from the discomfort of labor and delivery.

coprolalia Obtaining sexual pleasure from using "dirty" language; usually someone who indulges in it finds it is his or her only means of sexual gratification.

copulation See *coitus*.

corona The rim or crown of the penis where the glans rises slightly over the shaft.

corpora cavernosa The top two of the three cylinders of erectile tissue in the penis.

corpus The upper muscular division of the uterus.

corpus luteum A yellow glandular body formed in the ovary from the ruptured remains of the Graafian follicle; it secretes estrogens and progesterone to prepare the reproductive system for the ovum.

corpus spongiosum The bottommost of the three cylinders of erectile tissue in the penis, located under the corpora cavernosa.

couvade See *sympathetic pregnancy.*

covert male homosexual A male who leads a double lifestyle; he appears to be heterosexual and may be married and have children, but when away from home, he may engage in homosexual behavior.

Cowper's glands See *bulbourethral glands.*

crabs See *pubic lice.*

cremasteric muscles Muscles attached to the testes that contract to pull the testes closer to the body, thus warming them, or relax, lowering the testes, thus cooling them.

crowning The emergence of the baby's head into view during childbirth.

cryptorchidism A condition in which the testes fail to descend from the abdominal cavity to the scrotum before birth.

cunnilingus Oral stimulation of the female's genitals.

cyst In the breast, a sac formed when fluid becomes trapped in a lymph duct. In the ovary, a primary follicle that grows and does not rupture to release an egg. The cyst usually fills with fluid; some just become hard. Symptoms may include abdominal swelling, menstrual pain, and irregular cycles.

cystitis An infection of the urinary bladder caused by the bacterium *Escherichia coli,* which is normally present in the intestines and can spread into the urethra and pass into the bladder. Symptoms include painful urination and intercourse and the frequent urge to urinate.

darkfield examination A method of diagnosing syphilis. Fluid from a chancre is placed on a slide and examined by means of a darkfield microscope usually the spirochete can be seen.

delayed ejaculation See *retarded ejaculation.*

deprived homosexual See *situational homosexual.*

diaphragm A dome-shaped contraceptive device made of thin rubber with a flexible rubber-covered rim that is inserted into the vagina; it fits snugly over the cervix and provides a mechanical barrier to prevent the semen from entering the uterus. A diaphragm should always be used with a spermicidal cream or jelly.

diethylstilbestrol (DES) A synthetic estrogen that is taken orally after a woman has had unprotected intercourse in the middle of her cycle. FDA-approved for emergency use only. Also known as the "morning-after" pill.

differential association A term that refers to associating with persons who reinforce the beliefs of the childless.

dilation The opening of the cervix that results from the contractions of labor.

dilation and curettage (D & C) A surgical procedure used to treat menstrual problems and infertility. The cervical opening is dilated so that a curette can be inserted to scrape away the uterine lining. For abortions, the D & C has been replaced by vacuum curettage as the method of choice.

dildo An artificial penis that is usually made of rubber; it may be inserted into the vagina or anus by a partner or by oneself.

dispiriting relationships Relationships that result in a feeling of unimportance, worthlessness, isolation, frustration, and low self-esteem.

domestic partnership See *cohabitation.*

dominant partner In a sadomasochistic relationship, the dominant partner may whip, bite, pinch, defecate on, yell or swear at the other partner.

douche An ineffective contraceptive method in which a woman rinses out her vagina with water or another substance immediately after intercourse to wash away the sperm.

(the) "drip" See *gonorrhea.*

"dry orgasm" See *retrograde ejaculation.*

dyke A female who has masculine characteristics—short hair, stocky build and a "tough look"; she is frequently characterized as a homosexual.

dysmenorrhea Painful menstruation that may be caused by inflammation, constipation, psychological stress, and hormone imbalance.

dyspareunia Painful intercourse, usually affecting women who experience pain in the vagina, cervix, uterus, or bladder. In men, pain may occur in the penis, prostate, or seminal vesicles during ejaculation.

ectopic pregnancy Pregnancy that occurs when a fertilized ovum implants itself in any place other than the lining of the uterus; 96% are tubal pregnancies.

edema Water retention in the body, such as in the hands, face, ankles, wrists, and feet of a pregnant woman.

effacement A flattening and thinning of the cervix that takes place during the first stage of labor.

ejaculation The sudden expulsion of seminal fluid from the erect penis.

ejaculatory anhedonia A nonorgasmic ejaculation, or one that brings with it very little emotional or physical release.

ejaculatory duct A short, straight tube that passes into the prostate gland to open into the urethra.

ejaculatory impotence See *retarded ejaculation.*

ejaculatory incompetence See *retarded ejaculation.*

elective abortion An abortion performed at the request of the pregnant woman when there is no compelling medical reason for the abortion.

endometriosis The growth of endometrial tissue somewhere other than in the lining of the uterus; it is a frequent cause of infertility.

endometritis Inflammation of the uterine lining. Symptoms can include pelvic pain, a foul-smelling discharge, and tenderness during examination; sometimes there are no symptoms.

endometrium The inner lining of the uterus which consists of soft, spongy tissue that grows each month to prepare for the implantation of the fertilized egg.

engagement of the fetus See *lightening.*

epididymis A comma-shaped structure on the back and upper surface of the testes where the sperm mature.

epididymitis An inflammation of the epididymis that may cause painful swelling on the bottom of the testicle, blockage of the sperm to that testicle, and sterility. Epididymitis can result from a gonorrheal infection.

episiotomy A cut made in the perineum to facilitate the passage of the baby's head through the vagina and to prevent vaginal tissues and anal muscles from being injured. Many women are now questioning the validity of this procedure.

erectile dysfunction See *impotence.*

erection An involuntary process that occurs when the spongy layers inside the penis are engorged with blood and the penis swells and elongates.

erogenous zones Those parts of the body that are sexually sensitive to touch, especially the genital area, the breasts, the lips, the neck, the thighs, the buttocks, the ears, and the mouth.

eros lovestyle A lovestyle in which a person seeks others to whom he or she is powerfully attracted. An eros type values physical attraction, sex, and sex technique.

Escherichia coli The bacterium that causes cystitis.

estrogen(s) A group of female sex hormones that produces female secondary sex characteristics and affects the menstrual cycle. Also found in lesser amounts in males.

excitement phase The first of four stages in the sexual response cycle; the male response is an erection; the female response is vaginal lubrication and expansion, and engorgement of the vulva and breasts.

exhibitionism The exposure of the sexual organs to the opposite sex in situations in which exposure is socially defined as inappropriate and when the exposure, at least in part, is for the purpose of his or her own sexual arousal and gratification.

exhibitionist A person who participates in exhibitionism.

expansion A term that refers to enlarging the size of the family.

experiential celibate A person who practices celibacy as a sexual option before or after experiencing other varieties of sexual behavior.

extramarital sex Sexual interaction between a married person and someone other than that married person's spouse; adultery.

fallopian tubes See *oviducts.*

false pregnancy A condition in which a woman who is not pregnant but believes she is pregnant shows some of the signs and symptoms of pregnancy. Also known as pseudocyesis.

fellatio Oral stimulation of the male's genitals.

fertile Capable of producing offspring.

fetal alcohol syndrome A condition that affects a fetus when a pregnant woman consumes excessive amounts of alcohol. Fetal symptoms include abnormal smallness in the head size, poor coordination, behavior problems, and heart defects.

fetishism A state of being erotically aroused by objects, commonly articles of clothing while they are being worn, when they are separated from their owner's body, or when they are depicted in the media; also, one can have a fetish for a part of the body, such as breasts, buttocks, or legs.

fibroadenoma In the breast, a lump formed when fluid becomes trapped in a lymph duct.

fibroids Benign, slow-growing growths in the uterus that usually occur because the endometrial lining is not completely sloughed off each month. Fibroids may make childbirth difficult or may cause urinary-tract infections or menstrual irregularities.

fimbria   Fingerlike projections at the end of each oviduct into which the released ovum enters.

Flagyl   A trade name for the drug metronidazole, the most effective treatment for trichomoniasis.

foam   A spermicidal preparation that is deposited in the vagina near the cervix with an applicator. During intercourse, it is spread around, blocks the cervix, and becomes a mechanical barrier to sperm.

follicle-stimulating hormone (FSH)   A hormone secreted by the pituitary gland that stimulates the ovarian follicles in the female and sperm production in the male.

foreplay   Stimulating actions such as kissing, touching, and caressing used in the preliminary stages of sexual intercourse.

foreskin   Skin that covers the glans of the penis in uncircumcised men.

fornication   Sex between unmarried people.

fraternal twins   Twins that develop from two separate ova that are fertilized at the same time; they do not necessarily look alike and may be of different sexes.

frenulum   A delicate fold of skin that connects the foreskin to the underside of the glans of the penis.

frenum   See *frenulum.*

frigidity   A derogatory, ambiguous term previously used to describe orgasmic dysfunction or failure to achieve sexual arousal in women.

frottage   The act of obtaining sexual pleasure by rubbing or pressing the penis against a person, usually against the buttocks of a fully clothed woman.

frotteur   A person who performs frottage.

gay   See *homosexual.*

gender identity   The psychological sense of one's own masculinity or femininity. Among homosexuals, most males desire to be male and most females desire to be female.

genital herpes   A sexually transmitted disease that is usually caused by herpes simplex virus Type 2; it causes clustered blisters on the surface of the skin or mucous membranes. The Type 1 virus usually causes cold sores around the mouth.

genital warts   See *veneral warts.*

gigolos   Male heterosexual prostitutes who perform sexual services for women for a fee.

glans   The head of the penis.

goal   A statement of aim or purpose. Goals are the most important consideration in the formation of a partnership.

gonococcal arthritis   Arthritic pain in the joints, a condition caused by gonococci invading the bloodstream.

gonorrhea   A sexually transmitted disease that initially causes inflammation of the mucous membranes; it is the most widespread *reportable* communicable disease in this country. Also known as the "clap" and the "drip."

Graafian follicle   One of the immature primary follicles that balloons outward into full maturity and ruptures at ovulation to release an egg.

group marriage   A voluntary family group of three or more persons that is committed to and maintains an ongoing relationship with more than one person in what is regarded by the participants as "being married." Also known as multilateral marriage.

growing relationship   One that is developing and maturing.

gumma   An ulceration of a body organ that may occur in the tertiary stage of syphilis, three to seven years after infection.

gynecologist   A physician who specializes in the treatment of the problems of the female reproductive and sexual organs.

happiness   According to Immanuel Kant, the three grand essentials of happiness are something to do, someone to love, and something to hope for.

hermaphroditism   A condition in which a person is born with both male and female genitalia.

herpes   There are two types of herpes, Type 1 and Type 2. Both cause clustered blisters on the surface of the skin or mucous membranes and are caused by viral infection. Type 2 is the more serious of the two and is the one that is contracted through sexual contact.

heterosexual   A person who is sexually attracted to or engages in sexual activity primarily with members of the opposite gender.

homosexual   A person who is sexually attracted to or engages in sexual activity primarily with members of the same gender.

homosexuality   A preference for partners of the

same sex who arouse in fantasy and in sexual encounters. A person can engage in sexual activities with a person of the opposite sex and be aroused if he or she fantasizes these activities as taking place with a person of the same sex.

human chorionic gonadotropin (HCG) A hormone secreted in the urine early in pregnancy which makes the biological test for pregnancy possible.

hymen A thin membrane that stretches across the vaginal opening.

hypnosis A passive mind control technique characterized by dissociation from the immediate surroundings and a heightened susceptibility to suggestion.

hypogonadal A condition characterized by a lack of androgens as a result of a disease of the endocrine system and resulting in a reduction or loss of sexual vigor and sometimes negative emotional reactions such as depression.

hysterectomy Surgical removal of the uterus, either through the abdominal wall or through the vagina.

hysterotomy An abortion method used late in the second trimester of pregnancy when a woman's health is at risk. A small cesarean section is performed, and the fetus is removed.

identical twins Twins that develop from a single fertilized egg; they possess the same chromosomes and are always of the same sex.

I-messages Statements about the self, revelations of inner feelings and needs, and information not processed by others. I-messages have three components: a behavior, an effect, and a feeling.

imperforate hymen A hymen with no central perforation to allow the menstrual flow to leave the body; the hymen must be opened by incision.

impotence A male's inability to produce or maintain an erection sufficient for sexual intercourse in the majority of sexual contacts. Also known as erectile dysfunction.

incest Sexual relations between people related by birth.

induced abortion A method of abortion that is used late in the second trimester. See *induced labor.*

induced labor An abortion method used late in the second trimester of pregnancy that involves injecting a saline solution or prostaglandins into the amniotic sac; prostaglandins can also be inserted as a vaginal suppository or given intrave-

nously. All of the above means will initiate labor.

infertile Incapable of producing offspring.

information gathering An objective message sent without added feeling for the purpose of obtaining information about sexual behavior and lifestyle so that a person can make wise decisions.

inguinal canal A passageway through which the testes descend before birth.

inguinal hernia An abnormal protrusion through the inguinal canal, which is sometimes weakened after the testes descend through the canal before birth.

inspiriting relationships Relationships that lift the spirits, allowing one to experience joy, enthusiasm, passion, hope, satisfaction, and high self-esteem.

interception The prevention of implantation of the fertilized egg, such as with an intrauterine device (IUD).

interpersonal (partial) celibate A person who engages in masturbation, but no other form of sexual activity with others.

interstitial-cell-stimulating hormone (ICHS) A hormone secreted by the pituitary gland in the male that stimulates the maturation of sperm cells.

intimacy A personal and private closeness marked by free choice, mutuality, reciprocity, trust, and delight.

intrauterine device (IUD) A plastic or metal device that is inserted into the uterus for birth control.

introitus The opening to the vagina.

inverted nipples Nipples that are held in as opposed to protruding; women with inverted nipples can breast-feed.

investment A term that refers to putting effort and/or money into a venture that will be profitable, including a relationship.

involuntary childless couples Couples who are assumed to want children but who are unable to have them.

isthmus The middle, constricted area of the uterus.

john A male who pays for the services of a prostitute.

Kegel exercises Techniques intended to strengthen the female's pubococcygeal muscle, which runs from the pubic bone to the coccyx and contract involuntarily at orgasm.

keratitis   Inflammation of the cornea of the eye due to herpes; may lead to blindness.

Kwell   A prescription drug that is the most commonly known cure for lice. It comes in the form of a cream, shampoo, or lotion.

labia majora   The outer lips or heavy folds of skin surrounding the opening of the vagina.

labia minora   The two smaller lips or folds of skin located between the labia majora.

labor   Childbirth, which is divided into three stages: Stage 1 is the longest, consisting of contractions and the effacement and dilation of the cervix. Stage 2 is the delivery of the baby; and Stage 3, the expulsion of the placenta.

lactation   The production of milk in the mother's breasts following childbirth.

Lamaze technique   A program in prepared childbirth that emphasizes education, exercises, relaxation and controlled breathing.

"latency age"   See preadolescence.

L-dopa   A drug used to treat Parkinson's disease; men using this drug were reported to be in a constant state of sexual arousal. Occasionally the drug did produce priapism.

lesbianism   The term that is more often used to describe female homosexuals.

LeBoyer technique   A method of childbirth that emphasizes soft lights and sounds, submersion of the baby in warm water, and immediate skin-to-skin contact, all of which help the baby adjust to its new environment.

liability   A weak point, something that works to disadvantage.

libido   The sex drive.

lightening   The descent of the uterus at the beginning of the ninth month of pregnancy that indicates that the baby has begun to sink into the pelvis in preparation for birth. The medical term for this is engagement of the fetus.

"living together arrangements" (LTA)   See cohabitation.

longitudinal delivery   Lengthwise delivery of the child; 99% of babies are born this way.

ludus lovestyle   A lovestyle in which a person views love as a playful encounter. Ludus types have a low commitment to their lovers and seek involvement with several persons at one time.

lust murder   Murdering and mutilating another person to achieve sexual gratification.

madam   Manager of a brothel, often a former prostitute.

"making out"   See petting.

manic lovestyle   An obsession with love, characterized by powerful passion and a variety of partners.

masochism   A sexual variance in which a person receives sexual pleasure from being physically or psychologically hurt by the sexual partner. The opposite of sadism.

mastodynia   The swelling and painful tenderness of the breasts that accompanies the menstrual cycle.

masturbation   Self-stimulation of the genitals, either manually or by an object, for the purpose of achieving sexual pleasure.

mate swapping   See swinging.

meconium   The dark green or blackish matter discharged from the baby's bowels in the first days after birth; colostrum from the mother's breasts has a laxative effect on meconium.

medical model theory of homosexuality   An outmoded theory that held that homosexuality was an illness that should be cured.

menarche   The term used to describe the first menstrual cycle; it is not uncommon for girls to begin menstruation at age 9, but most begin their periods as teenagers.

menopause   Cessation of menstruation that usually occurs in women aged 48 to 52. The ovaries stop producing a monthly egg, and circulating levels of both estrogens and progesterone decrease. Surgical removal of the ovaries also results in menopause.

menorrhagia   Abnormally heavy menstrual flow that can be a symptom of disease, endocrine disorder, or abnormalities of the sexual organs.

menstrual cycle   The monthly cycle that prepares a woman's body for the possibility of pregnancy. Each cycle is divided into three phases: proliferative; secretory, or progestational; and menstrual.

menstrual flow   The lining of the uterus expelled each month that pregnancy does not occur. It consists of dead cells and a small quantity of blood and fluid.

microhemagglutination treponemal pallidum (MHA-TP)   A blood antibody test for syphilis that is considered the most reliable diagnostic procedure.

middle childhood   See preadolescence.

"mini-pill"   See progestin-only pill.

miscarriage   See spontaneous abortion.

Monilia   A yeastlike fungus that will multiply in the vagina if its environment is altered, causing itching, inflammation, and a white vaginal discharge that looks like cottage cheese. Now more commonly known as Candida.

moniliasis Yeast infection in the vagina caused by the Monilia (Candida) fungus.

mons veneris Pads of fatty tissue over the front of the pubic bone that serves as a protective cushion for the female reproductive organs.

"morning-after pill" See *diethylstilbestrol.*

morning erection An erection that is present when a man or boy awakens; it may be due to a full bladder and it often accompanies the dreaming stage of sleep.

morula The term for the fertilized egg as it divides into a mass of cells and travels down the oviduct.

motile Capable of movement, such as sperm capable of propelling themselves to reach the ovum.

mucus method This method of birth control requires a woman to chart the changes in her vaginal mucus secretions. As ovulation nears, the mucus becomes more abundant, clear, slippery, and stringy. This method can also be used to time intercourse for couples who desire to conceive.

multilateral marriage See *group marriage.*

multiple orgasm The capacity in some women to experience orgasm more than once during a single sexual response cycle.

mutual masturbation Stimulation of the genitals by another, either manually or by an object, for the purpose of achieving pleasure.

myometrium The muscular layer of the uterus.

natural childbirth See *prepared childbirth.* Synonymous with that term, but the authors prefer the term "prepared childbirth" because "natural childbirth" implies that the use of drugs is "unnatural."

"necking" See *petting.*

necrophile Someone who engages in necrophilia.

necrophilia Using a corpse to obtain sexual gratification.

Neisseria gonorrhoeae The bacterium responsible for gonorrhea; it can survive only in the warm mucus membranes that line the genitals, anus, and throat.

new marriage See *cohabitation.*

nipple The tip of the breast.

nocturnal emissions Spontaneous ejaculations which may occur during sleep. They are caused by changes in hormonal concentrations during puberty.

nonconsensual extramarital sex An extramarital relationship that is kept from the spouse.

nongonococcal urethritis (NGU) Inflammation of the urethra not caused by gonococcus bacteria. Also called nonspecific urethritis.

nonspecific urethritis (NSU) See *nongonococcal urethritis.*

nymphomania A condition in which a female has a compulsive, insatiable sexual appetite so as to interfere with all other concerns or interests. Known as satyriasis in the male.

obscenity Material that is either sexual or nonsexual that is abhorrent to one's accepted standards of morality.

obstetrician A physician who specializes in the care of women during pregnancy, labor and delivery, and the period immediately following.

Oedipal period According to Freudian theory, a child aged 3 or 4 becomes attracted to the opposite-sex parent, and manifests that attraction by wishes and fantasies; in a loving family these feelings disappear as a child learns to identify with the same-sex parent.

Oedipus complex In Freudian theory, the sexual attraction of a child for the opposite-sex parent, a stage which is usually outgrown during maturation.

oophorectomy Surgical removal of the ovaries.

open marriage A marriage in which both spouses are permitted to develop close relationships with persons outside of the marriage; these relationships may include intimate sexual and emotional involvement or transitory sex only.

orchidectomy The surgical removal of the testes, castration, usually as a treatment for cancer of the prostate gland.

orchiditis A condition caused by the mumps virus in post-pubescent males; the virus may cause the seminiferous tubules to swell and lose their function, which can result in sterility.

organic impotence Failure to maintain or achieve an erection due to physiological and chemical phenomena such as anatomical abnormalities in genital structure, problems of the nervous system, medications, surgery, spinal cord injuries, and excessive intake of drugs and alcohol.

orgasm An explosive discharge of neuromuscular tensions at the peak of sexual response, marked by rhythmic contractions and a sense of physiological and psychological release.

orgasmic dysfunction The inability of a woman to achieve orgasm. Also known as anorgasmia.

orgasmic phase The third of four stages in the sexual response cycle during which orgasm occurs.

orgasmic platform Vasocongestion of the outer third of the vagina and labia minora that occurs during the plateau phase of the female sexual response cycle.

orgy A party in which the nude participants engage in touching as well as various kinds of sexual acts with anyone who is around.

os The opening of the cervix.

ovarian cancer Cancer of the ovary, most prevalent among women who are: 40 to 50 years old, have a history of ectopic pregnancy or infertility, or who have endometriosis.

ovaries Two almond-shaped female sex glands that lie at the brim of the pelvis; they produce ova and secrete hormones.

overt homosexual A male who is open about his lifestyle.

oviducts Three- to five-inch trumpet-shaped tubes that transport the ovum to the uterus. Also called uterine tubes.

ovulation The release of a mature ovum from the Graafian follicle of the ovary.

Papanicolaou (Pap) smear A routine test for cervical cancer and other abnormalities that involves the laboratory analysis of tissue scraped from the cervix.

partial hysterectomy Surgical removal of most of the uterus; part of the cervix remains as well as the ovaries and oviducts. Ovulation occurs each month, and the ovary secretes estrogen.

parturition The entire process of childbirth.

pedophile A person who derives sexual pleasure from using a child as a sexual object.

pedophilia Child molesting; a form of sexual variation in which adults derive erotic pleasure from using children as sexual objects.

pelvic examination A medical examination that includes inspection of the external genitalia, a speculum examination, a bimanual vaginal examination, and a rectovaginal examination.

pelvic inflammatory disease (PID) An infection of the uterus and pelvic cavity. Symptoms are lower abdominal pain, nausea, vomiting, fever, irregular menstruation, and malaise.

penis The male organ of sexual pleasure, reproduction, and urination.

perineum The very sensitive area between the vagina and the anus of the female and the scrotum and the anus of the male.

petting Erotic physical contact that goes beyond kissing but stops short of sexual intercourse. Also known as "necking" or "making out."

pheromones Odors from the bodies of animals during fertile periods that are an important means of communication, frequently serving as a means of sexual arousal.

phimosis A condition in which the foreskin is so tight over the glans that it cannot be pulled back, causing painful intercourse.

photoinactivation A treatment method for genital herpes that is still being tested. Lesions are painted with light-sensitive dye and exposed to light, which inactivates the virus.

pimp A person who lives directly on the earnings of prostitutes.

placenta A disc-shaped organ formed on the wall of the uterus and connected to the fetus by an umbilical cord through which nutrients and waste products are exchanged with the mother.

polygamist A spouse with several mates.

polymorphous perverse A Freudian term for an infant; Freud considered newborns to be bisexuals who would respond pleasurably to any erotic stimulation.

polyps Long, tubelike protrusions that grow from mucous membranes inside the uterus or along the cervix. Symptoms are irregular menstrual periods, bleeding between periods, and a heavy flow.

pornography Material in literature, art, motion pictures, or other means of communication and expression that has been developed with the intention of evoking sexual interest and arousal.

postpartum period The first several weeks after birth; the woman may undergo rapid changes of mood.

potassium nitrate A diuretic, also known as saltpeter, that was used in boarding schools as an anaphrodisiac; it was ineffective.

plateau phase The second of four stages in the sexual response cycle; it immediately precedes orgasm.

pragma A lovestyle in which someone is likely to "date around" to find someone with certain special qualities.

preadolescence The age period from 8 to 12 also known as middle childhood or the "latency age." Freud believed that the sex drive was dormant during this period, but this theory has been disproved.

precoital fluid A slippery fluid secreted by the bulbourethral glands that can be noticed on the tip of the penis when a man is sexually aroused.

pregnancy rate A rate determined by the number of sexually active women out of 100% who would get pregnant in a year using a particular means of birth control. The pregnancy rate with no means of contraception is 80%.

premarital sex An outdated term with vague connotations that is meant to indicate that sex in marriage is the norm for sexual intercourse.

premature ejaculation A sexual difficulty in which a male has no control over the ejaculatory reflex, causing him to believe he is performing inadequately or is failing to satisfy his partner.

premature infant Any newborn baby who weighs less than 5½ pounds.

prenatal Before birth.

prepared childbirth Childbirth method which emphasizes education, relaxation, and controlled breathing to help a woman cope with the discomfort of labor and delivery.

prepuce See *foreskin.*

priapism A continual and pathological erection of the penis which is painful and is not accompanied by sexual desire.

primary follicles Podlike structures present in the ovary at birth that contain immature or unripened ova. During the reproductive years about 375 of the primary follicles are sufficiently developed to expel ova.

primary homosexuality The state of not having had any heterosexual experience.

primary impotence A sexual difficulty in which a man has *never* had the ability to maintain an erection for sexual intercourse.

primary orgasmic dysfunction A condition in which a woman has never had an orgasm by any method.

progesterone A hormone secreted by the corpus luteum whose function is to initiate the nourishing secretions for the egg in the oviduct, inhibit the contraction of the muscular layer of the uterus, stimulate the breast's ducts, and thicken the uterine lining to receive the egg.

progestin injections A contraceptive injection of a long-lasting progestin, usually Depo-Provera; 150 mg should last for more than three months.

progestin-only pill A contraceptive pill that contains small doses of progestin, a synthetic progesterone. The progestin-only pill *may* be safer than combined oral contraceptives because it contains no estrogen.

prolactin A milk-stimulating hormone secreted by the pituitary gland as soon as the placenta is removed during childbirth.

proliferate phase The first phase of the menstrual cycle when the follicle-stimulating hormone causes 15 to 20 primary follicles to grow in the ovaries.

prophylactic See *condom.*

prostate gland A gland located just beneath the bladder and surrounding the urethra that produces most of the seminal fluid released during ejaculation.

prostitute A person who engages in sexual acts for monetary rewards.

pseudocyesis See *false pregnancy.*

pseudomarriage See *cohabitation.*

psychic erection An erection that occurs because of thought and not tactile stimulation of the body.

psychogenic impotence Failure to maintain or achieve an erection due to psychological factors; the cause of 90% of all cases of impotency.

psychoprophylactic method A mind control technique popularized by Fernand Lamaze that emphasizes relaxation and controlled breathing to help a woman cope with the discomfort of labor and delivery.

puberty The stage of life when the reproductive organs become functional and secondary sexual characteristics develop.

pubic lice Yellowish gray insects the size of a pinhead that attach themselves to the pubic hair and suck the skin. Seen microscopically, they resemble their nickname, "crabs." They can be transmitted from close sexual contact or from infected clothing, sheets, or toilets.

pyromania Compulsive fire-setting, an example of a fetishistic pattern since fire has sexual connotations.

quadruplets Four children born at the same time; usually they are the result of two ova that separate and form two sets of identical twins.

quickening The stage of pregnancy in which the woman can feel the fetus kicking and moving in her uterus.

rape Sexual intercourse that occurs by force or deception, or because another person may be too incompetent to give consent.

rape trauma syndrome An immediate state of disorganization that results from an attempted or successful rape.

reaction formation   A phenomenon in which a person who secretly fears something, such as latent homosexuality, discriminates against homosexuals.

reactive factors   A term for persons who choose not to have children because of unhappy parental marriages, atypical experiences with siblings, and financial burdens.

reflex erection   An erection that results from effective tactile stimulation of the penis or genital area. A man with a spinal cord injury may be able to experience reflex erection.

refractory period   A period following orgasm when the male cannot become sexually excited to the point of erection.

relaxation   An important component of the Lamaze technique of prepared childbirth; it helps a woman to dissociate herself from the discomfort of labor and delivery.

religious celibate   A person who practices celibacy because of a specific ideology or belief.

resolution phase   The last of the four stages in the sexual response cycle in which the body returns to its normal, nonexcited state.

response cycle   A predictable pattern of sexual response in most men and women. There are four phases: excitement, plateau, orgasm, and resolution.

responsibility message   A message that communicates attitudes, beliefs, values, and feelings about sexuality, and which takes into account accurate information about sexuality.

retarded ejaculation   An inability in the male to ejaculate even though he desires to do so. Also known as ejaculatory incompetence, ejaculatory impotence or delayed ejaculation.

retrograde ejaculation   Orgasm without ejaculation; the semen is expelled into the bladder instead of out of the penis. This condition often occurs because of prostate surgery, illness, or the use of certain depressant drugs. Also known as "dry orgasm."

RhoGam   A drug that prevents an Rh-negative mother from developing antibodies that could attack the red blood cells of an Rh-positive child.

role   A role is a function assumed by someone.

rubber   See *condom*.

sadism   A sexual variance in which a person receives sexual pleasure by inflicting physical or psychological pain on the sexual partner. The opposite of masochism.

safe   See *condom*.

satyriasis   A condition in which a male has a compulsive, insatiable sexual appetite so as to interfere with all other concerns or interests. Known as nymphomania in the female.

scrotum   A saclike pouch in the groin area that holds the testes and regulates temperature for sperm production.

secondary homosexuality   A term that indicates that a person has had one or more heterosexual experiences.

secondary impotence   A sexual difficulty in which a man cannot maintain or perhaps achieve an erection, but who has succeeded at vaginal or rectal intercourse at least once.

secondary orgasmic dysfunction   A condition in which a woman has had an orgasm sometime in her life, but now cannot, at least with any predictability in coitus. Also known as situational orgasmic dysfunction.

selected perception   A tendency for a couple to focus on the disadvantages of having children without acknowledging any advantages.

self-identity   The criteria by which a person categorizes himself or herself.

semen   See *seminal fluid*.

Semans start-stop technique   A treatment for premature ejaculation in which a man signals his partner to halt genital contact when he feels the urge to ejaculate, which makes it possible for him to delay ejaculation and to learn to control it.

seminal fluid   A viscous fluid ejaculated through the penis that is composed of prostate secretion, which is whitish and alkaline, secretions of the seminal vesicles, which act as a nutrient, and sperm.

seminal vesicles   Two small glands at the ends of the vas deferens that secrete an alkaline fluid that is rich in fructose, a sugar nutrient that provides energy for sperm.

seminiferous tubules   A coiled network of tubes in the testes in which sperm are produced.

sensate focus exercises   Stroking and massage exercises that are used by couples as a form of sexual expression; these exercises are used as a basic treatment of many sexual dysfunctions.

sexual dysfunction   An impairment or ineffectiveness in sexual performance. Impotence, premature ejaculation and retarded ejaculation are male-related; orgasmic dysfunction and vaginismus are female-related. Painful intercourse and sexual disinterest can occur in both men and women.

sexually deviant behavior Sexual behavior directed at people other than the opposite sex or sexual acts not usually associated with coitus.

sexually transmitted diseases (STDs) Any disease whose mode of transmission is *almost always* by sexual contact.

sexual urethralism Sexual arousal obtained by stimulating the urethra with an object.

sexual variations Certain sexual behaviors that are outside the realm of marriage, are not traditional sexual intercourse, and which may be considered by others to be perverted or sexually deviant.

shaft The main part of the penis, also known as the body.

Siamese twins Twins who are born joined at any part of the body because a cell mass did not separate completely.

situational homosexual A person who engages in homosexual activity because of a particular situation, such as being placed in prison. Also known as a deprived homosexual.

situational orgasmic dysfunction See *secondary orgasmic dysfunction.*

smegma An accumulation of secretions on the glans of the penis.

societal ambivalence A strategy childless couples use to convince themselves that parents envy them.

sodomy An ambiguous legal term for a wide range of sexual variations, although it usually refers to anal intercourse.

spasmodic dysmenorrhea Painful menstruation due to too much progesterone in relation to estrogen. Symptoms include sharp pain in the lower abdomen, cramping, and nausea. Hormone therapy and childbirth alleviate the condition.

sperm The tiny male reproductive cell (or cells) that is capable of fertilizing the female egg and causing impregnation.

spermatogenesis Sperm production, which takes place in the seminiferous tubules.

sperm banks Storage places for frozen sperm, which can later be thawed and used for artificial insemination.

spermicidal preparation A foam, cream, jelly, or suppository containing a chemical that is deposited in the vagina near the cervix to kill or immobilize sperm.

spirochete See *Treponema pallidum.*

spontaneous abortion A miscarriage, or an expulsion of the embryo or fetus before it has reached the point of development at which it can survive.

"squeeze technique" A treatment for premature ejaculation in which a man signals his partner to squeeze his penis when he feels the urge to ejaculate, which makes it possible for him to delay ejaculation and to learn to control it.

Staphylococcus aureus A bacterium that causes toxic shock syndrome (TSS). The bacterium proliferates in the vaginas of menstruating women who use tampons, and probably secretes a toxin which enters the bloodstream to cause TSS.

statutory rape Sexual intercourse with a girl who is under the legal age of consent—regardless of whether or not consent has been granted.

sterile See *infertile.*

sterilization Any procedure (usually surgical) by which an individual is made incapable of producing offspring.

stigma A nipplelike protrusion on the surface of the Graafian follicle; it disintegrates at ovulation under the influence of the luteinizing hormone and releases the egg.

storge lovestyle A lovestyle in which a person builds relationships slowly, gradually comes to care for a partner, and tends to form stable, committed relationships.

stratum vasculare The spongy appearance of the uterus during pregnancy.

structure social situation Undesirable situations with children set up by couples as a means of confirming their belief that they don't want children.

submissive partner In a sadomasochistic relationship, the submissive partner is the recipient of the physically abusive behavior of the sexual partner.

suppository A spermicidal preparation that is deposited high in the vagina at least ten minutes before intercourse. It effervesces, forming a thick mechanical barrier.

surrogate A member of a sex therapy team who serves as a sexual partner for the individual who is under treatment.

surrogate marriage See *cohabitation.*

sympathetic pregnancy A phenomenon in which a man experiences the symptoms of pregnancy and birth: nausea, vomiting, and labor pains along with the woman. Also known as couvade.

syphilis A sexually transmitted disease that progresses through four stages if left untreated, and may result in death. However, it can be easily treated with penicillin.

swinging A form of consensual extramarital sex in which couples exchange spouses with other married couples. Also known as mate swapping.

telephone coprolalia Obscene talking to strangers or known persons on the telephone to achieve sexual gratification.

testes Male gonads inside the scrotum that secrete the male hormone testosterone and produce sperm.

testicle See *testes.*

testosterone A major male hormone produced by the testes; it maintains the secondary male sex characteristics.

test-tube baby A baby born as a result of the fertilization of an egg outside the woman's body. The fertilized egg is then implanted in the woman's uterus for growth and development.

therapeutic abortion An abortion performed because the mother's life is in danger or because there is a possibility of fetal abnormality.

"the shot" See *progestin injections.*

thrush A yeast infection in a baby's digestive system transmitted by the mother as the baby passes through her infected vagina. Thrush can develop in the throat of an infected woman's partner if cunnilingus is performed.

thyroid gland An endocrine gland located just below the larynx that secretes hormones that influence growth and stimulate activity in the nervous system.

toxemia A disease during pregnancy characterized by high blood pressure, edema, and rapid weight gain, all frequently resulting from malnutrition, and which can result in premature delivery.

toxic-shock syndrome (TSS) A serious, sometimes fatal flulike illness caused by a bacterium that finds a favorable environment for growth in the vaginas of menstruating women who use tampons. Women can almost entirely reduce the risk of TSS by not using tampons.

traditional marriage A marriage with rules that are set by society, concentrates on role expectations, and is concerned with social approval.

transition The final phase of the first stage of labor, which is marked by very strong, short contractions. The cervix is completely dilated.

transsexual A person who wishes to be or sincerely believes that he or she is a member of the opposite sex.

transverse position A rare (1-in-200) presentation in which the baby' shoulder, arm, or hand enters the birth canal first; a cesarean section may be indicated.

transvestism The wearing of clothes of the opposite sex in order to achieve sexual gratification.

Treponema pallidum A corkscrew-shaped bacterium, also known as a spirochete, that causes syphilis.

Tribadism One woman lying on top of another woman; they move up and down rhythmically to stimulate each other's clitoris.

Trichomonas vaginalis The single-celled organism responsible for many vaginal infections, including trichomoniasis. The organism has four tail-like strands that it uses to propel itself, and it survives only in the genitourinary system.

trichomoniasis A sexually transmitted disease that results from infection by *Trichomonas vaginalis,* an organism that can survive only in the genitourinary system. In males, there are rarely any symptoms, but there may be a white discharge from the urethra. In females, symptoms include vaginal discharge, itching, burning, and increased frequency of urination.

trimester A period of three months which marks the three major stages of fetal development and pregnancy.

triplets Three children born at the same time, who develop from either one, two, or three fertilized eggs; in most cases two eggs are involved.

trophoblast The small mass of cells that maintains the embryo in the first several days of its existence; the trophoblast later becomes a placenta.

tubal cauterization A procedure for sterilizing a female that involves burning the oviducts.

tubal ligation A surgical procedure for sterilizing a female that involves cutting and tying the oviducts.

tubal pregnancy A fertilized ovum that implants in the oviduct. If not detected, the condition may result in severe infection, heavy bleeding, shock, and possibly death.

"turn tricks" A slang term for the sexual favors performed by prostitutes.

umbilical cord A semitransparent jelly-like rope that is attached to the placenta from the fetus's navel, and through which oxygen, nutrients, and waste products are exchanged with the mother.

undescended testes See *cryptorchidism.*

urethra The tube through which urine passes from the bladder to the outside of the body. In males it also serves as a passageway for semen.

urethritis An inflammation of the urethra that causes a thick white, yellow, or yellow-green discharge, and may result from gonorrhea.

urinalysis A chemical or microscopic examination of the urine.

urophilia Sexual arousal from and erotic interest in urine; urophilia is closely related to sexual urethralism.

uterine cancer Cancer of the uterus. Women at risk have a history of uterine cancer in their families, diabetes, delayed menopause, irregular bleeding, and obesity.

uterine orgasm The second type of female orgasm experience described by Singer and Singer. It is characterized by a cumulative gasping type of breathing that culminates in an "involuntary breath-holding response, which occurs only after considerable diaphragmatic tension has been achieved."

uterine tubes See *oviducts.*

uterus The womb; the organ that receives the fertilized ovum, supports it during pregnancy, and contracts during childbirth.

vacuum curettage The most commonly used abortion procedure during the first trimester of pregnancy. The cervix is dilated, a vacuum aspirator is inserted into the uterus, and the fetus and some of the lining of the uterine wall is suctioned out.

vagina A muscular passageway lying between the bladder and the rectum, which serves as the female organ of intercourse, the birth canal, and the passageway for arriving sperm and the menstrual flow.

vaginal cancer Cancer of the vagina, which is most prevalent among women whose mothers took diethylstilbestrol (DES) during pregnancy to prevent miscarriage.

vaginal orgasm Orgasm achieved after vaginal stimulation. According to Masters and Johnson, there is no difference between a clitoral and vaginal orgasm.

vaginismus An intense and involuntary contraction of the muscles near the vaginal entrance that occurs when penetration is attempted.

vaginitis Inflammation of the vaginal walls caused by a variety of vaginal infections.

values clarification A process that helps people ascertain whether or not their decisions are in accordance with their life principles.

vas deferens Two long, thin cords that function as a passageway for sperm and as a place for sperm storage.

vasectomy A surgical procedure for sterilizing the male that involves cutting, tying, and coagulating the vas deferens.

vasocongestion The increased engorgement of blood in an area, such as in the erect penis.

venereal warts Dry wartlike growths that are caused by the same virus that produces warts on other parts of the body. Also known as genital warts, they are transmitted primarily by sexual, oral, and anal intercourse.

vestibule A space between the labia minora into which open the urethra, the vagina, and the ducts of the Bartholin's glands.

vibrator An oscillating device that can be used for stimulation in masturbation or in homosexual or heterosexual play.

voluntarily childless couples Couples assumed to be fertile but not inclined toward parenthood.

voyeur Someone who obtains sexual satisfaction from the act of peeping and the masturbation that accompanies it.

voyeurism The act of obtaining sexual gratification from looking at the bodies, sex organs, or sex acts of other persons. Voyeurism is considered a deviation when it is preferred to coitus.

vulva The external genitals of the female, including the mons veneris, the labia majora, the labia minora, the clitoris, the vestibule, the urethral opening, the introitus, the hymen, the perineum, and Bartholin's glands.

vulval orgasm The first type of female orgasm experience described by Singer and Singer. It is similar to the "involuntary rhythmic contractions of the orgasmic platform" noted by Masters and Johnson.

wet dreams See *nocturnal emissions.*

withdrawal See *coitus interruptus.*

womb See *uterus.*

yeast infection See *moniliasis.*

you-messages Blaming or shaming messages that close off openness.

zoophilia See *bestiality.*

Index

Page numbers in *italics* indicate illustrations; (t) denotes a table.